8th Ed

STANDARD GUIDE TO
SMALL-SIZE
U.S. PAPER MONEY
1928 TO DATE

Edited by
John Schwartz & Scott Lindquist

Based on the work of
Dean Oakes & John Schwartz

©2007 Krause Publications

Published by

krause publications
An Imprint of F+W Publications

700 East State Street • Iola, WI 54990-0001
715-445-2214 • 888-457-2873
www.krausebooks.com

Our toll-free number to place an order or obtain
a free catalog is (800) 258-0929.

ISSN 1555-5348
ISBN-13: 978-0-89689-575-1
ISBN-10: 0-89689-575-0

Designed by Sandi Morrison
Edited by Randy Thern

Printed in the United States of America

Table of Contents

Special Research Contributors

Mike Crabb	David Manley
Alex Delatola	Dean Oakes
Jim Hodgson	Dave Schlingman
Peter Huntoon	Gerald Glasser

Contributors

Mike Accavallo	John English	Mike Korchynsky	David Rollick
E.J. Aleo	Lawrence Falater	Robert Kotcher	Mark Roth
Harold Andrews	Harvey Fenton	H. D. Kruse	Rick Rounds
Will Arnold	Ken Ferguson	Bob Kvederas, Jr.	Dave Ruth
Bob Aspiazu	David L. Fien	Bob Kvederas, Sr.	Joe Sande
Donald W. Atkin	Kim Fisher	Tim Kyzivat	Jim Sazama
Ken Bachner	Tom Flynn	J. D. Larson	Howard Schein
Bill Bagwell	Dennis Forgue	Graham Lawrence	Thomas W.
Al Bailey	Jim Futrell	J. L. Laws	Schofield
Dick Balbaton	Danny S. Gauthier	Julian Leidman	David Scott
Greg Bannon	Bob Giamboi	Art Leister	Eugene R. Seger
Pat Barnes	Don Gilletti	James T. Lemon	Jackson Sellwood
Joe Barr	Herb Glover	David Leong	Don Severance
Fred Bart	Nathan Goldstein	Charles Lindquist	Micky Shipley
R.C. Beach	Tom Gregg	Roger Loecher	Jim Simek
Frank Bennett	Ron Gustafson	Francis Loo	Charlie Sloan
Larry Berg	Bruce Hagen	Timothy Luckey	Daryl Spelbring
Glen Burger	Jeff Haggerty	Ann Lundebo	David Spencer
Harlan Berk	John Hanik	Alvin Macomber	John Stassins
Scott Billings	Dan Hassard	Judd Maher	Lewis Stern
John L. Blair	Chuck Hayes	Steve Malast	Milton Stewart
Leon H. Bookman	Bob Hearn	Rocky Manning	Tom Surina
Carl Bombara	James Hedges	Jim Martin	R. Logan Talks
David E. Booth	Ron Hedglin	Peter Mayer	Mike Tauber
Paul Borys	Forrest Henry	Greg McNeal	Allen Teal
Wade Boughton	Gene Hessler	Scott McClure	Larry Thomas
Gary M. Brown	Shawn Hewitt	George T. McDuffie	Ronald Thomas
Bill Burd	Rick Hobson	Marc Michaelsen	Leon Thornton
Warren H. Burnside	Malcolm Holbrook	Michael Miuccio	Frank Trask
Brooks Burr	Bruce R. Holocek	Ray W. Morrow	Peter Treglia
Bill Bussey	Don Homesley	Mark Mraz	Bruce Tyson
Alan R. Camacho	Susan Hopson	Kevin Mullin	Blain Van Allen
Douglas Campbell	Richard L. Horst	Doug Murray	Bob Vandevender
Mark Canny	Joe Horka, Jr.	Greg Muselli	Martin Vink
Charles Cataldo	Lowell Horwedel	Musk	Randy Vogel
David Cieniewicz	Mark Hotz	David G. Nielson	Don Vosburgh
Henry Coalter	Steven A. Hubers	Joe O'Brien	Greg Voss
Tom Conklin	Dennis L. Huff	Jerry Oliver	Doug Walcutt
Lawrence Cookson	Arri Jacob	Bruce Ollis	H. M. Wallace
Terry Coyle	Steve Jennings	Jim Ondyk	R. E. Wallace
Daryl Crotts	Craig Johnson	Lawrence O'Neal	George Warner
Paul Crow	Mark Johnson	Dave Orshowitz	Rich Wasckiewicz
Paul Cuccia	Harry Jones	Charles Parrish	John Watson
Gary Dabbs	Jeff Jones	Baxter Worth	Kyle Wesley
Dean Davis	Glen Jorde	Paschal III	Timothy West
Greg Davis	Vincent J. Jurgaitis	Alex Perakis	Barry Wexler
John DeMaris	Dick Kalmbach	Steve Perakis	Harlan White
Tom Denly	Russell Kaye	Eustolio Perez	John Williams
Norman Dishman	Blake Keller	Carl Pietroboni	Robert Wilson
James V. Doiron	Don Kelly	Gayle Pike	Jim Wolfe
Mark Dombrowski	Gene Kelso	Thomas Poirier	Andrew Woodruff
Mike Dougherty	R. H. Klein	Phil Pollard	Glen Wright
Turner Douglas	Lyn Knight	Lou Rasera	Jamie Yakes
Ted Dumetz, Jr.	David Koble	Bob Reed	John Yasuk
Joel P. Dutenhoefer	Vince Kohlbecker	S. D. Reiss	Joe Zimmer
C. Keith Edison	Robert Kolasa	Bob Reithe	

Introduction

Welcome to the 8th edition of the Standard Guide to Small Size U.S. Paper Money. We hope that this, and subsequent editions, will further your interest and enjoyment in this growing collectible field of Small Size U.S. Paper Money.

This guide is a concerted effort of the collecting fraternity as a whole and is strongly based on the works of many of the pioneers in small size collecting, including but not limited to our current author, dating back to the first edition, John Schwartz, whose infectious excitement and interest in collecting is a necessary ingredient of any successful hobby publication. With his original partners, Leon Goodman and Chuck O'Donnell they wrote the first Standard Handbook of Modern US. Paper Money in 1968. Dean Oakes was the principal with whom John launched this latest successful series of guides.

For those who do not know Scott Lindquist, personally or professionally, he has been active as a dealer since 1981, both as a vest-pocket coin dealer and shop owner under the business name of The Coin Cellar. His beginnings in dealing in small size paper money started more as a practical necessity and grew to full time currency dealer in the early to mid 90's. After almost 20 years as a self-employed numismatist, he has been for the past eight years affiliated with Smythe and Company. In that time he has handled numerous small size rarities and attended every major auction possible under a heavy show and travel schedule. This experience, out in the trenches, week in and week out, is where values and rarity find themselves in dollar amounts. He does his best to translate those prices to the pages of this, the best and most complete small size reference for U.S. paper money issued from 1928 to date.

His personal goal with this work is to have it most accurately reflect true values to the best of his abilities in the pages to follow. He does not collect small size paper money nor does he use this book as a tool to adjust values for our benefit. It is in everyone's best interests in the long term to make this price guide as accurate as is humanly possible so that all may feel confident that the prices reflect true market values at the time of this writing. All the values are taken from auction, retail and wholesale data. Of' course, a rising tide floats all boats and it is the authors' hope that with accurate information and honest pricing in tow, newcomers will keep entering our collecting fraternity.

Gem Values and Third Part Grading (TPG)

The Large Size market has been on the straight upward value curve since 2002 with many gem notes doubling and tripling in value in just four to five years. Legitimate third party grading has for better or worse, increased the confidence of most buyers, and liquidity seems to be higher than ever before. Notes that used to auction for $2,000 ten years ago are, in some cases, trading at the $10,00-$20,000 level today. Small Size, to a lesser degree, has also seen an influx of activity, with prices rising to previously unheard of levels.

This has caused major changes in the market place. Notes that grade Gem Crisp Uncirculated (GCU) certified or not by a reputable service are bringing two and three times the price of a Choice Crisp Uncirculated (CCU) note. For this reason we will be adding Gem price columns in this and future editions, starting first with the most frequently traded types, i.e., Legal Tenders, Gold and Silver Certificates etc.

Gem prices in this edition are based on 'accurately graded' notes with the PMG 65 EPQ and PCGA 65-66 PPQ designations. Of course, properly graded 'raw' or unslabbed Gems also qualify. There are a lot of other grading services in the grading arena, but only these two services make an effort to remove themselves from conflict of interest, with PMG having only full time graders on staff that are not allowed to buy and sell banknotes. We strongly caution all buyers, collectors and dealers alike to ' buy the note not the holder' which simply means open your eyes. Just because there are respected third party graders doesn't remove dealers and collectors alike from the responsibility of basic due diligence in making their own sight seen assessment to verify that they agree with the grade assigned by the third party graders.

Choice uncirculated note values are given to represent properly graded raw and PMG EPQ and PCGS PPQ 63 through 64 designations. A non-EPQ or PPQ note implies something is wrong with the paper quality and the note is no longer original. This usually indicates that the note has been washed, flattened, pressed, pin hole repaired, re-embossed or otherwise processed. These less desirable notes lacking originality will bring prices commensurate with their respective quality problems at a discount below Choice Uncirculated. Please see the grading section for more details regarding grades and their respective values.

Scott's place in this publication began as a contributor to price updates starting with the 4th edition. We welcome any information regarding new highs and lows, misprints or what you may just consider a mistake that needs to be corrected. Please send your information to Scott's Smythe e-mail address: slindquist@smytheonline.com. With your help we look forward to the process of continuing to make this the most accurate and trusted U.S .Small Size Currency price guide.

GRADES: GEM CRISP UNCIRCULATED - GEM CU

This is a near perfect note with good paper and ink color, centering, margins, superior registration (how the front and back printing align to each other), crisp paper with original embossing intact and absolutely no evidence of repairs or tampering with the notes original qualities. Values listed in this guide are for properly graded PMG65EPQ and PCGS 65-66PPQ.

DISCLAIMER: THIS IS ONLY A GUIDE

No warranty is implied or expressed by the publisher or the authors of this price guide.

The prices listed are as general guide to value and do not represent an offer to buy or sell. Prices are compiled using empirical auction and retail asking prices from numerous sources known to the industry. Still, this is only a guide, as economic forces can cause dramatic price swings in relatively short periods of time. We ask the reader to investigate not only the prices listed in this reference, but to also find a numismatic professional to lend a hand in the acquisition and decision making process.

User's Guide

The first reduced size notes appeared on Jan. 10, 1929. Their origin is traced to Secretary of the Treasury MacVeagh, who served from 1909 to 1913 under President Taft. He appointed a committee that reported favorably on the advantages and savings from adoption of smaller size notes, identical in size to the Philippine currency which had proven highly successful. World War I and the fact that MacVeagh left office one week after accepting the committee recommendations apparently prevented adoption of the idea.

On August 20, 1925, Secretary of the Treasury Andrew W. Mellon appointed a committee to study the whole question of "currency design, printing operations, issuance, and related interests associated with replacing the large size currency with smaller notes." In May of 1927, Secretary Mellon accepted the recommendations of his committee and directed the Bureau of Engraving and Printing to implement the plan.

Classes of Small Size Issues

UNITED STATES NOTES, also called Legal Tender Notes, are the longest lived of U.S. currency, first authorized in the Act of Congress, May 3, 1878. The act required that an outstanding amount of $346,681,016 be maintained. Small LT notes have been issued in $1, $2, $5, and $100. Printed but not issued were the $10 and $20 denominations.

Only one issue of the small size LT $1 was printed, the series of 1928. On Aug. 10, 1966, the Treasury announced no more $2 bills (or U.S. notes) would be printed, and later discontinued the printing of $5 United States notes. The $100 U.S. note was printed in Series of 1966 and 1966A, with star notes printed for only the 1966 series. All small-size U.S. notes have red seals.

SILVER CERTIFICATES were authorized by Acts of Congress on Feb. 28, 1878, and on Aug. 4, 1886. The blue seal distinguishes this class of currency printed in denominations of $1, $5, and $10. The silver law of 1963, which was designed to free the Treasury stockpile of silver bullion (security backing up Silver Certificates) paved the way for obsolescence of this class of currency. The Treasury stopped the redemption of Silver Certificates in silver dollars in 1964 and discontinued bullion redemption on June 24, 1968, based on $1.29 per ounce.

GOLD CERTIFICATES first authorized by the Currency Act of March 3, 1863, have beautiful yellow seals. Gold certificates were issued in denominations of $10, $20, $50, $100, $500, $1,000, $5,000 and $10,000 for general circulation and in the $100,000 for inter-bank use. The $100,000 denomination with a portrait of Woodrow Wilson was Series of 1934.

All the regularly issued Gold Certificates were Series of 1928. Gold Certificates were printed for Series of 1928A and Series of 1934, but were never released and have since been destroyed. On Dec. 28, 1933, the Secretary of the Treasury issued an order forbidding the holding of Gold Certificates, and unlike gold coins, made no provision for collectors to hold them. Banks were ordered to turn in all stocks of Gold Certificates.

On April 24, 1964, Secretary Dillon removed restrictions against the holding of gold certificates.

FEDERAL RESERVE BANK NOTES, first authorized under Act of Dec. 23, 1913, bore an obligation by the issuing bank, rather than the United States. The notes were secured by U.S. Bonds deposited by the issuing bank with the Treasurer of the United States.

All small-size Federal Reserve Bank Notes are Series of 1929, and have a brown seal. Many of these notes are quite scarce (especially the star notes) and are avidly collected. According to the Treasury records, less than two million dollars is still outstanding for this series.

FEDERAL RESERVE NOTES, authorized by an Act of Congress on Dec. 23, 1913, bear the familiar green seal. These notes are the mainstay of our contemporary currency. Federal Reserve Notes are obligations of the United States and are a first lien on the assets of the issuing Federal Reserve Bank. In addition they are secured by a pledge of collateral equal to the face value of the notes. The collateral must consist of the following assets, alone or in any combination: [1] gold certificates, [2] Special Drawing Right Certificates, [3] United States Government Securities, and [4] "eligible paper" as described by statute.

Federal Reserve Notes are issued by the Federal Reserve Banks in denominations of $1, $2, $5, $10, $20, $50 and $100. On July 14, 1969, the Department of the Treasury announced that the issuance of $500, $1,000, $5,000 and $10,000 Federal Reserve Notes would be discontinued immediately because of the lack of demand.

NATIONAL BANK NOTES. President Lincoln signed the National Bank Act into law on February 25, 1863. The purpose of this legislation was to provide for a system of National Bank Note currency that would circulate freely. The currency was secured by United States bonds, which the issuing banks deposited with the U.S. Treasurer. Holders of the notes were protected from loss because if the bank failed, the bonds held by the Treasurer could be sold, and the proceeds used to redeem the outstanding currency.

More than $2.8 billion in small size National Bank Notes were issued between 1929 and 1935, all in the Series of 1929 bearing the federal signatures E. E. Jones, Register of the Treasury, and W.O. Woods, Treasurer. These notes were issued in denominations of $5, $10, $20, $50 and $100 by the national banks and bear the title and location of the bank to the left of the portrait, and the charter number of the bank just inside the right and left margins of the face. There were more than 6,000 issuing banks in 1929, representing all 48 states plus the territories of Alaska and Hawaii. Additional banks were organized between 1929 and 1935 that also issued these notes, and others failed or otherwise went out of business and ceased issuing. The result is that collectors are assured of countless varieties and some extreme rarities within this interesting series. National Bank Note collections commonly center on location themes and National Bank Note collecting represents one of the most dynamic and competitive phases of small note collecting.

The basic back and face designs of National Bank Notes were printed in sheets of 12, then cut vertically and overprinted with the bank information, brown seals and serial numbers. There are two types of Series of 1929 notes. The serial numbers on type 1 notes have both prefix and suffix letters whereas the type 2 notes have only a prefix letter. In addition, the charter numbers are printed in brown next to the serial number on type 2 notes.

The serial numbers on type 1 notes are sheet numbers. Consequently, all six notes in type 1 sheets have the same number, the difference being that the prefix letter cycled from A to F down the sheet. These were printed between 1929 and 1933. The serial numbers on type 2 notes are note numbers, and appear incremented down the sheets similar to other notes of the same vintage. These were printed between 1933 and 1935.

Series of 1929 National Bank Notes are not catalogued in this edition because a thorough listing by bank is beyond the scope of this work. You are referred to one of the comprehensive catalogs that treat this fascinating specialty in great detail such as the *Standard Catalog of U.S. National Bank Notes* by John Hickman and Dean Oakes (published by Krause Publications) or *National Bank Notes, A Guide With Prices* by Don Kelly.

Signature Combinations

All signatures on small currency appear on the face of the note. All United States Notes, Silver and Gold Certificates, and Federal Reserve Notes carry two signatures, the signature of the Treasurer of the United States at the lower left and the signature of the Secretary of the Treasury at the lower right.

National Bank Notes and Federal Reserve Bank Notes have four signatures. All have E.E. Jones, Register of the Treasury at the upper left and W.O. Woods, Treasurer, at the top right. In the lower left appears the signature of the cashier of the bank, and in the lower right, the signature of the president of the bank. Federal Reserve Bank Notes have the signature of the bank cashier in the lower left and the signature of the governor of the bank in the lower right, with the following exceptions: New York notes have the signature of the deputy governor in the lower left instead of the cashier; Chicago has the assistant deputy governor replacing the cashier's signature; and St. Louis has the signature of the controller replacing that of the cashier. See Appendix IV for a list of all signature combinations as they have appeared on small-size paper money.

Printing Paper Currency

Through the years, from the earliest times, people have used cut or scratched lines to decorate their most prized possessions. By the end of the Roman Empire, they had learned to fill little cut lines with a dark gummy substance, smoke the surface, then wipe off the plate and transfer the image to paper.

By the mid-15th century, this art had been most highly developed in both Italy and Germany, and one of the first to actually engrave in ferrous metal for printing was the German, Albrecht Durer. His fine work was printed from copper plates, first by hand rollers, then later on the copper plate printing press, which was invented about 1545.

Paper money of the finest quality was printed by copper plates in mid-17th century England. The first official paper money in America was issued by the Massachusetts Bay Colony in 1690 to pay soldiers. By the mid-18th century, several colonies were issuing very attractive notes.

However, no transfer process was available and all plates had to be recut or newly engraved by hand. It was impossible to make printing plates bearing two identical designs. Despite the very severe penalties for counterfeiting, it was fairly easy.

The end of the 18th century seems to be the beginning of the American banknote printing industry. Jacob Perkins of Massachusetts invented a method of punching lettering and designs into the walls of steel cylinders and crossing them with engraved intersecting lines. These were then rolled into copper plates, and multiple intaglio impressions of exact fidelity were produced.

In 1812, Asa Spencer of Connecticut patented an engine-turning device to ornament watches. A stationary point traced or cut an endless design of perfect regularity, and this was quickly recognized as an effective deterrent for foiling counterfeiters. Perkins purchased the patent rights to this machine in 1815 and introduced it to the banknote business.

The first paper money issued by the U.S. Government came into being by Act of Congress in 1861 and was the result of the need for financing the Civil War, a plan proposed by Secretary of the Treasury Salmon P. Chase [under President Lincoln] as both a system of taxation and one of floating loans. The Bureau of Engraving and Printing was established on Aug. 29, 1862.

Until recently, currency was produced from wet paper printed on intaglio plates. The wetting is required because of the extreme pressures necessary to force the paper down into the incised lines of the plates in order to pick up the ink deposited therein.

Intaglio means that the design is cut or incised into the plate as compared to the raised letters on the more familiar type of printing. Experiments as early as 1938 in methods of dry printing were conducted. Development of non-offset ink allowed the dry method to be used starting in 1952.

With the introduction of the small size currency in 1929, all plates were standardized at 12-subject size. This 12-subject plate was considered maximum size under the wet method of printing because of the shrinkage of the sheets during the alternate wetting and drying of the paper between the printing of the back and the printing of the face of the notes. It was also necessary during this period to place a tissue between each sheet of printed paper to prevent the offset of ink prior to drying.

The size of the plate was increased to 18 subjects following the development of non-offset green ink in 1950 and a black ink in 1952. The door then was opened for increasing the size of the plates. 18-subject plates were first used in August 1952, and by September 1953 all presses had been converted to 18-subjects. With the introduction of the dry paper method for printing, plate size was increased to the 32-subject plate currently used.

When a new note is to be issued, designs are submitted to the designers at the BEP, who prepare a final model. The final model must be approved by the Secretary of the Treasury. Photographic copies of the approved model are furnished to the engravers.

Engravers reproduce the currency designs in pieces of soft steel, known as dies, by working with steel cutting instruments, or gravers, and powerful magnifying glasses. Each separate design, such as the portrait, the vignette, the ornaments, and the lettering, is hand cut by an engraver who has been specially trained in that particular style. A geometric lathe is used to cut the intricate lacy ornaments and borders, and a ruling machine is used to cut the fine crosshatched lines in the portraits. It is practically impossible for an engraver to exactly reproduce his own work or that of another engraver.

When the hand-engraved pieces of soft steel, or dies, have been completed, they are cleaned, and then hardened by being heated in sodium cyanide and quickly dipped into brine. The design of each die is then transferred to a roll or cylinder of soft steel by placing the die on the bed of a transfer press and, under tremendous pressure, forcing the face of the soft roll into the intaglio engraving on the hard die.

The result is an exact duplicate of the original design standing out in relief on the face of the roll. To make a master die by the transfer process, the rolls from these several dies are passed separately over the soft die steel under great pressure. Different portions of the engraving are thereby united on the die in their proper positions. The master die is then finished and hardened and a master roll is made with all the designs necessary to make one note. An engraved steel master plate can then be made from the master roll on the transfer press.

The electrolytic process is now used for making plates for the printing of paper currency. The engraved steel master plate is placed in a nickel-plating bath and by means of electro-deposition another plate is built thereon to a required thickness. This plate is referred to as an alto, and when it is removed from the master, the design stands out in relief on a flat surface. A duplicate plate of the original steel master is then reproduced in the nickel-plating bath from this relief design. These duplicate plates, with the design in the intaglio or cut-in impression as on the original master, are then electrolytically plated with chromium and made ready for printing.

Serial Numbers

There are two different serial numbering systems on U.S. currency, one for Federal Reserve Notes, and another for all the other classes. On Federal Reserve Notes, the prefix letter is always the same as the bank letter. For example all notes issued by the Federal Reserve Bank of Boston have serials that begin with A. The suffix letters progressively cycle through the alphabet as notes are printed producing a stream of blocks that for Boston look like AA, AB, AC, AD etc.

On other classes of currency, numbering always begins with the AA block, but after the first 100 million notes the first letter to change is the prefix letter. As numbering progresses, the prefix letters cycle alphabetically until the ZA block is used up. At this time, the suffix letter is changed to B and the prefix letters begin another cycle at A again.

The letter O is not used in either the prefix or suffix positions on any U.S. currency.

When 12-subject sheets were serial numbered, the sheets were first cut in half vertically. Next the half sheets were fed into the numbering press and serial numbering progressed down the half sheet beginning with 00000001 on position A or G depending on which half of the sheet went first. 00000002 was on the B or H position, etc. The half sheet was then cut into individual notes, arranged in order mechanically, and the next half sheet was fed through.

Starting with the 18-subject sheets in 1952, the notes were numbered through the stack, that is consecutively from sheet to sheet. The notes on a sheet were numbered with skips equal to the number of sheets in the production unit. At that time, a standard production unit was 8000, so the numbers on the number one sheet progressed from 00000001, 00008001 through 00144001. The numbering within a production unit, then as now, actually went backwards so that the smallest numbers landed on the top of the completed stack. Once all the sheets were numbered, the notes were then separated.

The 32-subject notes are printed in four quadrants of eight notes. The upper left quadrant sheet position letters are A1 through H1, the lower left quadrant A2 through H2, the upper right quadrant is A3 through H3 and the lower right quadrant is A4 through H4. The numbering advances 20,000 numbers per position starting with position A1 through H4, then A2 through H2, A3 through H3 and finally A4 through H4. In 1981, the production unit was changed to 40,000 sheets so that now the numbering advances 40,000 numbers between positions.

Star Notes

On April 14, 1910, the director of the Bureau of Engraving and Printing wrote to the treasurer, Lee McClung, suggesting "that the Bureau be authorized to prepare a stock of notes numbered in sequence, distinguished from all other notes by a special letter or character printed before/after the serial number ... that these notes be substituted for defective specimens ... with notation on the pages indicating the package contained such substitutes."

The green light to proceed was given. Approval must have been anticipated, because on April 17, 1910, a rush order was sent to the American Numbering Company in Brooklyn, N.Y., specifying eight stars for use on automatic numbering blocks. The Bureau finished the first package with stars on June 20, 1910, and delivered them to Treasurer McClung on July 12, 1910. Thus the earliest possible star notes are those of 1910 with the Vernon-McClung signature. The first pack of stars was numbered ★75612001**A** through ★75612100**A** and were Series of 1899 $1 Silver Certificates.

It is inevitable that some misprints, smudged notes, or otherwise imperfect notes will be made during note production. At the time of examination, these imperfect notes are replaced by new notes that have a star on one end of the serial number. The percentage of spoiled notes is very small; hence the number of star notes is rather limited. In the early series of our small size notes, the spoilage percentage has been accurately estimated at less than 1% of total notes. No attempt is made to replace any defective note with the same serial number star note.

Star notes also are used to replace the 100 millionth note instead of a note with serial 00 000 000 as printed. We know of at least one instance where, through error, the note with serial **A**00 000 000**A** escaped replacement in the Bureau and was shown at the ANA convention in Boston, Mass., in 1973 by John Morrissey.

Blocks

A block refers to the prefix-suffix letter or star combination appearing in a serial number. For example, serial **F12345678A** is from the FA block. Likewise serial ★87654321**A** is from the ★**A** block. One popular way to collect small size currency is to collect all the blocks.

Groups

A group is a consecutive run of serial numbered notes within a given block that has some unique identity. For example, the $1 SC 1935A Hawaii and North Africa printings were interspersed within the same serial number sequence as regular blue seal notes. In the FC block, serial **F41952001C** to **F41964000C** were North Africa Issues and serials **F41964001C** through **F41976000C** were Hawaii Issues. Thus there are four groups in the FC block, one each of North Africa and Hawaii, with both leading and trailing blue seal printings.

Another interesting $1 SC block with groups is the 1935F and G printings in the BJ block. Serials **B00000001J** through **B54000000J** are 1935F, **B54000001J** through **B71640000J** are 1935G, **B71640001J** through **B72000000J** are 1935F again, and **B72000001J** through **B99999999J** are 1935G.

With the introduction of the Fort Worth $1 FRNs in the Series of 1988A, a few new groups have been created. For example, in the KC block, the first 93,600,000 were printed in Washington, D.C. and the last 6,400,000 were printed in Fort Worth and contain the distinctive FW prefix for the face plate letter.

Some types of group collecting have come and gone, their lost popularity being attributed to the variation being way too minor or the concept underlying the uniqueness of the group being too tedious. One example is the COPE/conventional craze that began with the introduction of Currency Overprinting and Processing Equipment (COPE) in the $1 Series of 1969B FRNs. The COPE serial numbers had a slightly different look than the serials printed from the same typeface on conventional older equipment. The Bureau published totals printed, separating the COPE and conventional serials. The collector had to have the list of numbers to tell what to collect! Another collectible group developed when the Bureau began producing star notes in the Federal Reserve series with serial numbering gaps within production printed serials. Some dedicated collectors tried to collect from each of the myriad of printed groups. Modern day mules might also be attempted to be assembled by some.

It turns out that if groups are to catch on, the variety must be readily distinguishable.

Plate Position Letters

The position of a note in a sheet is revealed by the plate letter that appears on the upper left corner on the face of the note on the 12-subject and 18-subject sheets, and the letter and number that appears in the upper left corner on the face of the 32-subject sheets.

Master Plate Number

The plate number appears in the margin of the sheet (similar to the plate number on a sheet of postage stamps) and is trimmed off during the cutting operation.

Plate Numbers

The tiny number in the lower right of both the face and back is called the plate check number for the cross-reference to the master plate number.

Some collectors find great enjoyment in trying to establish a consecutive run of these plate numbers, or finding notes with matching numbers on front and back, however, one must recognize that the Bureau does not use all numbers in a series. The face and back plate numbers are not related to each other.

Label Sets

Notes produced at the BEP are packaged in 40 packs of 100 notes each. This package, commonly called a brick, has wooden blocks placed at each end of the stack along with a label denoting contents. The brick is then bound with two steel straps. It is then wrapped in heavy Kraft paper and a duplicate label denoting contents affixed to one end of the brick with a label of the Treasury seal affixed to the other end. Until Series of 1974 the label showed the number of notes (4,000), the series year, the denomination of the notes inside, and the serial number of the first and last note.

With the Series 1974, the label remained the same except that it showed only the serial number of the first note in the brick. In recent years many collectors attempted to obtain these labels, with the first and last note in the brick and the term label set was applied.

Series Date

Prior to the Series of 1974, the series date on the face of each bill indicated the year in which the face design of the note was adopted. The capital letter following the series year indicates that a minor change was authorized in a particular series. Such a change occurred with a new Secretary of the Treasury or Treasurer of the United States. This policy was changed when William E. Simon became Secretary of the Treasury. He directed that the series year would be changed whenever there was a change in the Office of the Secretary of the Treasury. Now the series dates are advanced by one letter, or a new year is selected, the latter being more common recently. Consequently, each new signature now results in a surprise for the collector.

In God We Trust

"In God We Trust" owes its presence on United States coins and notes largely to the increased religious sentiment existing during the Civil War. Salmon P. Chase, then Secretary of the Treasury, received a number of appeals from devout persons throughout the country, urging that deity be recognized suitably on our coins in a manner similar to that commonly found on the coins of other nations.

On Nov. 20, 1861, Secretary Chase instructed the Director of the Mint at Philadelphia to prepare a motto "expressing this national recognition." The

Secretary wrote, "No nation can be strong except in the strength of God, or safe except in His defense." The motto first made its appearance on the two-cent coin, authorized by Act of Congress dated April 22, 1864. First appearance of the motto on our paper money was on the silver dollars shown on the back of the $5 1886.

A law passed by the 84th Congress and approved by President Eisenhower on July 11, 1955, provides that "In God We Trust" shall appear on all United States paper currency and coins. One-dollar bills bearing the inscription were first made available to the public at most of the country's banks on Oct. 1, 1957. As the Bureau of Engraving and Printing converted to the dry intaglio process of printing, the motto "In God We Trust" was included in the back design of all classes and denominations of paper currency.

Matthew H. Rothert, past President of the American Numismatic Association, presented the suggestion to Secretary of the Treasury George W. Humphrey in November 1953, and is credited with the ultimate adoption of the idea.

The $ Sign

There are many accounts of the origin of the $ sign. The most widely accepted explanation being that it is the result of evolution of the Mexican or Spanish "Ps" pieces of eight. The theory, derived from a study of old manuscripts, is that the "S" gradually came to be written over the "P" developing a close equivalent of the $ mark. It was widely used before the adoption of the United States dollar in 1785.

Mules

A mule is a note that has a micro size check number on one side and a macro size number on the other. Micro numbers measure 0.6mm high whereas the macro numbers are 1 mm high.

Mules came about with the adoption of macro plate check numbers beginning in January 1938. Mules flowed from the Bureau of Engraving and Printing for the next 15 years. They ceased in 1953 when the last of the 12-subject $50 and $100 Federal Reserve micro back plates were finally retired with the phasing out of 12-subject plates.

The change to macro numbers was of sufficient importance to the Bureau of Engraving and Printing that they advanced the series designations on the new macro face plates by one letter. For example, the $5 Silver Certificates went from Series of 1934 to 1934A, despite the fact that the treasury signatures remained Julian-Morganthau. The difference was entirely in the size of the plate check numbers.

During the transition to all macro plates, both micro and macro plates were in use, often side by side on the same press. This occurred because the Bureau had a policy of using up obsolete plates rather than scrapping them. Whenever micro faces were mated with macro backs, or macro faces were mated with micro backs, we had a mule.

As shown below, mules were created in every denomination from $1 to $10,000. In fact, high denomination notes were among the most commonly muled owing to large stocks of 12-subject high denomination micro back plates.

The first macro plate to go to press was the number 1 Series of 1935A $1 Silver Certificate face on January 6, 1938. The first $1 macro back, plate 930, did not go to press until January 28, 1938; consequently all the 1935A $1s printed between January 6 and January 27 were mules. Those sheets were competing with $5 1934A SCs for the distinction of being the first mules to be overprinted with serial numbers. It turns out that the first Series of 1934A $5 faces (macro) went to press on January 14, a week after the first $1s. All were mated with micro backs and these were the first $5 mules of any class.

The $5 SC sheets advanced to the serial numbering stage more quickly than the $1s. On January 25, the first mule to be serial numbered was a $5 SC bearing number **D**50352001**A**. The first $1 SC 1935A mule, **M**07668991**A**, was numbered the next day. Two days later on January 28, 1938, the first muled star note was printed, a $1 Series of 1935A with serial ★17076001**A**. Macro plates for the other classes and denominations gradually came on line in succeeding months.

By far, the most diverse mules involved the three $5 classes. Micro $5 face plates gradually wore out and the first to go were the SC Series of 1934 plates on August 18, 1938, next were the LT Series of 1928B plates on December 1, 1940, and finally the last Series of 1934 FRN (Richmond) on January 23, 1946. With the exception of two plates, the last of the micro $5 backs was retired on February 14, 1940. However, a stockpile of old preprinted micro backs continued to provide micro backs through about June of 1942.

Overlapping the depletion of $5 micro plates were the introductions of $5 macro plates in the following order: SC Series of 1934A faces on January 14, 1938, macro backs on March 16, 1938, LT Series of 1928C on May 31, 1939, and FRN Series of 1934A (New York) on July 31, 1941. The mix of these plates assured a highly varied $5 mule production for years.

A great added surprise came in 1944 when an unfinished, now ancient, $5 micro back plate bearing number 637 was discovered and completed on November 10, 1944. It first went to press on June 23, 1945 and was used rather continuously until June 16, 1949 when it was finally canceled. In the meantime, a second ancient plate was discovered, plate 629, which was already completed but which had never been used. It too was sent to press, but for a very short period from November 17, 1947 through February 2, 1948. These extraordinary plates produced a plethora of our rarest and most eagerly sought mules.

Back 637 produced the following mules: SC 1934A, B, C; LT 1928C, D, & E and FRN 1934A, B, C. In addition, this plate appears unmuled with FRN 1934 faces in blocks D-A, E-A, and J-A. Plate 629 produced mules in the following series: SC 1934C, LT 1928E, and FRN 1934C. All 629 mules are prized rarities. Many 637 mules are major rarities, especially the Series of 1934A FRNs which rank as the most elusive of all mule rarities. Plates 629 and 637 are responsible for all the $5 mules produced after January 1946.

Complete list of mules by type.

Denom.	Class	Series	Face	Back
$1	SC	1935	micro	macro
		1935	macro	micro
$2	LT	1928C	micro	macro
		1928D	macro	micro
$5	SC	1934	micro	macro
		1934A	macro	micro
		1934B	macro	micro
		1934C	macro	micro
	LT	1928B	micro	macro
		1928C	macro	micro
		1928D	macro	micro
		1928E	macro	micro
	FRN	1934 dark green seal	micro	macro
		1934 Hawaii	micro	macro
		1934A dark green seal	macro	micro
		1934B	macro	micro
		1934B NY 212*	intermediate	micro
		1934C	macro	micro
$10	SC	1934	micro	macro
		1934 North Africa	micro	macro
		1934A	macro	micro
		1934 light green seal	micro	macro
	FRN	1934 dark green seal	micro	macro
		1934A light green seal	macro	micro
		1934A dark green seal	macro	micro
$20	FRN	1934 dark green seal	micro	macro
		1934 Hawaii	micro	macro
		1934A light green seal**	macro	micro
		1934A dark green seal	macro	micro
		1934A Hawaii	macro	micro
$50	FRN	1934 dark green seal	micro	macro
		1934A dark green seal	macro	micro
		1934B	macro	micro
		1934C	macro	micro
		1934D	macro	micro
		1950	macro	micro
$100	FRN	1934 dark green seal	micro	macro
		1934A dark green seal	macro	micro
		1934B	macro	micro
		1934C	macro	micro
		1934D	macro	micro
		1950	macro	micro

$500, $1000, $5000, $10000 mules possible in all 1934 series.
Mule varieties involving late finished plates:

$10	SC	1934A 86, 87	macro	micro
$20	FRN	1934 204 dark green seal	micro	macro
		1934 204 Hawaii	micro	macro

*none reported
**may be possible from Chicago

Late Finished Plates

A small group of interesting but peculiar varieties came into being as a result of the conversion from micro to macro size plate check numbers, a conversion that began in January 1938. These are the notes printed from late finished plates. What happened was that the plates were assigned numbers and their manufacture was begun during the micro era. However, their completion was delayed until long after macro plate numbers were adopted. Consequently they carry macro plate numbers but the numbers fall decidedly in the micro range.

The following is a list of these most unusual plates.

Plate	No.	Date Begun	Date Finished	Dates Used	Total Notes
$1 back	470	Sep 1, 1936	May 13,1943	May 15, 1943- Jun 18,1943	2,402,700

Plate	No.	Date Begun	Date Finished	Dates Used	Total Notes
$5 SC 1934A	307	Apr 6, 1936	Jul 3, 1942	Jul 9, 1942- Jun 3, 1943	569,244
$10 SC 1934A	86	Jan 21, 1938	May 29, 1940	Jul 18,1940- Jun 29,1944	1,203,456
$10 SC 1934A	87	Feb 7, 1938	Sep 16,1938	Dec 5, 1939- Jan 16, 1940	83,100
$20 back	204	Dec 21, 1934	Mar 18,1944	Apr 4, 1944- Oct 2, 1946	3,328,728

You will see in the listings that these plates were responsible for a host of interesting and unusual varieties. By far the rarest are the $1 SC Series of 1935A notes from the 470 back. Notice that the $5 and $10 SC faces were completed as Series of 1934As which is consistent with their macro check numbers.

These varieties used to be called Trial Notes before the circumstances behind their manufacture became known.

Experimental Notes

The most well known experimental notes are the $1 SC 1935A R and S (regular and special) paper tests. Several such paper tests have been conducted over the years. The most well-documented include the $1 SC 1928A and 1928B XB, YB and ZB block notes, $1 SC 1935 AB, BB and CB block notes and recently the Natick paper test.

Approximately one million of the red R and S notes were placed in circulation in June 1944. Compilation of statistics was to be done as the notes were returned for redemption. However, the returns were so small that the volume never reached sufficient proportions for a valid analysis. The 1928A and 1928B experimentals, as well as the 1935 issue of experimentals were much better disguised. However, no test results seem to have been forthcoming.

New experiments conducted in 1981 on so-called Natick test paper resulted in the printing of $1 notes for Series 1977A (Richmond) serials **E** 76 800 001 **H** through **E** 80 640 000 **H**, a total of 3,840,000 notes; $1 Series 1977A (Richmond) serials **E** 07 052 001★ through **E** 07 060 000★, a total of 256,000 notes with a gap of 12,000 serial numbers between positions; and $10 Series 1977A notes for Richmond in August 1981 with serials **E** 05 772 001★ through **E** 05 780 000★.

The Treasury Seal

U.S. paper money of small size carries an imprint of the Treasury seal. It is the distinguishing mark which validates our currency, and in a manner of speaking is the authority, coupled with the expression of obligation and the two signatures that form a valid contract between the United States government and the holders of its currency. The color of the seal indicates the class of currency it adorns.

The Seal of the Treasury of North America is inscribed in Latin (Thesaur. Amer. Septent Sigil) around the seal. A square for rectitude, a key for safety, and a set of scales for equality are distinguishable features. A modern version with inscription in English and removal of some of the heraldry was approved and first appeared on the $100 U.S. Note Series in 1966. Treasury Order No. 212 dated January 29, 1968 and signed by Henry H. Fowler officially approved the new Treasury seal.

OLD SEAL   *NEW SEAL*

The Treasury considers that the creator of its seal probably was Francis Hopkinson, who is known to have submitted bills to the Congress in 1780 authorizing the design of departmental seals, including the Board of Treasury. Although it is not certain that Hopkinson was the designer, the seal is similar to others by him. Also obscured by the absence of historical proof is the reason for original wording that embraced all North America.

Federal Reserve Seal Color Varieties

There are two distinct treasury seal colors on both 1928 and 1934 series Federal Reserve Notes. These will be treated in turn.

The treasury seals were changed from a dark green to a vivid yellow green color sometime between 1930 and 1932. All the Series of 1928C and 1928D FRNs have the yellow green seal. Many $5, $10 and $20 Series of 1928B and quite a few high denomination Series of 1928 and 1928A plates were in use after the change so yellow green seals occur on notes from these plates as well. The change to the yellow green color was progressive and collectors have been able to assemble sets of notes showing many gradations between the old green and newer yellow green varieties.

The vivid yellow green seals were continued into the 1934 series. The color was again changed around the fall of 1938, this time to a pale blue green color. As with the 1928 change, this change was gradational so several different intermediate hues have been observed, particularly on the $10s and $20s. No $5 Series of 1934 yellow green seal mules were printed because there were no $5 FRN printings between May 20, 1937 and July 10, 1941. This period spanned both the introduction of macro backs and the seal color change, so when $5 printings resumed, the Series of 1934 mules that rolled off the presses all got pale blue green seals.

These seal color varieties have caused serious cataloging problems since the inception of this catalog, and we are taking major steps to sort through these problems with this edition. In doing so, we have gotten very precise with our definition of light (yellow) green seals. To be considered light the seal must be vivid yellow olive green only. All transitional intermediate seal colors have been categorized as dark. When in doubt, compare your note with a full vivid yellow olive green seal note only. Do not compare backwards, i.e., with a dark seal to see if yours is lighter. (They'll all come out light). Using this criteria, we hope that you will contribute serial number data to help us refine our steadily improving data base.

Subtle Design Changes On Federal Reserve Notes

The Federal Reserve Notes underwent substantial redesigns beginning with the following series: 1928, 1934, 1950 and 1963. The following is a list of important minor changes that have occurred over the years.

On 1928 series notes, the early issues have treasury seals which contain the number of the issuing bank. The number was changed to a letter beginning with the Series of 1928A $50 and $100 notes, and with the Series of 1928B $5, $10 and $20 notes. Only the letter was used in the seal for the high denomination notes.

The word "The" was dropped from the Federal Reserve seals beginning with the Series of 1934B issues.

A new vignette was adopted for the backs of the $20s during the Series of 1934C printings wherein the balcony was added to the White House, the shrubbery grew considerably, and the word "the" was added to the line under the vignette. Both varieties appear on Series of 1934C notes.

"IN GOD WE TRUST" was added to the backs as follows: Series of 1963 $5, $10, $20, and Series of 1963A $50 and $100.

The new treasury seal was adopted on the Series of 1969 notes.

Major Redesign On Federal Reserve Notes

With a primary goal to foil counterfeiters, the U.S. Treasury released the Series 1996 $100 Federal Reserve Note in early 1996, with a total redesign. Among the new significant features are the enlarged off-center portrait of Benjamin Franklin, the Franklin watermark, the use of color shifting inks, and a standard Federal Reserve Seal used for all districts with district designation of issuing bank indicated by a letter and number just below the upper left serial number. The additional letter preceding the serial number corresponds to the series, i.e., (A) represents Series 1996, (B) represents Series 1999, etc. Also found on the new designs are concentric fine line printing and microprinting. The back of the note still shows Independence Hall, but has also undergone major redesign. Beginning in late 2003, the Series 2004 $20 notes , followed by the $50 notes, utilizing colorized backgrounds were released. This was considered one step further in the effort to foil counterfeiters.

North African And Hawaii Series

United States Silver Certificates printed with the Treasury seal in yellow, rather than the usual blue, were used in the initial stages of America's World War II military operations in North Africa and Sicily. The distinctive seal was adopted to facilitate isolation of the currency in event that military reverses caused substantial amounts to fall into enemy hands. Denominations issued were $1, $5 and $10. Circulation of the yellow seal currency was confined for some time to the military zones of operation, but subsequently restrictions against its circulation in the United States were removed. Except for the yellow seal, it is identical with other Silver Certificates of the same vintage.

A specially marked U.S. currency was introduced into Hawaii in July 1942, as an economic defense against a possible Japanese occupation. The notes were overprinted "HAWAII" horizontally on the back and vertically at each end on the face. Only the overprinted notes were allowed in Hawaii after Aug. 14, 1942, except in rare instances approved by the Governor of Hawaii. Notes utilized for this purpose were the $1 Silver Certificate Series 1935A and the San Francisco Federal Reserve notes of $5 Series 1934 and 1934A, the $10 Series 1934A and the $20 Series 1934 and 1934A. All of the Hawaii overprinted currency carried brown seals and serial numbers and the Julian-Morgenthau signatures. The prohibition of unmarked currency in Hawaii remained in effect until Oct. 21, 1944.

Fancy Facts

Notes are 2.61 by 6.14 inches long. Laid end to end there would be approximately 11,900 notes per mile. Notes are .0043 inches thick, stacked there would be 233 notes per inch. 490 notes would weigh one pound, one million notes would be about a ton and would occupy about 42 cubic feet. The Bureau uses about 3,500 tons of paper and about 1,000 tons of ink each year.

How Paper Money Enters Circulation

The distribution of paper currency is made through the Federal Reserve banks and their branches. Member banks of the Federal Reserve System carry reserve accounts with the Federal Reserve bank of their district. When member banks need additional currency, they authorize the Federal Reserve Bank to charge their reserve account and ship the currency. The Federal Reserve banks will ship needed currency on request. Nonmember banks procure their currency through a correspondent member bank located in the same city with the Federal Reserve Bank.

Destruction Of Unfit Currency

When paper currency becomes worn and no longer fit for use, it is withdrawn from circulation, destroyed, and replaced by new notes. The worn notes are destroyed by incineration or pulverization. The destruction process is not complete until the notes have been reduced to an unidentifiable residue so that no recovery is possible.

Currency is verified as to genuineness, kind, value, and number of pieces before destruction. Dollar bills make up the bulk of the currency which is retired. One dollar bills normally last about 18 months, while higher-denomination bills last much longer.

Currencies in all denominations below $500 that are no longer fit for use are verified and destroyed at Federal Reserve banks and branches throughout the country, and by the United States Treasurer's Office, under procedures prescribed by the Department of the Treasury. Federal Reserve Notes in denominations of $500 and above are canceled with distinctive perforations and cut in half lengthwise. The lower halves are shipped to the Department of the Treasury in Washington, D.C. where they are verified and destroyed. The upper halves are retained by the Federal Reserve banks and destroyed after the banks are notified by the Treasury that the lower halves have been verified.

Exchange Of Mutilated Paper Currency

Lawfully held paper money of the United States which has been mutilated will be exchanged at its face value if clearly more than one half of the original note remains. Fragments of such mutilated currency which are not clearly more than one half of the original note will be exchanged at face value only if the Treasurer of the United States is satisfied that the missing portions have been totally destroyed. Correspondence regarding mutilated currency should be addressed to the Office of the Treasurer of the United States, Room 1123, Main Treasury Bldg., Washington, D.C. 20220.

Legal Tender

Public law 89-81, the Coinage Act of July 23, 1965, defines Legal Tender as follows:

"All coins and currencies of the United States (including Federal Reserve notes and circulating notes of Federal Reserve banks and national banking associations), regardless of when coined or issued, shall be legal tender for all debts, public and private, public charges, taxes, duties, and dues."

Fancy Numbers

Palindromes, or radar notes, are notes on which the serial number reads the same backwards or forwards, without regard to prefix or suffix letters. In addition to these, many collectors like ladders with serial numbers like 01 234 567 or down ladders such as 98 765 432 etc. Repeaters, such as 12 12 12 12 or 2222 3333 are very popular. Perhaps the most outstanding of the fancy numbers are those which have all eight digits the same, such as 11 111 111 or 44 444 444 etc.

Low Numbers

Serial numbers under 9999 are generally considered low numbers, with serial number 00 000 001 of course being perfection. Today, most collectors are quite happy to find a note starting with four zeroes, and delighted to find one with even more zeroes. Naturally the notes rise in price with the number of zeroes at the beginning.

Grading

We believe the following criteria will enable you to properly and accurately grade any note:

Choice Crisp Uncirculated A new bill, never used, clean and crisp, but may have minor pinholes and a corner tip fold not into design. Keep in mind that some notes in certain series were not clean and crisp when printed. The 1935A $1 Silver Certificate is a good example of this. Many of the 1935A's have a dirty look to the paper, some are quite limp and were so when originally issued. (CH CU) The values shown are for decently centered notes with an average grade of "Choice CU." Poorly centered notes would carry a lower value, while well centered examples would command higher values.

Extremely Fine About Uncirculated Note is still crisp but may show minor wrinkles or few dirt specks. No heavy folds or creases. No stains or severe dirty spots. Two or three light folds or creases. (EF-AU)

Very Fine Shows some use, but still has some crispness. May have a 4 or 5 heavy folds. Must have a uniformly nice appearance with only light soil. (VF)

Very Good-Fine Shows circulation, may have heavy folds or possibly creases that break the paper and moderate to heavy soiling. May have minor stains. (VG-F)

Good Entire note is there but may have tears. No crispness, may be dirty, stained, or have ink marking in field. Generally described as average circulated. (G)

Below these grades are fair and poor. Generally considered uncollectible except in the rarest notes.

Wide And Narrow Margins

$1 1935D Silver Certificates come with wide and narrow back designs. The green border below the large printed words "ONE DOLLAR" at the bottom of the back of the note is the identifying area. If this strip is thin, it is referred to as a "narrow" margin. If it is thick, it is called a wide margin.

The wide and narrow backs on $5 1928F US Notes, $5 1934D Silver Certificates and $5 1950 Federal Reserve Notes can be distinguished by the small circle on the lower right corner of the back of the bill. A careful examination of the photo reveals three double lines in the right half of the circle on the wide backs. The narrow back has only two double lines.

The wide and narrow backs on the $10 1934D Silver Certificates are distinguished by the ribbon through figure 10 in the bottom right corner of the back of the note. If there is an area of green between the end of the ribbon and the white margin at the edge of the note, it is a wide back. If this ribbon extends completely to the printed edge of the note, it is a narrow back.

Wide   Narrow

Many design changes, from wide to narrow were incorporated into notes, on both faces and backs, in the late 1940's. most design changes, from $2.00 to $100.00, occurred between series, not within, so no rarities are thus possible in those cases. But a few did involve variations within a series, as seen above, and now newly found and reported by Pete Hunsroon, also in $5.00 SC Series 1934 C Faces, $5.00 FRN Series 1934 C Faces, $10.00 FRN Series 1934 C Faces, and $20.00 FRN Series 1934D backs.

$5.00 Wide, Narrow, Wide II

$10.00 Narrow

$10.00 Wide

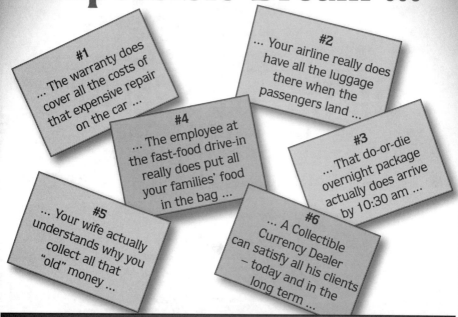

ONE DOLLAR NOTES

LEGAL TENDER

SERIES 1928 RED SEAL

PLATE NUMBERS: Face #1 - #36 (exceptions only #31 and #33-35).

SIGNATURES: W.O. Woods, W.H. Woodin

This series was printed in April and May 1933 but the majority were not released until the recession of 1948-49. These were then issued in Puerto Rico as an economy measure as follows:

Nov. 1948	40,000	**Jan. 1949**	500,000	**Feb. 1949**	40,000
Mar. 1949	42,000	**Apr. 1949**	144,000		

Puerto Rico was chosen to keep the "odd one-time" issue from causing sorting problems in the banks on the mainland.

Serial Numbers

Low	High	Notes Printed	VG	VF	CH CU	GEM
A00 000 001A	A01 872 012A	1,872,012	$100	$200	$550	$850
★00 000 002A	★00 007 892A	—	3,000	7,500	30,000*	40,000

*Lyn Knight Auction Dec 2, 2000 CH CU $35,000

$1 SILVER CERTIFICATES

SERIES 1928 BLUE SEAL

Obligation: "This certifies that there has been deposited in the Treasury of the United States of America One Silver Dollar payable to the bearer on demand."

Legend, Series 1928, 1928A, 1928B, 1928C and 1928D: "This certificate is receivable for all public dues and when so received may be reissued."

On Series 1928E: "This certificate is legal tender for all debts public and private."

PLATE NUMBERS: Face #2 - #1022. Back check numbers begin with #1.

SIGNATURES: H.T. Tate, A.W. Mellon

Serial numbers on both regular and star notes begin with 00 000 001.

Serial Numbers

Low	High	Notes Printed	VF	CH CU	GEM CU
A-A	H-A	638,296,908	$35	$80	$150
I-A	—	—	100	600	750
J-A	—	—	150	900	1,100
K-A	—	—	150	1,000	1,250
L52 107 065A high observed		—	225	1,500	2,000
★00 000 039A	★12 444 406A	—	125	800	1,200

SERIES 1928A BLUE SEAL

PLATE NUMBERS: Face #5 - #1814.
SIGNATURES: W.O. Woods, A.W. Mellon

Serial Numbers

Low	High	Notes Printed	VF	CH CU	GEM CU
D93 825 125A	—	2,267,809,500	$400	$2,200	$3,000
E-A	—	—	200	700	900
F-A	Z-A	—	30	75	125
A-B	F-B	—	30	75	125
G-B	H-B	—	30	85	125
I-B	—	—	60	200	300
—	J54 403 307B high observed	—	50	300	400
★08 571 642A	★37 217 680A	—	100	700	900

SERIES 1928A EXPERIMENTALS BLUE SEAL

The first major experimental group of small notes was printed in November 1932 and delivered to the Treasury for release into circulation in January and February of 1933, during the period of the $1.00 Series 1928A and 1928B. The experimental set was to determine the effect of changing the relative amounts of linen and cotton paper fibers. The **X-B** and **Y-B** groups were each printed on paper of different proportions of rag content with the **Z-B** group as the control, using the distinctive paper in regular use. The special numbers assigned to this experiment are given below.

The experimentals are randomly mixed between both Series 1928A and 1928B because they were serially numbered from a single number register. An estimate of quantities printed within each is not yet possible.

Serial Numbers

Low	High	Notes Printed	VG	VF	CH CU	GEM CU
X00 000 001B	X10 728 000B	10,728,000	$35	$75	$300	$450
Y00 000 001B	Y10 248 000B	10,248,000	35	75	225	325
Z00 000 001B	Z10 248 000B	10,248,000	45	85	300	400

SERIES 1928B EXPERIMENTALS BLUE SEAL

Serial Numbers

Low	High	VG	VF	CH CU	GEM CU
X00 000 001**B**	**X**10 728 000**B**	$40	$80	$275	$350
Y00 000 001**B**	**Y**10 248 000**B**	40	80	300	350
Z00 000 001**B**	**Z**10 248 000**B**	50	90	350	450

SERIES 1928B BLUE SEAL

PLATE NUMBERS: Face #2 - #567.

SIGNATURES: W.O. Woods, Ogden L. Mills

Serial Numbers

Low	High	Notes Printed	VF	CH CU	GEM CU
V51 000 001**A** official low	—	674,597,808	$100	$400	$500
V51 000 046**A** low observed	—	—	—	—	—
W-A	—	—	50	300	400
X-A	—	—	40	200	300
Y-A	—	—	40	125	225
Z-A	—	—	35	100	175
A-B	**J**53 997 572**B** high observed	—	35	75	150
★27 148 294**A**	★37 546 972**A**	—	300	1,600	2,200

SERIES 1928C BLUE SEAL

PLATE NUMBERS: Face #1 - #9 (numbers #5 and #10 were master plates and were not used).

SIGNATURES: W.O. Woods, W.H. Woodin

Serial Numbers

Low	High	Notes Printed	VG	VF	CH CU	GEM CU
B29 448 001**B** —		5,364,348	$150	$250	$750	$900
official low						
C-B	—	—	200	250	1,000	1,250
D-B	**I-B**	—	150	250	900	1,100
—	**J**47 096 952**B**	—	200	400	1,500	1,750
	high observed					
★33 390 295**A**	★36 774 073**A**	—	2,000	7,000	30,000	50,000

SERIES 1928D BLUE SEAL

PLATE NUMBERS: Face #1 - #49.

SIGNATURES: W.A. Julian, W.H. Woodin

Serial Numbers

Low	High	Notes Printed	VG	VF	CH CU	GEM CU
D82 596 001**B** —		14,451,372	$35	$95	$450	$550
official low						
F-B	—.	—	45	125	650	750
E-B G-B H-B	**I-B**	—	35	95	450	550
—	**J**54 890 954**B**	—	35	95	450	550
	high observed					
★35 006 672**A**	★37 368 075**A**	—	1,500	6,000	25,000	50,000

SERIES 1928E BLUE SEAL

PLATE NUMBERS: Face #1 - #12. #5 and #6 were masters.

SIGNATURES: W.A. Julian, Henry Morgenthau, Jr.

Serial Numbers

Low	High	Notes Printed	VG	VF	CH CU	GEM
F72 000 001B	J54 954 234B	3,519,324	$300	$800	$2,500	$3,250
★35 821 073A	—	—	10,000	16,000	50,000	90,000

The highest serial numbers printed for all 1928 series are **J**55 796 000**B** and ★37 560 000**A**.

SERIES 1934 BLUE SEAL

PLATE NUMBERS: Face #1 - #838. Back numbers end at #3096.

SIGNATURES: W.A. Julian, Henry Morgenthau, Jr.

Serial Numbers
Official Range

Low	High	Notes Printed	VF	CH CU	GEM CU
A00 000 001A	G82 176 000A	682,176,000	$35	$100	$150
★00 000 001A	★07 680 000A	7,680,000	175	1,000	1,400
(observed)	G82 012 459A	—	—	—	—
★00 000 065A	★07 660 451A	—	—	—	—

SERIES 1935 BLUE SEAL

Experimental notes were printed in this series which are identifiable by block letters **A-B**, **B-B** and **C-B**.

PLATE NUMBERS: Face #1 - #1391. Back #1 - #929.

SIGNATURES: W.A. Julian, Henry Morgenthau, Jr.

Serial Numbers

Low	High	Notes Printed	VF	CH CU	GEM CU
A00 000 001A	L-A	1,681,552,000	$5	$35	$55
M-A	—	—	7.50	35	55
N-A	—	—	15	75	100
P-A	—	—	25	150	175
Q-A	—	—	50	250	300
—	R81 552 000A official high	—	50	300	350
★00 005 551A	★22 313 807A	—	150	500	750

SERIES 1935 MULE BLUE SEAL

These are Series 1935 notes with macro back plate numbers (#930 or higher) and are actually Series 1935 faces printed on Series 1935A backs.

All series 1935 mules are scarce.

Serial Numbers

Low	High	Notes Printed	VF	CH CU	GEM CU
M81 121 635A		see above	$500	$1,500	$1,750
N-A	—		50	400	450
P-A	—		50	250	300
Q-A	R74 715 480A		50	200	250
★21 820 006A	★22 300 442A		1,500	5,000	7,500

SERIES 1935 EXPERIMENTALS BLUE SEAL

A paper experiment patterned after the $1.00 Series 1928A and 1928B set was again tried during the $1.00 Series 1935. In this case the printing began on March 16, 1937 on the **A-B** block, utilizing the distinctive paper with a special finish. The printing of this group ended April 28, 1937. Printing started again on November 26, 1937 with the **B-B** block using special paper. On December 1, 1937, the **C-B** block was begun on regular paper as the control, and both terminated on December 10th. These were all delivered within the year 1937. The special numbers assigned to this experiment are given below.

Serial Numbers

Low	High	Notes Printed	VF	CH CU	GEM CU
A00 000 001**B**	**A**06 180 000**B**	6,180,000	$50	$200	$275
B00 000 001**B**	**B**03 300 000**B**	3,300,000	150	650	750
C00 000 001**B**	**C**03 300 000**B**	3,300,000	100	650	750

SERIES 1935A MULE BLUE SEAL

These are Series 1935A notes with the micro back plate numbers (#2 and #436-929), and are actually Series 1935A faces printed on Series 1935 backs.

Serial Numbers

Low	High	VF	CH CU	GEM CU
M07 668 001**A**	—	—	—	—
official low printed January 26, 1938				
M07 777 770**A**	—	$5	$60	$75
low observed				
N-A	**T-A**	6	50	65
U-A	**W-A**	8	60	75
X-A	**Z-A**	15	150	175
A-B	—	25	250	300
B-B	—	75	400	500
C-B	—	25	200	300
D-B	—	100	750	900
—	**E**96 998 982**B**	300	1,200	—
	high observed			
★17 076 001**A**	★37 095 331**A**	125	550	750

(Official low star note printed January 28, 1938)

SERIES 1935A LATE FINISHED PLATE BLUE SEAL

SERIAL NUMBERS: (reported) **K**20 895 155**C** and **K**20 895 156**C**

PLATE NUMBER: Micro back #470.

TOTAL QUANTITY PRINTED: 2,402,700 notes.

Only four known. One of these is damaged.

VF+ example sold for $2,000 in 1996.

SERIES 1935A BLUE SEAL

PLATE NUMBERS: Face numbers begin at #1, starting January 6, 1938. Back numbers begin at #930, starting January 28, 1938.

SIGNATURES: W.A. Julian, Henry Morgenthau, Jr.

Serial Numbers

Low	High	VF	CH CU	GEM CU
M-A (only three notes known) **M**94 517 133**A**		$2,500	—	—
M52 262 049**A** sold for $8,250 in 1998.				
N-A	—	50	300	375
P-A	—	10	50	70
Q-A	**C-D**	3	15	25
—	**D**45 624 000**D** official high	7	30	45
★17 559 387**A** low observed	—	15	150	250
—	★02 651 672**B** high observed	35	225	350

HAWAII NOTES

SERIES 1935A BROWN SEAL

Serial Numbers

Low	High	Notes Printed	VG/F	VF	CH CU	GEM CU
Y68 628 001**B**	**Y**71 628 000**B**	3,000,000	$40	$50	$250	$350
Z99 000 001**B**	**Z**99 999 999**B**	1,000,000	75	150	1,000	1,500
A99 000 001**C**	**A**99 999 999**C**	1,000,000	75	200	1,750	3,000
C00 000 001**C**	**C**07 000 000**C**	7,000,000	40	60	200	350
F41 964 001**C**	**F**41 976 000**C**	12,000	100	180	700	1,000

Low	High	Notes Printed	VG/F	VF	CH CU	GEM CU
L75 996 001C	L78 996 000C	3,000,000	$30	$50	$200	$250
P31 992 001C	P37 032 000C	5,040,000	30	50	200	250
S39 996 001C	S54 996 000C	15,000,000	30	45	200	250
★64 812 001A	★64 860 000A	48,000	150	450	3,000	4,500
★66 084 001A	★66 108 000A	24,000	150	450	3,000	4,500
★70 260 001A	★70 332 000A	72,000	150	450	3,000	4,500
★87 360 001A	★87 408 000A	48,000	150	450	3,000	4,500
★91 128 001A	★91 140 000A	12,000	150	450	3,000	4,500
★64 812 607A	★91 139 361A	—	—	—	—	—
	observed range					

NORTH AFRICA NOTES

SERIES 1935A YELLOW SEAL

Serial Numbers

Low	High	Notes Printed	VG/F	VF	CH CU	GEM CU
B30 000 001C	B31 000 000C	1,000,000	$30	$50	$275	$400
B51 624 001C	B52 624 000C	1,000,000	30	50	275	400
B99 000 001C	B99 999 999C	1,000,000	30	50	275	400
C60 000 001C	C62 000 000C	2,000,000	30	50	275	400
C78 000 001C	C79 904 000C	1,904,000	30	50	275	400
F41 952 001C	F41 964 000C	12,000	75	150	550	850
I30 000 001C	I40 000 000C	10,000,000	30	50	275	400
R90 000 001C	R99 999 999C	10,000,000	30	50	275	400
★68 364 001A	★68 388 000A	24,000	150	400	3,000	5,000
★70 956 001A	★71 004 000A	48,000	150	400	3,000	5,000
★79 560 001A	★79 632 000A	72,000	150	400	3,000	5,000
★68 364 496A	★79 627 768A	—	—	—	—	—
	observed range					

"R & S" NOTES

SERIES 1935A EXPERIMENTAL R AND S BLUE SEAL

The best known of the experimental printings were the "R" and "S" overprint issues in the **S-C** block of Series 1935A. In this case, the red "R" was overprinted on the regular distinctive paper and the red "S" on a special paper. They were delivered June 20, 1944 and issued into circulation to test their comparative durabilities. No conclusive results were determined from the trial issue. (Bureau of Engraving and Printing records show that 12,000 star notes of each "R" and "S" were printed.)

The special numbers assigned to this experiment are given below.

"R" NOTES

Serial Numbers

Low	High	Notes Printed	VG/F	VF	CH CU	GEM CU
S70 884 001C	S72 068 000C	1,184,000	$70	$125	$500	$800
★91 176 001A	★91 188 000A	12,000	1,000	2,000	6,250	8,000
★91 177 120A	★91 187 706A observed	—	—	—	—	—

"S" NOTES

Low	High	Notes Printed	VG/F	VF	CH CU	GEM CU
S73 884 001C	S75 068 000C	1,184,000	$60	$115	$500	$800
★91 188 001A	★91 200 000A	12,000	1,000	2,000	6,250	8,000
★91 188 035A	★91 192 619A observed	—	—	—	—	—

SERIES 1935B BLUE SEAL

SIGNATURES: W.A. Julian, Fred M. Vinson

Serial Numbers

Low	High	Notes Printed	VF	CH CU	GEM CU
C93 384 001**D**	—	806,612,000	$45	$150	$200
D-D	**K-D**	—	4	20	35
L-D	—	—	5	25	40
M00 569 408**D**	**M**00 593 189**D**	—	500	1,500	—
—	**M**00 648 000**D** official high	—	—	—	—
★02 689 877**B**	★12 703 727**B** observed	—	65	300	400

SERIES 1935C BLUE SEAL

SIGNATURES: W.A. Julian, John W. Snyder

Serial Numbers

Low	High	Notes Printed	VF	CH CU	GEM CU
K99 996 001**D** official low	—	3,088,108,000	$50	$150	$225
L-D	**S-E**	—	3	15	30
T-E	—	—	4	20	35
—	**U**86 153 076**E**	—	5	50	65
★12 864 118**B**	★49 474 913**B**	—	20	90	130

$1 SILVER CERTIFICATES

SERIES 1935D WIDE BLUE SEAL

From 12 Subject Sheets

PLATE NUMBERS: Back #5015 or lower.

SIGNATURES: Georgia Neese Clark, John W. Snyder

1935D WIDE

1935D WIDE

Serial Numbers					
Low	**High**	**Notes Printed**	**VF**	**CH CU**	**GEM CU**
R88 104 001E	—	4,656,968,000*	$35	$150	$200
S-E	F-G	—	3	15	30
H-G	I-G	—	5	20	35
J-G	—	—	10	30	45
K-G	—	—	20	60	75
L-G	—	—	35	200	250
—	M88 986 086G	—	50	250	350
★49 603 597B low observed	—	—	15	150	200
—	★06 038 641C high observed	—	250	900	—

Includes all 1935D notes: All 12 subject sheets, and 146,944,000 in sheets of 18.

SERIES 1935D NARROW BLUE SEAL

From 12 Subject Sheets

PLATE NUMBERS: Back #5017 or higher.

Serial Numbers

Low	High	Notes Printed	VF	CH CU	GEM CU
U54 720 688E low observed	—	see above	$2,000	$6,000	$—
V-E	—	—	20	60	80
W-E	—	—	15	45	60
X-E	—	—	10	30	45
Y-E	Z-E	—	5	20	35
A-F	M98 128 000G	—	3	12	30
★55 213 765B low observed	—	—	15	50	100
—	★07 044 000C official high	—	25	115	200

1935D NARROW

SERIES 1935D BLUE SEAL (18 SUBJECT SHEETS)

PLATE NUMBERS: Face #7463 or higher (with some alternating back to 12 subject sheets).

Back #5689 or higher (with some alternating back to 12 subject sheets)

Serial Numbers

Low	High	Notes Printed	VF	CH CU	GEM CU
G00 000 001G	G99 999 999G	99,999,999	$8	$30	$60
N00 000 001G	N46 944 000G	46,944,000	8	40	70
★00 000 001D	★05 023 672D high observed	—	50	250	500

SERIES 1935E BLUE SEAL

SIGNATURES: Ivy Baker Priest, G.M. Humphrey

Serial Numbers

Low	High	Notes Printed	VF	CH CU	GEM CU
N46 944 001**G**	P54 185 771**I**	5,134,056,000	$3	$15	$25
★05 054 838**D**	—	—	5	20	35
low observed					
★-**E**	—	—	5	20	50
—	★57 024 556**F**	—	6	25	75
	high observed				

SERIES 1935F BLUE SEAL

SIGNATURES: Ivy Baker Priest, Robert B. Anderson

Serial Numbers

Low	High	Notes Printed	VF	CH CU	GEM CU
P81 000 001**I**	B54 000 000**J**	1,173,000,000	$4	$15	$25
B71 640 001**J**	B72 000 000**J**	360,000	150	900	—
★57 367 573**F**	—	—	6	20	40
low observed					
—	★10 542 728**G**	53,200,000	6	30	60
	high observed				

SERIES 1935G NO MOTTO BLUE SEAL

PLATE NUMBERS: Back #6786 or lower.

SIGNATURES: Elizabeth Rudel Smith, C. Douglas Dillon

Serial Numbers

Low	High	Notes Printed	VF	CH CU	GEM CU
B54 000 001J	B71 000 000J	17,000,000	$5	$20	$30
B71 000 001J	B71 640 000J	640,000	20	100	—
B72 000 001J	B99 999 999J	28,000,000	5	20	30
C00 000 001J	D48 960 000J	148,960,000	4	15	25
★10 455 957G	★19 024 276G	8,640,000	6	50	100

SERIES 1935G W/MOTTO BLUE SEAL

PLATE NUMBERS: Back #6787 or higher.

SIGNATURES: Same as 1935G without motto.

MOTTO: "In God We Trust" added to back above "ONE".

Serial Numbers

Low	High	Notes Printed	VF	CH CU	GEM CU
D48 960 001J	D80 280 000J	31,320,000	$10	$50	$75
★19 090 466G low observed	—	—	—	—	—
—	★20 149 712G high observed	1,080,000	50	225	325

SERIES 1935H BLUE SEAL

PLATE NUMBERS: Face #8648 or lower.

Back check #6876 or lower (last plates used for 18 subject sheets).

SIGNATURES: Kathryn O'Hay Granahan, C. Douglas Dillon

Serial Numbers

Low	High	Notes Printed	VF	CH CU	GEM CU
D80 280 001J	E10 800 000J	30,520,000	$4	$20	$35
★20 160 854G	—	—	—	—	—
low observed					
—	★21 596 000G	1,436,000	15	60	100
	official high				

SERIES 1957 BLUE SEAL

First of the 32 Subject Sheet

PLATE NUMBERS: Face and back numbers begin at #1 with 32 subject sheets.

SERIAL NUMBERS: Both regular and star numbers begin at 00 000 001**A**.

SIGNATURES: Ivy Baker Priest, Robert B. Anderson

Serial Numbers

Low	High	Notes Printed	VF	CH CU	GEM CU
A-A - Z-A and A-B		2,609,600,000	$2.50	$10	$20
J-A - K-A	—	—	3	15	25
—	B09 600 000B	—	40	150	225
★A, ★B, ★C		307,640,000	4	15	30
—	★07 640 000D	—	10	45	75

SERIES 1957A BLUE SEAL

SIGNATURES: Elizabeth Rudel Smith, C. Douglas Dillon

Serial Numbers

Low	High	Notes Printed	VF	CH CU	GEM CU
A00 000 001**A**	**Q**94 080 000**A**	1,594,000,000	$2.50	$8	$20
★00 000 001**A**	★94 720 000**A**	94,720,000	4	15	30

SERIES 1957B BLUE SEAL

PLATE NUMBERS: Face #789 was the official high. Back check #447 is highest known.

SIGNATURES: Kathryn O'Hay Granahan, C. Douglas Dillon

Serial Numbers

Low	High	Notes Printed	VF	CH CU	GEM CU
Q94 080 001**A**	—	718,400,000	$3	$15	$25
R-A - X-A	—	—	2.50	7	15
—	**Y**12 480 000**A**	—	2.50	10	20
★94 880 001**A**	—	—	10	45	60
—	★44 160 000**B**	49,280,000	4	15	25

In March 1964, Secretary of the Treasury Dillon halted the redemption of Silver Certificates in silver dollars and on June 24, 1968, redemption in silver bullion was discontinued.

FEDERAL RESERVE NOTES

SERIES 1963 GREEN SEAL

32 Subject Sheet

PLATE NUMBERS: Face numbers begin at #1. Back numbers continued from silver certificates.

SIGNATURES: Kathryn O'Hay Granahan, C. Douglas Dillon

	Blocks	Notes Printed	CH CU
BOSTON	A-A	87,680,000	$5
	A-★	6,400,000	10
NEW YORK	B-A, B-B	200,000,000	5
	B-C	19,200,000	150
	B-★	15,040,000	7
PHILADELPHIA	C-A	100,000,000	5
	C-B	23,680,000	20
	C-★	10,720,000	7
CLEVELAND	D-A	100,000,000	5
	D-B	8,200,000	125
	D-★	8,160,000	7
RICHMOND	E-A	100,000,000	5
	E-B	59,520,000	10
	E-★	12,000,000	8
ATLANTA	F-A	100,000,000	5
	F-B	100,000,000	10
	F-C	21,120,000	25
	F-★	18,880,000	8
CHICAGO	G-A	100,000,000	5
	G-B, G-C	179,360,000	10
	G-★	15,520,000	8
ST. LOUIS	H-A	99,840,000	5
	H-★	9,600,000	8
MINNEAPOLIS	I-A	44,800,000	5
	I-★	5,120,000	12
KANSAS CITY	J-A	88,960,000	5
	J-★	8,960,000	8
DALLAS	K-A	85,760,000	5
	K-★	8,960,000	8
SAN FRANCISCO	L-A	100,000,000	5
	L-B	100,000,000	10
	L-★	14,400,000	30

SERIES 1963A GREEN SEAL

SERIAL NUMBERS: All districts started both regular and star notes with serial 00 000 001.
SIGNATURES: Kathryn O'Hay Granahan, Henry H. Fowler

	Blocks	Notes Printed	CH CU
BOSTON	A-A	100,000,000	$4
	A-B	100,000,000	4
	A-C, A-D	119,840,000	5
	A-★	8,360,000	9
NEW YORK	B-A, B-E - B-G	350,600,000	4
	B-B	100,000,000	15
	B-C, B-D	200,000,000	4
	B-★	48,800,000	6
PHILADELPHIA	C-A - C-D	375,520,000	4
	C-★	26,240,000	6
CLEVELAND	D-A - D-D	337,120,000	4
	D-★	21,120,000	8
RICHMOND	E-A - E-F	632,000,000	4
	E-★	41,600,000	8
ATLANTA	F-A - F-G	636,480,000	4
	F-★	40,960,000	8
CHICAGO	G-A, G-D - G-H	284,480,000	4
	G-B, G-C	200,000,000	7
	G-★	52,640,000	8
ST. LOUIS	H-A, H-C	164,000,000	4
	H-B	100,000,000	7
	H-★	17,920,000	8
MINNEAPOLIS	I-A	100,000,000	4
	I-B	12,160,000	25
	I-★	7,040,000	10
KANSAS CITY	J-A - J-C	219,200,000	4
	J-★	14,720,000	8
DALLAS	K-A - K-C	288,960,000	4
	K-★	19,184,000	8
SAN FRANCISCO	L-A - L-F	576,800,000	4
	L-★	43,040,000	8

SERIES 1963B GREEN SEAL

SERIAL NUMBERS: Continued in sequence from previous series.
SIGNATURES: Kathryn O'Hay Granahan, Joseph W. Barr

	Serial Numbers		Notes Printed	CH CU
	Low	**High**		
NEW YORK	B50 600 001G	B80 640 000H	130,040,000	$5
	B48 800 001★	B52 480 000★	3,680,000	20
RICHMOND	E32 000 001F	E25 600 000G	73,600,000	5
	E41 600 001★	E44 800 000★	3,200,000	20
CHICAGO	G84 480 001H	G75 520 000I	91,040,000	5
	G52 640 001★	G55 040 000★	2,400,000	20
KANSAS CITY	J19 200 001C	J64 000 000C	44,800,000	6
SAN FRANCISCO	L76 800 001F	L83 200 000G	106,400,000	5
	L43 040 001★	L46 080 000★	3,040,000	20

SERIES 1969 GREEN SEAL

SERIAL NUMBERS: All districts started both regular and star notes with 00 000 001.
SIGNATURES: Dorothy Andrews Elston, David M. Kennedy

	Serial Numbers		Notes Printed	VF	CH CU
	Low	**High**			
BOSTON	A-A	—	99,200,000	—	$5
	A-★	A05 120 000★	5,120,000	—	8
NEW YORK	B-A	B-C	269,120,000	—	4
	B-★	B14 080 000★	13,760,000	—	8
PHILADELPHIA	C-A	—	68,480,000	—	5
	C-★	C03 360 000★	2,200,000	—	8
	C05 120 001★	C05 753 000★	416,000	50	200

(Late printing of 13,000 sheets) Following 1969A C-★)

Serial Numbers

	Low	High	Notes Printed	VF	CH CU
CLEVELAND	D-A	D-B	120,480,000	—	$4
	D-★	D05 760 000★	5,600,000	—	8
RICHMOND	E-A	E-C	250,560,000	—	4
	E-★	E10 880 000★	10,560,000	—	8
ATLANTA	F-A	F-B	186,120,000	—	4
	F-★	F07 680 000★	7,520,000	—	8
CHICAGO	G-A	G-D	359,520,000	—	4
	G-★	G12 160 000★	11,680,000	—	8
ST. LOUIS	H-A	—	74,880,000	—	5
	H-★	H03 840 000★	3,840,000	—	8
MINNEAPOLIS	I-A	—	48,000,000	—	6
	I-★	I01 920 000★	1,920,000	—	25
KANSAS CITY	J-A	—	95,360,000	—	5
	J-★	J05 760 000★	5,760,000	—	8
DALLAS	K-A	K-B	113,440,000	—	5
	K-★	K05 120 000★	4,960,000	—	8
SAN FRANCISCO	L-A	L-C	226,240,000	—	4
	L-★	L09 600 000★	9,280,000	—	8

SERIES 1969A GREEN SEAL

SERIAL NUMBERS: Regular notes continued in sequence from previous series. Star notes resumed with gaps in number sequence in all districts except E, H, and I.

SIGNATURES: Dorothy Andrews Kabis, David M. Kennedy

	Serial Numbers			
	Low	**High**	**Notes Printed**	**CH CU**
BOSTON	A99 200 001A	A99 999 999A	800,000	$20
	A00 000 001B	A39 680 000B	39,680,000	5
	A05 280 001★	A06 400 000★	1,120,000	12
NEW YORK	B69 120 001C	B91 520 000D	122,400,000	4
	B14 240 001★	B20 480 000★	6,240,000	8
PHILADELPHIA	C68 480 001A	C13 440 000B	44,960,000	5
	C03 360 001★	C05 120 000★	1,760,000	10
CLEVELAND	D20 480 001B	D50 560 000B	30,080,000	5
	D05 760 001★	D07 040 000★	1,280,000	10
RICHMOND	E50 560 001C	E16 640 000D	66,080,000	4
	E10 880 001★	E14 080 000★	3,200,000	8
ATLANTA	F85 120 001B	F55 680 000C	70,560,000	4
	F07 840 001★	F10 240 000★	2,400,000	8
CHICAGO	G59 520 001D	G35 200 000E	75,680,000	4
	G12 160 001★	G16 640 000★	4,480,000	8
ST. LOUIS	H74 880 001A	H16 300 000B	41,420,000	5
	H03 840 001★	H05 120 000★	1,280,000	10
MINNEAPOLIS	I48 000 001A	I69 760 000A	21,760,000	4
	I01 920 001★	I02 560 000★	640,000	30
KANSAS CITY	J95 360 001A	J99 999 999A	4,640,000	8
	J00 000 001B	J35 840 000B	35,840,000	5
	J05 920 001★	J07 040 000★	1,120,000	10
DALLAS	K13 440 001B	K40 960 000B	27,520,000	6
SAN FRANCISCO	L26 240 001C	L78 080 000C	51,840,000	4
	L09 600 001★	L13 440 000★	3,840,000	8

SERIES 1969B GREEN SEAL

SERIAL NUMBERS: All districts started both regular and star notes with serial 00 000 001, except for **G-★** and **I-★**.

SIGNATURES: Dorothy Andrews Kabis, John B. Connally

	Serial Numbers			
	Low	**High**	**Notes Printed**	**CH CU**
BOSTON	A-A	—	94,720,000	$5
	A-★	A01 920 000★	1,920,000	10
NEW YORK	B-A	B-D	329,440,000	4
	B-★	B07 040 000★	6,560,000	8
PHILADELPHIA	C-A	C-B	133,280,000	4
	C-★	C03 200 000★	3,040,000	8
CLEVELAND	D-A	—	91,520,000	5
	D-★	D04 480 000★	4,480,000	8
RICHMOND	E-A	E-B	180,000,000	4
	E-★	E03 840 000★	3,680,000	8
ATLANTA	F-A	F-B	170,400,000	4
	F-★	F03 840 000★	3,680,000	8
CHICAGO	G-A	G-B	200,000,000	4
	G-C	G04 480 000C	4,480,000	15
	G00 160 001★	G04 480 000★	4,160,000	6
ST. LOUIS	H-A	—	59,520,000	5
	H-★	H01 920 000★	1,920,000	10
MINNEAPOLIS	I-A	—	33,920,000	6
	I02 560 001★	I03 200 000★	640,000	35
KANSAS CITY	J-A	—	67,200,000	5
	J-★	J02 560 000★	2,560,000	8
DALLAS	K-A	K-B	116,640,000	5
	K-★	K05 120 000★	4,960,000	8
SAN FRANCISCO	L-A	L-B	200,000,000	4
	L-C	L08 960 000C	8,960,000	6
	L-★	L05 760 000★	5,440,000	8

SERIES 1969C GREEN SEAL

SERIAL NUMBERS: All districts continue in sequence from previous series printings for both regular and star notes, except for **E-★**, **F-★**, **G-★**, and **J-★** which start with gaps of 160,000 notes.

SIGNATURES: Romana Acosta Banuelos, John B. Connally

	Serial Numbers			
	Low	**High**	**Notes Printed**	**CH CU**
NEW YORK	B29 440 001D	B79 360 000D	49,920,000	$5
CLEVELAND	D91 520 001A	D99 999 999A	8,480,000	8
	D00 000 001B	D07 040 000B	7,040,000	8
	D04 480 001★	D05 120 000★	640,000	40
RICHMOND	E80 000 001B	E41 600 000C	61,600,000	5
	E04 000 001★	E04 480 000★	480,000	50
ATLANTA	F70 400 001B	F31 360 000C	60,960,000	5
	F04 000 001★	F07 680 000★	3,680,000	25
CHICAGO	G04 480 001C	G41 600 000D	137,120,000	5
	G04 640 001★	G06 388 000★	1,373,000	25
ST. LOUIS	H59 520 001A	H83 200 000A	23,680,000	6
	H01 920 001★	H02 560 000★	640,000	25
MINNEAPOLIS	I33 920 001A	I59 520 000A	25,600,000	6
	I00 320 001★	I03 840 000★	640,000	35
KANSAS CITY	J67 200 001A	J99 999 999A	32,800,000	5
	J00 000 001B	J05 760 000B	5,760,000	8
	J02 720 001★	J03 840 000★	1,120,000	25
DALLAS	K16 640 001B	K46 080 000B	29,440,000	6
	K05 120 001★	K05 760 000★	640,000	35
SAN FRANCISCO	L08 960 001C	L10 240 000D	101,280,000	5
	L05 760 001★	L08 320 000★	2,400,000	200

SERIES 1969D GREEN SEAL

SERIAL NUMBERS: All districts started regular notes with serial 00 000 001, and ran block printings through to 99 999 999.

SIGNATURES: Romana Acosta Banuelos, George P. Shultz

	Serial Numbers			
	Low	**High**	**Notes Printed**	**CH CU**
BOSTON	A-A	A-B	187,040,000	$5
	A00 000 001★	A01 280 000★	1,120,000	25
NEW YORK	B-A	B-E	468,480,000	5
	B00 160 001★	B05 120 000★	4,480,000	8
PHILADELPHIA	C-A	C-C	218,560,000	5
	C00 000 001★	C04 480 000★	4,160,000	8
CLEVELAND	D-A	D-B	161,440,000	5
	D00 000 001★	D02 560 000★	2,400,000	10
RICHMOND	E-A	E-D	374,240,000	5
	E00 160 001★	E08 960 000★	8,480,000	8
ATLANTA	F-A	F-D	377,440,000	5
	F00 000 001★	F05 760 000★	5,280,000	8
CHICAGO	G-A	G-D	378,080,000	5
	G00 000 001★	G05 750 000★	4,560,000	8
ST. LOUIS	H-A	H-B	168,480,000	5
	H00 000 001★	H01 920 000★	1,760,000	12
MINNEAPOLIS	I-A	—	83,200,000	6
KANSAS CITY	J-A	J-B	185,760,000	5
	J00 000 001★	J03 200 000★	3,040,000	8
DALLAS	K-A	K-B	158,240,000	5
	K00 000 001★	K06 400 000★	6,240,000	8
SAN FRANCISCO	L-A	L-D	400,000,000	5
	L-E	L00 640 000E	640,000	25
	L00 000 001★	L07 040 000★	6,400,000	8

SERIES 1974 GREEN SEAL

SERIAL NUMBERS: All districts started   regular notes with serial 00 000 001, and star notes with 00 160 000, except for **J-★**, which started from number 1.

SIGNATURES: Francine I. Neff, William E. Simon

PLATE NUMBERS: Faces begins with #1. Backs continues from previous series. Back 1472 is lowest observed. Back 905 is a BEP typesetting error, should be 1905.

	Serial Numbers			
	Low	**High**	**Notes Printed**	**CH CU**
BOSTON	A-A	A-C	269,760,000	$4
	A-★	A02 560 000★	1,728,000	10
NEW YORK	B-A	B-H	740,160,000	4
	B-★	B08 960 000★	5,808,000	7
PHILADELPHIA	C-A	C-C	300,000,000	4
	C-D	C08 960 000D	8,960,000	25
	C-★	C01 920 000★	1,600,000	30
CLEVELAND	D-A	D-C	240,960,000	4
	D-★	D01 280 000★	960,000	25
RICHMOND	E-A	E-G	644,160,000	4
	E-★	E05 760 000★	4,960,000	8
ATLANTA	F-A	F-F	599,680,000	4
	F-★	F07 680 000★	4,352,000	8
CHICAGO	G-A	G-E	473,600,000	4
	G-★	G07 040 000★	4,992,000	8
ST. LOUIS	H-A	H-C	291,520,000	4
	H-★	H03 200 000★	2,880,000	8
MINNEAPOLIS	I-A	I-B	144,160,000	4
	I-★	I00 640 000★	480,000	45
KANSAS CITY	J-A	J-C	223,520,000	4
	J-★	J03 200 000★	2,144,000	8
DALLAS	K-A	K-D	330,560,000	4
	K-★	K01 920 000★	1,216,600	15
SAN FRANCISCO	L-A	L-H	736,960,000	4
	L-★	L04 480 000★	3,520,000	8

SERIES 1977 GREEN SEAL

SERIAL NUMBERS: All districts started regular notes with serial 00 000 001.
SIGNATURES: Azie Taylor Morton, W.M. Blumenthal
PLATE NUMBERS: Numbers continued from previous series.

	Serial Numbers			
	Low	**High**	**Notes Printed**	**CH CU**
BOSTON	A-A	A88 320 000B	188,160,000	$4
	A00 016 001★	A03 840 000★	2,428,000	25
NEW YORK	B-A	B36 480 000G	635,520,000	4
	B00 012 001★	B11 520 000★	10,112,000	8
PHILADELPHIA	C-A	C99 840 000B	199,680,000	4
	C-C	C17 280 000C	17,280,000	15
	C00 016 001★	C05 760 000★	3,840,000	9
CLEVELAND	D-A	D99 840 000B	199,680,000	4
	D-C	D13 440 000C	13,440,000	15
	D00 012 001★	D05 760 000★	3,200,000	9
RICHMOND	E-A	E19 200 000E	418,560,000	4
	E00 016 001★	E07 680 000★	6,400,000	9
ATLANTA	F-A	F65 920 000F	565,120,000	4
	F00 012 001★	F09 600 000★	8,940,000	10
CHICAGO	G-A	G16 640 000G	615,680,000	4
	G00 016 001★	G10 240 000★	9,472,000	7
ST. LOUIS	H-A	H99 840 000B	199,680,000	4
	H00 000 001★	H02 560 000★	2,048,000	8
MINNEAPOLIS	I-A	I99 840 000A	99,840,000	4
	I-B	I15 360 000B	15,360,000	20
	I00 000 001★	I02 560 000★	2,560,000	10
KANSAS CITY	J-A	J23 680 000C	223,360,000	4
	J00 012 001★	J05 120 000★	3,760,000	9
DALLAS	K-A	K89 600 000C	289,280,000	4
	K00 012 001★	K06 400 000★	4,704,000	9
SAN FRANCISCO	L-A	L17 280 000F	516,480,000	4
	L00 012 001★	L08 960 000★	8,320,000	9

SERIES 1977A GREEN SEAL

SIGNATURES: Azie Taylor Morton, G. William Miller

PLATE NUMBERS: Highest face #2185. Highest back #3297, except for K-G mules, with low series 1981 backs.

SERIAL NUMBERS: All regular and star serials for this series continued in sequence from Series 1977, but stars continue with gaps in districts A, D, & F, with the exception of the Richmond star which reverted to 00 000 001. New York block B-A followed production of block B-L.

	Serial Numbers			
	Low	**High**	**Notes Printed**	**CH CU**
BOSTON	A-B	A-D	211,200,000	$4
	A04 496 001★	A08 960 000★	2,432,000	20
NEW YORK	B-G - B-L	B-A	592,000,000	4
	B-★	B22 400 000★	9,984,000	8
PHILADELPHIA	C-C	C-E	196,480,000	4
	C-★	C08 960 000★	2,688,000	10
CLEVELAND	D-C	D-D	174,720,000	4
	D05 772 001★	D09 600 000★	2,560,000	10
RICHMOND	E-E	E-H	377,560,000	4
	E00 000 001★	E07 680 000★	6,360,000	8
ATLANTA	F-F	F-J	396,160,000	4
	F09 616 001★	F16 000 000★	5,376,000	8
CHICAGO	G-G	G-I	250,880,000	4
	G-★	G12 800 000★	2,560,000	10
ST. LOUIS	H-C	—	99,840,000	4
	H-D	H03 840 000D	3,840,000	20
	H-★	H05 760 000★	5,760,000	8
MINNEAPOLIS	I-B	—	38,400,000	20
	I-★	I03 840 000★	1,024,000	20
KANSAS CITY	J-C	J-E	275,840,000	4
	J-★	J12 800 000★	4,864,000	8
DALLAS	K-C	K-F	309,760,000	4
	K-G	K03 840 000★	3,840,000	15
	K-G mule	—	—	75
	K-★	K12 800 000★	5,504,000	8
SAN FRANCISCO	L-F	L-J	433,280,000	4
	L-★	L15 360 000★	5,888,000	8

SERIES 1981 GREEN SEAL

SIGNATURES: Angela M. Buchanan, Donald T. Regan

PLATE NUMBERS: Both front and back numbers begin at 1, but some backs are found muled, using high numbered 1977A backs.

SERIAL NUMBERS: All districts started both regular and star notes with serial 00 000 001, except St. Louis and Minneapolis stars.

	Serial Numbers				
	Low	**High**	**Notes Printed**	**VF**	**CH CU**
BOSTON	A-A	A-C	299,520,000	—	$4
	A-D	—	9,600,000	—	8
	AE - AH	—	160,000	—	40
	uncut sheets only				
	A-★	A04 480 000★	3,200,000	—	15
NEW YORK	B-A	B-J	965,760,000	—	4
	B-★	B12 800 000★	11,760,000	—	12
PHILADELPHIA	C-A	C-D	360,320,000	—	4
	C-★	C 01 920 000★	1,536,000	—	125
CLEVELAND	D-A	D-C	295,680,000	—	4
	D-H	—	160,000	—	40
	uncut sheet only				
	D-★	D03 200 000★	1,792,000	—	12
RICHMOND	E-A	E-F	599,040,000	—	4
	E-G	—	6,400,000	—	100
	E-H	—	160,000	—	40
	uncut sheet only				
	E-★	E03 840 000★	3,840,000	—	20
ATLANTA	F-A	F-H	743,680,000	—	4
	F-★	F03 200 000★	3,200,000	—	15
CHICAGO	G-A	G-G	631,040,000	—	4
	G-★	G05 760 000★	4,544,000	—	15
ST. LOUIS	H-A	H-B	163,800,000	—	4
	H-C	—	160,000	—	40
	uncut sheet only				
	H-D	—	160,000	—	40
	uncut sheet only				
	H-E	—	160,000	—	40
	uncut sheet only				
	H00 008 001★	H01 920 000★	1,056,000	—	15
MINNEAPOLIS	I-A	—	70,400,000	—	5
	I-B	—	35,200,000	—	5
	I00 012 001★	I01 920 000★	1,152,000	—	20
KANSAS CITY	J-A	J-C	299,620,000	—	4

	Low	High	Notes Printed	VF	CH CU
	J-D	—	3,200,000	500	$1,500
	J-★	J03 840 000★	3,216,000	—	15
DALLAS	K-A	K-D	385,920,000	—	4
	K-★	K01 920 000★	1,920,000	—	15
SAN FRANCISCO	L-A	L-G	679,040,000	—	4
	L-★	L06 400 000★	4,992,000	—	12

SERIES 1981A GREEN SEAL

SERIAL NUMBERS: All districts start both regular and star notes with serial 00 000 001.

SIGNATURES: Katherine Davalos Ortega, Donald T. Regan

PLATE NUMBERS: Both front and back numbers begin at 1, but some backs are found muled using high numbered 1981 backs early in the run, and 1985 low numbered backs late in the run.

Serial Numbers

	Low	High	Notes Printed	VF	CH CU
BOSTON	A-A	A-B	198,400,000	—	$4
	A-C	A06 400 000C	6,400,000	—	10
NEW YORK	B-A	B-F	595,200,000	—	4
	B-★	B16 000 000★	9,088,000	—	15
PHILADELPHIA	C-A	—	99,200,000	—	4
	C-B	uncut sheets only	160,000	—	40
CLEVELAND	D-A	D-B	188,800,000	—	4
RICHMOND	E-A	E-E	496,000,000	—	4
	E-★	E06 400 000★	6,400,000	—	15
ATLANTA	F-A	F-E	483,200,000	—	4
CHICAGO	G-A	G-E	432,000,000	—	4
	G-★	G03 200 000★	3,200,000	—	15
ST. LOUIS	H-A	H-B	182,400,600	—	4
MINNEAPOLIS	I-A	—	99,200,000	—	4
	I-B	I03 200 000B	3,200,000	—	70
KANSAS CITY	J-A	J-B	176,000,000	—	4
DALLAS	K-A	K-B	188,800,000	—	4
	K-★	K03 200 000★	640,000	250	1,250
SAN FRANCISCO	L-A	L-G	659,200,000	—	4
	L-★	L03 200 000★	3,200,000	—	15

SERIES 1985 GREEN SEAL

SERIAL NUMBERS: All districts start both regular and star notes with serial 00 000 001, except Richmond stars.

SIGNATURES: Katherine Davalos Ortega, James A. Baker III

PLATE NUMBERS: Both front and back numbers begin at 1, though low numbered backs are only seen in mid run.

	Serial Numbers				
	Low	High	Notes Printed	VF	CH CU
BOSTON	A-A	A57 600 000F	553,600,000	—	$4
NEW YORK	B-A	B09 600 000T	1,836,800,000	—	4
PHILADELPHIA	C-A	C25 600 000E	422,400,000	—	4
CLEVELAND	D-A	D41 600 000G	636,800,000	—	4
RICHMOND	E-A	E99 200 000L	1,190,400,000	—	4
	E03 200 001★	E06 400 000★	3,200,000	—	15
ATLANTA	F-A	F25 600 000P	1,513,600,000	—	4
CHICAGO	G-A	G99 200 000L	1,190,400,000	—	4
	G-★	G09 600 000★	7,040,000	—	8
ST. LOUIS	H-A	H99 200 000D	300,800,000	—	4
	—	H03 200 000E	3,200,000	—	300
	H-★	H03 200 000★	640,000	250	1,200
MINNEAPOLIS	I-A	I48 000 000C	246,400,000	—	4
	I-D	uncut sheets only	96,000	—	75
	I-★	I03 200 000★	2,560,000	—	15
KANSAS CITY	J-A	J92 800 000D	396,800,000	—	4
DALLAS	K-A	K-H	790,200,000	—	4
	K-★	K03 200 000★	3,200,000	—	15
SAN FRANCISCO	L-A	L96 000 000T	1,980,800,000	—	4
	L-★	L09 600 000★	6,400,000	—	15

SERIES 1988 GREEN SEAL

SERIAL NUMBERS: All districts start both regular and star notes with serial 00 000 001.
SIGNATURES: Katherine Davalos Ortega, Nicholas F. Brady

	Serial Numbers			
	Low	**High**	**Notes Printed**	**CH CU**
BOSTON	A-A	A19 200 000C	214,400,000	$8
	A-★	A03 200 000★	3,200,000	15
NEW YORK	B-A	B38 400 000J	921,400,000	7
	B-★	B03 200 000★	2,560,000	15
PHILADELPHIA	C-A	C96 000 000A	96,000,000	8
CLEVELAND	D-A	D99 200 000B	198,400,000	8
RICHMOND	E-A	E44 800 000H	458,480,000	8
	E-★	E03 200 000★	2,688,000	15
ATLANTA	F-A	F92 800 000D	396,800,000	8
	F-★	F03 200 000★	640,000	1,400
CHICAGO	G-A	G25 600 000E	422,400,000	7
ST. LOUIS	H-A	H28 800 000B	128,000,000	8
MINNEAPOLIS	I-A	I64 000 000A	64,000,000	10
KANSAS CITY	J-A	J38 400 000B	137,600,000	7
	J-★	J03 200 000★	3,200,000	15
DALLAS	K-A	K80 000 000A	80,000,000	9
	K-★	K03 200 000★	1,248,000	30
SAN FRANCISCO	L-A	L99 200 000F	585,600,000	7
	L-★	L03 200 000★	3,200,000	15

SERIES 1988A GREEN SEAL

SERIAL NUMBERS: All districts start both regular and star notes with serial 00 000 001.
SIGNATURES: Catalina Vasquez Villalpando, Nicholas F. Brady
PRINTING FACILITY: All printings in Washington unless otherwise indicated. First appearances of notes printed in Fort Worth and denoted by "FW" preceding plate position letter and plate number in lower right of notes.

	Serial Numbers			
	Low	**High**	**Notes Printed**	**CH CU**
BOSTON	A-A	A-G	672,000,000	$4
NEW YORK	B-A	B-X	2,163,200,000	4
	B32 000 000L	B38 000 000L W	—	200
	B-★	B16 000 000★	14,080,000	9
PHILADELPHIA	C-A	C-E	473,600,000	4

	Low	High	Notes Printed	CH CU
CLEVELAND	**D-A**	**D-E**	460,800,000	$4
	D-★	**D**06 400 000★	6,400,000	10
RICHMOND	**E-A**	**E-Q**	1,504,600,000	4
	E-R	**E**06 400 000**R**	6,400,000	75
	E-★	**E**09 600 000★	9,600,000	10
ATLANTA	**F-A**	**F-M**	1,248,000,000	4
	F-N	**F-U** W/FW	672,000,000	4
	FN FW	—	12,800,000	400
	F-V	**F-Y**	371,200,000	4
	F-★	**F**12 800 000★	12,800,000	10
CHICAGO	**G-A - G-G, G-J,**		1,081,600,000	4
G-K, G-R, G-X		G-Y		
	G-H W/FW	—	—	4
	G-I W/FW	—	—	4
	G-L W/FW	—	—	4
	G-M FW	—	—	4
	G-N FW	—	—	4
	G-P W/FW	—	—	4
	G-Q W/FW	—	—	4
	G-S W/FW	—	—	4
	G-T FW	—	—	4
	G-U W/FW	—	—	4
	G-V W/FW	—	—	4
	G-W W/FW	—	—	4
	G-★ W/FW	**G**25 600 000★	25,600,000	9
ST. LOUIS	**H-A - H-C**	**H-G** W/FW	339,200,000	4
	H-D	**H-F** W/FW	334,800,000	4
	H-E FW	—	96,000,000	4
	H-H FW	—	—	—
	H-I	—	—	—
	H-★	**H**03 200 000★	3,200,000	10
MINNEAPOLIS	**I-A** W		672,000,000	4
	I-A FW		—	450
	I-B to **I-J**FW	—	—	4
	I-★ W/FW	**I**12 800 000★	12,800,000	25
KANSAS CITY	**J-A** W	—	76,800,000	4
	J-A FW	**J-D** FW	185,600,000	4
DALLAS	**K-A, K-B**/W	—	195,200,000	4
	K-A, K-B/FW	—	—	40
	K-C/W	—	—	175
	K-C/FW	—	96,000,000	4
	K-D	**K-I** FW	576,000,000	4
	K-★ FW	**K**03 200 000★	3,200,000	15
SAN FRANCISCO	**L-A**	**L-B**	192,000,000	4
	L-C W		89,600,000	4
	L89 600 001**C** FW**L**96 000 000**C**		6,400,000	400
	L-D	**L-P** FW	1,152,000,000	4

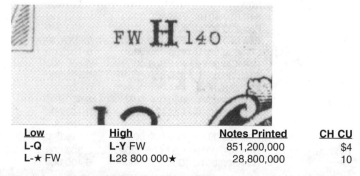

Low	High	Notes Printed	CH CU
L-Q	L-Y FW	851,200,000	$4
L-★ FW	L28 800 000★	28,800,000	10

SERIES 1988A WEB-FED PRESS PRINTINGS GREEN SEAL

With an initial press run in May, 1992, the Bureau of Engraving and Printing began testing the high volume Web-Fed intaglio currency press in actual production. With this press, both sides of the note are printed in a single pass of a continuous roll of paper from a printing cylinder of 96 subjects or notes.

Some obvious face design changes including the removal of the face plate letters and quadrant number. Plate numbers begin a new sequence on both face and back with #1. The back plate number has been relocated to the right of the word 'TRUST'.

Face plate numbers used: 1, 2, 3, 4, 5, 8, 9, 10.

Back plate numbers used: 1 through 8.

The compilation of the Web-Fed Press production data was enabled by the research of Jim Hodgson and Bob Vandevender.

The printings are as follows:

	Serial Numbers				
	Low	**High**	**Notes Printed**	**VF**	**CH CU**
BOSTON	A25 600 001E	A32 000 000E	6,400,000	—	$45
	A38 400 001E	A44 800 000E	6,400,000	—	45
	A57 600 001E	A64 000 000E	6,400,000	—	45
	A00 000 001F	A12 800 000F	12,800,000	—	45
	A83 200 001F	A96 000 000F	12,800,000	—	45
	A00 000 001G	A19 200 000G	19,200,000	—	45
NEW YORK	B32 000 001L	B38 400 000L	1,920,000	$400	1,500
PHILADELPHIA	C64 000 001A	C76 800 000A	12,800,000	—	55
RICHMOND	E44 800 001I	E64 000 000I	19,200,000	—	45
	E44 800 001K	E64 000 000K	19,200,000	—	45
ATLANTA	F70 400 001L	F76 800 000L	6,400,000	—	200
	F83 200 001L	F89 600 000L	6,400,000	—	200
	F00 000 001M	F06 400 000M	6,400,000	—	125

	Low	High	Notes Printed	VF	CH CU
	F57 600 001N	F76 800 000N	19,200,000	—	$150
	F51 200 001U	F57 600 000U	6,400,000	—	40
	F64 000 001U	F70 400 000U	6,400,000	—	40
	F89 600 001U	F96 000 000U	6,400,000	—	40
	F06 400 001V	F12 800 000V	6,400,000	—	40
	F19 200 001V	F25 600 000V	6,400,000	—	40
	F38 400 001V	F44 800 000V	6,400,000	—	40
	F57 600 001V	F64 000 000V	6,400,000	—	40
	F76 800 001V	F83 200 000V	6,400,000	—	40
	F89 600 001V	F96 000 000V	6,400,000	—	75
	F06 400 001★	F09 600 000★	640,000	$500	1,400
CHICAGO	G44 800 001P	G57 600 000P	12,800,000	—	100
	G44 800 001Q	G51 200 000Q	6,400,000	—	150

(Series 1988A discontinued in April 1994; Series 1993 began in April 1994.)

SERIES 1993 GREEN SEAL

SERIAL NUMBERS: All districts started numbering both regular and star notes with 00 000 001.

PLATE NUMBERS: Face and back numbers begin at #1.

SIGNATURES: Mary Ellen Withrow, Lloyd Bentsen

	Serial Numbers				
	Low	High	Notes Printed	VF	CH CU
BOSTON	A-A - A-B	A44 800 000B	140,800,000	—	$4
NEW YORK	B-A - B-H	B44 800 000H	716,800,000	—	3
	B-★	B09 600 000★	5,760,000	—	10
PHILADELPHIA	C-A	C70 400 000A	70,400,000	—	10
	C-★	C03 200 000★	640,000	30	200
CLEVELAND	D-A - D-B	D12 800 000B	108,800,000	—	4
RICHMOND	E-A - E-E	E76 800 000E	460,800,000	—	4
ATLANTA	F-A - F-H	F51 200 000H	723,200,000	—	4
	F-★	F09 600 000★	9,600,000	—	10
CHICAGO	G-A	G-G W	96,000,000	—	$3
	G-B - G-G FW	G32 000 000G	512,000,000	—	3
	G-★ FW	G08 960 000★	8,960,000	—	8
ST. LOUIS	H-A FW		96,000,000	—	4
	H-B - H-C FW	H25 600 000C	121,600,000	—	4
MINNEAPOLIS	I-A FW	I25 600 000A	25,600,000	—	175
DALLAS	K-A - K-E FW	K96 000 000E	480,000,000	—	4
	K-★ FW	K12 800 000★	12,800,000	—	10
SAN FRANCISCO	L-A - L-K W/FW	L89 600 000K	1,145,600,000	—	3
	L-C L51 200 001C	L64 000 000C	12,800,000	—	10

SERIES 1993 WEB-FED PRESS PRINTINGS GREEN SEAL

PLATE NUMBERS: Face number used: 1. Back numbers used: 8, 9, 10.

Serial Numbers

	Low	High	Notes Printed	CH CU
NEW YORK	B19 200 001H	B25 600 000H	6,400,000	$25
	B38 400 001H	B44 800 000H	6,400,000	25
PHILADELPHIA	C38 400 001A	C44 800 000A	6,400,000	15
	C51 200 001A	C57 600 000A	6,400,000	15

SERIES 1995 GREEN SEAL

SIGNATURES: Mary Ellen Withrow, Robert E. Rubin

PLATE NUMBERS: Both face and back numbers begin at #1.

SERIAL NUMBERS: All districts start both regular and star notes with 00 000 001.

Serial Numbers

	Low	High	Notes Printed	CH CU
BOSTON	A-A - A-M W	A96 000 000M	1,248,000,000	$3
	A-N W	A06 400 000N	6,400,000	15
	A-★ W	A15 360 000★	15,360,000	6
NEW YORK	B-A - B-Y W	B96 000 000Y	2,304,000,000	3
	B-★ W	B19 840 000★	19,840,000	5
PHILADELPHIA	C-A - C-F W	C76 800 000F	556,880,000	3
	C-★ W	C07 040 000★	7,040,000	6
CLEVELAND	D-A - D-R W/FW	D25 600 000R	1,561,600,000	3
	D-★ W	D07 040 000★	7,040,000	7
RICHMOND	E-A - E-S W	E96 000 000S	1,632,000,000	3
	E-T W	E06 400 000T	6,400,000	15
	E-★ W	E12 800 000★	7,040,000	7
ATLANTA	F-A - F-V W/FW	F57 600 000V	1,977,600,000	3
	F-★ W/FW	F22 400 000★	16,000,000	6
CHICAGO	G-A - G-Q W/FW	G19 200 000Q	1,459,200,000	3
	G-★ FW	G12 800 000★	10,240,000	6
ST. LOUIS	H-A - H-K FW	H64 000 000K	1,024,000,000	3
MINNEAPOLIS	I-A - I-N W/FW	I32 000 000N	1,280,000,000	3
	I-★ FW	I19 200 000★	14,080,000	6
KANSAS CITY	J-A - J-T W/FW	J83 200 000T	1,811,200,000	3
	J-★ FW	J06 400 000★	6,400,000	7
DALLAS	K-A - K-N FW	K70 400 000N	1,318,400,000	3
	K-★ FW	K03 360 000★	1,440,000	20
SAN FRANCISCO	L-A - L-Y W/FW	L96 000 000Y	2,304,000,000	3
	L-★ FW	L06 400 000★	6,400,000	6

SERIES 1995 WEB-FED PRESS PRINTINGS GREEN SEAL

PLATE NUMBERS: Face numbers used: 1, 2, 3, 4, 5, 6, 7. Back numbers used: 8, 9, 10, 12.

	Serial Numbers			
	Low	**High**	**Notes Printed**	**CH CU**
BOSTON	A32 000 001**C**	A38 400 000**C**	6,400,000	$20
	A38 400 001**C**	A44 800 000**C**	6,400,000	20
	A76 820 001**D**	A83 200 000**D**	5,760,000	35
NEW YORK	B32 000 001**H**	B38 400 000**H**	6,400,000	15
	B44 800 001**H**	B51 200 000**H**	6,400,000	15
CLEVELAND	D64 000 001**C**	D70 400 000**C**	6,400,000	15
ATLANTA	F83 200 001**D**	F89 600 000**D**	6,400,000	20
	F89 600 001**D**	F96 000 000**D**	6,400,000	20

The Web-Fed press trial operations were discontinued after the printing of the **A-D** run in December 1995, due to the bureau's inability to afford the resolution of problems in the peripheral issues connected to the printing operation.

SERIES 1999 GREEN SEAL

SIGNATURES: Mary Ellen Withrow, Lawrence H. Summers

PLATE NUMBERS: Both face and back numbers begin at #1.

SERIAL NUMBERS: All districts start both regular and star notes with 00 000 001.

	Serial Numbers			
	Low	**High**	**Notes Printed**	**CH CU**
BOSTON	A-A - A-G W	A76 800 000**G**	556,800,000	$2
	A-★ W	A00 640 000★	640,000	45
	A03 200 001★ W	A06 400 000★	3,200,000	6
NEW YORK	B-A - B-Q W	B57 600 000**Q**	1,497,600,000	2
	B-★ W	B09 600 000★	9,600,000	5

	Low	High	Notes Printed	CH CU
PHILADELPHIA	C-A - C-J W	C25 600 000J	1,062,400,000	$2
	C-★ W	C03 520 000★	3,520,000	5
	C06 400 001★ W	C07 040 000★	640,000	50
	C09 600 001★ W	C19 200 000★	9,600,000	3
CLEVELAND	D-A - D-C W	D76 800 000C	268,800,000	2
	D-★ W	D00 320 000★	320,000	50
	D03 200 001★ W	D03 520 000★	320,000	75
RICHMOND	E-A - E-H W	E76 800 000H	748,800,000	2
	E-★ W	E03 200 000★	3,200,000	6
	E03 200 001★ W	E03 840 000★	640,000	30
	E06 400 001★ W	E09 600 000★	3,200,000	6
ATLANTA	F-A - F-T W/FW	F64 000 000T	1,956,800,000	2
	F-M FW	F06 400 000M	6,400,000	15
	F89 600 001R W	F96 000 000R	6,400,000	10
	F-★ FW	F00 640 000★	640,000	85
CHICAGO	G-A -G-I FW	G96 000 000I	864,000,000	3
ST. LOUIS	H-A FW	H89 600 000A	89,600,000	4
	H00 000 001★ FW	H03 840 000★	3,840,000	150
	H06 400 001★	H09 600 000★	3,200,000	6
MINNEAPOLIS	I-A FW	I12 800 000A	12,800,000	10
KANSAS CITY	J-A - J-D FW	J51 200 000D	339,200,000	3
DALLAS	K-A - K-J FW	K70 400 000J	934,400,000	3
SAN FRANCISCO	L-A - L-W FW	L25 600 000W	1,920,000,000	3
	L-★ FW	L19 200 000★	19,840,000	5
	L19 200 001★ FW	L19 840 000★	640,000	35

SERIES 2001 GREEN SEAL

SIGNATURES: Rosario Marin, Paul H. O'Neill

PLATE NUMBERS: Both face and back numbers begin at #1.

SERIAL NUMBERS: All districts start both regular and star notes with 00 000 001, except Dallas stars.

	Serial Numbers			
	Low	High	Notes Printed	CH CU
BOSTON	A-A - A-E W	A64 000 000E	448,000,000	$2
	A-★ W	A00 320 000★	320,000	65
	A03 200 001★ W	A06 400 000★	6,400,000	5
NEW YORK	B-A - B-G W	B96 000 000G	672,000,000	2
	B-H W	B06 400 000H	6,400,000	35
PHILADELPHIA	C-A - C-F W	C70 400 000F	550,400,000	2
	C-★ W	C06 400 000★	6,400,000	6

	Low	High	Notes Printed	CH CU
CLEVELAND	D-A - D-D W	D19 200 000D	307,200,000	$2
RICHMOND	E-A W	E70 400 000A	70,400,000	2
ATLANTA	F-A - F-F W/FW	F57 600 000F	499,200,000	2
	F-★ W	F00 320 000★	320,000	75
	F03 200 001★ W	F06 400 000★	3,200,000	5
	F06 400 001★ FW	F09 600 000★	3,200,000	5
	F09 600 001★ FW	F10 240 000★	640,000	40
CHICAGO	G-A - G-D FW	G70 400 000D	332,800,000	2
	G-★ FW	G03 200 000★	3,200,000	5
	G03 200 001★ FW	G03 840 000★	640,000	40
	G06 400 001★ FW	G07 040 000★	640,000	40
ST. LOUIS	H-A - H-C W/FW	H83 200 000C	268,800,000	2
	H-★ W	H00 640 000★	640,000	75
MINNEAPOLIS	I-A W	I06 400 000A	6,400,000	15
	I06 400 001A FW	I64 000 000A	57,600,000	3
KANSAS CITY	J-A FW	J70 400 000A	70,400,000	2
	J70 400 001A W	J89 600 000A	19,200,000	12
	J89 600 001A FW	J96 000 000A	6,400,000	8
	J-B FW	J83 200 000B	83,200,000	2
DALLAS	K-A - K-D FW	K12 800 000D	300,800,000	2
	K03 200 001★ FW	K06 400 000★	3,200,000	6
SAN FRANCISCO	L-A - L-L FW	L96 000 000L	1,052,000,000	2
	L-★ FW	L03 200 000★	3,200,000	6

SERIES 2003 GREEN SEAL

SIGNATURES: Rosario Marin, John W. Snow

PLATE NUMBERS: Both face and back numbers begin at #1.

SERIAL NUMBERS: All districts start both regular and star notes with 00 000 001.

	Serial Numbers		Notes Printed	CH CU
	Low	High		
BOSTON	A-A - A-D W	A96 000 000D	384,000,000	$2
	A00000001★ W	A03 200 000★	3,200,000	6
NEW YORK	B-A - B-G W	B25 600 000G	601,600,000	2
	B00 000 001★ W	B00 320 000★	320,000	70
	B03 200 001★ W	B03 520 000★	320,000	70
	B06 400 001★ W	B11 520 000★	5,120,000	6
PHILADELPHIA	C-A - C-E W	C76 800 000E	460,800,000	2
	C99 000 001A FW(Sheets)		—	15
CLEVELAND	D-A - D-D W	D83 200 000D	371,200,000	2
	D00 000 001★ W	D00 320 000★	320,000	100
RICHMOND	E-A - E-J W	E89 600 000J	953,600,000	2
	E00 000 001★ W	E00 320 000★	320,000	50
	E03 200 001★ W	E06 400 000★	3,200,000	5
	E06 400 001★ W	E06 560 000★	160,000	100
	E09 600 001★ W	E12 800 000★	3,200,000	5
ATLANTA	F-A - F-C W/FW	F96 000 000C	147,200,000	2
	F-D W	F06 400 000D	6,400,000	10
	F06 400 001D W/FW	F96 000 000D	89,600,00	2
	F-E - F-L FW	F19 200 000L	921,600,000	2
	F00 000 0001★ W	F00 320 000★	320,000	75
	F03 200 001★ W	F06 400 000★	3,200,000	6
CHICAGO	G-A - G-H FW	G70 400 000H	646,400,000	2
	G00 000 001★ FW	G09 600 000★	10,240,000	5
	G09 600 001★ FW	G10240000★	640,000	35
ST. LOUIS	H-A - H-C FW	H76 800 000C	268,800,000	2
	H99 000 000A		—	15
MINNEAPOLIS	I-A - I-B FW	I51 200 000B	147,200,000	3
KANSAS CITY	J-A - J-B FW	J83 200 000B	179,200,000	2
	J99 000 000A		—	15
DALLAS	K-A - K-H FW	K32 000 000H	704,000,000	2
	K00 000 001★ FW	K03 200 000★	3,200,000	6
SAN FRANCISCO	L-A - L-N FW	L19 200 000N	1,267,200,000	2
	L00 000 001★ FW	L03 200 000★	3,200,000	6

SERIES 2003A GREEN SEAL

SIGNATURES: Anna Escobedo Cabral, John W. Snow
PLATE NUMBERS: Face and back numbers begin at #1.
SERIAL NUMBERS: All districts start both regular and star notes with 00 000 001.

Serial Numbers

	Low	High	Notes Printed	CH CU
BOSTON	A-A - A-D W	A12 800 000D	300,800,000	$2
NEW YORK	B-A - B-J W	B96 000 000J	960,000,000	2
	B00 000 001K W	B06 400 000K	6,400,000	10
	B00 000 001★ W	B00 320 000★	320,000	75
	B03 200 001★ W	B03 520 000★	320,000	50
	B06 400 001★ W	B12 800 000★	6,400,000	10
	B12 800 001★ W	B13 120 000★ (sheets)	320,000	50
PHILADELPHIA	C-A - C-C W	C32 000 000C	224,000,000	2
	C00 000 001★ W	C03 200 000★	3,200,000	10
	C03 200 001★ W	C03 520 000★ (sheets)	320,000	50
CLEVELAND	D-A - D-D W	D96 000 000D	384,000,000	2
	D00 000 001E W	D06 400 000E	6,400,000	10
RICHMOND	E-A - E-H W	E70 400 000H	742,400,000	2
	E00 000 001★ W	E00 320 000★ (sheets)	320,000	75
	E03 200 001★ W	E06 400 000★	3,200,000	6
ATLANTA	F-A - F-L w/FW	F96 000 000L	1,152,000,000	2
	F00 000 001M FWF06 400 000M		6,400,000	10
	F06 400 001M w/FWF89 600 000M		83,200,000	2
	F89 600 001M W	F96 000 000M	6,400,000	10
	F-N - F-P W	F64 000 000P	160,000,000	2
	F64 000 001P FWF70 400 000P		6,400,000	10
	F00 000 001★ W	F03 520 000★	3,520,000	5
	F06 400 001★ W	F06 720 000★ (sheets)	320,000	75
	F09 600 001★ w/FWF16 384 000★		6,784,000	5
CHICAGO	G-A - G-I FW	G83 200 000I	851,200,000	2
ST. LOUIS	H-A - H-B FW	H70 400 000B	166,400,000	2
MINNEAPOLIS	I00 000 001A FW I76 800 000A		76,800,000	2
KANSAS CITY	J-A - J-E FW	J64 000 000E	448,000,000	2
	J00 000 001★ FWJ03 200 000★		3,200,000	8
DALLAS	K-A - K-G FW	K96 000 000G	672,000,000	2
	K00 000 001H FWK06 400 000H		6,400,000	10
	K00 000 001★ FWK00 640 000★		640,000	50
	K03 200 001★ FWK03 840 000★ (sheets)		640,000	50
SAN FRANCISCO	L-A - L-Q FW	L76 800 000Q	1,516,800,000	2

SERIES 2006 GREEN SEAL

SIGNATURES: Anna Escobedo Cabral, Henry M. Paulson, Jr.
PLATE NUMBERS: Face and back numbers begin at #1.
SERIAL NUMBERS: All districts start both regular and star notes with 00 000 001.

	Serial Numbers			
	Low	**High**	**Notes Printed**	**CH CU**
BOSTON	A-A W	A44 800 000A	44,800,000	$2
NEW YORK	B-A - B-B W	B89 600 000B	185,600,000	2
PHILADELPHIA	C-A - C-C W	C06 400 000C	198,400,000	2
CLEVELAND	D-A W	D89 600 000A	89,600,000	2
RICHMOND	E-A W	E51 200 000A	51,200,000	2
ATLANTA	F-A - F-E FW	F32 000 000E	416,000,000	2
ST. LOUIS	H-A - H-B FW	H32 000 000B	128,000,000	2
MINNEAPOLIS	I-A FW	I70 400 000A	70,400,000	2
DALLAS	K-A FW	K06 400 000A	6,400,000	5
SAN FRANCISCO	L-A - L-D FW	L25 600 000D	313,600,000	2

TWO DOLLAR NOTES

LEGAL TENDER

SERIES 1928 RED SEAL

12 Subject

PLATE NUMBERS: Face #1 was not used. Face numbers #2 through #103. Back numbers are 'micro' type and begin at #1. Some notes are known without a back number.

SIGNATURES: H.T. Tate, A.W. Mellon

Serial Numbers

Low	High	Notes Printed	VF	CH CU	GEM CU
A00 000 001A	A57 010 459A	55,889,424	$25	$250	$350
★00 000 579A	★00 688 584A	—	400	2,200	3,000

SERIES 1928A RED SEAL

PLATE NUMBERS: Face #1 (master), #2 and #3 were not used. Face numbers #4 through #93.

SIGNATURES: W.O. Woods, A.W. Mellon

Serial Numbers

Low	High	Notes Printed	VG/F	VF	CH CU	GEM CU
A51 112 758A	A99 999 999A	46,859,136	$25	$60	$450	$700
B00 000 001A	B08 965 670A	—	30	60	600	1,000
★00 732 343A	★01 055 383A	—	350	1,500	10,000	—

SERIES 1928B RED SEAL

PLATE NUMBERS: Face #1 through #6 not used. Face numbers #7 through #42.

SIGNATURES: W.O. Woods, Ogden L. Mills

Serial Numbers

Low	High	Notes Printed	VG/F	VF	CH CU	GEM CU
A86 398 443A	—	9,001,632	$75	$200	$1,500	$2,000
—	B09 004 381A	—	60	175	1,200	1,800
H00 942 054A	H01 053 286A	—	14,000	25,000	—	85,000

Highest grades of only 7 star notes known is GEM. One AU and one GEM.

SERIES 1928C RED SEAL

PLATE NUMBERS: Face numbers #1 through #181, excluding #56 through #75 which were not used.

Back numbers end at #288 (high observed of the micro type).

SIGNATURES: W.A. Julian, Henry Morgenthau, Jr.

Serial Numbers

Low	High	Notes Printed	VF	CH CU	GEM CU
B09 008 001A	B99 999 999A	86,584,008	$20	$150	$250
C00 000 001A	C05 595 078A	—	40	325	425
★01 062 930A	★02 039 694A	—	700	3,000	—

SERIES 1928C MULE RED SEAL

These are Series 1928C notes with macro back plate numbers (#289 or higher), and are actually Series 1928C faces on Series 1928D backs, #289 through #294 observed.

Serial Numbers

Low	High	Notes Printed	VG/F	VF	GEM CU
B97 675 354A	B99 999 999A	—	$1,500	$2,500	—
C00 000 001A	C02 199 891A	—	1,500	2,500	—

SERIES 1928D MULE RED SEAL

These are Series 1928D notes with the micro back plate numbers (#288 or lower), and are actually Series 1928D faces on Series 1928C backs.

Serial Numbers

Low	High	Notes Printed	VF	CH CU	GEM CU
B87 580 373A	B99 999 999A	Included in	$50	$275	$400
C00 000 001A	C55 064 693A	1928D total.	15	85	125
★01 911 287A	★02 619 482A	—	350	1,400	2,000

SERIES 1928D RED SEAL

PLATE NUMBERS: Face numbers #182 through #401. Back numbers begin at #289.
SIGNATURES: W.A. Julian, Henry Morgenthau, Jr.

Serial Numbers

Low	High	Notes Printed	VF	CH CU	GEM CU
B83 988 001A	B99 999 999A	146,381,364	$1,000	—	—
B97 283 825A	Low observed	—	—	—	—
C00 000 001A	D35 443 700A	—	15	$80	110
★01 972 969A observed	★03 215 773A	—	100	700	1,000

SERIES 1928E RED SEAL

PLATE NUMBERS: Face numbers #403 through #414.
SIGNATURES: W.A. Julian, Fred M. Vinson

Serial Numbers

Low	High	Notes Printed	VF	CH CU	GEM CU
D29 712 001A	D39 591 186A	6,480,000	$25	$150	$250
★03 212 775A	★03 227 372A	—	2,800	10,000	14,000

SERIES 1928F RED SEAL

PLATE NUMBERS: Face numbers #440 through #462.
SIGNATURES: W.A. Julian, John W. Snyder

Serial Numbers Official

Low	High	Notes Printed	VF	CH CU	GEM CU
D36 192 001A	D82 673 798A	42,360,000	$15	$75	$125
★03 236 520A	★03 644 508A	—	125	650	1,000

SERIES 1928G RED SEAL

PLATE NUMBERS: Face numbers #483 through #516. Back numbers end at #390 (last number used on 12 subject sheets).
SIGNATURES: Georgia Neese Clark, John W. Snyder

Serial Numbers Official

Low	High	Notes Printed	VF	CH CU	GEM CU
D78 552 001A	E30 760 000A	52,208,000	$15	$75	$115
★03 651 150A	★04 137 953A	—	100	600	900
official high	—	—	—	—	—
★04 152 000A					

SERIES 1953 RED SEAL

PLATE NUMBERS: Face check numbers begin at #1 (#8 was not used). Back numbers begin at #391 (First number used on 18 subject sheets).

SIGNATURES: Ivy Baker Priest, G.M. Humphrey

Serial Numbers Official

Low	High	Notes Printed	VF	CH CU	GEM CU
A00 000 001A	A45 360 000A	45,360,000	$9	$25	$55
★00 000 001A	★02 160 000A	2,160,000	20	100	175

SERIES 1953A RED SEAL

SIGNATURES: Ivy Baker Priest, Robert B. Anderson

Serial Numbers Official

Low	High	Notes Printed	VF	CH CU	GEM CU
A45 360 001A	A63 360 000A	18,000,000	$8	$25	$45
★02 160 001A	★02 880 000A	720,000	20	100	150

SERIES 1953B RED SEAL

SIGNATURES: Elizabeth Rudel Smith, C. Douglas Dillon

Serial Numbers Official

Low	High	Notes Printed	VF	CH CU	GEM CU
A63 360 001A	A74 160 000A	10,800,000	$7	$20	$45
★02 880 001A	★03 600 000A	720,000	15	75	150

SERIES 1953C RED SEAL

SIGNATURES: Kathryn O'Hay Granahan, C. Douglas Dillon

PLATE NUMBERS: Back numbers used on 18 subject sheets end at #412. Face numbers used on 18 subject sheets end at #16.

Serial Numbers Official

Low	High	Notes Printed	VF	CH CU	GEM CU
A74 160 001A	A79 920 000A	5,760,000	$7	$20	$45
★03 600 001A	★03 960 000A	360,000	20	80	150

SERIES 1963 RED SEAL

PLATE SERIALS: Both face and back numbers on 32 subject sheets begin at #1.
SIGNATURES: Kathryn O'Hay Granahan, C. Douglas Dillon

Serial Numbers Official

Low	High	Notes Printed	VF	CH CU	GEM CU
A00 000 001A	A15 360 000A	15,360,000	$7	$20	$40
★00 000 001A	★00 640 000A	640,000	12	50	75

SERIES 1963A RED SEAL

PLATE NUMBERS: Both face and back numbers end at #3.
SIGNATURES: Kathryn O'Hay Granahan, Henry H. Fowler

Serial Numbers Official

Low	High	Notes Printed	VF	CH CU	GEM CU
A15 360 001A	A18 560 000A	3,200,000	$7	$20	$40
★00 640 001A	★01 280 000A	640,000	20	100	150

The printing of the $2 United States Note terminated with Series 1963A.

FEDERAL RESERVE NOTES

SERIES 1976 GREEN SEAL

SIGNATURES: Francine I. Neff, William E. Simon

PLATE NUMBERS: Face numbers 1 through 80, 93, 94 and 98. Back numbers 1 through 78, 84 and 100.

	Serial Numbers			
	Low	**High**	**Notes Printed**	**CH CU**
BOSTON	A00 000 001**A**	A29 440 000**A**	29,440,000	$8
	A00 000 001★	A01 280 000★	1,280,000	15
NEW YORK	B00 000 001**A**	B67 200 000**A**	67,200,000	7
	B00 000 001★	B02 560 000★	2,560,000	20
	B-B	—	—	30
	uncut sheets only			
	B-C	—	—	30
	uncut sheets only			
PHILADELPHIA	C00 000 001**A**	C33 280 000**A**	33,800,000	6
	C00 000 001★	C01 280 000★	1,280,000	15
CLEVELAND	D00 000 001**A**	D31 360 000**A**	31,630,000	7
	D00 000 001★	D01 280 000★	1,280,000	25
RICHMOND	E00 000 001**A**	E56 960 000**A**	56,960,000	7
	E99 840 000**B**	E99 999 960**B**	160,000	30
	E-B	—	—	—
	uncut sheets only			
	E00 000 001★	E00 640 000★	640,000	75

	Low	High	Notes Printed	CH CU
ATLANTA	F00 000 001**A**	F60 800 000**A**	60,800,000	$6
	F00 000 001★	F01 280 000★	1,280,000	20
CHICAGO	G00 000 001**A**	G82 316 054**A**	84,480,000	$6
	G00 000 001★	G01 280 000★	1,280,000	60
ST. LOUIS	H00 000 001**A**	H39 040 000**A**	39,040,000	7
	H00 000 001★	H01 280 000★	1,280,000	15
MINNEAPOLIS	I00 000 001**A**	I23 680 000**A**	23,680,000	12
	I-B	—	200,000	30
	uncut sheets only			
	I-C	—	200,000	30
	uncut sheets only			
	I00 000 001★	I00 640 000★	640,000	275
KANSAS CITY	J00 000 001**A**	J24 960 000**A**	24,960,000	18
	J00 000 001★	J00 640 000★	640,000	200
DALLAS	K00 000 001**A**	K41 600 000**A**	41,600,000	8
	K00 000 001★	K01 280 000★	1,280,000	25
SAN FRANCISCO	L00 000 001**A**	L82 560 000**A**	82,5600	6
	L00 000 001★	L01 920 000★	1,920,000	35

SERIES 1995 GREEN SEAL

SIGNATURES: Mary Ellen Withrow, Robert E. Rubin
PLATE NUMBERS: Both face and back numbers start at #1.
PRINTING FACILITY: All notes printed in Fort Worth.

	Serial Numbers			
	Low	High	Notes Printed	CH CU
ATLANTA	F00 000 001**A**	F57 600 000**B**	153,600,000	$4
	F-C through F-H	—	—	35
	uncut sheets only			
	F00 000 001★	F05 760 000★	1,280,000	12

MILENNIUM NOTES

	Low	High	Notes Printed	CH CU
BOSTON	A-★	A20 009 999★	9,999	$75
NEW YORK	B-★	B20 009 999★	9,999	50

	Low	High	Notes Printed	CH CU
PHILADELPHIA	C-★	C20 009 999★	9,999	$50
CLEVELAND	D-★	D20 009 999★	9,999	50
RICHMOND	E-★	E20 009 999★	9,999	50
ATLANTA	F-★	F20 009 999★	9,999	75
CHICAGO	G-★	G20 009 999★	9,999	50
ST. LOUIS	H-★	H20 009 999★	9,999	50
MINNEAPOLIS	I-★	I20 009 999★	9,999	50
KANSAS CITY	J-★	J20 009 999★	9,999	50
DALLAS	K-★	K20 009 999★	9,999	50
SAN FRANCISCO	L-★	L20 009 999★	9,999	50

SERIES 2003 GREEN SEAL

SIGNATURES: Rosario Marin, John W. Snow

PLATE NUMBERS: Both face and back numbers begin at #1.

SERIAL NUMBERS: All districts start regular star notes with 00 000 001.

Serial Numbers			
	Low	High	Notes Printed	CH CU
BOSTON	A-★ W	A00 016 000★	16,000	$20

	Low	High	Notes Printed	CH CU
NEW YORK	B-★ W	B00 016 000★	16,000	$20
PHILADELPHIA	C-★ W	C00 016 000★	16,000	20
CLEVELAND	D-★ W	D00 016 000★	16,000	20
RICHMOND	E-★ W	E00 016 000★	16,000	20
ATLANTA	F-★ W	F00 016 000★	16,000	20
CHICAGO	G-★ W	G00 016 000★	16,000	20
ST. LOUIS	H-★ W	H00 016 000★	16,000	20
MINNEAPOLIS	I-A - I-B FW	I25 600 000B	121,600,000	5
	I-★ FW	I03 840 000★	3,840,000	10
	I-★ W	I00 016 000★	16,000	20
KANSAS CITY	J-★ W	J00 016 000★	16,000	20
DALLAS	K-★ W	K00 016 000★	16,000	20
SAN FRANCISCO	L-★ W	L00 016 000★	16,000	20

SERIES 2003A GREEN SEAL

SIGNATURES: Anna Escobedo Cabral, John W. Snow
PLATE NUMBERS: Both face and back numbers begin at #1.
SERIAL NUMBERS: All districts start regular and star notes with 00 000 001.
PRINTING FACILITY: All notes printed in Fort Worth.

	Serial Numbers Low	High	Notes Printed	CH CU
BOSTON	A-A	A12 800 000A	12,800,000	$5
NEW YORK	B-A	B25 600 000A	25,600,000	5
PHILADELPHIA	C-A	C06 400 000A	6,400,000	10
CLEVELAND	D-A	D19 200 000A	19,200,000	15
RICHMOND	E-A	E19 200 000A	19,200,000	5
ATLANTA	F-A	F19 200 000A	19,200,000	5
	F-★	F00 320 000★ (sheets)	320,000	125
CHICAGO	G-A	G25 600 000A	25,600,000	5
ST. LOUIS	H-A	H06 400 000A	6,400,000	10
MINNEAPOLIS	I-A	I06 400 000A	6,400,000	10
KANSAS CITY	J-A	J12 800 000A	12,800,000	5
DALLAS	K-A	K12 800 000A	12,800,000	5
SAN FRANCISCO	L-A	L64 000 000A	64,000,000	5

FIVE DOLLAR NOTES

FEDERAL RESERVE BANK NOTES

SERIES 1929 BROWN SEAL

SERIAL NUMBERS: Figures shown below are the official high numbers. All districts started both regular and star notes with serial 00 000 001. Bureau of Engraving and Printing information is incomplete on star serial numbers, as are reports of high observed serial numbers.

PLATE NUMBERS: Face numbers #1 through #356.

SIGNATURES: E.E. Jones, W.O. Woods, and the Federal Reserve Bank Cashier or Controller or the Deputy or Assistant Deputy Governor, with the Governor.

Collectors are requested to supply information on star serial numbers.

	Serial Numbers		Notes			
	Low	High	Printed	VF	CH CU	GEM CU
BOSTON	A00 000 001A	A02 687 815A	3,180,000	$45	$200	$350
	A00 000 001★	A00 023 607★	36,000	1,200	8,000	—
NEW YORK	B00 000 003A	B02 090 355A	2,100,000	40	250	450
	B00 004 660★	B00 007 123★	24,000	1,500	5,000	—
PHILADELPHIA	C00 000 002A	C03 022 801A	3,096,000	40	200	350
	C00 000 034★	C00 022 801★	36,000	600	5,000	—
CLEVELAND	D00 000 006A	D04 196 975A	4,236,000	40	200	350
	D00 011 417★	D00 040 079★	60,000	500	4,000	—
RICHMOND	Not Printed.	—	—	—	—	—
ATLANTA	F00 000 001A	F01 661 390A	1,884,000	45	400	500
	F00 001 066★	F00 021 941★	24,000	600	4,500	—
CHICAGO	G00 000 002A	G05 800 042A	5,988,000	40	175	400
	G00 000 673★	G00 075 808★	84,000	500	3,500	—
ST. LOUIS	H00 000 003A	H00 271 261A	276,000	800	5,000	—
	H00 012 021★	H00 013 227★	24,000	10,000	20,000	—
MINNEAPOLIS	I00 000 020A	I00 679 114A	684,000	100	1,250	—
	I00 000 005★	I00 007 220★	24,000	3,000	8,000	—
KANSAS CITY	J00 000 004A	J02 398 810A	2,460,000	45	250	450
	J00 006 560★	J00 034 254★	48,000	600	5,000	—
DALLAS	K00 000 008A	K00 848 049A	996,000	60	275	450
	K00 003 021★	K00 009 423★	24,000	11,000	—	—
SAN FRANCISCO	L00 000 100A	L00 359 006A	360,000	2,500	12,000	—
	L-★	—	24,000	—	—	—
	Not Reported.					

US/LEGAL TENDER

SERIES 1928 RED SEAL

PLATE NUMBERS: Face #4 through #408; face #1 through #3 were not used. Back numbers are micro type and begin at #1.

SIGNATURES: W.O. Woods, A.W. Mellon

Serial numbers are those that have been observed.

Serial Numbers

Low	High	Notes Printed	VF	CH CU	GEM CU
A00 000 001A	C-A	267,209,616	$20	$125	$200
	D14 579 201A high observed	—	400	2,000	3,000
★00 007 777A	★03 282 332A observed	—	300	3,500	5,000

SERIES 1928A RED SEAL

PLATE NUMBERS: Face #3 through #122, #174 and #175. (Face #1, #2 and #123 through #173 were not used).

SIGNATURES: W.O. Woods, Ogden L. Mills

Serial Numbers

Low	High	Notes Printed	VG/F	VF	CH CU	GEM CU
C29 334 214A	D15 142 278A	58,194,600	—	$25	$175	$400
★02 821 949A	★03 330 983A	—	800	1,500	7,500	—

SERIES 1928B MULE RED SEAL

Macro back numbers 939 or higher.

Serial Numbers

Low	High	Notes Printed	VF	CH CU	GEM CU
E09 764 160A	E79 977 997A	included below	$30	$200	$300
★04 795 133A	★05 187 780A	—	2,500	9,000	12,000

SERIES 1928B RED SEAL

PLATE NUMBERS: Face #1 through #287. Back numbers end at #938 (High of the micro type).

SIGNATURES: W.A. Julian, Henry Morgenthau, Jr.

Serial Numbers

Low	High	Notes Printed	VF	CH CU	GEM CU
D15 228 001A	E68 326 448A	147,827,340	$15	$75	$150
★03 409 448A	★05 042 742A	—	240	1,200	1,800

SERIES 1928C MULE RED SEAL

PLATE NUMBERS: Face #288 through #522.

Micro back numbers 938 or lower. All **G-A** mules have back #637.

Serial Numbers

Low	High	Notes Printed	VF	CH CU	GEM CU
E41 395 929A	E97 543 866A	included below	$25	$125	$200
F00 577 379A	F03 922 924A	—	1,000	3,000	—
G41 283 312A	G57 843 456A	—	1,400	3,500	—
★04 928 514A	★05 602 636A	—	750	4,500	—

SERIES 1928C RED SEAL

PLATE NUMBERS: Face #288 through #522. Back numbers begin at #939.

SIGNATURES: W.A. Julian, Henry Morgenthau, Jr.

Serial Numbers

Low	High	Notes Printed	VF	CH CU	GEM CU
E41 395 429A	G57 877 893A	214,735,765	$20	$75	$125
★04 997 858A	★07 074 007A	—	175	1,000	1,500

SERIES 1928D MULE RED SEAL

PLATE NUMBERS: Face #524 through #550. Micro back number 637.

Serial Numbers

Low	High	Notes Printed	VF	CH CU	GEM CU
G54 832 909A	G65 998 344A	included below	$500	$3,500	—

SERIES 1928D RED SEAL

PLATE NUMBERS: Face #524 through #550. Back #939 or higher.

SIGNATURES: W.A. Julian, Fred M. Vinson

Serial Numbers

Low	High	Notes Printed	VG/F	VF	CH CU	GEM CU
G50 628 001A	G66 781 666A	9,297,120	$15	$50	$250	$300
★07 093 577A	★07 174 715A	96,000	600	1,500	5,000	—

SERIES 1928E MULE RED SEAL

PLATE NUMBERS: Face #566 through #627. Micro back numbers 629 and 637. 629 is at least 10 times scarcer than 637, appears only in block H-A, and commands a premium of 3 to 4 times an H-A with 637 back.

Serial Numbers

Low	High	Notes Printed	VF	CH CU	GEM CU
G70 465 356A	H50 445 154A	included below	$400	$1,200	$1,700
★07 281 117A		—	15,000	—	—
(unique) - back plate #637					

SERIES 1928E RED SEAL

PLATE NUMBERS: Face #566 through #627.

SIGNATURES: W.A. Julian, John W. Snyder

Serial Numbers

Low	High	Notes Printed	VF	CH CU	GEM CU
G62 496 001A	H77 577 770A	109,952,760	$20	$90	$180
★07 177 415A	★08 697 470A	—	200	1,500	2,000
★07 176 001A official low					

SERIES 1928F RED SEAL

SIGNATURES: Georgia Neese Clark, John W. Snyder

WIDE 1

PLATE NUMBERS: Face #628 through #683. Back number 2006 or lower.

Serial Numbers

Low	High	Notes Printed	VF	CH CU	GEM CU
H71 592 001A	I79 320 200A	104,194,704	$17	$75	$100
★08 396 104A	★09 677 247A	—	120	850	1,200

NARROW

PLATE NUMBERS: Back number 2007 through 2066.

Serial Numbers

Low	High	Notes Printed	VF	CH CU	GEM CU
I51 752 715A	I75 479 000A	included above	$35	$150	$200
★09 419 479A	★09 658 306A	—	1,000	4,000	—

WIDE II

PLATE NUMBERS: Back number 2067 through 2096.

Serial Numbers

Low	High	Notes Printed	VF	CH CU	GEM CU
I69 897 697A	I79 394 789A	included above	$50	$175	$225
★09 541 928A	★09 672 795A	—	2,000	8,000	—

Official ending serial numbers for 1928F are I79 468 000A and ★09 744 000A.

SERIES 1953 RED SEAL

PLATE NUMBERS: Face numbers begin at #1. Back numbers begin at #2094 (low of 18 subject sheets).

SIGNATURES: Ivy Baker Priest, G.M. Humphrey

Serial Numbers Official

Low	High	Notes Printed	VF	CH CU	GEM CU
A00 000 001**A**	—	120,880,000	$12	$40	$60
—	**B**20 880 000**A**	—	15	60	75
★00 000 001**A**	★05 760 000**A**	5,760,000	60	300	500

SERIES 1953A RED SEAL

SIGNATURES: Ivy Baker Priest, Robert B. Anderson

Serial Numbers Official

Low	High	Notes Printed	VF	CH CU	GEM CU
B20 880 001**A**	—	90,280,000	$12	$35	$50
—	**C**11 160 000**A**	—	12	40	60
★05 760 001**A**	★11 160 000**A**	5,400,000	40	225	300

SERIES 1953B RED SEAL

SIGNATURES: Elizabeth Rudel Smith, C. Douglas Dillon

Serial Numbers Official

Low	High	Notes Printed	VF	CH CU	GEM CU
C11 160 001A	C55 800 000A	44,640,000	$12	$35	$50
★11 160 001A	★13 320 000A	2,160,000	40	200	300

SERIES 1953C RED SEAL

PLATE NUMBERS: Face numbers on 18 subject sheets end at #44. Back numbers on 18 subject sheets end at #2587.

SIGNATURES: Kathryn O'Hay Granahan, C. Douglas Dillon

Serial Numbers Official

Low	High	Notes Printed	VF	CH CU	GEM CU
C55 800 001A	C64 440 000A	8,640,000	$15	$50	$75
★13 320 001A	★13 664 118A high observed	—	80	400	600

SERIES 1963 RED SEAL

PLATE NUMBERS: The range of the face numbers made for 32 subject sheets is #1 through #10. Back number range #1 through #9.

SIGNATURES: Kathryn O'Hay Granahan, C. Douglas Dillon

Serial Numbers Official

Low	High	Notes Printed	VF	CH CU	GEM CU
A00 000 001**A**	**A**63 360 000**A**	63,360,000	$12	$30	$60
★00 000 001**A**	★03 840 000**A**	3,840,000	20	100	175

SILVER CERTIFICATES

SERIES 1934 BLUE SEAL

Lincoln photo by Mathew Brady Feb. 9, 1864. Original glass plate negative presented to Library of Congress in 1953 by Louis Rabinowitz.

PLATE NUMBERS: Face numbers range #1 - #561. Back numbers below #938 (micro size).

SIGNATURES: W.A. Julian, Henry Morgenthau, Jr.

Serial Numbers

Low	High	Notes Printed	VF	CH CU	GEM CU
A00 000 001**A**	**D**99 999 999**A**	356,352,000	$10	$60	$90
—	**E**51 445 583**A** high observed	—	200	1,500	1,900
★00 002 350**A**	★03 995 572**A**	3,960,000	80	600	900

SERIES 1934 MULE BLUE SEAL

PLATE NUMBERS: These are Series 1934 Notes with large back numbers, and are 1934 faces on 1934A backs. Macro back numbers #939 or higher.

Serial Numbers

Low	High	Notes Printed	VF	CH CU	GEM CU
E06 094 905A	E53 049 647A	included above	$250	$1,000	$1,500

SERIES 1934A MULE BLUE SEAL

These are Series 1934A notes with micro back plate numbers, and are actually Series 1934A faces on Series 1934 backs.

PLATE NUMBERS: Back numbers 938 or less (micro size).

SERIAL NUMBERS: D50 352 001A official low-Printed January 25, 1938.

SIGNATURES: W.A. Julian, Henry Morgenthau, Jr.

Serial Numbers

Low	High	Notes Printed	VF	CH CU	GEM CU
D56 173 786A	G-A	included below	$10	$60	$125
H-A	—	—	500	—	—
IA & JA unknown	—	—	—	—	—
K-A Bp 637 only	—	—	100	500	—
—	L24 664 250A (back plate #637)— high observed		150	500	—
★03 594 833A	★06 414 028A	—	95	550	700

SERIES 1934A BLUE SEAL

PLATE NUMBERS: Face number range is #562 - #1765. Back numbers begin at #939.

Serial Numbers

Low	High	Notes Printed	VF	CH CU	GEM CU
E10 554 653A	—	740,128,000*	$10	$50	$75
low observed					
F-A	K-A	—	10	40	75
—	L27 130 229A	—	15	80	100
	high observed				
★04 599 105A	★11 656 719A	—	60	325	500

*Includes all types of 1934A Series

SERIES 1934A LATE FINISHED FACE PLATE 307 BLUE SEAL

Serial Numbers

Low	High	Notes Printed	VF	CH CU	GEM CU
K18 979 685A	K53 978 344A	569,244*	$900	$2,250	$3,500
★10 846 330A (unique)		—	—	—	—

*Includes 1934A North Africa

The plate 307 blue seal is estimated to be rarer than the plate 307 yellow seal by a ratio of 30:1.

NORTH AFRICA NOTES

SERIES 1934A YELLOW SEAL

PLATE NUMBERS: Back numbers begin at 939.

Serial Numbers

Low	High	Notes Printed	VF	CH CU	GEM CU
K34 188 001A	K34 508 000A	320,000	$80	$350	$550
K36 420 001A	K36 740 000A	320,000	80	350	550
K37 464 001A	K37 784 000A	320,000	80	350	550
K40 068 001A	K42 068 000A	2,000,000	80	350	550
K43 152 001A	K44 852 000A	1,700,000	80	350	550
K53 984 001A	K65 984 000A	12,000,000	80	350	550
★10 548 001A	★10 568 158A	20,000	400	3,000	4,000
★10 716 001A	★10 764 000A	48,000	400	3,000	4,000
★10 884 001A	★11 016 000A	32,000	400	3,000	4,000
★10 549 061A	★11 015 131A	—	—	—	—
	low and high observed				

SERIES 1934A LATE FINISHED FACE PLATE 307 (NORTH AFRICA)

Serial Numbers	Notes Printed	VF	CH CU	GEM CU
K40 927 103A	K63 440 982A	$100	$750	—
★10 896 399A	see 1934A pl. 307	—	—	—
low observed				
★11 010 487A	—	600	4,000	—
high observed				

SILVER CERTIFICATES

SERIES 1934B MULE BLUE SEAL

These are Series 1934B notes with micro back check numbers, and are actually Series 1934B faces on Series 1934 backs.

PLATE NUMBERS: Back number used is #637 (micro size).

SIGNATURES: W.A. Julian, Fred M. Vinson

Serial Numbers

Low	High	Notes Printed	VF	CH CU	GEM CU
K90 480 001A	—	included below	$300	$2,000	—
—	L84 069 273A	—	200	1,000	—
★11 665 158A	★12 418 103A	—	1,500	5,000	—

SERIES 1934B BLUE SEAL

PLATE NUMBERS: Face numbers #1769 - #1826. Back #939 and higher.

Serial Numbers

Low	High	Notes Printed	VF	CH CU	GEM CU
K89 400 165A	—	60,328,000	$25	$200	$250
L00 000 001A	L99 999 999A	—	15	90	150
	M33 301 809A	—	300	2,000	3,000
★11 412 691A	★12 418 105A	—	200	2,750	3,500

SERIES 1934C MULE BLUE SEAL - WIDE FACE

These are Series 1934C notes with only micro back plate numbers noted below, and are actually Series 1934C faces on Series 1934 backs.

PLATE NUMBERS: Primary back number used #637 (micro size). Back number 629 is at least 10 times scarcer than 637, and commands a premium of 3 to 4 times higher.

Serial Numbers Observed

Low	High	Notes Printed	VF	CH CU	GEM CU
L29 451 093A	P72 850 478A	included below	$60	$250	$400
★13 803 080A	★15 714 460A	—	700	2,000	3,000

SERIES 1934C MULE BLUE SEAL - NARROW FACE

These are Mules as described directly above.

FACE PLATE NUMBERS: Narrow face plate numbers 2028, 2029, 2030, and 2031 only. (Introduced in August 1948)

BACK PLATE NUMBERS: Micro back number 637 has been observed in all blocks shown.

Serial Numbers Observed

Low	High	Notes Printed	VF	CH CU
N85 978 601**A**	N94 678 133**A**	included below	$300	$1,200
P16 330 226**A**	—	—	—	—
★-A	(unique) (637 back)	—	—	—

SERIES 1934C BLUE SEAL - WIDE FACE

PLATE NUMBERS: Face check numbers #1875 - #2026. Back number 939 and higher.

SIGNATURES: W.A. Julian, John W. Snyder

Serial Numbers Observed

Low	High	Notes Printed	VF	CH CU	GEM CU
L49 546 170**A**	—	372,328,000	$15	$50	$75
M-A through	**Q**65 450 107**A**	—	12	40	65
★11 977 515**A**	★17 687 718**A**	—	50	300	425

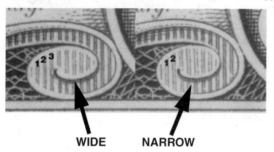

WIDE   NARROW

SERIES 1934C BLUE SEAL - NARROW FACE

PLATE NUMBERS: Narrow face plates were introduced in August 1948 on face plate numbers 2028, 2029, 2030 and 2031 only.

Serial Numbers Observed

Low	High	Notes Printed	VF	CH CU
N-A - P-A	Q-A	(+ or -) 2 1/2% of 1934C total	$50	$300
★-A	—	—	Rare	—

Note: Serial number submissions are requested for both Narrow regular and Mules.

SERIES 1934D BLUE SEAL

SIGNATURES: Georgia Neese Clark, John W. Snyder

Serial Numbers Official

Low	High	Notes Printed
Q23 136 001**A**	**V**14 796 000**A**	491,666,000
★16 884 788**A**	★23 088 000**A**	—
low observed		

WIDE I

PLATE NUMBERS: Face numbers #2035 - #2171. Back number 2006 or lower.

Serial Numbers Observed

Low	High	Notes Printed	VF	CH CU	GEM CU
Q24 783 484**A**		see above	$10	$40	$70
	V14 681 741**A**		15	80.00	125
★16 884 788**A**	★23 056 385**A**	—	50	400	

NARROW

PLATE NUMBERS: Back numbers 2007 through 2066.

Serial Numbers Observed

Low	High	Notes Printed	VF	CH CU	GEM CU
T43 892 772**A**	**U**-**A**	see above	$20	$60	$80
—	**V**14 536 251**A**	—	30	120	150
★17 687 712**A**	★23 052 308**A**	—	75	600	—

WIDE II

PLATE NUMBERS: Back numbers 2067 through 2096.

Serial Numbers Observed

Low	High	Notes Printed	VF	CH CU	GEM CU
U37 326 477A	—	see above	$20	$90	$175
—	V14 374 928A	—	35	200	300
★22 017 567A	★23 034 317A	—	150	1,200	1,700

SERIES 1953 BLUE SEAL

PLATE NUMBERS: Face numbers begin at #1. Back numbers begin at #2097 (First number used on 18 subject sheets).

SIGNATURES: Ivy Baker Priest, G.M. Humphrey

Serial Numbers Official

Low	High	Notes Printed	VF	CH CU	GEM CU
A00 000 001A	D39 600 000A	339,600,000	$10	$27	$50
★00 000 001A	★15 120 000A	15,120,000	25	120	200
★00 000 029A (observed)					

SERIES 1953A BLUE SEAL

SIGNATURES: Ivy Baker Priest, Robert B. Anderson

Serial Numbers Official

Low	High	Notes Printed	VF	CH CU	GEM CU
D39 600 001A	F72 000 000A	232,400,000	$10	$27	$50
★15 120 001A	★28 080 000A	12,960,000	20	95	150

SERIES 1953B BLUE SEAL

SIGNATURES: Elizabeth Rudel Smith, C. Douglas Dillon

Serial Numbers Official

Low	High	Notes Printed	VF	CH CU	GEM CU
F72 000 001A	G45 000 000A	73,000,000	$10	$25	$50
★28 080 001A	★31 320 000A	3,240,000	3,500	14,000	17,500

This series was only released in part. **G-A** printed but not released.
F81 904 366A and ★**28 428 881A** highest observed

SERIES 1953C BLUE SEAL

PLATE NUMBERS: Face numbers of 18 subject sheets end at #97. Back numbers on 18 subject sheets end at #2587.

SIGNATURES: Kathryn O'Hay Granahan, C. Douglas Dillon

NOTE: This series was printed but not released. The Bureau actually exhibits an uncut sheet of star notes.

Serial Numbers Official

Low	High	Notes Printed
G45 000 001A	H35 640 000A	90,640,000
★31 320 001A	★35 640 000A	4,320,000

FEDERAL RESERVE NOTES
SERIES 1928 GREEN SEAL

SERIAL NUMBERS: All districts started both regular and star notes with 00 000 001.
Bureau of Engraving and Printing information is incomplete on ending serial numbers.
PLATE NUMBERS: Both face and back numbers begin at #1.
SIGNATURES: H.T. Tate, A.W. Mellon

Single and double digit low serial numbers are valued at three to four times regular prices.

	Serial Numbers					
	Low	**High**	**Notes Printed**	**VF**	**CH CU**	**GEM CU**
BOSTON	A00 000 012A	A07 452 161A	8,025,300	$70	$500	$750
	A00 000 740★	A00 283 715★	—	1,200	4,000	—
NEW YORK	B00 314 371A	B50 764 007A	14,701,884	$50	$300	450
	B00 099 527★	B00 163 827★	—	400	1,250	2,000
PHILADELPHIA	C00 000 063A	C27 758 611A	11,819,712	50	350	450
	C00 000 002★	C00 217 187★	—	700	2,500	—

	Low	**High**	**Notes Printed**	**VF**	**CH CU**	**GEM CU**
CLEVELAND	D00 000 030A	D13 179 914A	9,049,000	$40	$250	$325
	D00 004 940★	D00 192 724★	—	450	2,000	—
RICHMOND	E02 126 178A	E06 022 463A	6,027,660	70	750	1,250
	E00 022 434★	E00 085 392★	—	1,000	5,000	—
ATLANTA	F00 075 734A	F11 087 392A	10,964,400	60	400	600
	F00 000 284★	F00 227 802★	—	1,000	4,000	—

	Low	High	Notes Printed	VF	CH CU	GEM CU
CHICAGO	G00 000 001A	G23 387 298A	12,326,052	35	250	$350
	G00 000 393★	G00 445 680★	—	200	1,250	2,000
ST. LOUIS	H00 000 001A	H04 220 853A	4,675,200	60	300	450
	H00 020 486★	H00 113 707★	—	500	3,000	—
MINNEAPOLIS	I00 000 001A	I03 953 188A	4,284,300	200	1,400	2,000
	I00 027 531★	I00 071 060★	—	2,000	6,000	—
KANSAS CITY	J00 000 222A	J05 245 344A	4,480,800	80	500	700
	J00 014 423★	J00 137 993★	—	800	3,000	—
DALLAS	K00 000 001A	K09 084 633A	8,137,824	50	200	350
	K00 014 742★	K00 113 419★	—	1,200	4,000	—
SAN FRANCISCO	L00 000 025A	L11 189 914A	9,792,000	70	350	500
	L00 000 099★	L00 121 873★	—	1,500	5,000	—

SERIES 1928A GREEN SEAL

SERIAL NUMBERS: All districts continued from previous series with regular and star notes.
PLATE NUMBERS: Face numbers begin with #1.
SIGNATURES: W.O. Woods, A.W. Mellon

Serial Numbers

	Low	High	Notes Printed	VF	CH CU	GEM CU
BOSTON	A06 494 816A	A16 638 789A	7,404,352	$100	$800	—
	A00 323 962★	A00 417 508★	—	1,000	3,500	—
NEW YORK	B09 734 051A	B54 038 970A	43,210,696	35	250	350
	B00 243 238★	B00 827 434★	—	800	2,000	—
PHILADELPHIA	C06 466 940A	C32 769 554A	10,806,012	50	250	400
	C00 218 478★	C00 350 766★	—	1,000	3,500	—
CLEVELAND	D06 848 181A	D14 684 486A	6,822,000	50	225	350
	D00 243 855★	D00 304 339★	—	400	2,500	—
RICHMOND	E06 887 809A	E11 658 510A	2,409,900	60	350	500
	E00 126 303★	E00 127 185★	—	2,000	6,000	—
ATLANTA	F04 404 550A	F17 171 469A	3,537,600	100	450	750
	F00 252 029★		—	2,000	6,000	—

	Low	High	Notes Printed	VF	CH CU	GEM CU
CHICAGO	G07 874 283A	G49 855 759A	37,882,176	35	200	$325
	G00 247 663★	G00 649 815★	—	300	1,250	2,250
ST. LOUIS	H05 022 380A	H09 947 974A	2,731,824	50	300	450
	H00 162 702★	—	—	2,000	7,000	—
MINNEAPOLIS	I04 188 101A	I04 925 962A	652,800	400	2,000	—
	I-★ not reported—			—	—	—
KANSAS CITY	J04 822 495A	J08 269 784A	3,572,400	60	450	650
	J-★ not reported—			—	—	—
DALLAS	K05 632 501A	K09 423 371A	2,564,400	200	2,500	—
	K00 130 714★	K00 134 737★	—	3,000	—	—
SAN FRANCISCO	L08 676 061A	L17 233 258A	6,565,500	50	300	450
	L00 275 230★	L00 350 766★	—	2,000	—	—

SERIES 1928B DARK GREEN SEAL

SERIAL NUMBERS: All districts continued sequence from previous series with regular and star notes.

PLATE NUMBERS: Face numbers begin with #1.

SIGNATURES: W.O. Woods, A.W. Mellon

	Serial Numbers				
	Low	High	Notes Printed	VF	CH CU
BOSTON	A15 921 412A	A29 010 354A	28,430,724	$20	$90
	A00 425 259★	—	—	500	2,000
NEW YORK	B54 024 182A	B81 942 241A	51,157,536	20	90
	B00 902 593★	—	—	500	1,500
PHILADELPHIA	C21 695 184A	C37 243 781A	25,698,396	20	75
	C00 401 030★	C00 491 525★	—	300	1,000
CLEVELAND	D15 828 264A	D30 400 320A	24,874,272	20	90
	D00 364 555★	D00 388 595★	—	500	2,000
RICHMOND	E08 343 197A	E17 325 584A	15,151,932	20	100
	E00 085 392★	E00 180 533★	—	500	2,000
ATLANTA	F14 337 964A	F22 552 512A	13,386,420	20	100
	F00 272 092★	F00 333 663★	—	300	2,000

	Low	High	Notes Printed	VF	CH CU
CHICAGO	G45 649 832A	G48 798 031A	17,157,036	$20	$100
	G-★	—	—	—	—
ST. LOUIS	H06 221 967A	H22 086 727A	20,251,716	20	90
	H00 216 303★	H00 299 543★	—	300	1,500
MINNEAPOLIS	I04 692 029A	I08 295 799A	6,954,060	50	200
	I00 101 208★	I00 101 557★	—	1,000	5,000
KANSAS CITY	J08 602 028A	J11 815 054A	10,677,636	40	300
	J-★	—	—	—	—
DALLAS	K09 680 545A	K12 115 181A	4,334,400	40	150
	K-★	—	—	—	—
SAN FRANCISCO	L17 023 713A	L34 508 985A	28,840,080	20	90
	L00 308 937★	L00 439 971★	—	500	2,000

SERIES 1928B VIVID YELLOW LIGHT GREEN SEAL

SERIAL NUMBERS: All districts continued sequence from dark green seal variety above.

TOTAL NOTES PRINTED: This information is found in previous section and includes both light and dark seal varieties of Series 1928B. High official star serial numbers are listed, but only a fraction of these were actually used.

	Serial Numbers				
	Low	High	Notes Printed	VF	CH CU
BOSTON	A-A	—	—	—	—
	A-★	A00 612 000★	—	—	—
NEW YORK	B-A	—	—	—	—
	B-★	B01 284 000★	—	—	—
PHILADELPHIA	C38 171 567A	—	—	100	500
	C-★	C00 636 000★	—	—	—
CLEVELAND	D31 531 690A	—	—	100	500
	—	D00 576 000★	—	—	—
RICHMOND	E-A	—	—	—	—
	E-★	E00 288 000★	—	—	—
ATLANTA	F23 227 169A	F28 452 147A	—	40	250
	F00 346 221★	F00 372 000★	—	1,000	—
CHICAGO	G-A	—	—	—	—
	G-★	G00 852 000★	—	—	—
ST. LOUIS	H19 096 985A	H27 889 570A	—	40	200
	H00 315 765★	H00 360 000★	—	700	3,000
MINNEAPOLIS	I-A	—	—	50	300
	I-★	I00 144 000★	—	—	—
KANSAS CITY	J-A	J-A	—	50	225
	J-★	J00 240 000★	—	—	—
DALLAS	K-A	—	—	—	—
	K-★	K00 180 000★	—	—	—
SAN FRANCISCO	L36 890 483A	L41 165 862A	—	50	250
	L00 406 647★	L00 576 000★	—	1,000	—

SERIES 1928C LIGHT VIVID YELLOW-GREEN SEAL

SERIAL NUMBERS: Districts printed continued sequence from previous series. Of those printed, only 1.2 million were released.

PLATE NUMBERS: Face numbers range for Atlanta is #1 through #8.

SIGNATURES: W.O. Woods, Ogden L. Mills

	Serial Numbers				
	Low	**High**	**Notes Printed**	**VF**	**CH CU**
CLEVELAND	D-A	unknown	3,293,640	—	—

	Low	**High**	**Notes Printed**	**VF**	**CH CU**	**GEM CU**
ATLANTA	F23 798 011A	F28 651 253A	2,056,200	$1,000	$4,000	—
	F-★	unknown	—	—	—	—
SAN FRANCISCO	L-A	unknown	266,304	—	—	—

SERIES 1928D LIGHT VIVID YELLOW-GREEN SEAL

SERIAL NUMBERS: District printed continued sequence from previous series.

PLATE NUMBERS: Face range #1 through #14. High observed is #9.

SIGNATURES: W.O. Woods, W.H. Woodin

	Serial Numbers				
	Low	**High**	**Notes Printed**	**VF**	**CH CU**	**GEM CU**
ATLANTA	F26 282 729A	F28 617 186A	1,281,600	$2,500	$6,000	—
	F-★	unknown	—	—	—	—

SERIES 1934 LIGHT VIVID YELLOW-GREEN SEAL

SERIAL NUMBERS: All districts started both regular and star notes with 00 000 001.

PLATE NUMBERS: Face numbers begin at #1. Back numbers continue from Series 1928D.

SIGNATURES: W.A. Julian, Henry Morgenthau, Jr.

	Serial Numbers					
	Low	**High**	**Notes Printed**	**VF**	**CH CU**	**GEM CU**
BOSTON	A00 166 741A	A05 996 125A	30,510,036	$15	$90	$125
	A00 009 413★	A00 021 382★	—	100	1,000	1,500
NEW YORK	B00 000 003A	B14 832 000A	47,888,760	$15	$100	125
	B00 007 363★	B00 129 358★	—	100	700	1,000
PHILADELPHIA	C00 000 003A	C06 720 000A	47,327,760	$15	$80	$100
	C00 007 356★	C00 068 215★	—	200	1,200	1,750
CLEVELAND	D00 000 002A	D05 400 000A	62,237,508	15	80	120
	D-★	—	—	—	—	—
RICHMOND	E00 019 527A	E04 992 000A	62,128,000	15	90	—
	E00 021 980★	—	—	150	1,200	—
ATLANTA	F01 750 536A	F12 000 000A	22,811,916	15	100	—
	F00 012 697★	—	—	200	1,200	—
CHICAGO	G00 020 996A	G09 732 000A	31,299,156	15	80	—
	G00 003 957★	G00 082 098★	—	100	700	—
ST. LOUIS	H00 000 003A	H10 368 000A	48,737,280	15	80	—
	H00 010 633★	H00 084 202★	—	150	1,000	—
MINNEAPOLIS	I00 196 641A	I04 920 000A	16,795,392	25	130	—
	I00 010 363★	I00 028 690★	—	150	1,200	—
KANSAS CITY	J00 000 003A	J03 000 000A	31,854,432	15	70	—
	J00 017 331★	J00 031 557★	—	150	1,200	—
DALLAS	K00 000 001A	K08 352 000A	33,332,208	15	100	—
	K-★	—	—	200	1,500	—
SAN FRANCISCO	L01 632 856A	L12 396 000A	39,324,168	15	80	—
	L00 005 324★	L00 038 412★	—	100	900	—

SERIES 1934 DARK BLUE-GREEN SEAL

PLATE NUMBERS: Micro back numbers 938 and lower, includes #637.

NOTE: Back plate 637 non mule DGS varieties are known on B, D, E and J districts. These backplates 637 varieties command substantial premiums, with only seven specimens known at this time.

	Serial Numbers					
	Low	**High**	**Notes Printed**	**VF**	**CH CU**	**GEM CU**
BOSTON	A06 060 971A	A06 121 190A	see above	75	500	—
	A00 049 210★	A00 088 170★	—	300	1,000	—
NEW YORK	B15 001 763A	B15 945 749A	—	50	300	—
		B66 598 277B (#637)	—	500	1,500	—
	B00 140 120★	—	—	250	800	—
PHILADELPHIA	C06 756 383A	C07 506 484A	—	50	300	—
	C00 092 007★	C00 095 717★	—	250	800	—
CLEVELAND	D53 788 157A (#637)	D56 475 697A (#637)	—	500	1,500	—
	D00 074 756★	—	—	250	1,000	—
RICHMOND	E04 996 687A	E61 241 842A (#637)	—	75	400	—
	E-★	—	—	—	—	—
ATLANTA	F12 119 799A	F12 410 419A	—	75	400	—
	F00 124 917★	F00 129 590★	—	300	750	—
CHICAGO	G09 760 267A	G11 048 850A	—	50	250	—
	G00 107 933★	G00 117 396★	—	300	800	—
ST. LOUIS	H10 373 570A	H10 905 473A	—	200	600	—
	H00 122 348★	—	—	350	1,000	—
MINNEAPOLIS	I04 947 199A	I10 382 816A	—	100	350	500
	I00 054 386★	I00 091 074★	—	400	1,000	—
KANSAS CITY	J03 138 409A	J27 826 430A (#637)	—	350	1,000	—
	J00 050 246★	J00 077 594★	—	—	—	—
DALLAS	K08 400 591A	K08 458 167A	—	300	1,000	—
	K00 063 645★	K00 091 576★	—	—	—	—
SAN FRANCISCO	L12 400 561A	L13 161 190A	—	100	—	—
	L00 129 365★	L00 143 053★	—	300	1,000	—

SERIES 1934 MULE DARK BLUE-GREEN SEAL

PLATE NUMBERS: Macro back numbers 939 and higher. These are series 1934 notes with larger back numbers and are 1934 faces on 1934A backs.

Quantities included with 1934 Light Green Seal.

	Serial Numbers				
	Low	**High**	**Notes Printed**	**VF**	**CH CU**
BOSTON	A06 036 173A	A37 361 644A	see above	$15	$65
	A00 102 497★	A00 538 857★	—	100	400
NEW YORK	B17 676 495A	—	—	15	50
	—	B72 677 449B	—	15	50
	B00 238 289★	B01 604 259★	—	100	350
PHILADELPHIA	C07 732 843A	C64 460 348A	—	15	60
	C00 076 251★	C00 626 791★	—	100	400
CLEVELAND	D07 651 389A	D58 601 293A	—	$15	$50
	D00 140 234★	D00 728 450★	—	100	400
RICHMOND	E05 643 293A	E60 362 871A	—	15	70
	E00 139 846★	E00 725 816★	—	100	450
ATLANTA	F13 222 904A	F68 164 863A	—	15	60
	F00 201 702★	F00 822 602★	—	100	500
CHICAGO	G12 120 900A	G58 557 297A	—	15	50
	G00 127 644★	G00 565 215★	—	100	300
ST. LOUIS	H11 192 532A	H50 974 371A	—	15	50
	H00 149 245★	H00 656 124★	—	100	350
MINNEAPOLIS	I05 570 480A	I15 555 946A	—	20	70
	I00 120 928★	I00 195 510★	—	200	800
KANSAS CITY	J03 138 409A	J31 057 520A	—	15	50
	J00 328 853★	J00 391 305★ (only 2 known)	—	300	1,000
DALLAS	K08 717 394A	K31 181 840A	—	20	75
	K00 143 582★	K00 366 164★	—	100	500
SAN FRANCISCO	L14 996 001A	L77 547 571A	—	15	50
	L00 211 277★	L00 631 393★	—	100	500

HAWAII NOTES

The word "Hawaii" is overprinted in black on both face and back. Seals and serial numbers are printed in brown ink.

Official Print Runs – All Varieties Included

Serial Numbers

Low	High	Notes Printed
L12 396 001A	L14 996 000A	2,600,000
L19 776 001A	L20 176 000A	400,000
L46 404 001A	L47 804 000A	1,400,000
L54 072 001A	L56 088 000A	2,016,000
L66 132 001A	L69 132 000A	3,000,000
L00 120 001★	L00 192 000★	72,000
L00 852 001★	L00 856 000★	4,000
L00 892 001★	L00 896 000★	4,000

SERIES 1934 HAWAII BROWN SEAL

PLATE NUMBERS: Back numbers 938 or lower.
SIGNATURES: Same as Series 1934 Green Seal notes.

Serial Numbers

Low	High	VG/F	VF	CH CU	GEM CU
L12 400 561**A**	L13 161 190**A**	$100	$250	$2,500	$5,000
L00 120 001★	L00 144 000★	2,000	4,500	16,000	—
L00 130 185★	L00 136 115★ (observed)	—		—	—

SERIES 1934 MULE HAWAII BROWN SEAL

PLATE NUMBERS: Back numbers 939 or higher.

Serial Numbers

Low	High	Notes Printed	VF	CH CU	GEM CU
L12 658 305**A**	L56 086 791**A** (observed)	—	$125	$1,100	$1,600
L00 130 818★	L00 191 631★	48,000	3,500	12,000	—

SERIES 1934A HAWAII BROWN SEAL

PLATE NUMBERS: Back numbers 939 or higher.

SIGNATURES: Same as Series 1934A Green Seal notes.

Serial Numbers

Low	High	Notes Printed	VF	CH CU	GEM CU
L46 434 463A	L69 132 000A	—	$125	$1,000	$1,500
L00 854 313★	L00 894 083★	—	8,500	—	—

FEDERAL RESERVE NOTES

SERIES 1934A MULE GREEN SEAL

SERIAL NUMBERS: All districts continued sequence from previous series.

PLATE NUMBERS: All have back #637.

	Serial Numbers				
	Low	High	Notes Printed	VF	CH CU
NEW YORK	B63 063 567A	B84 656 980B	see below	$300	$1,000
PHILADELPHIA	C68 173 332A	C69 052 070A	—	400	1,200
CHICAGO	G80 536 253A	G06 763 402B	—	300	1,000
	G01 399 038★	—	—	1,000	3,000
ST. LOUIS	H39 621 679A	H49 106 308A	—	400	1,000
SAN FRANCISCO	L32 664 147A	—	—	400	1,200
	L01 212 949★	—	—	1,000	3,000

SERIES 1934A GREEN SEAL

SERIAL NUMBERS: All districts continued sequence from previous series.
PLATE NUMBERS: Back numbers begin at 939.
SIGNATURES: W.A. Julian, Henry Morgenthau, Jr.

	Serial Numbers				
	Low	**High**	**Notes Printed**	**VF**	**CH CU**
BOSTON	A21 342 253A	A51 153 931A	23,231,568	$15	$40
	A00 389 629★	A00 615 539★	—	65	450
NEW YORK	B22 682 753A	—	143,199,336	15	40
	—	B98 640 063B	—	15	40
	B00 357 438★	B02 259 425★	—	50	400
PHILADELPHIA	C27 010 066A	C73 940 411A	30,691,632	15	40
	C00 554 825★	C00 925 000★	—	50	450
CLEVELAND	D13 264 438A	D63 150 769A	1,610,676	50	300
	D00 832 431★	—	—	100	550
RICHMOND	E46 358 248A	E67 314 357A	6,555,168	15	125
	E00 782 182★	—	—	75	500
ATLANTA	F17 523 826A	F70 628 235A	22,811,916	40	200
	F00 299 341★	F00 380 260★	—	100	600
CHICAGO	G21 939 262A	G17 101 268B	88,376,376	15	40
	G00 382 596★	G01 517 060★	—	50	400
ST. LOUIS	H39 411 474A	H53 023 304A	7,843,852	15	50
	H00 521 917★	H00 618 363★	—	75	400
SAN FRANCISCO	L24 794 922A	—	—	15	40
	—	L00 793 914B	72,118,452	50	200
	L00 683 876★	L01 219 181★	—	50	400

No regular or star notes were printed for Minneapolis, Kansas City or Dallas.

SERIES 1934B MULE GREEN SEAL

These are actually Series 1934B faces on Series 1934 backs. (All back plate #637).

SERIAL NUMBERS: All districts continued sequence from previous series.

	Serial Numbers				
	Low	**High**	**Notes Printed**	**VF**	**CH CU**
BOSTON	A54 375 901A	—	included above	$200	$600
NEW YORK	B80 851 374B	B96 537 324B	included above	150	500
PHILADELPHIA	C77 160 838A	—	included above	200	600
CLEVELAND	D60 641 001A	D63 813 881A	included above	150	600
	D00 761 254★	—	—	600	2,000
CHICAGO	G20 502 474B	G21 370 363B	included above	150	500
ST. LOUIS	H53 328 667A	H58 149 736A	included above	200	1,000
MINNEAPOLIS	I15 920 841A	I18 105 713A	—	300	1,000
SAN FRANCISCO	L01 597 562B	L02 967 122B	included above	150	600
	L01 359 866★	L01 359 867★	included above	500	2,000

SERIES 1934B GREEN SEAL

SERIAL NUMBERS: All districts continued sequence from previous series.

PLATE NUMBERS: Back number 939 and higher.

SIGNATURES: W.A. Julian, Fred M. Vinson

	Serial Numbers				
	Low	**High**	**Notes Printed**	**VF**	**CH CU**
BOSTON	A51 927 351A	A57 018 223A	3,457,800	$15	$125
	A00 678 614★	A00 679 364★	—	200	1,000
NEW YORK	B75 425 469B	B95 741 965B	14,099,580	15	80
	B02 162 784★	B02 514 381★	—	120	700
PHILADELPHIA	C72 036 043A	C81 112 559A	8,306,820	15	80
	C00 938 264★	C01 026 003★	—	250	700
CLEVELAND	D57 994 351A	D70 315 211A	11,348,184	15	80
	D00 683 876★	D01 022 514★	—	150	700
RICHMOND	E66 963 050A	E72 106 406A	5,902,848	15	125
	E-★	—	—	—	—
ATLANTA	F68 864 061A	F72 376 837A	4,314,048	45	300
	F00 900 821★	—	—	200	1,000
CHICAGO	G13 186 858B	G25 042 572B	9,070,932	15	100
	G01 643 051★	—	—	200	1,000
ST. LOUIS	H53 492 931A	H71 547 955A	4,307,712	20	100
	H00 680 501★	H00 753 479★	—	150	700

	Low	High	Notes Printed	VF	CH CU
MINNEAPOLIS	I15 477 261A	I17 833 992A	2,482,600	$25	$150
	I00 216 331★	I00 232 537★	—	150	800
KANSAS CITY	J31 736 195A	J32 227 785A	64,000	1,500	4,000
	J-★	unknown	—	—	Rare
DALLAS	None printed.				
SAN FRANCISCO	L95 336 592A	—	—	15	90
	L03 750 526B	L04 384 760B	9,910,296	15	100
	L01 282 426★	L01 371 471★	—	900	2,000

SERIES 1934B ENGRAVING ERROR FACE PLATE 212 GREEN SEAL

PLATE NUMBER: Face plate number 212.

	Serial Numbers				
	Low	High	Notes Printed	VF	CH CU
NEW YORK	B73 706 585B	B92 932 697B	included above	$175	$600
	B02 335 987★	—	—	1,500	2,500

SERIES 1934C MULE GREEN SEAL

These are actually Series 1934C faces on Series 1934 backs. (Back plates #629 and #637).

	Serial Numbers					
	Low	High	Notes Printed	VF	CH CU	GEM CU
BOSTON	A54 870 831A	A60 476 989A	included below	$200	$800	—
NEW YORK	B22 594 851C	B39 857 132C	included below	200	800	—
	B45 409 229C	BP 629		— 1,500	—	1,200
PHILADELPHIA	C95 791 219A	—	included below	200	900	—
	—	C01 183 611B		— 200	900	—
	C	BP 629		1,500	—	1,500
CLEVELAND	D76 605 379A	D85 217 832A	included below	200	800	—
RICHMOND	E92 093 059A	—	included below	200	900	—
CHICAGO	G31 475 153B	G64 883 578B	included below	200	800	—
	G45 417 717B	BP 629		— 1,500	—	—
ST. LOUIS	H67 840 193A	H70 831 511A		— 200	900	—
MINNEAPOLIS	I20 058 699A	—	included below	300	1,100	—
KANSAS CITY	J31 266 251A	J35 162 625A	included below	200	800	—
SAN FRANCISCO	L07 782 787B	—	included below	300	1,100	—

SERIES 1934C GREEN SEAL - WIDE FACE

SERIAL NUMBERS: All districts continued sequence from previous series.
PLATE NUMBERS: Back numbers 939 and higher.
SIGNATURES: W.A. Julian, John W. Snyder

	Serial Numbers				
	Low	**High**	**Notes Printed**	**VF**	**CH CU**
BOSTON	A54 946 387A	A69 368 687A	14,332,299	$15	$75
	A00 729 711★	A00 904 062★	—	100	900
NEW YORK	B96 552 273B	—	74,383,248	35	125
	—	B71 534 698C	—	15	75
	B02 444 953★	B03 314 656★	—	100	700
PHILADELPHIA	C80 431 346A	—	22,879,212	15	75
	—	C05 721 259B	—	15	85
	C01 083 169★	C01 347 517★	—	100	900
CLEVELAND	D69 301 787A	D89 748 520A	19,898,256	15	75
	D00 933 393★	D01 126 904★	—	80	750
RICHMOND	—	E93 983 925A	23,800,524	15	75
	E00 988 099★	E01 212 448★	—	100	900
ATLANTA	F74 457 032A	F95 223 927A	23,572,968	15	75
	F01 055 135★	F01 156 544★	—	100	1,000
CHICAGO	G23 755 809B	G90 821 246B	60,598,812	15	75
	G01 634 180★	G02 763 794★	—	100	700
ST. LOUIS	H58 447 911A	—	20,393,340	15	75
	—	H07 551 780B	—	25	100
	H00 784 303★	H00 954 900★	—	100	800

	Low	High	Notes Printed	VF	CH CU
MINNEAPOLIS	I18 468 703A	I22 609 277A	5,089,200	$30	$150
	I00 310 738★	I100 323 068★	—	200	1,200
KANSAS CITY	J31 066 282A	J37 650 223A	8,313,504	15	90
	J00 453 442★	J00 527 874★	—	100	900
DALLAS	K31 715 222A	K37 276 203A	5,107,800	25	100
	K00 398 273★	—	—	200	1,200
SAN FRANCISCO	L05 994 335B	L12 353 862B	9,451,944	15	85
	L01 431 170★	L01 589 520★	—	100	900

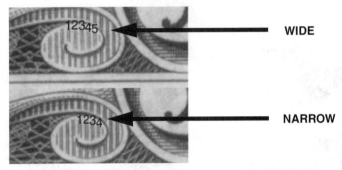

WIDE

NARROW

SERIES 1934C GREEN SEAL - NARROW FACE

PLATE NUMBERS: Narrow face plates were introduced in April, 1949 on face plates made for New York district, #298 to 303 only.

Serial Numbers

	Low	High	Notes Printed	VF	CH CU
NEW YORK	B-C	—	(+ or -) 12% of N.Y. figure	4 known	Scarce
	B03 478 435★	—	—	—	—
	(unique)				

SERIES 1934D GREEN SEAL

SERIAL NUMBERS: All districts continued sequence from previous series. High star numbers shown indicate official end of print run.

SIGNATURES: Georgia Neese Clark, John W. Snyder

Serial Numbers

	Low	High	Notes Printed	VF	CH CU
BOSTON	A68 486 900A	A80 384 786A	12,660,552	$15	$90
	A00 937 183★	A01 052 000★	—	100	800
NEW YORK	B57 783 928C	—	50,976,576	12	75

	Low	High	Notes Printed	VF	CH CU	GEM CU
	—	B12 352 539D	—	$12	$75	—
	B03 272 517★	B03 888 000★	—	90	600	—
PHILADELPHIA	C02 491 319B	C14 815 748B	12,106,740	15	85	—
	C01 406 655★	C01 500 000★	—	125	800	—
CLEVELAND	D65 673 725A	D98 133 349A	8,969,052	15	90	—
	D01 033 988★	D01 284 000★	—	150	1,500	—
	—	D01 225 679★ high observed	—	—	—	—
RICHMOND	E94 054 703A	—	13,333,032	35	125	—
	—	E07 136 921B	—	35	125	—
	E01 354 750★	E01 428 000★	—	125	1,500	—
ATLANTA	F95 002 632A	—	9,599,352	250	800	1,000
	—	F04 742 170B	—	250	800	1,000
	—	F01 380 000★	—	500	3,000	—
CHICAGO	G80 874 865B	—	36,601,680	12	75	—
	—	G16 249 094C	—	12	75	—
	G02 609 785★	G02 916 000★	—	100	500	—
ST. LOUIS	H76 423 572A	—	8,093,412	15	75	—
	H01 033 988★	H01 176 000★	—	125	800	—
MINNEAPOLIS	I23 483 891A	I26 397 991A	3,954,900	60	600	800
	I00 333 838★	I00 372 000★	—	600	2,000	—
KANSAS CITY	J38 565 670A	J44 891 392A	6,538,740	$20	100	—
	—	J00 568 000★	—	125	900	—
DALLAS	K33 950 138A	K40 668 433A	4,139,016	20	200	—
	K00 493 278★	K00 496 000★	—	200	900	—
SAN FRANCISCO	L12 681 010B	L23 645 029B	11,704,200	15	100	—
	L01 516 720★	L01 644 000★	—	125	900	—

SERIES 1950 WIDE GREEN SEAL

SERIAL NUMBERS: All districts started both regular and star notes with 00 000 001. High numbers shown are official for Series 1950 (all varieties).

PLATE NUMBERS: Face numbers begin at #1. Back numbers 2006 or lower.

SIGNATURES: Georgia Neese Clark, John W. Snyder

Serial Numbers

	Low	High	Notes Printed	VF	CH CU	GEM CU
BOSTON	A00 000 024A	A30 672 000A	30,672,000	$10	$45	$60
	A00 037 701★	A00 204 036★	408,000	60	400	500
NEW YORK	B00 000 003A	—	106,768,000	10	35	45
	—	B06 768 000B	—	15	50	70
	B00 020 000★	B01 464 000★	1,464,000	50	300	400
PHILADELPHIA	C00 000 004A	C44 784 000A	44,784,000	10	40	50
	C00 191 078★	C00 338 661★	600,000	60	350	450
CLEVELAND	D00 000 005A	D54 000 000A	54,000,000	10	40	50
	D00 071 579★	D00 542 878★	744,000	60	350	450
RICHMOND	E00 000 099A	E47 088 000A	47,088,000	10	45	60
	E00 337 923★	E00 684 000★	684,000	75	300	400
ATLANTA	F05 078 620A	F52 416 000A	52,416,000	10	45	60
	F00 000 005★	F00 377 646★	696,000	60	350	450
CHICAGO	G00 000 014A	G85 104 000A	85,104,000	10	30	40
	G00 408 074★	G01 176 000★	1,176,000	60	250	350
ST. LOUIS	H00 000 002A	H36 864 000A	36,864,000	10	45	60
	H00 000 486★	H00 552 000★	552,000	60	300	400
MINNEAPOLIS	I00 000 007A	I11 796 000A	11,796,000	15	60	85
	I00 024 470★	I00 144 000★	144,000	150	700	800
KANSAS CITY	J00 006 000A	J25 428 000A	25,428,000	12	45	60
	J00 000 009★	J00 360 000★	360,000	60	300	400
DALLAS	K03 116 659A	K22 848 000A	22,848,000	10	60	80
	—	K00 372 000★	372,000	100	400	500
SAN FRANCISCO	L00 000 100A	L55 008 000A	55,008,000	10	50	70
	L00 127 755★	L00 744 000★	744,000	80	300	400

SERIES 1950 NARROW GREEN SEAL

PLATE NUMBERS: Back numbers range #2007-2066.

Serial Numbers

	Low	High	Notes Printed	VF	CH CU	GEM CU
BOSTON	A17 738 425A	A29 017 643A	included above	$15	$75	$100
NEW YORK	B68 131 945A	—	included above	12	40	60
	—	B06 725 410B	—	15	100	150
	B00 824 357★	B01 375 357★	—	75	450	600
PHILADELPHIA	C25 191 174A	C43 652 958A	included above	12	40	60
	C00 429 930★	C00 484 377★	—	75	450	600
CLEVELAND	D35 967 165A	D53 997 798A	included above	12	40	60
	D00 488 030★	D00 717 430★	—	75	400	600
RICHMOND	E27 648 294A	E46 969 425A	included above	12	50	75
	E00 428 303★	E00 512 611★	—	75	450	600
ATLANTA	F36 965 675A	F42 342 240A	included above	15	100	150
CHICAGO	G47 113 378A	G81 018 210A	included above	12	40	60
	G00 964 200★	—	—	75	450	600
ST. LOUIS	H17 703 471A	H36 639 659A	included above	$12	$50	75
	H00 479 995★	—	—	75	450	600
MINNEAPOLIS	I06 328 008A	I11 527 084A	included above	15	100	125
KANSAS CITY	J12 455 195A	J24 466 242A	included above	12	50	75
DALLAS	K11 256 625A	K22 220 544A	included above	12	100	150
SAN FRANCISCO	L38 391 131A	L53 873 260A	included above	12	100	150
	L00 640 807★	L00 667 972★	—	75	450	600

SERIES 1950 WIDE II GREEN SEAL

PLATE NUMBERS: Face numbers end at #144. Back numbers range #2067-#2096. Both are highest of 12 subject sheets.

Serial Numbers

	Low	High	Notes Printed	VF	CH CU	GEM CU
BOSTON	A24 311 603A	A25 366 951A	included above	$17	$70	$90
NEW YORK	B71 738 407A	—	included above	17	50	80
	—	B04 905 193B	—	20	90	120
	B00 995 156★	—	—	1,000	—	—
PHILADELPHIA	C32 438 915A	C43 549 397A	included above	17	60	90
	C00 411 755★	C00 562 150★	—	600	3,000	—
CLEVELAND	D35 864 001A	D51 155 493A	included above	15	60	90
	D00 670 420★	—	—	850	4,000	5,000
RICHMOND	E36 507 409A	E46 170 089A	included above	15	70	100
ATLANTA	F42 342 238A	F42 342 239A	included above	17	100	140
CHICAGO	G57 723 984A	G81 917 195A	included above	15	70	100
ST. LOUIS	H25 443 568A	H36 598 750A	included above	15	60	90
MINNEAPOLIS	I11 111 108A	—	included above	20	125	175
KANSAS CITY	J15 643 836A	J21 041 939A	included above	15	70	90
DALLAS	K14 779 309A	K20 575 016A	included above	100	500	—
SAN FRANCISCO	L35 178 698A	L52 328 098A	included above	14	70	100
	L00 489 451★	L00 538 171★	included above	600	3,000	—

SERIES 1950A GREEN SEAL

SERIAL NUMBERS: All numbers shown are official.

PLATE NUMBERS: Face numbers begin at #145. Back numbers begin at #2097. Both lowest of 18 subject sheets.

SIGNATURES: Ivy Baker Priest, G.M. Humphrey

	Serial Numbers			
	Low	**High**	**Notes Printed**	**CH CU**
BOSTON	A30 672 001A	A84 240 000A	53,568,000	$25
	A00 432 001★	A03 240 000★	2,808,000	75
NEW YORK	B06 768 001B	—	186,472,000	20
	—	B93 240 000C	—	20
	B01 584 001★	B10 800 000★	9,216,000	60
PHILADELPHIA	C44 784 001A	—	79,616,000	25
	—	C14 400 000B	—	25
	C00 720 001★	C05 040 000★	4,320,000	75
CLEVELAND	D54 000 001A	D99 360 000A	45,360,000	25
	D00 864 001★	D03 240 000★	2,376,000	75
RICHMOND	E47 088 001A	—	76,672,000	25
	—	E23 760 000B	—	25
	E00 720 001★	E06 120 000★	5,400,000	75
ATLANTA	F52 416 001A	—	86,464,000	25
	—	F38 880 000B	—	25
	F00 720 001★	F05 760 000★	5,040,000	75

	Low	**High**	**Notes Printed**	**CH CU**
CHICAGO	G85 104 001**A**	—	129,296,000	$20
	G-B		—	20
	—	G14 400 000**C**	—	20
	G01 296 001★	G07 560 000★	6,284,000	75
ST. LOUIS	H36 864 001**A**	H91 800 000**A**	54,936,000	25
	H00 576 001★	H03 960 000★	3,384,000	150
MINNEAPOLIS	I11 808 001**A**	I23 040 000**A**	11,232,000	45
	I00 144 001★	I01 008 000★	864,000	300
KANSAS CITY	J25 488 001**A**	J55 440 000**A**	29,952,000	25
	J00 432 001★	J02 520 000★	2,088,000	100
DALLAS	K22 896 001**A**	K47 880 000**A**	24,984 000	40
	K00 432 001★	K01 800 000★	1,368,000	150
SAN FRANCISCO	L55 008 001**A**	—	90,712,000	25
	—	L45 720 000**B**	—	25
	L00 864 001★	L07 200 000★	6,336,000	75

SERIES 1950B GREEN SEAL

SERIAL NUMBERS: All numbers shown are official.

SIGNATURES: Ivy Baker Priest, Robert B. Anderson

	Serial Numbers			
	Low	**High**	**Notes Printed**	**CH CU**
BOSTON	A84 240 001**A**	—	30,880,000	$30
	—	A15 120 000**B**	—	30
	A03 240 001★	A05 760 000★	2,520,000	75

	Low	High	Notes Printed	CH CU
NEW YORK	B93 240 001C	—	85,960,000	$30
	—	B79 200 000D	—	30
	B10 800 001★	B15 480 000★	4,680,000	65
PHILADELPHIA	C14 400 001B	C57 960 000B	43,560,000	30
	C05 040 001★	C07 920 000★	2,880,000	75
CLEVELAND	D99 360 001A	—	640,000	1,800
	—	D38 160 000B	38,160,000	30
	D03 240 001★	D06 120 000★	2,880,000	75
RICHMOND	E23 760 001B	E76 680 000B	52,920,000	30
	E06 120 001★	E09 000 000★	2,880,000	100
ATLANTA	F38 880 001B	—	80,560,000	25
	—	F19 440 000C	—	30
	F05 760 001★	F09 720 000★	3,960,000	90
CHICAGO	G14 400 001C	—	104,320,000	30
	—	G18 720 000D	—	30
	G07 560 001★	G13 680 000★	6,120,000	60
ST. LOUIS	H91 800 001A	—	25,840,000	30
	—	H17 640 000B	—	30
	H03 960 001★	H05 400 000★	1,440,000	80
MINNEAPOLIS	I23 040 001A	I43 920 000A	20,880,000	40
	I01 008 001★	I01 800 000★	792,000	150
KANSAS CITY	J55 440 001A	J87 840 000A	32,400,000	30
	J02 520 001★	J05 040 000★	2,520,000	75
DALLAS	K47 880 001A	K99 999 999A	52,119,999	25
	K01 800 001★	K05 040 000★	3,240,000	75
SAN FRANCISCO	L45 720 001B	—	56,080,000	30
	—	L01 800 000C	—	60
	L07 200 001★	L10 800 000★	3,600,000	80

SERIES 1950C GREEN SEAL

SERIAL NUMBERS: All numbers shown are official.

SIGNATURES: Elizabeth Rudel Smith, C. Douglas Dillon

	Serial Numbers			
	Low	High	Notes Printed	CH CU
BOSTON	A15 120 001B	A36 000 000B	20,880,000	$25
	A05 760 001★	A06 480 000★	720,000	225
NEW YORK	B79 200 001D	—	47,440,000	20
	—	B26 640 000E	—	20
	B15 480 001★	B18 360 000★	2,880,000	60
PHILADELPHIA	C57 960 001B	C87 480 000B	29,520,000	20
	C07 920 001★	C09 720 000★	1,800,000	100
CLEVELAND	D38 160 001B	D72 000 000B	33,840,000	25
	D06 120 001★	D07 920 000★	1,800,000	100

	Low	High	Notes Printed	CH CU
RICHMOND	E76 680 001B	—	33,400,000	$20
	—	E10 080 000C	—	20
	E09 000 001★	E11 160 000★	2,160,000	140
ATLANTA	F19 440 001C	F73 800 000C	54,360,000	$20
	F09 720 001★	F12 960 000★	3,240,000	100
CHICAGO	G18 720 001D	G75 600 000D	56,880,000	20
	G13 680 001★	G16 920 000★	3,240,000	100
ST. LOUIS	H17 640 001B	H40 320 000B	22,680,000	30
	H05 400 001★	H06 120 000★	720,000	150
MINNEAPOLIS	I43 920 001A	I56 880 000A	12,960,000	50
	I01 800 001★	I02 520 000★	720,000	200
KANSAS CITY	J87 840 001A	—	24,760,000	20
	—	J12 600 000B	—	20
	J05 040 001★	J06 840 000★	1,800,000	100
DALLAS	K00 000 001B	K03 960 000B	3,960,000	75
	K05 040 001★	K05 400 000★	360,000	200
SAN FRANCISCO	L01 800 001C	L27 720 000C	25,920,000	20
	L10 800 001★	L12 240 000★	1,440,000	175

SERIES 1950D GREEN SEAL

SERIAL NUMBERS: All numbers shown are official.

SIGNATURES: Kathryn O'Hay Granahan, C. Douglas Dillon

	Serial Numbers			
	Low	High	Notes Printed	CH CU
BOSTON	A36 000 001B	A61 200 000B	25,200,000	$25
	A06 480 001★	A07 560 000★	1,080,000	100
NEW YORK	B26 640 001E	—	102,160,000	20
	—	B28 800 000F	—	20
	B18 360 001★	B23 400 000★	5,040,000	60
PHILADELPHIA	C87 480 001B	—	21,520,000	20
	—	C09 000 000C	—	20
	C09 720 001★	C10 800 000★	1,080,000	70
CLEVELAND	D72 000 001B	D95 400 000B	23,400,000	20
	D07 920 001★	D09 000 000★	1,080,000	100
RICHMOND	E10 080 001C	E52 560 000C	42,480,000	25
	E11 160 001★	E12 960 000★	1,800,000	100
ATLANTA	F73 800 001C	—	35,200,000	25
	—	F09 000 000D	—	30
	F12 960 001★	F14 760 000★	1,800,000	100

	Low	High	Notes Printed	CH CU
CHICAGO	G75 600 001D	—	67,240,000	$20
	—	G42 840 000E	—	20
	G16 920 001★	G20 520 000★	3,600,000	60
ST. LOUIS	H40 320 001B	H60 480 000B	20,160,000	20
	H06 120 001★	H06 840 000★	720,000	100
MINNEAPOLIS	I56 880 001A	I64 800 000A	7,920,000	35
	I02 520 001★	I02 880 000★	360,000	200
KANSAS CITY	J12 600 001B	J23 760 000B	11,160,000	20
	J06 840 001★	J07 560 000★	720,000	100
DALLAS	K03 960 001B	K11 160 000B	7,200,000	30
	K05 400 001★	K05 760 000★	360,000	175
SAN FRANCISCO	L27 720 001C	L81 000 000C	53,280,000	20
	L12 240 001★	L15 840 000★	3,600,000	100

SERIES 1950E GREEN SEAL

SERIAL NUMBERS: All numbers shown are official.

PLATE NUMBERS: Face numbers on 18 subject sheets end at #436. Back numbers on 18 subject sheets end at #2587.

SIGNATURES: Kathryn O'Hay Granahan, Henry H. Fowler

Serial Numbers

	Low	High	Notes Printed	CH CU	GEM CU
NEW YORK	B28 800 001F	—	82,000,000	$35	$55
	—	B10 800 000G	—	35	55
	B23 400 001★	B30 223 913★	7,200,000 est.	90	145
CHICAGO	G42 840 001E	G57 600 000E	14,760,000	75	100
	G20 520 001★	G21 600 000★	1,080,000	300	400
SAN FRANCISCO	L81 000 001C	—	24,400,000	50	75
	—	L05 400 000D	—	100	150
	L15 840 001★	L17 640 000★	1,800,000	250	350

SERIES 1963 GREEN SEAL

SERIAL NUMBERS: All districts started both regular and star notes with 00 000 001.

PLATE NUMBERS: Both face and back numbers begin at #1 with 32 subject sheets. Motto "IN GOD WE TRUST" added to back.

SIGNATURES: Kathryn O'Hay Granahan, C. Douglas Dillon

| | Serial Numbers | | | |
	Low	High	Notes Printed	CH CU
BOSTON	A-A	—	4,480,000	$30
	A-★	—	640,000	90
NEW YORK	B-A	—	12,160,000	25
	B-★	—	1,280,000	60
PHILADELPHIA	C-A	—	8,320,000	25
	C-★	—	1,920,000	50
CLEVELAND	D-A	—	10,240,000	25
	D-★	—	1,920,000	50
ATLANTA	F-A	—	17,920,000	25
	F-★	—	2,560,000	50
CHICAGO	G-A	—	22,400,000	25
	G-★	—	3,200,000	50
ST. LOUIS	H-A	—	14,080,000	25
	H-★	—	1,920,000	50
KANSAS CITY	J-A	—	1,920,000	30
	J-★	—	640,000	75
DALLAS	K-A	—	5,760,000	30
	K-★	—	1,920,000	60
SAN FRANCISCO	L-A	—	18,560,000	25
	L-★	—	1,920,000	50

SERIES 1963A GREEN SEAL

SERIAL NUMBERS: All districts continued sequence from previous series.
SIGNATURES: Kathryn O'Hay Granahan, Henry H. Fowler

	Serial Numbers			
	Low	**High**	**Notes Printed**	**CH CU**
BOSTON	A04 480 001A	A81 920 000A	77,440,000	$20
	A00 640 001★	A06 400 000★	5,760,000	40
NEW YORK	B12 160 001A	—	85,160,000	15
	B-B	B10 240 000B	10,240,000	20
	B01 280 001★	B08 960 000★	7,040,000	30
PHILADELPHIA	C08 320 001A	—	91,680,000	15
	C-B	C14 720 000B	14,720,000	20
	C01 920 001★	C12 160 000★	8,320,000	30
CLEVELAND	D10 240 001A	D94 080 000A	83,840,000	15
	D01 920 001★	D08 960 000★	7,040,000	25
RICHMOND	E-A	E18 560 000B	18,560,000	20
	E00 000 001★	E10 880 000★	10,880,000	30
ATLANTA	F17 920 001A	—	82,080,000	15
	F-B	F35 840 000B	35,840,000	15
	F02 560 001★	F12 160 000★	9,600,000	40
CHICAGO	G22 400 001A	—	77,600,000	15
	G-B	—	99,999,999	15
	G-C	G35 840 000C	35,840,000	15
	G03 200 001★	G19 840 000★	16,640,000	25

	Low	High	Notes Printed	CH CU
ST. LOUIS	H14 080 001**A**	H71 040 000**A**	56,960,000	$20
	H01 920 001★	H07 040 000★	5,120,000	40
MINNEAPOLIS	I00 000 001**A**	I32 640 000**A**	32,640,000	25
	I00 000 001★	I03 200 000★	3,200,000	60
KANSAS CITY	J01 920 001**A**	J56 960 000**A**	55,040,000	20
	J00 640 001★	J06 400 000★	5,760,000	40
DALLAS	K05 760 001**A**	K69 760 000**A**	64,000,000	20
	K01 920 001★	K05 760 000★	3,340,000	40
SAN FRANCISCO	L18 560 001**A**	—	81,440,000	15
	L-B	L47 860 000**B**	47,860,000	15
	L01 920 001★	L14 073 000★	12,153,000	30

SERIES 1969 GREEN SEAL

SERIAL NUMBERS: All districts started both regular and star notes with 00 000 001.

PLATE NUMBERS: Face numbers begin at #1. Back numbers continue from previous series.

SIGNATURES: Dorothy Andrews Elston, David M. Kennedy

	Serial Numbers			
	Low	High	Notes Printed	CH CU
BOSTON	**A-A**	—	51,200,000	$20
	A00 000 001★	A01 920 000★	1,920,000	50
NEW YORK	**B-A**	—	99,999,999	15
	B-B	—	98,560,000	15
	B00 000 001★	B08 960 000★	8,800,000	25
PHILADELPHIA	**C-A**	—	60,120,000	15
	C00 000 001★	C02 560 000★	2,560,000	30
CLEVELAND	**D-A**	—	56,320,000	15
	D00 000 001★	D02 560 000★	2,560,000	30
RICHMOND	**E-A**	—	84,480,000	15
	E00 000 001★	E03 200 000★	3,200,000	30
ATLANTA	**F-A**	—	84,480,000	15
	F00 000 001★	F03 840 000★	3,840,000	30
CHICAGO	**G-A**	—	99,999,999	15
	G-B	—	25,600,000	15
	G00 000 001★	G05 120 000★	5,120,000	30

	Low	High	Notes Printed	CH CU
ST. LOUIS	H-A	—	27,520,000	$20
	H00 000 001★	H01 280 000★	1,280,000	50
MINNEAPOLIS	I-A	—	16,640,000	25
	I00 000 001★	I00 640 000★	640,000	75
KANSAS CITY	J-A	—	48,640,000	15
	J00 000 001★	J03 192 000★	3,192,000	30
DALLAS	K-A	—	39,680,000	15
	K00 000 001★	K01 920 000★	1,920,000	40
SAN FRANCISCO	L-A	—	99,999,999	15
	L-B	—	3,840,000	35
	L00 000 001★	L04 480 000★	4,320,000	40

SERIES 1969A GREEN SEAL

SERIAL NUMBERS: All districts continued sequence from previous series.

SIGNATURES: Dorothy Andrews Kabis, John B. Connally

Serial Numbers

	Low	High	Notes Printed	CH CU
BOSTON	A51 200 001A	A74 240 000A	23,040,000	$20
	A01 920 001★	A03 200 000★	1,280,000	60
NEW YORK	B98 560 001B	—	1,440,000	60
	—	B60 800 000C	60,800,000	20
	B09 120 001★	B10 880 000★	1,760,000	50
PHILADELPHIA	C60 120 001A	—	39,880,000	20
	—	C01 280 000B	1,280,000	60
	C02 650 001★	C04 480 000★	1,760,000	50
CLEVELAND	D56 320 001A	D77 440 000A	21,120,000	20
	D02 560 001★	D03 200 000★	640,000	70
RICHMOND	E84 480 001A	—	15,520,000	20
	—	E22 400 000B	22,400,000	20
	E03 360 001★	E04 480 000★	1,120,000	60
ATLANTA	F84 480 001A	—	15,520,000	20
	—	F09 600 000B	9,600,000	25
	F04 000 001★	F04 480 000★	480,000	90
CHICAGO	G25 600 001B	G86 400 000B	60,800,000	20
	G05 120 001★	G07 040 000★	1,920,000	50
ST. LOUIS	H27 520 001A	H42 880 000A	15,360,000	20
	H01 280 001★	H01 920 000★	640,000	70

	Low	High	Notes Printed	CH CU
MINNEAPOLIS	I16 640 001**A**	I25 600 000**A**	8,960,000	$30
	I00 640 001★	I01 280 000★	640,000	80
KANSAS CITY	J48 640 001**A**	J66 560 000**A**	17,920,000	20
	J03 200 001★	J03 840 000★	640,000	70
DALLAS	K39 680 001**A**	K60 800 000**A**	21,120,000	25
	K01 920 001★	K02 560 000★	640,000	70
SAN FRANCISCO	L03 840 001**B**	L48 640 000**B**	44,800,000	20
	L04 480 001★	L06 400 000★	1,920,000	60

SERIES 1969B GREEN SEAL

SERIAL NUMBERS: Official ranges shown below follow sequence from previous series.

SIGNATURES: Romana Acosta Banuelos, John B. Connally

	Serial Numbers			
	Low	High	Notes Printed	CH CU
BOSTON	A74 240 001**A**	A80 000 000**A**	5,760,000	$100
NEW YORK	B60 800 001**C**	B95 360 000**C**	34,560,000	75
	B10 880 001★	B11 520 000★	640,000	200
PHILADELPHIA	C01 280 001**B**	C06 400 000**B**	5,120,000	100
CLEVELAND	D77 440 001**A**	D89 600 000**A**	12,160,000	80
RICHMOND	E22 400 001**B**	E37 760 000**B**	15,360,000	80
	E04 480 001★	E05 120 000★	640,000	200
ATLANTA	F09 600 001**B**	F28 160 000**B**	18,560,000	75
	F04 480 001★	F05 120 000★	640,000	200
CHICAGO	G86 400 001**B**	—	13,600,000	75
	—	G13 440 000**C**	13,440,000	75
	G07 200 001★	G07 680 000★	480,000	200
ST. LOUIS	H42 880 001**A**	H48 000 000**A**	5,120,000	100
MINNEAPOLIS	I25 600 001**A**	I33 920 000**A**	8,320,000	100
KANSAS CITY	J66 560 001**A**	J74 880 000**A**	8,320,000	100
	J03 840 001★	J04 480 000★	640,000	200
DALLAS	K60 800 001**A**	K72 960 000**A**	12,160,000	80
SAN FRANCISCO	L48 640 001**B**	L72 320 000**B**	23,680,000	60
	L06 400 001★	L07 040 000★	640,000	200

SERIES 1969C GREEN SEAL

SERIAL NUMBERS: Official ranges shown below. Regular notes are in sequence from previous series. Star notes continue from last prior printing.

SIGNATURES: Romana Acosta Banuelos, George P. Shultz

	Serial Numbers			
	Low	**High**	**Notes Printed**	**CH CU**
BOSTON	A80 000 001A	—	20,000,000	$20
	—	A30 720 000B	30,720,000	20
	A03 200 001★	A05 120 000★	1,920,000	60
NEW YORK	B95 360 001C	—	4,640,000	40
	B-D	—	99,840,000	20
	—	B15 360 000E	15,360,000	25
	B11 520 001★	B13 920 000★	2,400,000	40
PHILADELPHIA	C06 400 001B	C60 160 000B	53,760,000	20
	C04 480 001★	C05 760 000★	1,280,000	45
CLEVELAND	D89 600 001A	—	10,400,000	25
	—	D33 280 000B	33,280,000	20
	D03 200 001★	D03 680 000★	480,000	65
		D03 754 155★ (observed)		
RICHMOND	E37 760 001B	—	62,240,000	20
	—	E11 520 000C	11,520,000	25
	E05 120 000★	E05 760 000★	640,000	60
ATLANTA	F28 160 001B	—	71,840,000	20
	—	F09 600 000C	9,600,000	25
	F05 120 001★	F08 320 000★	3,200,000	40
CHICAGO	G13 440 001C	G67 840 000C	54,400,000	20
	G-★	—	none printed	—
ST. LOUIS	H48 000 001A	H86 400 000A	38,400,000	20
	H01 920 001★	H03 200 000★	1,280,000	50
MINNEAPOLIS	I33 920 001A	I45 400 000A	11,520,000	35
KANSAS CITY	J74 880 001A	—	25,120,000	20
	—	J16 000 000B	16,000,000	20
	J04 480 001★	J06 400 000★	1,920,000	50
DALLAS	K72 960 001A	—	27,040,000	20
	—	K14 080 000B	14,080,000	20
	K02 560 001★	K04 480 000★	1,920,000	60
SAN FRANCISCO	L72 320 001B	—	27,680,000	20
	—	L57 120 000C	57,120,000	20
	L07 040 001★	L10 240 000★	3,200,000	50

SERIES 1974 GREEN SEAL

SIGNATURES: Francine I. Neff, William E. Simon

SERIAL NUMBERS: All districts continue in sequence from previous series.

PLATE NUMBERS: All continue from previous series.

	Serial Numbers			
	Low	**High**	**Notes Printed**	**CH CU**
BOSTON	A30 720 001B	A88 960 000B	58,240,000	$15
	A05 120 001★	A06 588 000★	1,468,000	50
NEW YORK	B15 600 001E	—	84,640,999	15
	—	B68 480 000F	68,480,000	15
	B13 920 001★	B16 736 000★	2,816,000	40
		B17 239 060★ (observed)		
PHILADELPHIA	C60 160 001B	—	39,840,000	15
	—	C14 080 000C	14,080,000	15
	C05 760 001★	C08 320 000★	2,560,000	40
	C05 256 843★ (observed)			
CLEVELAND	D33 280 001B	—	66,200,000	15
	—	D11 520 000C	11,520,000	15
	D03 840 001★	D05 760 000★	1,920,000	40
RICHMOND	E11 520 001C	—	88,480,000	15
	—	E46 720 000D	46,720,000	15
	E05 760 001★	E07 680 000★	1,920,000	45
ATLANTA	F09 600 001C	—	90,400,000	15
	—	F37 120 000D	37,120,000	15
	F08 320 001★	F11 520 000★	3,200,000	40
CHICAGO	G67 840 001C	—	32,160,000	15
	—	G63 360 000D	63,360,000	15
	G07 680 001★	G14 080 000★	6,400,000	35
ST. LOUIS	H86 400 001A	—	14,720,000	15
	—	H51 200 000B	51,200,000	15
	H03 200 001★	H03 840 000★	640,000	70
		H04 417 864★ (observed)		
MINNEAPOLIS	I45 440 001A	I87 040 000A	41,600,000	15
	I01 280 001★	I03 840 000★	2,560,000	40
KANSAS CITY	J16 000 001B	J58 240 000B	42,240,000	15
	J06 400 001★	J08 448 000★	2,048,000	40
DALLAS	K14 080 001B	K71 680 000B	57,600,000	15
	K04 480 001★	K06 262 000★	1,782,000	50
SAN FRANCISCO	L57 120 001C	—	42,880,000	15
	—	L92 800 000D	92,800,000	15
	L10 240 001★	L16 000 000★	5,760,000	40

SERIES 1977 GREEN SEAL

SIGNATURES: Azie Taylor Morton, W.M. Blumenthal
SERIAL NUMBERS: All districts, regular notes only, begin at 00 000 001.
PLATE NUMBERS: Face and back numbers continue from previous series.

	Serial Numbers			
	Low	**High**	**Notes Printed**	**CH CU**
BOSTON	A-A	—	60,800,000	$15
	A00 016 001★	A03 200 000★	256,000	100
NEW YORK	B-A	—	99,840,000	15
	B-B	—	83,200,000	15
	B00 016 001★	B05 120 000★	2,560,000	40
PHILADELPHIA	C-A	—	78,280,000	15
	C00 000 001★	C01 280 000★	1,280,000	50
CLEVELAND	D-A	—	76,160,000	15
	D00 016 001★	D03 200 000★	864,000	60
RICHMOND	E-A	—	99,840,000	15
	E-B	—	10,880,000	18
	E00 016 001★	E03 840 000★	2,816,000	50
ATLANTA	F-A	—	99,840,000	15
	F-B	—	27,520,000	15
	F00 012 001★	F02 560 000★	1,792,000	50
CHICAGO	G-A	—	99,840,000	15
	G-B	—	77,440,000	15
	G00 016 001★	G03 840 000★	2,944,000	40
ST. LOUIS	H-A	—	46,080,000	15
	H00 016 001★	H00 640 000★	128,000	150
MINNEAPOLIS	I-A	—	21,760,000	15
KANSAS CITY	J-A	—	78,080,000	15
	J00 008 001★	J01 920 000★	1,024,000	50
DALLAS	K-A	—	60,800,000	15
	K00 016 001★	K02 560 000★	1,024,000	50
SAN FRANCISCO	L-A	—	99,840,000	15
	L-B	—	44,800,000	15
	L00 012 001★	L04 480 000★	1,816,000	50

SERIES 1977A GREEN SEAL

SIGNATURES: Azie Taylor Morton, G. William Miller

SERIAL NUMBERS: All districts continue sequence from previous series, except Minn. Stars.

PLATE NUMBERS: All districts continue sequence from previous series.

	Serial Numbers			
	Low	**High**	**Notes Printed**	**CH CU**
BOSTON	A-A	—	39,040,000	$15
	A-B	—	8,960,000	20
	A03 216 001★	A04 480 000★	512,000	200
NEW YORK	B-B	—	16,640,000	15
	B-C	—	97,280,000	15
	B05 136 001★	B08 320 000★	1,152,000	70
PHILADELPHIA	C-A	—	21,120,000	15
	C-B	—	34,560,000	15
	C01 292 001★	C02 560 000★	640,000	100
CLEVELAND	D-A	—	27,744,000	15
	D-B	—	32,000,000	15
	D03 216 001★	D06 400 000★	1,280,000	80
RICHMOND	E-B	—	77,440,000	10
	E03 856 001★	E05 120 000★	768,000	300
ATLANTA	F-B	—	72,320,000	10
	F-C	—	3,840,000	10
	F02 576 001★	F05 120 000★	512,000	80
CHICAGO	G-B	—	22,800,000	15
	G-C	—	58,880,000	15
	G03 844 001★	G06 400 000★	1,152,000	70
ST. LOUIS	H-A	—	32,000,000	15
	H00 656 001★	H02 560 000★	640,000	60
MINNEAPOLIS	I-A	—	10,240,000	20
	I00 016 001★	I00 640 000★	128,000	175
KANSAS CITY	J-A	—	21,760,000	15
	J-B	—	30,720,000	15
	J01 928 001★	J03 200 000★	1,024,000	90
DALLAS	K-A	—	39,040,000	15
	K-B	—	37,120,000	15
	K02 576 001★	K05 760 000★	1,920,000	70
SAN FRANCISCO	L-B	—	55,040,000	15
	L-C	—	42,240,000	15
	L04 480 001★	L06 400 000★	1,152,000	90

SERIES 1981 GREEN SEAL

SIGNATURES: Angela M. Buchanan, Donald T. Regan

PLATE NUMBERS: Back numbers continue from previous series. Face numbers begin at #1.

SERIAL NUMBERS: Regular notes begin with 00 000 001, Star notes vary, and begin as shown below. B Blocks in seven districts restarted at 00 000 001 prior to completion of the A Blocks. Four districts did the same as they started their C Blocks.

	Serial Numbers			
	Low	**High**	**Notes Printed**	**CH CU**
BOSTON	A-A	—	51,200,000	$30
	A-B	—	22,400,000	30
	A00 019 501★	A00 640 000★	16,000	—
NEW YORK	B-A	—	99,840,000	25
	B-B	—	99,840,000	25
	B-C	—	51,200,000	25
	B00 000 001★	B01 280 000★	1,280,000	125
PHILADELPHIA	C-A	—	61,440,000	25
	C-B	—	12,800,000	35
	C00 000 001★	C00 640 000★	640,000	175
CLEVELAND	D-A	—	92,160,000	25
	D-B	—	38,400,000	30
	D00 016 001★	D01 280 000★	384,000	175
RICHMOND	E-A	—	99,840,000	25
	E-B	—	40,960,000	25
	E-C	—	35,200,000	30
	E00 008 001★	E01 920 000★	1,664,000	150
ATLANTA	F-A	—	99,840,000	25
	F-B	—	20,480,000	30
	F-C	—	19,200,000	30
	F00 000 001★	F01 280 000★	768,000	175
CHICAGO	G-A	—	99,840,000	25
	G-B	—	44,800,000	25
	G-C	—	41,600,000	25
	G00 000 001★	G01 280 000★	1,280,000	100
ST. LOUIS	H-A	—	35,840,000	30
	H-B	—	22,400,000	30
	H00 012 001★	H00 640 000★	256,000	200
MINNEAPOLIS	I-A	—	21,760,000	50
	I-B	—	9,600,000	55
	I00 016 001★	I00 640 000★	128,000	250
KANSAS CITY	J-A	—	85,760,000	30
	J-B	—	25,600,000	30
	J00 012 001★	J01 280 000★	272,000	150
DALLAS	K-A	—	57,600,000	30

	Low	High	Notes Printed	CH CU
	K-B	—	38,400,000	$32
	K00 000 001★	K00 640 000★	640,000	120
SAN FRANCISCO	L-A	—	99,840,000	25
	L-B	—	76,800,000	30
	L-C	—	64,000,000	30
	L00 000 001★	L02 560 000★	1,792,000	80

SERIES 1981A GREEN SEAL

SIGNATURES: Katherine Davalos Ortega, Donald T. Regan
PLATE NUMBERS: Face and back numbers continue from previous series.
SERIAL NUMBERS: All blocks begin at 00 000 001.

	Serial Numbers			
	Low	High	Notes Printed	CH CU
BOSTON	A-A	—	54,400,000	$50
NEW YORK	B-A	—	99,200,000	40
	—	B-B	12,800,000	50
	B00 000 001★	B03 200 000★	3,200,000	150
PHILADELPHIA	C-A	—	25,600,000	50
CLEVELAND	D-A	—	51,200,000	50
RICHMOND	E-A	—	96,000,000	45
ATLANTA	F-A	—	99,200,000	45
	—	F-B	3,200,000	50
CHICAGO	G-A	—	99,200,000	40
	—	G-B	16,000,000	50
ST. LOUIS	H-A	—	32,000,000	50
MINNEAPOLIS	I-A	—	19,200,000	50
KANSAS CITY	J-A	—	48,000,000	50
DALLAS	K-A	—	35,200,000	90
SAN FRANCISCO	L-A	—	99,200,000	55
	—	L-B	51,200,000	60
	L00 000 001★	L03 200 000★	3,200,000	125

SERIES 1985 GREEN SEAL

SERIAL NUMBERS: All districts started numbering notes with 00 000 001, except G-★.
PLATE NUMBERS: Back numbers continue from previous series. Face numbers begin at #1.
SIGNATURES: Katherine Davalos Ortega, James A. Baker III

	Serial Numbers			
	Low	**High**	**Notes Printed**	**CH CU**
BOSTON	A-A	—	99,200,000	$15
	—	A92 800 000B	92,800,000	15
NEW YORK	B-A	—	448,000,000	15
	B-B	—	—	15
	B-C	—	—	15
	B-D	—	—	15
	—	B51 200 000E	—	15
	B00 000 001★	B03 200 000★	256,000	150
PHILADELPHIA	C-A	—	99,200,000	15
	—	C70 400 000B	70,400,000	15
	C00 000 001★	C03 200 000★	3,200,000	100
CLEVELAND	D-A	—	99,200,000	15
	D-B	—	99,200,000	15
	—	D16 000 000C	16,000,000	15
RICHMOND	E-A	—	323,800,000	15
	E-B	—	—	15
	E-C	—	—	15
	—	E35 200 000D	—	15
	E00 000 001★	E03 200 000★	1,280,000	125
ATLANTA	F-A	—	343,000,000	15
	F-B	—	—	15
	F-C	—	—	15
	—	F54 400 000D	—	15
	F00 000 001★	F06 400 000★	3,840,000	80

	Low	High	Notes Printed	CH CU
CHICAGO	G-A	—	336,600,000	$15
	G-B	—	—	15
	G-C	—	—	15
	—	G48 000 000D	—	15
	G00 000 001★	G06 400 000★	3,584,000	75
ST. LOUIS	H-A	—	128,000,000	15
	—	H28 800 000B	—	15
MINNEAPOLIS	I-A	—	172,800,000	15
	—	I73 600 000B	—	30
KANSAS CITY	J-A	—	134,400,000	15
	—	J35 200 000B	—	15
DALLAS	K-A	—	176,000,000	15
	—	K76 800 000B	—	15
	K00 000 001★	K03 200 000★	3,200,000	110
SAN FRANCISCO	L-A	—	457,600,000	15
	L-B	—	—	15
	L-C	—	—	15
	L-D	—	—	15
	—	L60 800 000E	—	15
	L00 000 001★	L03 200 000★	2,256,000	100

SERIES 1988 GREEN SEAL

SIGNATURES: Katherine Davalos Ortega, Nicholas F. Brady

SERIAL NUMBERS: All districts, regulars and stars, begin at 00 000 001.

PLATE NUMBERS: Back numbers continue from previous series. Face numbers begin at #1.

	Serial Numbers			
	Low	High	Notes Printed	CH CU
BOSTON	A-A	—	86,400,000	$15
	A-★	A03 200 000★	768,000	120
NEW YORK	B-A	—	99,200,000	15
	—	B-B	96,000,000	15
	B-★	B03 200 000★	3,200,000	75
PHILADELPHIA	C-A	—	54,400,000	15
CLEVELAND	D-A	—	99,200,000	15
	—	D-B	12,800,000	25
RICHMOND	E-A	—	99,200,000	20
	—	E-B	32,000,000	10
ATLANTA	F-A	—	99,200,000	15
	—	F-B	38,400,000	15
	F-★	F06 400 000★	2,048,000	75
CHICAGO	G-A	—	99,200,000	15
	—	G-B	35,200,000	15
ST. LOUIS	H-A	—	51,200,000	15
MINNEAPOLIS	I-A	—	9,600,000	40
KANSAS CITY	J-A	—	44,800,000	15
DALLAS	K-A	—	54,400,000	15
SAN FRANCISCO	L-A	—	70,400,000	15

SERIES 1988A GREEN SEAL

SERIAL NUMBERS: All districts started numbering notes with 00 000 001. Fort Worth printings are interspersed with standard Washington D.C. issues.

PLATE NUMBERS: Face numbers begin at #1. Back numbers continue from previous series.

SIGNATURES: Catalina Vasquez Villalpando, Nicholas F. Brady

	Serial Numbers			
	Low	High	Notes Printed	CH CU
BOSTON	A-A W	—	96,000,000	$15
	A-B W	—	44,800,000	15
	A-★ W	A03 200 000★	3,200,000	40
NEW YORK	B-A, B-G W	—	640,000,000	15
	B-★ W	B06 400 000★	4,608,000	40
PHILADELPHIA	C-A W/FW	—	96,000,000	15
	C-B W	—	25,600,000	15

	Low	High	Notes Printed	CH CU
CLEVELAND	**D-A** W	—	96,000,000	$15
	D-B W	—	96,000,000	15
	D-C W	—	38,400,000	15
	D-★ W	**D**06 406 000★	5,120,000	40
RICHMOND	**E-A, E-E** W	—	480,000,000	15
	E-F W	—	6,400,000	30
	E-★ W	**E**09 600 000★	2,640,000	40
ATLANTA	**F-A** W	—	96,000,000	15
	F-B W/FW	—	96,000,000	15
	F-C FW	—	96,000,000	15
	F-D W/FW	—	96,800,000	15
	—	**F**70 050 825**E** FW	89,600,000	15
	F-★ W/FW	**F**09 600 000★	3,280,000	40
CHICAGO	**G-A** W	**G-G**	633,600,000	15
	G-H W	**G**06 400 000**H**	6,400,000	30
	G-H FW	**G**83 200 000**H**	66,800,000	15
	G-★ FW	**G**03 200 000★	1,280,000	50
ST. LOUIS	**H-A, H-B** W	—	166,400,000	15
	H-★ W	**H**03 200 000★	1,280,000	50
MINNEAPOLIS	**I-A** W	—	73,600,000	15
	I-★ W	**I**03 200 000★	128,000	250
KANSAS CITY	**J-A** W/FW	—	96,000,000	15
	J-B W	—	44,800,000	15
DALLAS	**K-A** W	**K**89 600 000**A**	89,600,000	15
	K-A FW	**K**96 000 000**A**	6,400,000	30
	K-B W/FW	—	76,800,000	15
SAN FRANCISCO	**L-A**	**L-G** W/FW	652,800,000	15
	L-H W	—	19,200,000	20
	L-★ FW	**L**03 200 000★	3,200,000	40

SERIES 1993 GREEN SEAL

SERIAL NUMBERS: All districts started numbering both regular and star notes with 00 000 001.
PLATE NUMBERS: Face numbers begin at #1. Back numbers continue from previous series.
SIGNATURES: Mary Ellen Withrow, Lloyd Bentsen

| | Serial Numbers | | | |
	Low	High	Notes Printed	CH CU
BOSTON	A-A W	A19 200 000A	19,200,000	$15
NEW YORK	B-A W	—	96,000,000	15
	B-B W	B06 400 000B	6,400,000	20
	B-★ W	B03 206 000★	3,200,000	40
PHILADELPHIA	C-A W	C38 400 000A	38,400,000	15
RICHMOND	E-A W	E76 800 000A	76,800,000	15
	E-★ W	E03 200 000★	3,200,000	60
ATLANTA	F-A W	F70 400 000A	70,400,000	15
CHICAGO	G-A FW	G64 000 000A	64,000,000	15
	G-★ FW	G01 280 000★	1,280,000	50
ST. LOUIS	H-A FW	H64 000 000A	64,000,000	15
	H-★ FW	H03 200 000★	3,200,000	40
MINNEAPOLIS	I-A FW	I06 400 000A	6,400,000	500
KANSAS CITY	J-A FW	J32 000 000A	32,000,000	15
DALLAS	K-A FW	K57 600 000A	57,600,000	15
SAN FRANCISCO	L-A, L-B FW	L89 600 000B	185,600,000	15
	L-★ FW	L02 560 000★	2,560,000	45

SERIES 1995 GREEN SEAL

SIGNATURES: Mary Ellen Withrow, Robert E. Rubin

PLATE NUMBERS: Face numbers begin at #1. Back numbers continue from previous series, creating mules, then start #1 in mid-series.

SERIAL NUMBERS: Both regular and star notes begin at 00 000 001.
  Note: Blocks H-D through H-K, that begin with H88880001 and end at 88888888, were printed in Fort Worth and sold in sheet form by the BEP as 8 note "Prosperity Sheets" at $88 each.

	Serial Numbers		Notes Printed	CH CU
	Low	**High**		
BOSTON	A-A - A-C W/FW	A25 600 000C	217,600,000	$20
	A-★ W	A00 640 000★	640,000	125
NEW YORK	B-A - B-F W/FW	B32 000 000F	512,000,000	20
	B-★ W	B05 120 000★	3,840,000	40
PHILADELPHIA	C-A - C-B W/FW	C70 400 000B	166,400,000	20
CLEVELAND	D-A - D-C W/FW	D19 200 000C	211,200,000	20
	D-★ FW	D03 200 000★	3,200,000	45
RICHMOND	E-A - E-E W/FW	E25 600 000E	409,600,000	20
ATLANTA	F-A - F-G W/FW	F51 200 000G	627,200,000	20
	F-★ FW	F00 384 000★	384,000	125
CHICAGO	G-A - G-F FW	G38 400 000F	518,400,000	20
	G-★ FW	G09 600 000★	9,600,000	35
ST. LOUIS	H-A - H-C FW	H12 800 000C	204,800,000	20
MINNEAPOLIS	I-A FW	I70 400 000A	70,400,000	25
KANSAS CITY	J-A - J-B FW	J64 000 000B	160,000,000	20
DALLAS	K-A - K-C FW	K70 400 000C	262,400,000	20
SAN FRANCISCO	L-A - L-H FW	L96 000 000H	768,000,000	20

SERIES 1999 GREEN SEAL

SIGNATURES: Mary Ellen Withrow, Lawrence H. Summers
PLATE NUMBERS: Both face and back numbers begin at #1.
SERIAL NUMBERS: Both regular and star notes begin at 00 000 001.

	Serial Numbers			
	Low	**High**	**Notes Printed**	**CH CU**
BOSTON	**BA-A** W/FW	**BA**96 000 000**A**	96,000,000	$15
	BA-B FW	**BA**06 400 000**B**	6,400,000	45
	BA-★ FW	**BA**03 200 000★	3,200,000	30
NEW YORK	**BB-A - BB-C** W/FW	**BB**44 800 000**C**	236,800,000	15
	BB-★ FW	**BB**03 840 000★	3,840,000	30
PHILADELPHIA	**BC-A - BC-B** W/FW	**BC**51 200 000**B**	147,200,000	15
CLEVELAND	**BD-A** W/FW	**BD**70 400 000**A**	70,400,000	15
RICHMOND	**BE-A - BE-C** W/FW	**BE**70 400 000**C**	262,400,000	15
	BE-★ W	**BE**00 035 200★	35,200	100
	BE03 200 001★ W	**BE**03 328 000★	128,000	85
	BE06 400 001★ W	**BE**06 656 000★	256,000	75
	BE12 800 001★ W	**BE**14 720 000★	1,920,000	50
	BE16 000 001★ W	**BE**16 320 000★	320,000	75
	BE19 200 001★ FW	**BE**22 400 000★	3,200,000	30
ATLANTA	**BF-A - BF-C** FW	**BF**19 200 000**C**	211,200,000	15
	BF-★ FW	**BF**00 035 200★	35,200	100
	BF03 200 001★ FW			
		BF03 840 000★	640,000	40
	BF09 600 001★ FW			
		BF19 840 000★	10,240,000	30
CHICAGO	**BG-A - BG-B** FW	**BG**44 800 000**B**	140,800,000	15
	BG-★ FW	**BG**03 200 000★	3,200,000	30
ST. LOUIS	**BH-A** FW	**BH**44 800 000**A**	44,800,000	15
MINNEAPOLIS	**BI-A** FW	**BI**12 800 000**A**	12,800,000	25
KANSAS CITY	**BJ-A** FW	**BJ**32 000 000**A**	32,000,000	15
	BJ-★ FW	**BJ**03 200 000★	3,200,000	35
DALLAS	**BK-A - BK-B**FW	**BK**25 600 000**B**	121,600,000	15
	BK-★ FW	**BK**03 200 000★	3,200,000	35
SAN FRANCISCO	**BL-A - BL-C** FW	**BL**51 200 000**C**	243,200,000	15

SERIES 2001 GREEN SEAL

SIGNATURES: Rosario Marin, Paul H. O'Neill
PLATE NUMBERS: Both face and back numbers begin at #1.
SERIAL NUMBERS: All districts start both regular and star notes with 00 000 001.
PRINTING FACILITY: All notes were printed in Fort Worth.

	Serial Numbers			
	Low	**High**	**Notes Printed**	**CH CU**
BOSTON	CA-A - CA-B	CA32 000 000B	128,000,000	$15
NEW YORK	CB-A - CB-B	CB25 600 000B	121,600,000	15
PHILADELPHIA	CC-A	CC64 000 000A	64,000,000	15
CLEVELAND	CD-A	CD83 200 000A	83,200,000	15
RICHMOND	CE-A	CE51 200 000A	51,200,000	20
ATLANTA	CF-A - CF-C	CF32 000 000C	224,000,000	15
CHICAGO	CG-A - CG-C	CG51 200 000C	243,200,000	15
ST. LOUIS	CH-A	CH96 000 000A	96,000,000	15
	CH-B	CH06 400 000B	6,400,000	25
MINNEAPOLIS	CI-A	CI32 000 000A	32,000,000	20
KANSAS CITY	CJ-A	CJ96 000 000A	96,000,000	15
	CJ-B	CJ06 400 000B	6,400,000	20
DALLAS	CK-A - CK-C	CK19 200 000C	211,200,000	15
	CK-★	CK03 200 000★	3,200,000	35
SAN FRANCISCO	CL-A - CL-D	CL12 800 000D	300,800,000	15
	CL-★	CL05 120 000★	5,120,000	30

SERIES 2003 GREEN SEAL

SIGNATURES: Rosario Marin, John W. Snow
PLATE NUMBERS: Both face and back numbers begin at #1.
SERIAL NUMBERS: All districts start with 00 000 001.

	Serial Numbers		Notes Printed	CH CU
	Low	High		
BOSTON	DA-A W/FW	DA57 600 000A	57,600,000	$15
NEW YORK	DB-A-DB-B FW	DB51 200 000A	147,200,000	15
PHILADELPHIA	DC-A W/FW	DC70 400 000A	70,400,000	15
CLEVELAND	DD-A W/FW	DD64 000 000A	64,000,000	15
RICHMOND	DE-A - DE-B FW	DE12 800 000B	108,800,000	15
ATLANTA	DF-A FW	DF96 000 000A	96,000,000	15
	DF-B W	DF89 600 000B	89,600,000	15
CHICAGO	DG-A FW	DG89 600 000A	89,600,000	15
	DG89 600 001A W			
		DG96 000 000A	6,400,000	25
	DG-B W	DG25 600 000B	25,600,000	15
	DG-★ W	DG01 280 000★	1,280,000	40
	DG03 200 001★ W			
		DG03 520 000★	320,000	75
ST. LOUIS	DH-A FW	DH51 200 000A	51,200,000	15
MINNEAPOLIS	DI-A FW	DI32 000 000A	32,000,000	20
KANSAS CITY	DJ-A FW	DJ51 200 000A	51,200,000	15
DALLAS	DK-A FW	DK96 000 000A	96,000,000	15
SAN FRANCISCO	DL-A - DL-D FW	D12 800 000D	300,800,000	15
	DL-★ FW	DL03 200 000★	3,200,000	35
	DL03 200 001★	DL03 520 000★(Sheets)	320,000	65
	DL06 400 001★ FW	DL09 600 000★	3,200,000	35

SERIES 2003A GREEN SEAL

SIGNATURES: Anna Escobedo Cabral, John W. Snow
PLATE NUMBERS: Both face and back numbers begin at #1.
SERIAL NUMBERS: All districts start with 00 000 001, for both regular and star notes.
PRINTING FACILITY: All notes were printed in Fort Worth.

	Serial Numbers			
	Low	**High**	**Notes Printed**	**CH CU**
BOSTON	FA-A	FA12 800 000B	108,800,000	$15
NEW YORK	FB-A	FB64 000 000C	256,000,000	15
	FB-★	FB00 640 000★(Sheets)	640,000	75
PHILADELPHIA	FC-A	FC25 600 000B	121,600,000	15
CLEVELAND	FD-A	FD25 600 000B	121,600,000	15
RICHMOND	FE-A	FE96 000 000B	192,000,000	15
ATLANTA	FF-A	FF44 800 000B	140,800,000	15
	FF-★	FF04 652 000★	4,352,000	50
CHICAGO	FG-A	FG25 600 000B	121,600,000	15
	FG-★	FG00 640 000★(Notes)	640,000	75
ST. LOUIS	FH-A	FH83 200 000A	83,200,000	15
MINNEAPOLIS	FI-A	FI19 200 000A	19,200,000	20
KANSAS CITY	FJ-A	FJ96 000 000A	96,000,000	15
	FJ-B	FJ06 400 000B	6,400,000	25
DALLAS	FK-A	FK76 800 000B	172,800,000	15
SAN FRANCISCO	FL-A	FL25 600 000D	313,600,000	15

SERIES 2006 GREEN SEAL

SIGNATURES: Anna Escobedo Cabral, Henry M. Paulson, Jr.
PLATE NUMBERS: Both face and back numbers begin at #1.
SERIAL NUMBERS: All districts start with 00 000 001, for both regular and star notes.
PRINTING FACILITY: All notes were printed in Fort Worth.

	Serial Numbers			
	Low	**High**	**Notes Printed**	**CH CU**
ATLANTA	HF-A- HF-B	HF57 600 000B	153,600,000	$15
CHICAGO	HG-A	HG12 800 000B	106,800,000	15
MINNEAPOLIS	HI-A	HI25 600 000A	25,600,000	15

TEN DOLLAR NOTES

GOLD CERTIFICATES

SERIES 1928 GOLD SEAL

PLATE NUMBERS: Face #1 through #290.

SIGNATURES: W.O. Woods, A.W. Mellon

Serial Numbers

Low	High	Notes Printed	VG	VF	CH CU	GEM CU
A00 000 001A	A99 999 999A	99,999,999	$110	$190	$750	1,250
B00 000 001A	B30 812 000A	30,812,000	175	350	1,700	2,250
★00 009 213A	★01 530 786A	—	300	800	5,000	—

SERIES 1928A GOLD SEAL

Serial Numbers

Low	High	Notes Printed	VG/F	CH CU
B30 802 001A	B33 346 000A	2,544,000	—	unknown

SIGNATURES: W.O. Woods, Ogden L. Mills

NOTE: Although BEP records indicate that 2,544,000 notes were DELIVERED, it is believed that all are in storage vaults in the basement of the Main Treasury Building, Washington, D.C., and that none were released to the public.

TREASURY REMOVES RESTRICTIONS ON
UNITED STATES GOLD CERTIFICATES ISSUED BEFORE 1934

On April 24, 1964, the Secretary of the Treasury issued Regulations removing all restrictions on the acquisition or holding of gold certificates which were issued by the United States Government prior to January 30, 1934. The main effect of this action will be to permit collectors to hold this type of currency.

"The restrictions which are being eliminated are considered no longer necessary or desirable. Under the laws enacted in 1934, these pre-1934 gold certificates are not redeemable in gold. They will, of course, continue to be exchangeable at face value for other currency of the United States."

The new Regulation authorizing the holding of gold certificates applies only to United States gold certificates issued prior to January 30, 1934. The holding of any other type of gold certificates, including any issued by foreigners against gold held on deposit abroad, continues to be prohibited. Also, the status of the special series gold certificates issued by the U.S. Treasury only to the Federal Reserve system for reserve purposes is not affected.

FEDERAL RESERVE BANK NOTES

SERIES 1929 BROWN SEAL

SERIAL NUMBERS: Figures shown below are the official high numbers. All districts started both regular and star notes with 00 000 001. Bureau of Engraving and Printing information is incomplete on star serial numbers, as are reports of high observed serial numbers.

PLATE NUMBERS: Face numbers within the range #1 through #290.

SIGNATURES: E.E. Jones, W.O. Woods

Also the Federal Reserve Bank Cashier or Controller or the Deputy or Assistant Deputy Governor, with the Governor.

	Serial Numbers					
	Low	**High**	**Notes Printed**	**VF**	**CH CU**	**GEM CU**
BOSTON	A00 000 001A	A01 589 097A	1,680,000	$50	$250	$400
	A00 001 088★	A00 018 782★	24,000	4,000	10,000	—
NEW YORK	B00 000 039A	B05 556 000A	5,556,000	45	225	325
	B00 001 634★	B00 070 700★	76,000	300	2,000	—
PHILADELPHIA	C00 000 002A	C01 287 352A	1,416,000	45	275	400
	C00 001 567★	C00 012 526★	24,000	700	2,500	—
CLEVELAND	D00 000 001A	D02 339 544A	2,412,000	40	250	350
	D00 000 252★	D00 023 401★	36,000	375	2,500	—
RICHMOND	E00 000 003A	E01 187 948A	1,356,000	70	500	750
	E00 015 295★	E00 020 104★	24,000	1,600	9,000	—
ATLANTA	F00 000 002A	F00 743 512A	1,056,000	50	400	600
	F00 001 463★	F00 005 926★	36,000	2,500	—	—
CHICAGO	G00 000 002A	G02 987 306A	3,156,000	45	200	350
	G00 000 826★	G00 006 988★	12,000	2,000	—	—
ST. LOUIS	H00 000 022A	H01 509 310A	1,584,000	50	200	350
	H00 000 547★	H00 035 771★	36,000	350	2,400	—
MINNEAPOLIS	I00 000 652A	I00 587 702A	588,000	70	300	500
	I00 000 066★	I00 022 474★	24,000	1,350	3,500	—
KANSAS CITY	J00 000 008A	J01 230 537A	1,284,000	40	200	400
	J00 000 538★	J00 027 622★	36,000	450	2,600	—
DALLAS	K00 000 002A	K00 454 600A	504,000	400	2,500	—
	K00 000 183★	K00 003 609★	12,000	7,000	—	—
SAN FRANCISCO	L00 000 100A	L01 036 903A	1,080,000	150	3,000	—
	L00 000 889★	L00 015 245★	36,000	1,500	—	—

LEGAL TENDER

SERIES 1928 RED SEAL

SERIAL NUMBERS: No Bureau record of printing.

PLATE NUMBERS: Face and back number 1.

SIGNATURES: W.O. Woods, W.H. Woodin

One specimen of this note was displayed at the Chicago World's Fair in 1933 (along with a $20 note).

SILVER CERTIFICATES

SERIES 1933 BLUE SEAL

PLATE NUMBERS: Face #1 only.

SIGNATURES: W.A. Julian, W.H. Woodin

Serial Numbers

Low	High	Notes Printed	VF	CH CU	GEM CU
A00 000 001A	—	216,000	$6,000	$20,000	$2,500
A00 216 000A					
★00 000 002A	This note (VF) sold privately in excess of $50,000.				
	A00 137 766A	—	—	—	—
	high observed				

SERIES 1933A BLUE SEAL

PLATE NUMBERS: Face #1 only.
SIGNATURES: W.A. Julian, Henry Morgenthau, Jr.

Serial Numbers

Low	High	Notes Printed	VF	CH CU
A00 216 001A	A00 552 000A	336,000	—	—

In November 1935, 368,000 $10.00 silver certificates were destroyed. Reports indicate that 156,000 Series 1933 and 60,000 Series 1933A were released and that the balance of 60,000 1933 and 308,000 of the 1933A were destroyed. However, these reports are believed to be inaccurate since NO 1933A regular notes have ever been reported. It is likely that the destruction included the entire printing of 1933A.

Perhaps the most desired notes in the small series Silver Certificates are Series of 1933 and 1933A $10.00 notes. Issued in the year 1933, their manufacture was cut short by the Administration's change in the silver policy. These two (1933 and 1933A) are the only certificates mentioning the word "coin" as such. The Series of 1933 were issued just prior to Woodin's retirement (signatures W.A. Julian and W.H. Woodin). This $10.00 differs from all other Silver Certificates, being inscribed "The United States of America-Ten Dollars-payable in silver coin to bearer on demand." No mention is made of the deposit of the silver. Only a few plates were prepared and only face check #1 is known. Later in the year Series 1933A was printed, Morgenthau's name replacing that of Woodin. A proof of a 12-subject sheet is in the Smithsonian Archives. The bureau occasionally exhibits its 12-subject sheet of specimen notes, but no one has ever verified the existence of an issued note.

SERIES 1934 BLUE SEAL

PLATE NUMBERS: Back numbers #584 (micro size) and lower.

SIGNATURES: W.A. Julian, Henry Morgenthau, Jr.

DESIGN: Face design for Series 1934 through 1934D shows a large blue 10 to left of portrait of Hamilton, blue Treasury seal at right. Back design same as 1933. Face and back plate numbers doubled in size for Series 1934A and beyond.

Serial Numbers

Low	High	Notes Printed	VF	CH CU	GEM CU
A00 000 001**A**	**A**85 651 458**A**	88,692,864	$40	$165	$210
	B16877749**A**		500	—	—
★00 000 013**A**	★00 939 068**A**	all types of Series 1934	200	1,300	1,800

SERIES 1934 MULE BLUE SEAL

These are series 1934 notes with the larger back plate numbers (585 or higher), and are actually Series 1934 Faces on Series 1934A Backs.

Serial Numbers

Low	High	Notes Printed	VF	CH CU	GEM CU
A31 648 080**A**	**A**91 044 000**A**	included above	$45	$200	$275
B00 904 000**A**	**B**01 130 170**A**	—	400	1,000	—
—	**B**16 924 554**A**	—	500	—	—
★00 557 484**A**	★01 401 498**A**	—	250	2,000	2,500

NORTH AFRICA

SERIES 1934 NORTH AFRICA MULE YELLOW SEAL

PLATE NUMBERS: Back number 585 or higher. Face numbers 116, 122, 123, 125, 126, and 127.

SIGNATURES: W.A. Julian, Henry Morgenthau, Jr.

Serial Numbers

Low	High	Notes Printed	VF	CH CU	GEM CU
A91 061 041**A** I		—	$5,000	$25,000	—
Low observed					
	B07 562 664**A**	—	5,000	25,000	—
	high observed				
★01 122 388**A**	Note sold (VF) in 1998 in excess of $50,000				

Only 24 CU specimens are known. One circulated star note is known.

SERIES 1934A MULE BLUE SEAL

These are Series 1934A notes with the Micro Back Plate Numbers (#584 or lower) and are actually Series 1934A Faces on Series 1934 Backs.

PLATE NUMBERS: Back numbers used #404, 523, 553, and 578.

Serial Numbers

Low	High	Notes Printed	VF	CH CU	GEM CU
A74 452 813**A**	**A**90 577 124**A**	included above	$150	$750	—

SERIES 1934A BLUE SEAL

PLATE NUMBERS: Face numbers range #129-210.

Serial Numbers

Low	High	Notes Printed	VF	CH CU	GEM CU
A74 761 305**A**	**A**91 044 000**A**	42,346,428	$45	$250	$300
B00 904 001**A**	**B**01 564 000**A**	660,000	50	350	400
B13 564 001**A**	**B**26 878 328**A**	—	40	200	250
★00 951 347**A**	★01 547 059**A**	—	300	2,250	2,750

SERIES 1934A NORTH AFRICA YELLOW SEAL

PLATE NUMBERS: Face #129-209. Back #585 and higher.

SIGNATURES: Same as Series 1934

Serial Numbers

Low	High	Notes Printed	VF	CH CU	GEM CU
A91 044 001A	B00 904 000A official	9,860,000	$90	$450	$700
B01 564 001A	B13 564 000A official	12,000,000	90	450	700
★01 008 001A	★01 284 000A official	276,000	300	2,500	—
★01 008 704A	★01 282 762A observed	—	—	—	—

SERIES 1934A
NORTH AFRICA LATE FINISHED FACE PLATE 86 YELLOW SEAL

Serial Numbers

Low	High	Notes Printed	VF	CH CU	GEM CU
A91 816 519A	B13 159 277A included above	$75	$450	—
★01 010 325A	★01 254 541A —	750	2,500	—

SERIES 1934A
LATE FINISHED FACE PLATE 86 BLUE SEAL

Serial Numbers

Low	High	Notes Printed	VF	CH CU	GEM CU
A84 958 136A	B21 912 244A included above	$100	$600	—
★00 950 578A	★01 485 388A —	1,000	7,500	—

SERIES 1934A
MULE LATE FINISHED FACE PLATE 86 BLUE SEAL

PLATE NUMBERS: Face number 86. Back numbers 404, 553, and 578.

Serial Numbers

Low	High	Notes Printed	VF	CH CU	GEM CU
A84 899 119A	A90 853 724A included above	$200	$2,500	—

SERIES 1934A LATE FINISHED FACE PLATE 87 BLUE SEAL

Serial Numbers

Low	High	Notes Printed	VF	CH CU	GEM CU
A77 166 221A	A78 646 447A included above	$1,000	$4,000	—

SERIES 1934A MULE LATE FINISHED FACE PLATE 87 BLUE SEAL

PLATE NUMBERS: Face number 87. Back numbers 404, 553 and 578.

Serial Numbers

Low	High	Notes Printed	VF	CH CU	GEM CU
A77 425 715A	A78 491 508A included above	$1,000	$5,000	—

SILVER CERTIFICATES

SERIES 1934B BLUE SEAL

PLATE NUMBERS: Face #211 only.

SIGNATURES: W.A. Julian, Fred M. Vinson

Serial Numbers

Low	High	Notes Printed	VF	CH CU	GEM CU
B15 432 001A	B21 521 396A	337,740	$250	$2,500	$3,500
★01 333 331A	★01 505 683A	—	2,500	15,000	—

SERIES 1934C BLUE SEAL

PLATE NUMBERS: Face numbers #214-232.

SIGNATURES: W.A. Julian, John W. Snyder

Serial Numbers

Low	High	Notes Printed	VF	CH CU	GEM CU
B16 848 001A	B46 108 395A	20,032,632	$30	$150	$225
★01 410 277A	★01 787 573A	—	100	750	1,000

$10.00 Wide   **$10.00 Narrow**

SERIES 1934D WIDE BLUE SEAL

PLATE NUMBERS: Face numbers range (both groups) #233-#252. Back numbers #1389 or lower.

SIGNATURES: Georgia Neese Clark, John W. Snyder

Serial Numbers Official

Low	High	Notes Printed	VF	CH CU	GEM CU
B38 556 589A	B50 196 000A	11,801,112	$40	$275	$350
★01 788 051A	★01 938 566A high observed	—	400	4,500	6,000

SERIES 1934D NARROW BLUE SEAL

PLATE NUMBERS: Back numbers range #1390-1456 (Last of the 12 subject sheets).

Serial Numbers Official

Low	High	Notes Printed	VF	CH CU	GEM CU
B47 556 045A	B50 196 000A	included above	$100	$800	$1,200
★01 932 430A	★01 939 976A	—	4,000	12,000	15,000
★01 940 000A official high	—	—	—	—	—

SERIES 1953 BLUE SEAL

PLATE NUMBERS: Face numbers begin at #1. Back numbers begin at #1448 (low of 18 subject sheets).

SIGNATURES: Ivy Baker Priest, G.M. Humphrey

Serial Numbers

Low	High	Notes Printed	VF	CH CU	GEM CU
A00 000 001A	A10 440 000A	10,440,000	$50	$250	$325
★00 000 001A	★00 576 000A	576,000	100	900	1,200

SERIES 1953A BLUE SEAL

SIGNATURES: Ivy Baker Priest, Robert B. Anderson

Serial Numbers

Low	High	Notes Printed	VF	CH CU	GEM CU
A10 440 001A	A11 520 000A	1,080,000	$70	$400	$575
★00 576 001A	★00 720 000A	144,000	150	1,600	2,000

SERIES 1953B BLUE SEAL

PLATE NUMBERS: Face numbers on 18 subject sheets end at #5. Back numbers on 18 subject sheets end at #1839.

SIGNATURES: Elizabeth Rudel Smith, C. Douglas Dillon

Serial Numbers

Low	High	Notes Printed	VF	CH CU	GEM CU
A11 520 001A	A12 240 000A	720,000	$50	$250	$350

No star notes printed.

FEDERAL RESERVE NOTES

SERIES 1928 GREEN SEAL

SERIAL NUMBERS: All serial numbers of both regular and star notes begin with 00 000 001.
PLATE NUMBERS: All face and back numbers begin with #1.
SIGNATURES: H.T. Tate, A.W. Mellon

Single and double digit low serial numbers are valued at three to four times regular price.

	Serial Numbers				
	Low	**High**	**Notes Printed**	**VF**	**CH CU**
BOSTON	A00 000 012A	A09 599 336A	9,804,552	$75	$500
	A00 066 470★	A00 398 506★	—	500	2,500

	Low	**High**	**Notes Printed**	**VF**	**CH CU**
NEW YORK	B00 172 246A	B10 556 466A	11,295,796	$40	$250
	B00 000 191★	B00 103 597★	—	300	1,000
PHILADELPHIA	C00 002 803A	C10 847 487A	8,114,412	50	350
	C00 056 902★	C00 220 723★	—	300	1,500
CLEVELAND	D00 000 032A	D10 155 856A	7,570,680	40	250
	D00 000 996★	D00 200 157★	—	300	1,250
RICHMOND	E00 002 544A	E06 022 463A	4,534,800	50	650
	E00 014 229★	E00 114 911★	—	1,250	5,000
ATLANTA	F00 002 821A	F08 682 361A	6,807,720	50	350
	F00 002 821★	F00 141 537★	—	500	3,250
CHICAGO	G00 001 200A	G12 342 348A	8,130,000	$60	250
	G00 000 042★	G00 304 040★	—	300	1,500

	Low	High	Notes Printed	VF	CH CU
ST. LOUIS	H00 000 012A	H05 157 636A	4,124,400	$60	$250
	H00 015 245★	H00 146 517★	—	250	1,500
MINNEAPOLIS	I00 000 001A	I03 879 838A	3,874,440	75	600
	I00 004 587★	I00 057 287★	—	500	2,000
KANSAS CITY	J00 000 039A	J04 655 326A	3,620,400	60	300
	J00 000 177★	J00 136 235★	—	300	1,750
DALLAS	K00 000 010A	K04 557 496A	4,855,500	60	650
	K00 000 177★	K00 096 000★	96,000	1,500	5,000
SAN FRANCISCO	L00 002 222A	L06 022 631A	7,086,900	50	400
	L00 029 182★	L00 136 294★	—	1,200	4,000

SERIES 1928A GREEN SEAL

SERIAL NUMBERS: All districts continued sequence from previous series. Face plates start with #1. Backs continue from previous series.

SIGNATURES: W.O. Woods, A.W. Mellon

Serial Numbers

	Low	High	Notes Printed	VF	CH CU
BOSTON	A08 555 834A	A12 711 116A	2,893,440	$125	$900
	A00 253 475★	A00 256 761★	—	4,000	—
NEW YORK	B08 442 103A	B29 501 191A	18,631,056	70	300
	B00 196 427★	B00 668 377★	—	500	2,000
PHILADELPHIA	C06 666 666A	C10 654 696A	2,710,680	50	500
	C00 225 770★	—	—	2,000	5,000
CLEVELAND	D05 108 991A	D15 256 075A	5,610,000	50	300
	D00 138 930★	D00 208 267★	—	500	2,500
RICHMOND	E04 672 279A	E07 298 125A	552,300	125	1,500
	E00 074 456★	E00 124 932★	—	1,000	—
ATLANTA	F04 152 285A	F09 362 464A	3,033,780	50	450
	F00 159 856★	—	—	1,500	—
CHICAGO	G06 063 114A	G25 989 476A	8,715,000	50	350
	G00 252 073★	G00 302 346★	—	400	1,500
ST. LOUIS	H03 552 311A	H05 151 623A	531,600	75	350
	H00 062 759★	H00 113 789★	—	500	1,500
MINNEAPOLIS	I03 649 469A	I03 998 386A	102,600	1,000	4,000
	I-★ not reported —		—	—

	Low	High	Notes Printed	VF	CH CU
KANSAS CITY	J03 286 412A	J04 286 834A	410,400	$750	—
	J-★ not reported—		—	—	—
DALLAS	K04 095 111A	K05 989 989A	961,800	400	2,500
SAN FRANCISCO	L07 063 176A	L10 856 679A	2,547,900	100	750
	L00 149 457★	—	—	400	1,600

SERIES 1928B DARK GREEN SEAL

SERIAL NUMBERS: All districts continued sequence from previous series.

SIGNATURES: W.O. Woods, A.W. Mellon

	Serial Numbers				
	Low	High	Notes Printed	VF	CH CU
BOSTON	A13 126 812A	A36 496 744A	33,218,088	$20	$100
	A00 323 424★	A00 514 869★	—	120	900
NEW YORK	B27 480 893A	B55 653 950A	44,458,308	20	90
	B00 494 815★	B00 523 883★	—	150	1,100
PHILADELPHIA	C10 062 953A	C24 235 634A	22,689,216	20	100
	C00 239 922★	—	—	150	1,000
CLEVELAND	D12 776 479A	D26 585 122A	17,418,024	20	100
	D00 195 443★	D00 302 202★	—	100	900
RICHMOND	E05 323 470A	E13 594 714A	12,714,504	20	120
	E00 124 932★	E00 195 443★	—	200	1,000
ATLANTA	F09 563 762A	F11 496 429A	5,246,700	20	120
	F00 176 034★	—	36,000	150	1,100
CHICAGO	G15 708 491A	G35 915 392A	38,035,000	20	85
	G00 316 826★	G00 559 530★	—	100	600
ST. LOUIS	H03 833 892A	H09 917 580A	10,814,664	20	100
	H00 124 721★	—	—	150	1,100
MINNEAPOLIS	I03 927 054A	I05 855 065A	5,294,460	20	120
	I00 077 380★	—	—	150	1,100
KANSAS CITY	J04 061 739A	J08 820 387A	7,748,040	20	90
	J-★	—	48,000	300	2,400
DALLAS	K06 391 440A	K08 319 882A	3,396,096	75	250
SAN FRANCISCO	L09 279 596A	L18 289 932A	22,695,300	20	90
	L00 208 244★	L00 293 758★	—	120	1,100

SERIES 1928B LIGHT VIVID YELLOW-GREEN SEAL

SERIAL NUMBERS: All districts continue sequence from 1928 dark green seal variety. High official star serial numbers are listed just below the high observed star serial numbers.

	Serial Numbers				
	Low	**High**	**Notes Printed**	**VF**	**CH CU**
BOSTON	A39 082 484A	A42 392 748A	included above	$25	$150
	A00 524 128★	A00 568 003★	—	150	1,000
	—	A00 624 000★	—	—	—
NEW YORK	—	B73 268 799A	included above	25	125
	B00 701 701★	B00 820 798★	—	150	800
	—	B00 852 000★	—	—	—
PHILADELPHIA	C23 763 754A	C39 744 939A	included above	25	125
	C00 328 478★	C00 329 103★	—	150	1,000
	—	C00 372 000★	—	—	—
CLEVELAND	D25 814 418A	D29 461 240A	included above	25	125
	D00 346 433★	D00 409 156★	—	120	1,000
	—	D00 420 000★	—	—	—
RICHMOND	E13 972 621A	E17 356 591A	included above	25	125
	E-★	—	—	200	1,000
	—	E00 216 000★	—	—	—
ATLANTA	F12 449 218A	F14 532 556A	included above	25	150
	F00 180 922★	—	—	200	1,000
	—	F00 204 000★	—	—	—
CHICAGO	G37 539 928A	G54 564 239A	included above	25	85
	G00 385 789★	G00 650 082★	—	100	600
	—	G00 672 000★	—	—	—
ST. LOUIS	H10 443 608A	H15 359 793A	included above	25	125
	H00 131 528★	H00 161 189★	—	150	1,000
	—	H00 192 000★	—	—	—
MINNEAPOLIS	I06 039 187A	I08 890 366A	included above	25	150
	I00 085 944★	I00 086 956★	—	200	1,000
	—	I00 120 000★	—	—	—
KANSAS CITY	J08 842 745A	J11 625 049A	included above	25	125
	J00 161 181★	J00 192 000★	—	200	1,000
DALLAS	K-A	—	included above	—	—
SAN FRANCISCO	L18 656 585A	L23 275 830A	included above	25	125
	—	L00 306 615★	—	150	1,000
	—	L00 312 000★	—	—	—

SERIES 1928C LIGHT VIVID YELLOW-GREEN SEAL

SERIAL NUMBERS: Districts printed continued sequence from previous series.

SIGNATURES: W.O. Woods, Ogden L. Mills

Serial Numbers

	Low	High	Notes Printed	VF	CH CU	GEM CU
NEW YORK	B69 216 300A	B73 932 140A	2,902,678	$100	$600	$1,000
CLEVELAND	D28 979 453A	D30 433 442A	1,230,428	600	3,500	4,500
	D00 404 401★	D00 405 892★	—15,000		50,000	—
	—	D00 420 000★	official high	—	—	—
RICHMOND	E16 516 319A	E17 554 338A	304,800	3,000	10,500	15,000
ATLANTA	none reported	—	688,380	—	—	—
CHICAGO	G44 181 072A	G54 885 265A	2,423,400	100	625	1,000

SERIES 1934 LIGHT VIVID YELLOW-GREEN SEAL

SERIAL NUMBERS: Both regular and star notes begin at 00 000 001.

PLATE NUMBERS: Face numbers begin with number 1. Back numbers continue from previous series.

SIGNATURES: W.A. Julian, Henry Morgenthau, Jr.

Total 1934 quantities printed listed under dark green seal series 1934.

Serial Numbers

	Low	High	Notes Printed	VF	CH CU
BOSTON	A00 060 273A	A21 304 868A	—	$20	$100
	A00 079 393★	A00 274 745★	—	80	800
NEW YORK	B00 000 003A	B74 735 451A	—	20	75
	B00 043 761★	B00 581 530★	—	100	650

	Low	High	Notes Printed	VF	CH CU
PHILADELPHIA	C00 000 005A	C14 386 107A	—	$20	$100
	C00 020 020★	C00 209 892★	—	100	800
CLEVELAND	D00 000 003A	D14 187 607A	—	20	100
	D00 007 123★	D00 154 216★	—	100	900
RICHMOND	E00 000 001A	E06 350 892A	—	20	120
	E00 023 280★	—	—	300	1,500
ATLANTA	F00 461 550A	F10 509 569A	—	30	150
	F00 023 231★	F00 052 036★	—	200	1,100
CHICAGO	G00 001 771A	G34 592 204A	—	20	100
	G00 040 505★	—	—	65	800
ST. LOUIS	H00 030 906A	H08 784 236A	—	20	120
	H00 005 346★	H00 137 913★	—	100	800
MINNEAPOLIS	I00 040 238A	I08 333 187A	—	20	150
	I00 008 963★	I00 073 777★	—	300	1,200
KANSAS CITY	J00 212 305A	J01 409 290A	—	20	100
	J00 012 904★	J00 075 712★	—	100	900
DALLAS	K00 309 695A	K02 371 046A	—	20	400
	K-★	—	—	300	1,800
SAN FRANCISCO	L00 242 668A	L16 347 529A	—	20	100
	L00 022 408★	L00 108 655★	—	200	1,500

SERIES 1934 DARK BLUE-GREEN SEAL

SERIAL NUMBERS: All districts continue sequence from 1934 light vivid yellow-green seal variety.

PLATE NUMBERS: Face numbers and back numbers continue from 1934 light vivid yellow-green seals up to back number 584.

Quantities include all types and variations.

SIGNATURES: W.A. Julian, Henry Morgenthau, Jr.

	Serial Numbers				
	Low	High	Notes Printed	VF	CH CU
BOSTON	A24 853 268A	A43 886 186A	46,276,152	$20	$100
	A00 309 090★	A00 599 085★	—	100	500
NEW YORK	B75 403 258A	B93 067 909A	—	15	75
	B04 420 169B	B09 971 355B	117,298,008	50	100
	B00 511 809★	B01 321 512★	795,826	60	300
PHILADELPHIA	C14 964 541A	C40 023 082A	34,770,768	15	75
	C00 226 168★	C00 396 514★	—	80	400
CLEVELAND	D17 673 101A	D26 499 575A	28,764,108	15	75
	D00 258 536★	D00 312 892★	—	100	450
RICHMOND	E11 422 882A	E16 333 750A	16,437,252	15	100
	E-★	—	—	150	700
ATLANTA	F10 464 968A	F28 851 008A	20,656,872	15	75
	F-★	—	—	150	700
CHICAGO	—	G73 692 498A	69,972,064	15	75
	G00 204 995★	G00 782 752★	—	75	375
ST. LOUIS	H07 296 150A	H20 299 417A	22,593,204	15	90
	H00 159 082★	H00 312 325★	—	80	450

	Low	High	Notes Printed	VF	CH CU
MINNEAPOLIS	I07 405 455A	I11 368 326A	16,840,980	$15	$120
	I00 123 464★	I00 123 866★	—	125	500
KANSAS CITY	J02 882 622A	J26 262 020A	22,627,824	15	75
	J00 174 654★	J00 891 972★	—	70	400
DALLAS	K02 879 500A	K07 952 929A	21,403,488	15	100
SAN FRANCISCO	L19 241 988A	L32 120 664A	37,402,308	15	75
	L00 382 103★	L00 491 987★	—	75	400

SERIES 1934 MULE DARK BLUE-GREEN SEAL

PLATE NUMBERS: Back check numbers 585 and higher.

Serial Numbers

	Low	High	Notes Printed	VF	CH CU
BOSTON	A33 222 723A	A36 720 011A	see above	$20	$50
	A-★	—	—	60	500
NEW YORK	B99 259 354A	B99 975 334A	—	70	200
	B03 735 856B	—	—	70	200
	B01 240 250★	—	—	80	600
PHILADELPHIA	C24 994 911A	C35 839 892A	—	20	50
	C00 153 760★	C00 290 943★	—	60	700
CLEVELAND	D47 320 233A	—	—	20	50
	D-★	—	—	60	500
RICHMOND	E15 838 080A	—	—	20	50
	E00 168 005★	—	—	75	525
ATLANTA	F19 533 829A	F95 924 589A	—	20	50
	F00 336 930★	F01 186 761★	—	50	500
CHICAGO	G53 547 096A	G74 057 546A	—	20	40
	G00 778 732★	G00 932 540★	—	50	500
ST. LOUIS	H15 796 074A	H23 671 097A	—	20	50
	H00 245 528★	H00 282 967★	—	60	600
MINNEAPOLIS	I09 243 549A	I31 039 744A	—	$20	50
	I00 302 548★	I00 379 022★	—	75	600
KANSAS CITY	J13 531 167A	J45 772 513A	—	20	50
	J00 189 869★	J00 646 641★	—	60	500
DALLAS	K09 964 715A	K39 837 504A	—	20	50
	K00 297 430★	K00 353 560★	—	60	500
SAN FRANCISCO	L30 726 913A	L36 866 420A	—	20	50
	L00 393 872★	L00 573 116★	—	60	500

SERIES 1934A MULE GREEN SEAL

SERIAL NUMBERS: All districts continued sequence from previous series.
PLATE NUMBERS: Back numbers 584 and lower.
SIGNATURES: W.A. Julian, Henry Morgenthau, Jr.

	Serial Numbers				
	Low	**High**	**Notes Printed**	**VF**	**CH CU**
BOSTON	A42 585 050A	A62 535 662A	see above	$25	$200
	A-★	—	—	—	—
NEW YORK	B02 997 501B	B74 184 901B	—	25	100
	B01 117 228★	B01 439 995★	—	225	800
PHILADELPHIA	C31 934 000A	C40 083 516A	—	25	100
	C00 396 514★	C00 457 415★	—	225	900
CLEVELAND	D27 564 857A	D50 366 255A	—	25	150
	D00 390 853★	—	—	—	—
RICHMOND	E16 396 469A	E24 997 557A	—	25	200
	E-★	—	—	—	—
ATLANTA	F13 953 881A	F16 766 480A	—	25	250
	F-★	—	—	—	—
CHICAGO	G58 564 719A	G98 991 329A	—	25	100
	G01 880 033B	G04 065 027B	—	150	500
	G00 844 199★	G01 050 020★	—	225	800
ST. LOUIS	H-A	—	—	—	—
	H-★	—	—	—	—
MINNEAPOLIS	I10 866 264A	I15 365 852A	—	25	225
	I-★	—	—	—	—
KANSAS CITY	J-A	—	—	—	—
	J-★	—	—	—	—
DALLAS	K-A	—	—	—	—
	K-★	—	—	—	—
SAN FRANCISCO	L35 181 194A	L36 687 863A	—	50	225
	L-★	—	—	—	—

SERIES 1934A GREEN SEAL

SERIAL NUMBERS: All districts continued sequence from previous series.

PLATE NUMBERS: Back numbers begin at 585.

SIGNATURES: W.A. Julian, Henry Morgenthau, Jr.

	Serial Numbers				
	Low	**High**	**Notes Printed**	**VF**	**CH CU**
BOSTON	A48 747 019A	—	104,540,088	$11	$40
	—	A44 222 363B	—	11	40
	A00 605 352★	A01 801 501★	—	30	250
NEW YORK	B15 273 644B	—	281,940,996	11	40
	B-C	—	—	11	40
	—	B90 870 463D	—	11	40
	B01 558 862★	B05 097 497★	—	35	200
PHILADELPHIA	C32 791 370A	—	95,338,032	11	40
	—	C27 992 286B	—	11	40
	C00 376 834★	C01 523 585★	—	30	250
CLEVELAND	D33 849 644A	—	93,332,004	11	40
	—	D16 897 839B	—	15	45
	D00 443 789★	D01 515 627★	—	30	250
RICHMOND	E17 288 754A	—	101,037,912	11	40
	—	E14 497 070B	—	12.50	40
	E00 369 502★	E01 455 171★	—	40	250
ATLANTA	F15 665 042A	F97 932 586A	85,478,160	11	40
	F03 361 159B	F03 361 160B	—	200	500
	F00 282 524★	F01 235 695★	—	30	400
CHICAGO	G70 175 527A	—	177,295,960	11	25
	G-B	—	—	11	25
	—	G37 851 417C	—	11	25
	G00 783 328★	G03 144 001★	—	35	200
ST. LOUIS	H21 555 664A	H69 807 802A	50,694,312	11	40
	H00 348 164★	H00 857 792★	—	40	250
MINNEAPOLIS	I09 243 570A	I31 945 441A	16,340,016	15	50
	I00 182 459★	I00 379 905★	—	50	400
KANSAS CITY	J18 160 353A	J52 984 711A	31,069,978	11	40
	J00 237 441★	J00 658 987★	—	40	250
DALLAS	K13 954 086A	K46 508 148A	28,263,156	11	45
	K00 171 229★	K00 342 700★	—	75	400
SAN FRANCISCO	L34 990 684A	—	125,537,592	11	45
	—	L56 227 931B	—	11	45
	L00 555 617★	L02 195 312★	—	60	300

HAWAII NOTES

SERIES 1934A BROWN SEAL

SIGNATURES: Same as Series 1934A Green Seal Notes.

Serial Numbers Official

Low	High	Notes Printed	VG-F	VF	CH CU	GEM CU
L65 856 001**A**	L66 456 000**A**	600,000	$75	$125	$1,300	$2,250
L67 476 001**A**	L69 076 000**A**	1,600,000	75	125	1,300	2,250
L69 736 001**A**	L71 336 000**A**	1,600,000	75	125	1,300	2,250
L77 052 001**A**	L77 172 000**A**	120,000	75	125	1,300	2,250
L11 160 001**B**	L12 664 000**B**	1,504,000	75	125	1,300	2,250
L28 212 001**B**	L29 712 000**B**	1,500,000	75	125	1,300	2,250
L43 032 001**B**	L45 532 000**B**	2,500,000	75	125	1,300	2,250
L50 292 001**B**	L51 292 000**B**	1,000,000	75	125	1,300	2,250
L00 900 001★	L00 996 000★	96,000	1,000	1,500	10,000	—
L02 008 001★	L02 012 000★	4,000	1,250	2,000	12,000	—
L02 040 001★	L02 048 000★	8,000	1,250	2,000	12,000	—
	L02 048 925★(Observed)					

FEDERAL RESERVE NOTES

SERIES 1934B GREEN SEAL

SERIAL NUMBERS: All districts continued sequence from previous series.

SIGNATURES: W.A. Julian, Fred M. Vinson

	Serial Numbers				
	Low	**High**	**Notes Printed**	**VF**	**CH CU**
BOSTON	A38 659 831B	A46 068 132B	3,999,600	$30	$150
	A01 820 686★	A01 897 603★	—	125	700
NEW YORK	B75 316 369D	—	—	25	75
	—	B17 311 144E	34,815,948	25	75
	B05 092 596★	B05 660 947★	—	70	450
PHILADELPHIA	C22 408 785B	C35 564 386B	10,339,020	25	100
	C01 506 231★	C01 660 619★	—	100	700
CLEVELAND	D17 711 381B	D29 697 457B	1,394,700	40	200
	D00 713 068★	D01 577 755★	—	250	1,250
RICHMOND	E11 800 489B	E17 995 646B	4,018,272	30	175
	E01 532 800★	—	—	175	900
ATLANTA	F98 652 001A (official)				
	F98 897 597A	F99 986 763A	—	300	2,000
	F00 012 420B	F08 434 271B	6,746,076	25	100
	F01 295 129★	—	—	250	1,000
CHICAGO	G31 631 360C	G48 967 953C	18,130,836	25	75
	G03 032 893★	G03 237 729★	—	70	450
ST. LOUIS	H69 891 088A	H78 814 225A	6,849,348	30	100
	H00 879 214★	H00 952 702★	—	125	700
MINNEAPOLIS	I31 401 771A	I33 682 979A	2,254,800	40	150
	I00 411 219★	—	—	250	1,500
KANSAS CITY	J50 864 742A	J54 813 813A	3,835,764	30	125
	J00 696 592★	J00 729 624★	—	125	700
DALLAS	K46 673 651A	K49 430 212A	3,085,200	40	150
	K00 588 386★	K00 628 433★	—	150	1,500
SAN FRANCISCO	L54 276 070B	L63 525 795B	9,076,800	30	100
	L02 264 852★	L02 274 853★	—	100	700

SERIES 1934C GREEN SEAL - WIDE FACE

SIGNATURES: W.A. Julian, John W. Snyder

	Serial Numbers				
	Low	**High**	**Notes Printed**	**VF**	**CH CU**
BOSTON	A46 727 409B	A89 677 869B	42,431,404	$12	$50
	A01 993 200★	A02 576 330★	—	60	400
NEW YORK	B14 341 429E	—	—	12	40
	—	B79 629 354F	115,675,644	12	40
	B05 666 897★	B07 813 576★	—	40	300
PHILADELPHIA	C33 527 514B	C81 049 029B	46,874,760	12	40
	C01 651 127★	C03 260 509★	—	50	400
CLEVELAND	D19 581 685B	D60 450 693B	33,240,000	12	45
	D01 613 832★	D02 347 709★	—	60	400
RICHMOND	E18 515 459B	E60 388 949B	37,422,600	12	50
	E01 577 111★	E02 123 769★	—	60	500
ATLANTA	F10 012 993B	F51 072 323B	44,838,264	12	50
	F01 344 359★	F02 052 434★	—	60	500
CHICAGO	G49 390 360C	—	105,875,412	12	40
	—	G56 214 961D	—	12	40
	G03 365 550★	G05 361 175★	—	40	300
ST. LOUIS	H75 861 252A	—	—	12	50
	—	H08 645 013B	36,541,404	12	50
	H01 139 716★	H01 556 190★	—	60	400
MINNEAPOLIS	I33 985 183A	I43 165 262A	11,944,848	12	75
	I00 449 979★	I00 596 950★	—	200	1,000
KANSAS CITY	J54 943 948A	J76 918 162A	20,874,072	12	50
	J00 833 311★	J01 162 394★	—	30	400
DALLAS	K50 804 411A	K74 108 012A	25,642,620	12	50
	K00 715 370★	K01 007 384★	—	70	450
SAN FRANCISCO	L64 548 208B	—	—	12	40
	—	L07 215 023C	49,164,480	12	50
	L02 390 457★	L02 575 030★	—	60	500

Wide

Narrow

Wide

SERIES 1934C GREEN SEAL - NARROW FACE

PLATE NUMBERS: Narrow face plates were introduced only on face plates #86, 87, 88 and 89, made for Kansas City in December 1949.

Serial Numbers

	Low	High	Notes Printed	VF	CH CU
KANSAS CITY	J73 832 613A	J74 737 213A	included in K.C. above	—	—
	J-★	—	—	—	—

SERIES 1934D GREEN SEAL

SERIAL NUMBERS: All districts continued sequence from previous series.

SIGNATURES: Georgia Neese Clark, John W. Snyder

Serial Numbers

	Low	High	Notes Printed	VF	CH CU
BOSTON	A89 660 775B	—	—	$15	$60
	—	A08 687 876C	19,917,900	15	60
	A02 696 109★	A02 938 568★	—	100	700
NEW YORK	B24 491 097F	B82 977 478F	64,067,904	12	50
	B07 677 496★	B08 337 511★	—	50	450
PHILADELPHIA	C75 769 379B	C94 609 249B	18,432,000	15	60
	C02 424 474★	C02 596 068★	—	70	500
CLEVELAND	D63 413 560B	D78 155 990B	20,291,316	15	60
	D02 341 252★	D02 550 742★	—	70	550

	Low	High	Notes Printed	VF	CH CU
RICHMOND	E53 277 056B	E70 888 045B	18,090,312	$15	$60
	E02 284 763★	—	—	500	1,500
ATLANTA	F50 388 847B	F65 986 683B	17,064,816	15	60
	F02 137 363★	F02 270 202★	—	100	900
CHICAGO	G47 665 115D	—	—	12	50
	—	G01 426 854E	55,943,844	15	75
	G05 113 043★	G05 665 693★	—	50	450
ST. LOUIS	H08 749 772B	H22 822 525B	15,828,048	20	90
	H01 587 975★	H01 767 546★	—	100	800
MINNEAPOLIS	I44 420 066A	I49 054 613A	5,237,220	40	125
	I00 606 556★	I00 662 768★	—	250	1,400
KANSAS CITY	J74 877 813A	J81 778 613A	7,992,000	25	100
	J01 157 532★	J01 178 082★	—	100	800
DALLAS	K73 073 191A	K80 705 334A	7,178,196	25	100
	K01 089 187★	—	—	300	1,400
SAN FRANCISCO	L06 545 257C	L27 559 874C	23,956,584	15	75
	L03 304 041★	—	—	300	1,200

SERIES 1950 WIDE GREEN SEAL

SERIAL NUMBERS: All districts both regular and star notes begin with 00 000 001. Official 1950 high serials for both varieties are shown below.

PLATE NUMBERS: Face numbers begin at #1. Back #1389 and lower.

SIGNATURES: Georgia Neese Clark, John W. Snyder

Notes printed shown below include both Wide and Narrow varieties of this series.

Serial Numbers Official

	Low	High	Notes Printed	VF	CH CU
BOSTON	A00 000 001A	A70 992 000A	70,992,000	$12	$80
	A00 006 794★	A01 008 000★	1,008,000	60	500
NEW YORK	B00 000 001A	—	99,999,999	2	75
	B-B	—	99,999,999	12	75
	—	B18 576 000C	18,576,000	12	100
	B00 838 900★	B03 168 000★	2,568,000	50	400
PHILADELPHIA	C00 000 001A	C76 320 000A	76,320,000	12	75
	C00 170 931★	C01 008 000★	1,008,000	60	500
CLEVELAND	D00 000 001A	D76 320 000A	76,320,000	12	75
	D00 057 812★	D01 008 000★	1,008,000	60	500
RICHMOND	E00 000 001A	E61 776 000A	61,776,000	12	75
	E00 390 446★	E00 876 000★	876,000	80	500

	Low	High	Notes Printed	VF	CH CU
ATLANTA	F00 000 001A	F63 792 000A	63,792,000	$12	$75
	—	F00 864 000★	864,000	80	500
CHICAGO	G00 000 001A	—	99,999,999	12	70
	—	G61 056 000B	61,056,000	12	70
	G00 002 101★	G02 088 000★	2,088,000	50	500
ST. LOUIS	H00 000 001A	H47 808 000A	47,808,000	12	75
	H00 012 570★	H00 648 000★	648,000	80	600
MINNEAPOLIS	I00 000 001A	I18 864 000A	18,864,000	12	90
	I00 125 830★	I00 252 000★	252,000	150	900
KANSAS CITY	J00 000 001A	J36 332 000A	36,332,000	12	75
	J00 178 200★	J00 456 000★	456,000	80	600
DALLAS	K00 000 077A	K33 264 000A	33,264,000	12	75
	K00 021 119★	K00 480 000★	480,000	80	600
SAN FRANCISCO	L00 000 001A	L76 896 000A	76,896,000	12	75
	L00 028 524★	L01 152 000★	1,152,000	60	600

SERIES 1950 NARROW GREEN SEAL

PLATE NUMBERS: Back numbers 1390-1456 (Last of the 12 subject sheets).

Serial Numbers

	Low	High	Notes Printed	VF	CH CU
BOSTON	A41 691 014A	A65 931 748A	see above	$25	$150
	A00 738 597★	A00 893 802★	—	150	750
NEW YORK	B41 715 573B	—	—	25	150
	—	B17 034 049C	—	75	600
	—	B02 213 030★	—	150	750
PHILADELPHIA	C45 571 678A	C74 610 569A	—	25	150
	C00 612 404★	C00 768 251★	—	150	750
CLEVELAND	D48 081 316A	D73 362 602A	—	25	150
	D00 820 570★	—	—	150	750
RICHMOND	E43 772 722A	E53 905 422A	—	25	150
	E00 744 397★	E00 765 688★	—	150	750
ATLANTA	F46 651 804A	F50 120 991A	—	30	150
CHICAGO	G96 --- ---A	—	—	—	—
	G10 793 067B	G52 719 263B	—	25	150
	G01 191 814★	G01 413 337★	—	150	750
ST. LOUIS	H27 407 447A	H46 745 726A	—	25	150
	H00 443 068★	H00 516 252★	—	150	750
MINNEAPOLIS	I11 433 063A	I17 068 904A	—	30	200
	I00 203 309★	I00 210 831★	—	200	1,000
KANSAS CITY	J20 405 730A	J32 420 498A	—	25	175
	J00 277 729★	J00 375 239★	—	150	750
DALLAS	K18 202 369A	K31 415 982A	—	25	175
	K00 214 035★	K00 339 998★	—	150	750
SAN FRANCISCO	L54 597 305A	L66 999 612A	—	25	150
	L00 850 039★	—	—	150	750

SERIES 1950A GREEN SEAL

SERIAL NUMBERS: All numbers shown are official and continue in sequence from previous series.

SIGNATURES: Ivy Baker Priest, G.M. Humphrey

	Serial Numbers				
	Low	**High**	**Notes Printed**	**VF**	**CH CU**
BOSTON	A70 992 001A	—	104,248,000	$12	$70
	—	A75 240 000B	—	12	70
	A01 008 001★	A06 120 000★	5,112,000	40	250
NEW YORK	B18 576 001C	B-D, B-E	356,664,000	12	70
	—	B75 240 000F	—	12	70
	B03 168 001★	B20 160 000★	16,992,000	40	150
PHILADELPHIA	C76 320 001A	—	73,920,000	12	90
	—	C48 240 000B	—	12	70
	C01 008 001★	C04 680 000★	3,672,000	40	300
CLEVELAND	D76 032 001A	—	75,088,000	12	60
	—	D51 120 000B	—	12	70
	D01 008 001★	D04 680 000★	3,672,000	40	300
RICHMOND	E61 776 001A	—	82,144,000	12	70
	—	E43 920 000B	—	12	70
	E01 008 001★	E05 400 000★	4,392,000	40	300
ATLANTA	F63 792 001A	—	73,288,000	12	90
	—	F37 080 000B	—	12	70
	F00 864 001★	F04 680 000★	3,816,000	40	300
CHICAGO	G61 056 001B	G-C	235,064,000	12	60
	—	G96 120 000D	—	12	60
	G02 160 001★	G13 320 000★	11,160,000	40	250
		G13 643 180★(observed)			
ST. LOUIS	H47 808 001A	H94 320 000A	46,512,000	12	60
	H00 720 001★	H03 600 000★	2,880,000	40	250
MINNEAPOLIS	I18 864 001A	I27 000 000A	8,136,000	12	100
	I00 288 001★	I00 720 000★	482,000	40	300
KANSAS CITY	J36 432 001A	J61 920 000A	25,488,000	12	70
	J00 576 001★	J02 880 000★	2,304,000	40	300
DALLAS	K33 264 001A	K55 080 000A	21,816,000	12	70
	K00 576 001★	K02 160 000★	1,584,000	40	350
SAN FRANCISCO	L76 896 001A	—	101,584,000	12	60
	—	L78 480 000B	—	12	60
	L01 152 001★	L07 560 000★	6,408,000	40	200

SERIES 1950B GREEN SEAL

SIGNATURES: Ivy Baker Priest, Robert B. Anderson

	Serial Numbers			
	Low	**High**	**Notes Printed**	**CH CU**
BOSTON	A75 240 001B	—	49,240,000	$40
	—	A24 480 000C	—	40
	A06 120 001★	A09 000 000★	2,880,000	150
NEW YORK	B75 240 001F	B-G	170,840,000	35
	—	B46 080 000H	—	35
	B20 160 001★	B28 440 000★	8,280,000	125
PHILADELPHIA	C48 240 001B	—	66,880,000	35
	—	C15 120 000C	—	35
	C04 680 001★	C07 920 000★	3,240,000	150
CLEVELAND	D51 120 001B	—	55,360,000	40
	—	D06 480 000C	—	45
	D04 680 001★	D07 560 000★	2,880,000	150
RICHMOND	E43 920 001B	E95 040 000B	51,120,000	40
	E05 400 001★	E08 280 000★	2,880,000	150
ATLANTA	F37 080 001B	—	66,520,000	35
	—	F03 600 000C	—	75
	F04 680 001★	F07 560 000★	2,880,000	150
CHICAGO	G96 120 001D	G-E	165,080,000	35
	—	G61 200 000F	—	32
	G13 680 001★	G20 160 000★	6,480,000	125
ST. LOUIS	H94 320 001A	—	33,040,000	40
	—	H27 360 000B	—	40
	H03 600 001★	H05 400 000★	1,800,000	170
MINNEAPOLIS	I27 000 001A	I40 320 000A	13,320,000	40
	I00 720 001★	I01 440 000★	720,000	300
KANSAS CITY	J61 920 001A	J95 400 000A	33,480,000	40
	J02 880 001★	J05 400 000★	2,520,000	150
DALLAS	K55 080 001A	K81 360 000A	26,280,000	40
	K02 160 001★	K03 600 000★	1,440,000	300
SAN FRANCISCO	L78 480 001B	—	55,000,000	40
	—	L33 480 000C	—	40
	L07 560 001★	L10 440 000★	2,880,000	150

SERIES 1950C GREEN SEAL

SIGNATURES: Elizabeth Rudel Smith, C. Douglas Dillon

	Serial Numbers			
	Low	**High**	**Notes Printed**	**CH CU**
BOSTON	A24 480 001C	A75 600 000C	51,120,000	$50
	A09 000 001★	A11 160 000★	2,160,000	300
NEW YORK	B46 080 001H	—	120,520,000	50
	—	B66 600 000I	—	50
	B28 440 001★	B35 280 000★	6,840,000	200
PHILADELPHIA	C15 120 001C	C40 320 000C	25,200,000	50
	C07 920 001★	C08 640 000★	720,000	300
CLEVELAND	D06 480 001C	D39 600 000C	33,120,000	75
	D07 560 001★	D09 360 000★	1,800,000	300
RICHMOND	E95 040 001B	—	45,640,000	55
	—	E40 680 000C	—	50
	E08 280 001★	E10 080 000★	1,800,000	350
ATLANTA	F03 600 001C	F42 480 000C	38,800,000	50
	F07 560 001★	F09 360 000★	1,800,000	350
CHICAGO	G61 200 001F	—	69,400,000	50
	—	G30 600 000G	—	50
	G20 160 001★	G23 760 000★	3,600,000	150
ST. LOUIS	H27 360 001B	H50 400 000B	23,040,000	75
	H05 400 001★	H06 480 000★	1,080,000	250
MINNEAPOLIS	I40 320 001A	I49 320 000A	9,000,000	85
	I01 440 001★	I02 160 000★	720,000	300

	Low	High	Notes Printed	CH CU
KANSAS CITY	J95 400 001A	—	23,320,000	$90
	—	J18 720 000B	—	75
	J05 680 001★	J06 480 000★	800,000	250
DALLAS	K81 360 001A	K99 000 000A	17,640,000	75
	K03 600 001★	K04 320 000★	720,000	250
SAN FRANCISCO	L33 480 001C	L69 120 000C	35,640,000	85
	L10 440 001★	L12 240 000★	1,800,000	250

SERIES 1950D GREEN SEAL

SIGNATURES: Kathryn O'Hay Granahan, C. Douglas Dillon

Serial Numbers

	Low	High	Notes Printed	CH CU
BOSTON	A75 600 001C	—	38,800,000	$50
	—	A14 400 000D	—	50
	A11 160 001★	A12 960 000★	1,800,000	200
NEW YORK	B66 600 001I	B-J	150,320,000	45
	—	B16 920 000K	—	45
	B35 280 001★	B42 120 000★	6,840,000	150
PHILADELPHIA	C40 320 001C	C59 400 000C	19,080,000	55
	C08 640 001★	C09 720 000★	1,080,000	200
CLEVELAND	D39 600 001C	D63 720 000C	24,120,000	55
	D09 360 001★	D10 800 000★	1,440,000	200
RICHMOND	E40 680 001C	E74 520 000C	33,840,000	55
	E10 080 001★	E11 520 000★	1,440,000	250
		E11 572 280★ (observed)		
ATLANTA	F42 480 001C	F78 480 000C	36,000,000	50
	F09 360 001★	F10 800 000★	1,440,000	250
CHICAGO	G30 600 001G	—	115,480,000	50
	—	G46 080 000H	—	50
	G23 760 001★	G28 800 000★	5,040,000	150
ST. LOUIS	H50 400 001B	H60 840 000B	10,440,000	55
	H06 480 001★	H07 200 000★	720,000	50
MINNEAPOLIS	none printed	—	—	—
KANSAS CITY	J18 720 001B	J34 200 000B	15,480,000	50
	J06 480 001★	J07 560 000★	1,080,000	250
DALLAS	K99 000 001A	—	18,280,000	75
	—	K17 280 000B	—	50
	K04 600 001★	K05 400 000★	800,000	275
SAN FRANCISCO	L69 120 001C	—	62,560,000	50
	—	L31 680 000D	—	50
	L12 240 001★	L15 840 000★	3,600,000	240

SERIES 1950E GREEN SEAL

PLATE NUMBERS: Highest face used #512. Highest back used #1839. (Last of 18 subject sheets)

SIGNATURES: Kathryn O'Hay Granahan, Henry H. Fowler

	Serial Numbers				
	Low	**High**	**Notes Printed**	**CH CU**	**GEM CU**
NEW YORK	B16 920 001K	B54 720 000K	37,800,000	$100	$125
	B42 120 001★	B44 821 038★	2,880,000	300	400
CHICAGO	G46 080 001H	—	65,080,000	100	125
	—	G11 160 000I	—	125	150
	G28 800 001★	G33 120 000★	4,320,000	300	400
SAN FRANCISCO	L31 680 001D	L48 960 000D	17,280,000	125	150
	L15 840 001★	L16 560 000★	720,000	400	600

SERIES 1963 GREEN SEAL

SERIAL NUMBERS: All serial numbers of both regular and star notes begin with 00 000 001.

PLATE NUMBERS: Face and back check begin with #1. Motto "IN GOD WE TRUST" added to back.

SIGNATURES: Kathryn O'Hay Granahan, C. Douglas Dillon

	Serial Numbers	**Notes Printed**	**CH CU**
BOSTON	A-A	5,760,000	$50
	A-★	640,000	120
NEW YORK	B-A	24,960,000	50
	B-★	1,920,000	80

	Serial Numbers	Notes Printed	CH CU
PHILADELPHIA	C-A	6,400,000	$50
	C-★	1,280,000	80
CLEVELAND	D-A	7,040,000	50
	D-★	640,000	100
RICHMOND	E-A	4,480,000	50
	E-★	640,000	120
ATLANTA	F-A	10,880,000	50
	F-★	1,280,000	80
CHICAGO	G-A	35,200,000	50
	G-★	2,560,000	80
ST. LOUIS	H-A	13,440,000	75
	H-★	1,280,000	80
MINNEAPOLIS	not issued	—	—
KANSAS CITY	J00 000 077A	3,840,000	70
	J00 000 077★	640,000	120
	J00 000 002★	—	—
DALLAS	K-A	5,120,000	70
	K-★	640,000	120
SAN FRANCISCO	L-A	14,080,000	60
	L-★	1,280,000	100

SERIES 1963A GREEN SEAL

SERIAL NUMBERS: All districts continue sequence from previous series.

SIGNATURES: Kathryn O'Hay Granahan, Henry H. Fowler

	Serial Numbers		Notes Printed	CH CU
	Low	**High**		
BOSTON	A05 760 001A	A99 999 999A	94,240,000	$40
	A00 000 001B	A37 120 000B	37,120,000	40
	A00 640 001★	A07 040 000★	6,400,000	75
NEW YORK	B24 960 001A	—	75,040,000	37.50
	B-B	—	99,999,999	37.50
	—	B24 320 000C	24,320,000	37.50
	B01 920 000★	B11 520 000★	9,600,000	70

	Low	High	Notes Printed	CH CU
PHILADELPHIA	C06 400 001A	—	93,600,000	$37.50
	—	C06 400 000B	6,400,000	50
	C01 280 001★	C05 760 000★	4,480,000	70
CLEVELAND	D07 040 001A	D80 000 000A	72,960,000	37.50
	D00 064 001★	D04 480 000★	3,840,000	70
RICHMOND	E04 480 001A	—	95,520,000	37.50
	—	E19 200 000B	14,720,000	37.50
	E00 640 001★	E05 760 000★	5,120,000	70
ATLANTA	F10 880 001A	F90 880 000A	80,000,000	37.50
	F01 280 001★	F05 120 000★	3,840,000	70
CHICAGO	G35 200 001A	—	64,800,000	37.50
	G-B	—	99,999,999	37.50
	—	G37 200 000C	37,200,000	37.50
	G02 560 001★	G12 160 000★	9,600,000	70
ST. LOUIS	H13 440 001A	H56 960 000A	43,520,000	37.50
	H01 280 001★	H03 200 000★	1,920,000	70
MINNEAPOLIS	I00 000 001A	I16 640 000A	16,640,000	37.50
	I00 000 001★	I00 640 000★	640,000	90
KANSAS CITY	J03 840 001A	J35 200 000A	31,260,000	37.50
	J00 640 001★	J02 560 000★	1,920,000	70
DALLAS	K05 120 001A	K56 320 000A	51,200,000	37.50
	K00 640 001★	K02 560 000★	1,920,000	70
SAN FRANCISCO	L14 080 001A	—	87,200,000	37.50
	—	L01 280 000B	—	50
	L01 280 001★	L06 400 000★	5,120,000	70

SERIES 1969 GREEN SEAL

SERIAL NUMBERS: All serial numbers of both regular and star notes begin with 00 000 001.

SIGNATURES: Dorothy Andrews Elston, David M. Kennedy

	Serial Numbers	Notes Printed	CH CU
BOSTON	A-A	74,880,000	$37.50
	A-★	2,560,000	70
NEW YORK	B-A	99,999,999	37.50
	B-B	99,999,999	37.50

	Serial Numbers	Notes Printed	CH CU
	B-C	47,360,000	$37.50
	B-★	10,240,000	70
PHILADELPHIA	C-A	56,960,000	37.50
	C-★	2,560,000	70
CLEVELAND	D-A	57,600,000	37.50
	D-★	2,560,000	100
RICHMOND	E-A	56,960,000	37.50
	E-★	2,560,000	100
ATLANTA	F-A	53,760,000	37.50
	F-★	2,560,000	70
CHICAGO	G-A	99,999,999	37.50
	G-B	42,240,000	37.50
	G-★	6,400,000	70
ST. LOUIS	H-A	22,400,000	37.50
	H-★	640,000	200
MINNEAPOLIS	I-A	12,800,000	37.50
	I-★	1,280,000	70
KANSAS CITY	J-A	31,360,000	37.50
	J-★	1,280,000	70
DALLAS	K-A	30,080,000	37.50
	K-★	1,280,000	70
SAN FRANCISCO	L-A	56,320,000	37.50
	L-★	3,185,000	70

SERIES 1969A GREEN SEAL

SERIAL NUMBERS: All districts continue sequence from previous series.
SIGNATURES: Dorothy Andrews Kabis, John B. Connally

	Serial Numbers		Notes Printed	CH CU
	Low	High		
BOSTON	A74 880 001A	—	27,120,000	$35
	—	A16 000 000B	16,000,000	35
	A02 560 001★	A04 480 000★	1,920,000	60

	Low	High	Notes Printed	CH CU
NEW YORK	B47 360 001C	—	52,240,000	$35
	—	B59 520 000D	59,520,000	35
	B10 240 001★	B14 080 000★	3,840,000	60
PHILADELPHIA	C56 960 001A	C81 280 000A	24,320,000	45
	C01 920 001★	C03 840 000★	1,920,000	60
CLEVELAND	D57 600 001A	D81 280 000A	23,680,000	45
	D02 560 001★	D03 836 000★	1,276,000	60
RICHMOND	E56 960 001A	E82 560 000A	25,600,000	40
	E02 560 001★	E03 200 000★	640,000	75
ATLANTA	F53 760 001A	F74 240 000A	20,480,000	45
	F02 560 000★	F03 200 000★	640,000	75
CHICAGO	G42 240 001B	—	47,760,000	35
	—	G22 400 000C	22,400,000	35
	G06 400 001★	G08 960 000★	3,560,000	60
ST. LOUIS	H22 400 001A	H37 760 000A	15,360,000	35
	H00 640 001★	H01 280 000★	640,000	75
MINNEAPOLIS	I12 800 001A	I21 120 000A	8,320,000	45
	No star notes printed.—		—	—
KANSAS CITY	J31 360 001A	J42 240 000A	10,880,000	40
	No star notes printed.			
DALLAS	K30 080 001A	K50 560 000A	20,480,000	45
	K01 280 001★	K01 920 000★	640,000	60
SAN FRANCISCO	L56 320 001A	L83 840 000A	27,520,000	40
	L03 200 001★	L04 480,000★	1,280,000	75

SERIES 1969B GREEN SEAL

SERIAL NUMBERS: All districts continue sequence from previous series.

SIGNATURES: Romana Acosta Banuelos, John B. Connally

Serial Numbers

	Low	High	Notes Printed	CH CU
BOSTON	A16 000 001B	A32 640 000B	16,640,000	$175
	No star notes printed.—		—	—
NEW YORK	B59 520 001D	—	60,320,000	150
	—	B19 840 000E	—	150
	B14 080 001★	B16 000 000★	1,920,000	200
	—	B15 799 442★	—	—
PHILADELPHIA	C81 280 001A	C93 080 000A	12,800,000	150
		C96 262 606A (observed)		
	No star notes printed.			

	Low	High	Notes Printed	CH CU
CLEVELAND	**D**81 280 001**A**	**D**94 080 000**A**	12,800,000	$150
	No star notes printed.			
RICHMOND	**E**82 560 001**A**	**E**94 720 000**A**	12,160,000	150
	E03 200 001★	**E**03 840 000★	640,000	350
	E03 299 199★	**E**03 324 719★	—	—
ATLANTA	**F**74 240 001**A**	**F**87 680 000**A**	13,440,000	150
	F03 200 001★	**F**03 840 000★	640,000	300
	—	**F**03 795 505★	—	—
CHICAGO	**G**22 400 001**C**	**G**55 040 000**C**	32,640,000	150
	G08 960 001★		1,040,000	250
	—	**G**09 821 505★	—	—
ST. LOUIS	**H**37 760 001**A**	**H**46 720 000**A**	8,960,000	150
	H01 280 001★	**H**02 560 000★	1,280,000	250
	H01 571 111★	—	—	—
MINNEAPOLIS	**I**21 120 001**A**	**I**24 320 000**A**	3,200,000	225
	No star notes printed.			
KANSAS CITY	**J**42 240 001**A**	**J**47 360 000**A**	5,120,000	175
	J01 280 001★	**J**01 920 000★	640,000	350
DALLAS	**K**50 560 001**A**	**K**56 320 000**A**	5,760,000	150
	No star notes printed.			
SAN FRANCISCO	**L**83 840 001**A**	—	23,840,000	150
	—	**L**07 680 000**B**	—	150
	L04 000 001★	**L**05 120 000★	640,000	350

SERIES 1969C GREEN SEAL

SERIAL NUMBERS: All districts continue sequence from previous series.

SIGNATURES: Romana Acosta Banuelos, George P. Shultz

	Serial Numbers			
	Low	High	Notes Printed	CH CU
BOSTON	**A**32 640 001**B**	**A**77 440 000**B**	44,800,000	$40
	A04 480 001★	**A**05 120 000★	640,000	125
NEW YORK	**B**19 840 001**E**	—	81,160,000	40
	B-F	—	99,999,999	40
	—	**B**23 040 000**G**	23,040,000	40
	B16 000 001★	**B**23 040 000★	7,040,000	75
PHILADELPHIA	**C**97 280 000**A**	—	2,720,000	50
	—	**C**67 200 000**B**	67,200,000	50
	C03 840 001★	**C**05 120 000★	1,280,000	80

	Low	High	Notes Printed	CH CU
CLEVELAND	D94 080 001**A**	—	5,920,000	$40
	—	D40 960 000**B**	40,960,000	40
	D03 836 001★	D06 400 000★	2,564,000	80
RICHMOND	E94 720 001**A**	—	5,280,000	40
	—	E40 320 000**B**	40,320,000	40
	E03 840 001★	E05 120 000★	1,280,000	100
ATLANTA	F87 680 001**A**	—	12,320,000	40
	—	F33 920 000**B**	33,920,000	40
	F03 840 001★	F05 760 000★	1,920,000	80
CHICAGO	G55 040 001**C**	—	44,960,000	40
	—	G10 240 000**D**	10,240,000	40
	G10 000 001★	G10 880 000★	880,000	100
ST. LOUIS	H46 720 001**A**	H76 520 000**A**	29,800,000	40
	H02 560 001★	H03 840 000★	1,280,000	100
MINNEAPOLIS	I24 320 001**A**	I35 840 000**A**	11,520,000	40
	I01 280 001★	I01 920 000★	640,000	140
KANSAS CITY	J47 360 001**A**	J70 400 000**A**	23,040,000	40
	J01 920 001★	J02 560 000★	640,000	120
DALLAS	K56 320 001**A**	K81 280 000**A**	24,960,000	40
	K01 920 000★	K02 560 000★	640,000	120
SAN FRANCISCO	L07 680 001**B**	L65 650 000**B**	56,960,000	40
	L05 120 001★	L05 760 000★	640,000	120

SERIES 1974 GREEN SEAL

SIGNATURES: Francine I. Neff, William E. Simon

SERIAL NUMBERS: Continued from previous series.

Serial Numbers

	Low	High	Notes Printed	CH CU
BOSTON	A77 440 001**B**	A99 999 999**B**	22,559,999	$35
	A00 000 001**C**	A81 920 000**C**	81,920,000	35
	A05 120 001★	A07 680 000★	2,048,000	70
NEW YORK	B23 040 001**G**	B99 999 999**G**	76,960,000	35
	B-H	—	99,999,999	35
	B00 000 00**I**	B62 080 000**I**	62,080,000	35
	B23 040 001★	B27 520 000★	3,712,000	70
PHILADELPHIA	C67 200 001**B**	C99 999 999**B**	32,799,999	35
	C00 000 001**C**	C36 480 000**C**	36,480,000	35
	C05 120 001★	C07 680 000★	2,560,000	70
CLEVELAND	D40 960 001**B**	D99 999 999**B**	59,039,999	35
	D00 000 001**C**	D23 040 000**C**	23,040,000	35

	Low	High	Notes Printed	CH CU
	D06 400 001★	D07 936 807★	640,000	$70
RICHMOND	E40 320 001B	E99 999 999B	59,680,000	40
	E00 000 001C	E46 080 000C	46,080,000	40
	E05 120 001★	E07 040 000★	1,920,000	60
ATLANTA	F33 920 001B	F99 840 000B	65,920,000	35
	F00 000 001C	F09 600 000C	9,600,000	35
	F05 760 001★	F08 960 000★	3,200,000	65
CHICAGO	G10 240 001D	G99 840 000D	89,600,000	35
	G00 000 001E	G14 720 000E	14,720,000	35
	G10 880 001★	G15 360 000★	4,096,000	55
ST. LOUIS	H76 520 001A	H99 999 999A	23,480,000	35
	H00 000 001B	H21 760 000B	21,760,000	35
	H03 840 001★	H05 120 000★	1,280,000	85
MINNEAPOLIS	I35 840 001A	I61 440 000A	25,600,000	35
	I01 920 000★	I03 840 000★	896,000	120

	Low	High	Notes Printed	CH CU
KANSAS CITY	J70 400 001A	J94 720 000A	24,320,000	$35
	J02 560 001★	J03 200 000★	640,000	60
DALLAS	K81 280 001A	K99 999 999A	18,720,000	35
	K00 000 001B	K21 120 000B	21,120,000	35
	K02 560 001★	K04 480 000★	1,920,000	60
SAN FRANCISCO	L64 640 001B	L99 999 999B	35,360,000	35
	L00 000 001C	L35 200 000C	35,200,000	35
	L05 760 001★	L07 680 000★	1,920,000	60

SERIES 1977 GREEN SEAL

SIGNATURES: Azie Taylor Morton, W.M. Blumenthal
SERIAL NUMBERS: All districts started regular notes with 00 000 001.
PLATE NUMBERS: Continued from previous series.

	Serial Numbers			
	Low	**High**	**Notes Printed**	**CH CU**
BOSTON	A00 000 001A	A96 640 000A	96,640,000	$40
	A00 012 001★	A03 840 000★	2,698,000	100
NEW YORK	B00 000 001A	—	99,840,000	$40
	B-B	—	99,840,000	40
	—	B77 440 000C	77,440,000	40
	B00 016 001★	B08 960 000★	7,168,000	60
PHILADELPHIA	C00 000 001A	C83 200 000A	83,200,000	40
	C00 000 001★	C01 280 000★	896,000	110
CLEVELAND	D00 000 001A	D83 200 000A	83,200,000	40
	D00 016 001★	D01 280 000★	768,000	110
RICHMOND	E00 000 001A	E71 040 000A	71,040,000	40
	E00 000 001★	E02 560 000★	1,920,000	100
ATLANTA	F00 000 001A	F88 960 000A	88,960,000	40
	F00 000 001★	F01 920 000★	1,536,000	80
CHICAGO	G00 000 001A	G99 840 000A	99,840,000	40
	G00 000 001B	G74 880 000B	74,880,000	40
	G00 016 001★	G06 400 000★	3,968,000	75
ST. LOUIS	H00 000 001A	H46 720 000A	46,720,000	40
	H00 012 001★	H01 280 000★	896,000	90
MINNEAPOLIS	I00 000 001A	I10 240 000A	10,240,000	50
	I00 012 001★	I00 640 000★	256,000	150
KANSAS CITY	J00 000 001A	J50 560 000A	50,560,000	40
	J00 012 001★	J01 280 000★	896,000	90
DALLAS	K00 000 001A	K53 760 000A	53,760,000	40
	K00 000 001★	K00 640 000★	640,000	100
SAN FRANCISCO	L00 000 001A	L73 600 000A	73,600,000	40
	L00 012 001★	L02 560 000★	1,792,000	80

SERIES 1977A GREEN SEAL

SIGNATURES: Azie Taylor Morton, G. William Miller
SERIAL NUMBERS: Continued in sequence from previous series.
PLATE NUMBERS: Continued from previous series.

Serial Numbers

	Low	High	Notes Printed	CH CU
BOSTON	A96 640 000A	A99 840 000A	3,200,000	$50
	A00 000 001B	A80 640 000B	80,640,000	35
	A03 848 001★	A06 400 000★	1,664,000	100
NEW YORK	B77 440 001C	B99 840 000C	22,400,000	35
	B-D	—	88,840,000	35
	B-E	—	99,840,000	35
	—	B37 200 000F	37,200,000	35
	B08 960 001★	B16 000 000★	5,248,000	60
PHILADELPHIA	C83 200 001A	C99 840 000A	16,640,000	35
	C00 000 001B	C79 360 000B	79,360,000	35
	C01 296 001★	C03 840 000★	2,048,000	70
CLEVELAND	D83 200 001A	D99 840 000A	16,640,000	35
	D00 000 001B	D28 160 000B	28,160,000	35
	D01 288 001★	D04 480 000★	2,048,000	70
RICHMOND	E71 040 001A	E99 840 000A	28,800,000	35
	E00 000 001B	E75 520 000B	75,520,000	35
	E02 576 001★	E07 040 000★	3,072,000	80
ATLANTA	F88 960 001A	F99 840 000A	10,880,000	35
	F00 000 001B	F23 040 000B	23,040,000	35
	F01 920 001★	F02 560 000★	640,000	150
	—	F02 793 644★ (observed)	—	—
CHICAGO	G74 880 001B	G99 840 000B	24,960,000	35
	G00 000 001C	G83 200 000C	83,200,000	35
	G06 400 001★	G10 240 000★	3,200,000	65
ST. LOUIS	H46 720 001A	H74 240 000A	27,520,000	35
	H01 292 001★	H02 560 000★	640,000	100
MINNEAPOLIS	I10 240 001A	I14 920 000A	7,680,000	35
	I00 656 001★	I01 280 000★	128,000	135
KANSAS CITY	J50 560 001A	J90 880 000A	4,032,000	50
	J01 296 001★	J05 760 000★	2,136,000	90
DALLAS	K53 760 001A	K99 840 000A	46,080,000	35
	K00 000 001B	K14 080 000B	14,080,000	35
	K00 640 001★	K05 760 000★	4,224,000	60
SAN FRANCISCO	L73 600 001A	L99 840 000A	26,240,000	35
	L00 000 001B	L33 280 000B	33,280,000	35
	L02 572 001★	L05 760 000★	1,792,000	70

SERIES 1981 GREEN SEAL

SIGNATURES: Angela M. Buchanan, Donald T. Regan

SERIAL NUMBERS: Regular notes begin with 00 000 001, star notes vary, and begin as shown below. B Blocks in ten districts restarted at 00 000 001 prior to completion of the blocks, as did Chicago also for the C Block, and New York for the E Block.

	Serial Numbers			
	Low	**High**	**Notes Printed**	**CH CU**
BOSTON	A-A	—	92,160,000	$40
	A-B	—	80,000,000	40
	A00 000 001★	A01 280 000★	1,280,000	100
NEW YORK	B-A	—	99,840,000	40
	B-B	—	99,840,000	40
	B-C	—	66,560,000	40
	B-D	—	99,840,000	40
	B-E	—	35,200,000	50
	B00 000 001★	B01 920 000★	1,920,000	125
PHILADELPHIA	C-A	—	62,720,000	45
	C-B	—	32,000,000	50
	C00 008 001★	C00 640 000★	384,000	125
CLEVELAND	D-A	—	46,080,000	45
	D-B	—	22,400,000	50
	D00 000 001★	D01 280 000★	896,000	120
RICHMOND	E-A	—	90,880,000	40
	E-B	—	32,000,000	50
	E00 019 001★	E03 200 000★	2,576,000	100
ATLANTA	F-A	—	40,960,000	45
	F-B	—	32,000,000	50
	F00 000 001★	F01 920 000★	1,536,000	100
CHICAGO	G-A	—	99,840,000	40
	G-B	—	25,600,000	50
	G-C	—	54,400,000	45
	G00 000 001★	G01 280 000★	1,280,000	100
ST. LOUIS	H-A	—	33,280,000	50
	H-B	—	22,400,000	50
MINNEAPOLIS	I-A	—	7,680,000	60
	I-B	—	16,000,000	50
	I00 012 001★	I00 640 000★	256,000	150
KANSAS CITY	J-A	—	43,520,000	45
	J-B	—	9,600,000	55
DALLAS	K-A	—	21,760,000	50
	K-B	—	28,800,000	50

	Low	High	Notes Printed	CH CU
SAN FRANCISCO	L-A	—	96,000,000	$40
	L-B	—	48,000,000	45
	L00 000 001★	L01 280 000★	1,280,000	100

SERIES 1981A GREEN SEAL

SIGNATURES: Katherine Davalos Ortega, Donald T. Regan
SERIAL NUMBERS: Both regular and stars start with 00 000 001.

	Serial Numbers			
	Low	High	Notes Printed	CH CU
BOSTON	A-A	—	99,200,000	$45
	A-B	—	12,800,000	45
NEW YORK	B-A, B-C	—	259,000,000	40
	B00 000 001★	B03 200 000★	768,000	400
PHILADELPHIA	C-A	—	48,000,000	45
CLEVELAND	D-A	—	60,800,000	45
RICHMOND	E-A	—	92,800,000	40
	—	E03 200 000★	3,200,000	100
ATLANTA	F-A	—	73,600,000	40
	F00 000 001★	F03 200 000★	3,200,000	100
CHICAGO	G-A	—	99,200,000	40
ST. LOUIS	H-A	—	25,600,000	40
MINNEAPOLIS	I-A	—	19,200,000	65
KANSAS CITY	J-A	—	48,000,000	40
DALLAS	K-A	—	48,000,000	40
SAN FRANCISCO	L-A	—	92,800,000	40
	L-B	—	16,000,000	45

SERIES 1985 GREEN SEAL

SIGNATURES: Katherine Davalos Ortega, James A. Baker III
SERIAL NUMBERS: Both regular and star notes begin with 00 000 001.

	Serial Numbers			
	Low	**High**	**Notes Printed**	**CH CU**
BOSTON	A-A - A-B - A-C	—	99,200,000 ea.	$35
	A-D	—	83,100,000	35
	A-★	A09 600 000★	7,296,000	60
NEW YORK	B-A - B-B - B-C - B-D	B-I	99,200,000 ea.	35
	B-J	—	96,400,000	35
	B-K	—	38,400,000	35
	B-★	B03 200 000★	2,560,000	60
PHILADELPHIA	C-A	—	99,200,000	35
	C-B	—	64,000,000	35
CLEVELAND	D-A - D-B - D-C	—	99,200,000 ea.	35
	D-D	—	6,400,000	45
	D-★	D03 200 000★	2,688,000	95
RICHMOND	E-A	—	99,200,000	35
	E-B	—	99,200,000	35
	E-C	—	12,800,000	40
ATLANTA	F-A - F-B	F-C	99,200,000 ea.	35
	F-★	F03 200 000★	384,000	150
CHICAGO	G-A - G-B - G-C	—	99,200,000 ea.	35
	G-D	—	60,800,000	35
ST. LOUIS	H-A	—	99,200,000	35
	H-B	—	32,000,000	35
	H-★	H03 200 000★	3,200,000	70
MINNEAPOLIS	I-A	—	64,000,000	35
KANSAS CITY	J-A	—	86,400,000	35
DALLAS	K-A	—	99,200,000	35
	K-B	—	16,000,000	40
	K-★	K06 400 000★	3,136,000	80
SAN FRANCISCO	L-A - L-B - L-C	—	99,200,000 ea.	35
	L-D	—	3,200,000	45
	L-★	L03 200 000★	2,688,000	80

SERIES 1988A GREEN SEAL

SIGNATURES: Catalina Vasquez Villalpando, Nicholas F. Brady

PLATE NUMBERS: Both face and back numbers begin at #1, with some muling from previous series on backs found early in this issue.

SERIAL NUMBERS: Both regular and star notes begin at 00 000 001.

	Serial Numbers			
	Low	**High**	**Notes Printed**	**CH CU**
BOSTON	A-A	—	96,000,000	$35
	A-B	—	96,000,000	35
	A-C	—	6,400,000	45
	A-★	A09 600 000★	6,480,000	100
NEW YORK	B-A - B-D	—	339,200,000	35
	B-★	B03 200 000★	2,688,000	100
PHILADELPHIA	C-A	—	57,600,000	35
CLEVELAND	D-A - D-B	—	128,000,000	35
	D03 198 469★	D03 200 000★	2,432,000	100
RICHMOND	E-A	—	96,000,000	35
	E-B	—	9,600,000	35
ATLANTA	F-A - F-C	—	236,800,000	35
CHICAGO	G-A - G-C	—	192,000,000	35
ST. LOUIS	H-A	—	70,400,000	35
MINNEAPOLIS	I-A	—	19,200,000	35
KANSAS CITY	J-A	—	51,200,000	35
DALLAS	K-A	—	96,000,000	35
	K-B	—	19,200,000	40
SAN FRANCISCO	L-A - L-C	—	192,000,000	35
	L-★	L03 200 000★	2,560,000	100

SERIES 1990 GREEN SEAL

SIGNATURES: Catalina Vasquez Villalpando, Nicholas F. Brady

PLATE NUMBERS: Face numbers begin at #1. Back numbers continue sequence from previous series.

SERIAL NUMBERS: Both regular and star notes begin at 00 000 001.

(Series 1990 introduced the anti-counterfeiting security thread and the micro size printing around the portrait.)

	Serial Numbers			
	Low	**High**	**Notes Printed**	**CH CU**
BOSTON	A-A	—	96,000,000	$20
	A-B	—	32,000,000	20
NEW YORK	B-A - B-H	—	742,400,000	20
	B-★	B19 200 000★	16,784,000	60
PHILADELPHIA	C-A	—	19,200,000	20
	C-★	C03 200 000★	2,560,000	60
CLEVELAND	D-A	—	89,000,000	20
RICHMOND	E-A	—	96,000,000	20
	E-B	—	9,600,000	40
ATLANTA	F-A - F-B	—	160,000,000	20
CHICAGO	G-A - G-C	—	288,000,000	20
	G-D	—	19,200,000	20
	G-★	G03 200 000★	2,560,000	65
ST. LOUIS	H-A	—	70,400,000	20
	H-★	H03 200 000★	1,920,000	75
MINNEAPOLIS	I-A	—	12,800,000	20
KANSAS CITY	J-A	—	70,400,000	20
DALLAS	K-A	—	57,600,000	20
SAN FRANCISCO	L-A	—	83,200,000	20

SERIES 1993 GREEN SEAL

SIGNATURES: Mary Ellen Withrow, Lloyd Bentsen

PLATE NUMBERS: Face numbers begin at #1. Back numbers continue from previous series, creating mules, then start at #1 in mid-series.

SERIAL NUMBERS: Both regular and star notes begin at 00 000 001.

	Serial Numbers		Notes Printed	CH CU
	Low	**High**		
BOSTON	A-A - A-B	A51 200 000B	147,200,000	$20
NEW YORK	B-A - B-E	B76 800 000E	564,000,000	20
	B-★	B03 200 000★	3,200,000	55
PHILADELPHIA	C-A - C-B	C19 200 000B	115,200,000	20
	C-★	C01 920 000★	1,920,000	60
CLEVELAND	D-A, D-B	D44 800 000B	140,800,000	20
ATLANTA	F-A, F-B	F25 600 000B	121,600,000	20
CHICAGO	G-A, G-B	G32 000 000B	128,000,000	20
	G-★	G03 200 000★	3,200,000	50
ST. LOUIS	H-A	H38 400 000A	38,400,000	20
KANSAS CITY	J-A	J19 200 000A	19,200,000	20
SAN FRANCISCO	L-A	L76 800 000A	76,800,000	20

SERIES 1995 GREEN SEAL

SIGNATURES: Mary Ellen Withrow, Robert E. Rubin

PLATE NUMBERS: Both face and back numbers begin at #1.

SERIAL NUMBERS: Both regular and star notes begin at 00 000 001.

Serial Numbers

	Low	High	Notes Printed	CH CU
BOSTON	A-A - A-B W	A96 000 000B	192,000,000	$25
NEW YORK	B-A - B-E W/FW	B06 400 000E	390,400,000	25
PHILADELPHIA	C-A - C-B W/FW	C51 200 000B	147,200,000	25
CLEVELAND	D-A W/FW	D25 600 000B	121,600,000	25
	D-★ FW	D01 920 000★	1,920,000	50
RICHMOND	E-A - E-C W/FW	E96 000 000C	288,000,000	20
	E-★ W	E01 280 000★	1,280,000	60
ATLANTA	F-A, F-E W/FW	F64 000 000E	448,000,000	20
	F-★ W	F00 640 000★	640,000	75
	F03 200 001★ FWF03 520 000★		320,000	100
CHICAGO	G-A, G-E FW	G64 000 000E	448,000,000	20
	G-★ FW	G03 200 000★	3,200,000	40
ST. LOUIS	H-A - H-B FW	H57 600 000B	51,200,000	20
	H-★ FW	H06 400 000★	6,400,000	45
MINNEAPOLIS	I-A FW	I70 400 000A	70,400,000	35
KANSAS CITY	J-A - J-B FW	J51 200 000B	147,200,000	20
DALLAS	K-A - K-B FW	K96 00 000B	192,000,000	20
SAN FRANCISCO	L-A - L-C FW	L83 200 000C	275,000,000	20
	L-★ FW	L03 200 000★	3,200,000	50

SERIES 1999 GREEN SEAL

SIGNATURES: Mary Ellen Withrow, Lawrence H. Summers
PLATE NUMBERS: Both face and back numbers begin at #1.
SERIAL NUMBERS: Both regular and star notes begin at 00 000 001.

	Serial Numbers			
	Low	**High**	**Notes Printed**	**CH CU**
BOSTON	BA-A W	BA83 200 000A	83,200,000	$20
	BA-★ FW	BA03 200 000★	3,200,000	45
NEW YORK	BB-A - BB-C W	BB96 000 000C	288,000,000	20
	BB-★ FW	BB03 200 000★	3,200,000	45
PHILADELPHIA	BC-A W	BC64 000 000A	64,000,000	20
	BC-★ W	BC06 400 000★	3,520,000	40
CLEVELAND	BD-A W	BD51 200 000A	51,200,000	20
	BD-★ W	BD03 520 000★	2,240,000	45
RICHMOND	BE-A W	BE96 000 000A	96,000,000	20
	BE-B W	BE12 800 000B	12,800,000	25
	BE-★ W	BE03 840 000★	675,200	60
ATLANTA	BF-A - BF-B W/FW	BF89 600 000B	185,600,000	20
	BF-★ FW	BF19 840 000★	14,115,200	30
CHICAGO	BG-A - BG-B W/FW	BG32 000 000B	128,000,000	20
ST. LOUIS	BH-A W	BH38 400 000A	38,400,000	20
MINNEAPOLIS	BI-A W	BI06 400 000A	6,400,000	100
KANSAS CITY	BJ-A FW	BJ06 400 000A	6,400,000	30
	BJ-A W	BJ19 200 000A	12,800,000	25
	BJ-A FW	BJ64 000 000A	44,800,000	20

	Low	High	Notes Printed	CH CU
DALLAS	BK-A - BK-B W/FW	BK76 800 000B	172,800,000	$20
	BK-★ FW	BK12 800 000★	12,800,000	30
SAN FRANCISCO	BL-A W/FW	BL76 800 000A	76,800,000	20

SERIES 2001 GREEN SEAL

SIGNATURES: Rosario Marin, Paul H. O'Neill

PLATE NUMBERS: Both face and back numbers begin at #1, except Washington backs, which continue in sequence from previous series.

SERIAL NUMBERS: All districts start both regular and star notes with 00 000 001.

Serial Numbers

	Low	High	Notes Printed	CH CU
BOSTON	CA-A - CA-B W/FW	CA70 400 000B	166,400,000	$20
NEW YORK	CB-A - CB-C W/FW	CB51 200 000C	243,200,000	20
	CB-★ W	CB00 320 000★	320,000	100
PHILADELPHIA	CC-A - CC-B W	CC12 800 000B	108,800,000	20
CLEVELAND	CD-A W	CD57 600 000A	57,600,000	20
	CD-★ W	CD01 280 000★	1,280,000	40
RICHMOND	CE-A - CE-B W/FW	CE44 800 000B	140,800,000	20
ATLANTA	CF-A W/FW	CF83 200 000A	83,200,000	20
CHICAGO	CG-A - CG-B FW	CG64 000 000B	160,000,000	20
	CG-★ W	CG00 640 000★	640,000	75
ST. LOUIS	CH-A W/FW	CH32 000 000A	32,000,000	25
MINNEAPOLIS	CI-A FW	CI32 000 000A	32,000,000	25
	CI 32 000 001A W	CI38 400 000A	6,400,000	30
DALLAS	CK-A FW	CK38 400 000A	38,400,000	25
	CK-★ FW	CK03 200 000★	3,200,000	35
SAN FRANCISCO	CL-★ FW	CL03 200 000★	3,200,000	35

SERIES 2003 GREEN SEAL

SIGNATURES: Rosario Marin, John W. Snow

PLATE NUMBERS: Both face and back numbers begin at #1.

SERIAL NUMBERS: All districts start both regular and star notes with 00 000 001.

	Serial Numbers			
	Low	**High**	**Notes Printed**	**CH CU**
BOSTON	DA-A W/FW	DA64 000 000A	64,000,000	$20
	DA-★ W	DA00 416 000★ (sheets)	416,000	150
NEW YORK	DB-A W/FW	DB51 200 000B	147,200,000	20
PHILADELPHIA	DC-A W/FW	DC76 800 000A	76,800,000	20
CLEVELAND	DD-A W/FW	DD70 400 000A	70,400,000	20
	DD-★ W	DD01 280 000★	1,280,000	75
RICHMOND	DE-A W/FW	DE83 200 000A	83,200,000	20
ATLANTA	DF-A W/FW	DF38 400 000B	134,400,000	20
CHICAGO	DG-A W/FW	DG51 200 000B	147,200,000	20
ST. LOUIS	DH-A W	DH38 400 000A	38,400,000	20
	DH-★ W	DH00 128 000★(sheets)	128,000	200
	DH03 200 001★ W	DH03 840 000★	640,000	100
MINNEAPOLIS	DI-A W	DI06 400 000A	6,400,000	40
	DI06 400 001A FW	DI12 800 000A	6,400,000	40
	DI09 126 903AW (observed)			
KANSAS CITY	DJ-A W	DJ51 200 000A	51,200,000	20
	DJ-★ W	DJ01 920 000★	1,920,000	75
DALLAS	DK-A W	DK76 800 000A	76,800,000	20
	DK-★ W	DK00 320 000★	320,000	150
SAN FRANCISCO	DL-A W	DL12 800 000B	108,800,000	20

SERIES 2004A GREEN SEAL (COLORIZED)

SIGNATURES: Anna Escobedo Cabral, John W. Snow
PLATE NUMBERS: Face and back numbers begin at #1.
SERIAL NUMBERS: All districts start both regular and star notes with 00 000 001.
PRINTING FACILITY: All notes were printed in Fort Worth.

	Serial Numbers			
	Low	**High**	**Notes Printed**	**CH CU**
BOSTON	GA-A	GA51 200 000A	51,200,000	$20
	GA-★	GA03 200 000★	3,200,000	50
NEW YORK	GB-A	GB57 600 000B	153,600,000	20
	GB-★	GB00 640 000★ (sheets)	640,000	100
PHILADELPHA	GC-A	GC64 000 000A	64,000,000	20
CLEVELAND	GD-A	GD44 800 000A	44,800,000	20
RICHMOND	GE-A	GE70 400 000A	70,400,000	20
ATLANTA	GF-A	GF38 400 000B	134,400,000	20
	GF-★	GF00 009 600★ (sheets)	9,600	200
CHICAGO	GG-A	GG96 000 000A	96,000,000	20
ST. LOUIS	GH-A	GH38 400 000A	38,400,000	20
MINNEAPOLIS	GI-A	GI12 800 000A	12,800,000	25
KANSAS CITY	GJ-A	GJ38 400 000A	38,400,000	20
DALLAS	GK-A	GK57 600 000A	57,600,000	20
SAN FRANCISCO	GL-A	GL89 600 000A	89,600,000	20
	GL-★	GL00 128 000★ (sheets)	128,000	150
	GL03 200 001★	GL03 712 000★ (notes)	512,000	100
	GL06 400 001★	GL11 520 000★	5,120,000	50

TWENTY DOLLAR NOTES

LEGAL TENDER

SERIES 1928 RED SEAL

SERIAL NUMBERS: No Bureau record of printing.

PLATE NUMBERS: Face and back check number #1.

SIGNATURES: W.O. Woods, W.H. Woodin

One specimen of this note was printed and displayed at the Chicago World's Fair in 1933. No notes were ever printed for issue.

GOLD CERTIFICATES

SERIES 1928 GOLD SEAL

PLATE NUMBERS: Face #1 through #174.

SIGNATURES: W.O. Woods, A.W. Mellon

Serial Numbers

Low	High	Notes Printed	VG	VF	CH CU	GEM CU
A00 000 001A	A66 204 000A	66,204,000	$125	$200	$900	$2,000
★00 000 365A	★00 488 307A	—	350	800	8,000	14,000

SERIES 1928A GOLD SEAL

SIGNATURES: W.O. Woods, Ogden L. Mills

Notes were printed but were never issued.

FEDERAL RESERVE BANK NOTES

SERIES 1929 BROWN SEAL

SERIAL NUMBERS: Both regular and star notes start with 00 000 001.
PLATE NUMBERS: Face numbers begin with #1.
SIGNATURES: Same as $5 FRBN

	Serial Numbers					
	Low	**High**	**Notes Printed**	**VF**	**CH CU**	**GEM CU**
BOSTON	A00 000 005A	A00 950 299A	972,000	$50	$375	$500
	A00 005 439★	A00 007 503★	24,000	2,000	—	—
NEW YORK	B00 000 003A	B02 502 592A	2,568,000	45	200	350
	B00 000 913★	B00 019 499★	24,000	425	—	—
PHILADELPHIA	C00 000 008A	C00 952 824A	1,008,000	55	250	400
	C00 000 043★	C00 015 903★	24,000	350	—	—
CLEVELAND	D00 000 003A	D00 997 398A	1,020,000	45	350	500
	D00 000 899★	D00 005 823★	24,000	3,000	—	—
RICHMOND	E00 000 002A	E01 617 979A	1,632,000	45	400	550
	E00 000 042★	E00 011 748★	24,000	675	3,500	—
ATLANTA	F00 000 001A	F00 957 086A	960,000	70	650	950
	F00 001 066★	F00 007 648★	8,000	2,000	—	—
CHICAGO	G00 000 013A	G01 967 998A	2,028,000	45	200	350
	G00 000 013★	G00 003 990★	12,000	1,800	—	—
ST. LOUIS	H00 000 014A	H00 369 354A	444,000	55	300	425
	H00 000 170★	H00 029 267★	24,000	475	3,000	—
MINNEAPOLIS	I00 000 022A	I00 861 573A	864,000	50	250	450
	I00 000 029★	I00 003 963★	12,000	1,300	5,000	—
KANSAS CITY	J00 000 006A	J00 599 572A	612,000	70	650	950
	J00 001 159★	J00 006 536★	24,000	700	—	—
DALLAS	K00 000 009A	K00 435 383A	468,000	500	2,500	—
	K00 000 455★	K00 005 691★	24,000	8,000	—	—
SAN FRANCISCO	L00 000 514A	L00 820 189A	888,000	125	750	1,000
	L00 004 103★	L00 007 271★	24,000	4,500	—	—

FEDERAL RESERVE NOTES

SERIES 1928 GREEN SEAL

SERIAL NUMBERS: All serial numbers of both regular and star notes begin with 00 000 001.

PLATE NUMBERS: Face and back numbers begin with #1.

SIGNATURES: H.T. Tate, A.W. Mellon

Single and double digit low serial numbers are valued at three to four times regular prices.

	Serial Numbers				
	Low	**High**	**Notes Printed**	**VF**	**CH CU**
BOSTON	A00 000 019A	A03 392 017A	3,790,880	$250	$2,500
	A00 004 453★	A00 071 909★	—	300	5,000
NEW YORK	B00 085 952A	B14 586 399A	12,797,100	70	300
	B00 006 020★	B00 142 510★	—	200	2,000
PHILADELPHIA	C00 000 037A	C03 945 267A	3,797,200	70	300
	C00 010 620★	C00 066 363★	—	300	2,000
CLEVELAND	D00 000 020A	D10 896 826A	10,626,900	50	200
	D00 009 327★	D00 146 506★	—	150	1,500
RICHMOND	E00 000 011A	E03 361 569A	4,119,600	70	250
	E00 008 974★	E00 047 239★	—	500	3,000
ATLANTA	F00 093 466A	F03 833 076A	3,842,388	80	300
	F00 000 408★	F00 048 959★	76,000	425	3,000
CHICAGO	G00 000 050A	G12 356 570A	10,891,740	$50	200
	G00 005 572★	G00 129 353★	—	150	1,650
ST. LOUIS	H00 000 012A	H04 485 554A	2,523,300	50	225
	H00 008 407★	H00 043 852★	—	300	2,500

	Low	High	Notes Printed	VF	CH CU
MINNEAPOLIS	I00 000 066A	I03 383 699A	2,633,100	50	$250
	I00 000 823★	I00 046 890★	—	425	2,750
KANSAS CITY	J00 000 080A	J02 602 170A	2,584,500	50	200
	J00 013 973★	J00 047 323★	—	300	2,000
DALLAS	K00 000 010A	K01 508 023A	1,568,500	100	1,000
	K00 000 816★	K00 014 063★	72,000	2,000	6,500
SAN FRANCISCO	L00 049 872A	L07 679 892A	8,404,800	50	300
	L00 040 433★	L00 111 862★	—	300	2,000

SERIES 1928A GREEN SEAL

SERIAL NUMBERS: All districts continued sequence from previous series.

PLATE NUMBERS: Face numbers begin with #1. Back numbers continue from previous series.

SIGNATURES: W.O. Woods, A.W. Mellon

	Serial Numbers				
	Low	High	Notes Printed	VF	CH CU
BOSTON	A03 995 549A	A05 222 537A	1,293,900	$200	—
	A-★	—	—	—	1,500
NEW YORK	B10 058 013A	B12 186 753A	1,055,800	150	700
	B00 118 389★	—	—	2,500	—
PHILADELPHIA	C03 729 477A	C05 496 678A	1,717,200	100	600
	C00 076 388★	—	—	2,500	—
CLEVELAND	D09 287 881A	D10 933 548A	625,200	100	600
	D-★	—	—	—	—
RICHMOND	E03 274 876A	E06 413 199A	1,534,500	100	600
	E00 050 002★	E00 063 147★	—	2,000	—
ATLANTA	F03 825 719A	F05 054 657A	1,442,400	60	400
	F-★	—	—	—	—
CHICAGO	G09 545 579A	G13 654 684A	822,000	60	400
	G00 127 902★	—	—	2,500	—
ST. LOUIS	H02 031 755A	H03 461 672A	573,500	100	600
	H-★	—	—	—	—
KANSAS CITY	J02 352 404A	J02 708 315A	113,900	$150	500
	J-★	—	—	—	—
DALLAS	K01 513 107A	K02 584 558A	1,032,000	100	600
	K-★	—	—	1,000	—

SERIES 1928B DARK GREEN SEAL

SERIAL NUMBERS: All districts continued from previous series.
SIGNATURES: W.O. Woods, A.W. Mellon

	Serial Numbers					
	Low	**High**	**Notes Printed**	**VF**	**CH CU**	**GEM CU**
BOSTON	A03 925 587A	A08 272 736A	7,749,636	$40	$100	$150
	A-★	—	—	250	1,200	
NEW YORK	B12 604 892A	—	19,448,436	40	80	100
	B00 163 574★	B00 196 360★	—	250	1,000	
PHILADELPHIA	C05 663 082A	C09 953 894A	8,095,548	40	100	125
	C00 085 243★	C00 090 459★	—	250	1,500	
CLEVELAND	D11 111 488A	—	11,684,548	40	90	120
	D-★	—	—	250	1,500	
RICHMOND	E05 231 386A	E07 386 430A	4,413,900	40	240	—
	E-★	—	—	250	1,500	
ATLANTA	F04 450 179A	F05 557 667A	2,390,240	200	1,000	—
	F-★	—	—	250	1,500	
CHICAGO	G10 541 757A	G19 893 492A	17,220,276	40	80	100
	G00 125 953★	G00 170 621★	—	250	1,000	
ST. LOUIS	H02 963 737A	H04 852 408A	3,834,600	45	100	125
	H00 075 525★	—	—	250	1,000	
MINNEAPOLIS	I02 607 389A	I03 123 555A	3,298,920	45	160	—
	I-★	—	—	250	2,000	
KANSAS CITY	J02 758 206A	J05 026 574A	4,941,252	40	90	125
	J-★	—	—	250	1,500	
DALLAS	K02 643 964A	K03 162 614A	2,406,060	45	200	—
	K-★	—	—	250	1,500	
SAN FRANCISCO	L09 067 732A	L12 018 423A	9,689,124	40	100	125
	L00 106 084★	L00 119 027★	—	250	1,500	

SERIES 1928B LIGHT VIVID YELLOW-GREEN SEAL

SERIAL NUMBERS: All districts continue sequence from 1928B Dark Green Seal variety. High official star serial numbers are listed below.

Serial Numbers

	Low	High	Notes Printed	VF	CH CU	GEM CU
BOSTON	A08 117 892A	A09 183 361A	included above	$50	$150	200
	A00 079 928★	A00 144 000★	—	200	1,100	—
NEW YORK	B24 685 189A	B30 238 010A	included above	40	125	175
	B00 247 977★	B00 276 000★	—	200	1,000	—
PHILADELPHIA	C09 593 677A	C10 740 130A	included above	40	125	200
	—	C00 120 000★	—	300	1,200	—
CLEVELAND	D16 055 703A	D17 019 068A	included above	40	125	200
	—	D00 216 000★	—	250	1,200	—
RICHMOND	E08 691 942A	E09 501 081A	included above	42	150	250
	E00 076 335★	E00 096 000★	—	350	1,200	—
CHICAGO	G19 800 009A	G25 194 159A	included above	40	110	150
	—	G00 264 000★	—	200	1,000	—
ST. LOUIS	H05 143 648A	H06 348 822A	included above	42	110	150
	—	H00 096 000★	—	300	1,100	—
MINNEAPOLIS	I03 125 342A	I04 685 145A	included above	42	150	250
	—	I00 072 000★	—	400	1,500	—
KANSAS CITY	J05 649 937A	J06 023 572A	included above	40	125	175
	—	J00 084 000★	84,000	350	1,200	—
SAN FRANCISCO	L12 991 538A	L16 475 545A	included above	40	150	—
	L00 146 938★	L00 204 000★	—	200	1,100	—

SERIES 1928C LIGHT VIVID YELLOW-GREEN SEAL

SERIAL NUMBERS: All districts continued sequence from previous series.

SIGNATURES: W.O. Woods, Ogden L. Mills

Serial Numbers

	Low	High	Notes Printed	VF	CH CU	GEM CU
CHICAGO	G23 419 620A	G25 230 425A	3,363,300	$650	$2,000	$3,500
SAN FRANCISCO	L15 631 459A	L16 479 243A	1,420,200	900	5,000	7,000

SERIES 1934 LIGHT VIVID YELLOW-GREEN SEAL

SERIAL NUMBERS: Both regular and star notes begin at 00 000 001.

PLATE NUMBERS: Face numbers begin with #1. Back numbers continue from previous series.

SIGNATURES: W. A. Julian, Henry Morgenthau, Jr.

Total 1934 quantities printed are listed under Dark Green seal Series 1934.

	Serial Numbers				
	Low	**High**	**Notes Printed**	**VF**	**CH CU**
BOSTON	A00 165 174A	A03 506 903A	included below	$35	$100
	A00 009 175★	A00 049 627★	—	150	1,000
NEW YORK	B00 000 004A	B15 983 666A	—	35	100
	B00 000 002★	B00 123 819★	—	110	800
PHILADELPHIA	C00 050 443A	C04 981 012A	—	35	100
	C00 005 656★	C00 092 870★	—	125	1,000
CLEVELAND	D00 000 100A	D09 259 559A	—	35	100
	D00 005 029★	D00 151 901★	—	125	1,000
RICHMOND	E00 000 001A	—	—	35	100
	E00 003 138★	—	—	125	1,000
ATLANTA	F00 025 080A	F02 602 167A	—	35	100
	F00 000 682★	F00 022 682★	—	100	1,200
CHICAGO	G00 494 587A	G13 333 932A	—	35	100
	G00 003 506★	G00 073 409★	—	100	800
ST. LOUIS	H00 240 277A	H03 686 668A	—	35	100
	H00 004 756★	H00 030 821★	—	120	1,200
MINNEAPOLIS	I00 022 436A	I02 855 305A	—	35	150
	I00 000 300★	I00 033 655★	36,000	200	1,800
KANSAS CITY	J00 054 968A	J03 432 025A	—	35	100
	J00 008 961★	—	—	150	1,200
DALLAS	K00 540 625A	K01 317 205A	—	35	100
	K00 000 001★	K00 011 988★	—	150	1,500
SAN FRANCISCO	L00 502 985A	—	—	35	100
	L00 010 125★	L00 065 413★	—	120	1,200

SERIES 1934 DARK BLUE-GREEN SEAL

SERIAL NUMBERS: All districts continue sequence from 1934 Light Vivid Yellow-Green seal variety.

PLATE NUMBERS: Face numbers and back numbers continue from previous series, up to 317.

SIGNATURES: W.A. Julian, Henry Morgenthau, Jr.

	Serial Numbers Low	High	Notes Printed	VF	CH CU
BOSTON	A04 248 125A	A22 709 575A	37,673,068	$30	$85
	A00 061 772★	A00 213 662★	—	80	600
NEW YORK	B16 712 592A	B26 660 574A	27,573,264	30	75
	B00 162 434★	B00 671 541★	—	80	600
PHILADELPHIA	C07 488 199A	C16 141 761A	53,209,968	30	85
	C00 100 031★	C00 269 153★	—	80	600
CLEVELAND	D09 757 473A	D52 931 743A	48,301,416	30	85
	D00 199 746★	D00 356 048★	—	80	600
RICHMOND	E10 000 132A	E18 390 497A	36,259,224	30	85
	E00 120 116★	E00 179 183★	—	120	800
ATLANTA	F02 602 258A	F40 500 918A	41,547,660	30	85
	F00 061 250★	F00 099 791★	—	120	800
CHICAGO	G16 371 183A	G27 321 818A	20,777,832	30	85
	G00 131 843★	G00 283 317★	—	80	600
ST. LOUIS	H04 043 864A	H10 282 544A	27,174,552	30	85
	H00 052 619★	H00 077 405★	—	80	600
MINNEAPOLIS	I03 507 046A	I08 828 247A	16,795,116	30	85
	I00 036 265★	I00 105 300★	—	80	700
KANSAS CITY	J03 740 292A	J09 426 845A	28,865,304	30	85
	J00 041 176★	J00 129 787★	—	80	600
DALLAS	K03 704 038A	K19 684 093A	20,852,160	30	85
	K00 033 195★	—		120	800
SAN FRANCISCO	L09 415 444A	L14 477 859A	32,203,956	30	85
	L00 091 288★	L00 234 002★	—	120	800

SERIES 1934 DARK BLUE-GREEN SEAL MULE

PLATE NUMBERS: Back #318 or higher.

	Serial Numbers Low	High	Notes Printed	VF	CH CU
BOSTON	A14 861 926A	A39 229 242A	included above	$25	$70
	A00 299 745★	A00 367 445★	—	80	600
NEW YORK	B10 745 706A		included above	80	200
PHILADELPHIA	C17 025 718A	C46 581 327A	included above	25	60
	C00 269 153★	C00 464 657★	—	80	600
CLEVELAND	D30 843 925A	D67 315 063A	included above	25	60
	D00 258 726★	D00 639 751★	—	80	600
RICHMOND	E27 389 681A	E71 326 000A	included above	25	60
	E00 337 214★	E00 658 597★	—	80	600
ATLANTA	F09 564 746A	F42 167 541A	included above	25	60
	F00 162 952★	F00 479 515★	—	80	600
ST. LOUIS	H09 430 712A	H29 004 060A	included above	25	60
	H00 112 536★	H00 269 679★	—	80	600
MINNEAPOLIS	I07 925 554A	I16 816 777A	included above	25	60
	I00 112 380★	I00 194 959★	—	80	600
KANSAS CITY	J08 858 537A	J29 785 870A	included above	25	60
	J00 106 196★	J00 279 073★	—	80	600
DALLAS	K02 533 586A	K20 845 000A	included above	25	60
	K00 040 468★	K00 188 210★	—	80	600

	Low	High	Notes Printed	VF	CH CU
SAN FRANCISCO	L26 073 762**A**	L98 971 789**A**	included above	$25	$60
	L00 856 878**B**	L17 180 439**B**	—	75	160
	L00 572 343★	L01 157 528★	—	80	600

HAWAII NOTES

Official Print Runs - All Varieties Included

Serial Numbers

Low	High	Notes Printed
L30 540 001**A**	L31 090 000**A**	550,000
L31 632 001**A**	L32 032 000**A**	400,000
L33 420 001**A**	L34 220 000**A**	800,000
L56 412 001**A**	L56 912 000**A**	500,000
L60 588 001**A**	L61 592 000**A**	1,004,000
L67 984 001**A**	L69 976 000**A**	1,992,000
L76 980 001**A**	L78 480 000**A**	1,500,000
L85 536 001**A**	L90 036 000**A**	4,500,000
L00 360 001★	L00 368 000★	8,000
L00 372 001★	L00 376 000★	4,000
L00 432 001★	L00 444 000★	12,000
L00 852 001★	L00 876 000★	24,000
L00 972 001★	L00 976 000★	4,000

SERIES 1934 BROWN SEAL

PLATE NUMBERS: Back numbers 317 or lower.

SIGNATURES: W.A. Julian, Henry Morgenthau, Jr.

Serial Numbers

Low	High	Notes Printed	VF	CH CU
L31 657 803**A**	L56 729 843**A**	—	$1,600	$8,000

SERIES 1934 MULE-HAWAII BROWN SEAL

PLATE NUMBERS: Back number 318 and higher.

Serial Numbers

Low	High	VG/F	VF	CH CU
L30 549 325**A**	L89 614 996**A**	$100	$200	$7,500
L00 361 137★	L00 874 734★	1,500	4,000	20,000

SERIES 1934 HAWAII LATE FINISHED BACK #204 BROWN SEAL

PLATE NUMBERS: Back #204.

Serial Numbers

Low	High	Notes Printed	VG/F	VF	CH CU
L85 583 901**A**	L89 374 858**A**	—	$150	$500	$8,000

FEDERAL RESERVE NOTES

SERIES 1934 LATE FINISHED BACK #204 GREEN SEAL

PLATE NUMBERS: Back #204.

TOTAL QUANTITY PRINTED: 3,328,728 (Includes both 1934 and 1934A green seal and Hawaii brown seal.)

	Serial Numbers				
	Low	High	Notes Printed	VF	CH CU
PHILADELPHIA	C39 801 518**A**	C42 844 550**A**	included above	$150	$400
CLEVELAND	D62 357 648**A**	D67 074 936**A**	included above	150	400
RICHMOND	E48 287 195**A**	E57 805 065**A**	included above	150	400
ATLANTA	F29 339 734**A**	F40 058 750**A**	included above	150	400
ST. LOUIS	H20 309 291**A**	H27 244 074**A**	included above	150	500
MINNEAPOLIS	I14 852 234**A**	I16 641 606**A**	included above	150	500
KANSAS CITY	J19 436 527**A**	J24 406 598**A**	included above	120	400
DALLAS	K14 338 320**A**	K19 684 093**A**	included above	120	400
SAN FRANCISCO	L10 171 157**B**	L10 278 775**B**	included above	120	400

SERIES 1934A MULE GREEN SEAL

SERIAL NUMBERS: All districts continued sequence from previous series.

PLATE NUMBERS: Back number 317 and lower.

SIGNATURES: W.A. Julian, Henry Morgenthau, Jr.

	Serial Numbers				
	Low	High	Notes Printed	VF	CH CU
BOSTON	A22 043 427**A**	—	—	$50	$150
NEW YORK	B23 106 740**A**	B56 384 416**A**	—	50	125
	B00 217 237★	B00 426 523★	—	300	1,500
CLEVELAND	D19 327 582**A**	D29 656 473**A**	—	50	125
	D00 270 746★	—	—	300	1,500
RICHMOND	E17 813 384**A**	E31 617 341**A**	—	50	125
CHICAGO	G19 150 006**A**	G58 128 561**A**	—	50	125
	G00 207 062★	G00 557 359★	—	300	1,500
ST. LOUIS	H11 841 224**A**	—	—	70	150
MINNEAPOLIS	I09 054 582**A**	I09 689 683**A**	—	70	150
KANSAS CITY	J08 554 475**A**	J10 824 605**A**	—	70	150
DALLAS	K05 540 674**A**	—	—	70	150
SAN FRANCISCO	L16 550 678**A**	L26 073 756**A**	—	50	125
	L00 176 920★	L00 221 644★	—	400	1,500

SERIES 1934A GREEN SEAL

SERIAL NUMBERS: All districts continued sequence from previous series.
PLATE NUMBERS: Back numbers begin at 318.
SIGNATURES: W.A. Julian, Henry Morgenthau, Jr.
 Quantities include all varieties.

	Serial Numbers				
	Low	High	Notes Printed	VF	CH CU
BOSTON	A19 373 046A	A30 901 104A	3,202,416	$30	$75
	A00 197 111★	A00 245 112★	—	100	500
NEW YORK	B39 636 227A	—	102,555,538	25	60
	—	B32 958 367B	—	25	60
	B00 468 332★	B01 434 837★	—	60	500
PHILADELPHIA	C21 627 204A	C50 540 853A	3,371,316	25	75
	C00 220 996★	C00 405 883★	—	70	500
CLEVELAND	D29 825 865A	D65 244 983A	23,475,108	25	75
	D00 213 039★	D00 539 515★	—	60	500
RICHMOND	E26 975 894A	E76 376 415A	46,816,224	25	75
	E00 342 217★	E00 662 786★	—	70	500
ATLANTA	F16 058 930A	F47 661 653A	6,756,816	27	75
	F00 143 745★	F00 554 423★	—	65	500
CHICAGO	G01 034 925A	G94 212 527A	91,141,452	25	60
	G00 666 802B	G07 815 480B	—	25	60
	G00 383 825★	G01 115 663★	—	60	500
ST. LOUIS	H11 841 224A	H35 769 437A	3,701,568	30	75
	H00 155 177★	H00 316 483★	—	70	500
MINNEAPOLIS	I08 877 647A	I11 830 101A	1,162,500	35	100
	I00 133 725★	—	—	100	550
KANSAS CITY	J12 259 434A	J29 057 491A	3,221,184	30	75
	J00 151 021★	J00 338 286★	—	70	500
DALLAS	K18 905 575A	K20 975 837A	2,531,700	30	75
	K-★	—	—	100	650
SAN FRANCISCO	L17 570 455A	—	94,454,112	25	75
	—	L35 359 756B	—	25	75
	L00 211 778★	L01 282 058★	—	60	500

HAWAII NOTES

SERIES 1934A MULE HAWAII BROWN SEAL

PLATE NUMBERS: Back numbers 317 or lower.
SIGNATURES: Same as Series 1934 Green Seal Notes.

	Serial Numbers					
	Low	**High**	**VG/F**	**VF**	**CH CU**	**GEM CU**
SAN FRANCISCO	L30 567 214A	L34 174 516A	$100	$250	$2,000	$4,500
	L00 361 329★	L00 441 242★	1,500	3,600	20,000	—

SERIES 1934A HAWAIII BROWN SEAL

PLATE NUMBERS: Back numbers 318 or higher.
SIGNATURES: Same as Series 1934 Hawaii Above

	Serial Numbers					
	Low	**High**	**VG/F**	**VF**	**CH CU**	**GEM CU**
SAN FRANCISCO	L30 569 896A	L90 031 844A	$50	$100	$1,500	$2,750
	L00 360 472★	L00 975 271★	1,000	1,750	15,000	—

SERIES 1934A LATE FINISHED BACK #204 HAWAII BROWN SEAL

PLATE NUMBERS: Back #204.

	Serial Numbers					
	Low	**High**	**VG/F**	**VF**	**CH CU**	**GEM CU**
SAN FRANCISCO	L85 580 844A	L89 846 438A	$100	$150	$1,500	—
	L04 031 927B	—	150	500	2,000	—

FEDERAL RESERVE NOTES

SERIES 1934A LATE FINISHED BACK #204 GREEN SEAL

PLATE NUMBERS: Back #204.

	Serial Numbers			
	Low	**High**	**VF**	**CH CU**
NEW YORK	B79 437 329A	B82 924 365A	$100	$300
	B02 408 783B	B14 661 059B	100	300
	B01 073 069★	B01 464 313★	—	1,000
PHILADELPHIA	C40 361 306A	—	100	300
CLEVELAND	D65 887 957A	—	100	300
RICHMOND	E49 992 136A	E76 690 574A	100	300
	E00 530 871★	—	—	1,500
CHICAGO	G96 959 019B	G99 928 976A	100	600
ST. LOUIS	H22 077 287A	—	100	300
SAN FRANCISCO	L02 269 795B	L84 396 375B	100	300

SERIES 1934B LATE FINISHED BACK #204 GREEN SEAL

PLATE NUMBERS: Back #204.

	Serial Numbers				
	Low	**High**	**Notes Printed**	**VF**	**CH CU**
NEW YORK	B33 433 725B	B37 011 030B	—	$150	$400
	B01 496 889★	—	—	500	1,500
PHILADELPHIA	C48 563 705A	—	—	150	400
RICHMOND	E82 031 705A	—	—	150	500
ATLANTA	F51 285 715A	—	—	150	400
CHICAGO	G14 602 589B	—	—	150	400
ST. LOUIS	H31 794 426A	H34 362 055A	—	150	400
DALLAS	K24 459 402A	K24 964 183A	—	150	400

SERIES 1934B GREEN SEAL

SERIAL NUMBERS: All districts continued sequence from previous series.
PLATE NUMBERS: Back #318 and higher.
SIGNATURES: W.A. Julian, Fred M. Vinson

	Serial Numbers				
	Low	**High**	**Notes Printed**	**VF**	**CH CU**
BOSTON	A38 471 752A	A42 242 548A	3,904,800	$30	$100
	A00 387 152★	A00 423 466★	—	150	900
NEW YORK	B17 408 148B	B41 671 693B	14,876,436	27.50	80
	B01 318 080★	B01 524 958★	—	90	700
PHILADELPHIA	C46 212 262A	C52 312 048A	3,271,452	30	100
	C00 469 975★	C00 537 549★	—	120	750
CLEVELAND	D17 450 524A	D71 450 524A	2,814,600	30	125
	D00 677 994★	D00 695 683★	—	150	750
RICHMOND	E72 879 805A	E82 979 964A	9,451,632	27.50	100
	E00 776 313★	E00 868 014★	—	120	750
ATLANTA	F45 139 820A	F53 664 202A	6,887,640	30	100
	F00 510 299★	F00 560 062★	—	120	900
CHICAGO	G06 668 282B	G17 457 299B	9,084,600	27.50	70
	G01 124 759★	G01 251 074★	—	90	700
ST. LOUIS	H29 626 392A	H35 150 402A	5,817,300	30	100
	H00 297 011★	H00 366 854★	—	120	750
MINNEAPOLIS	I16 407 235A	I19 331 895A	2,304,800	30	100
	I00 189 973★	I00 227 388★	—	150	900
KANSAS CITY	J29 279 402A	J32 770 825A	3,524,244	30	100
	J00 316 929★	J00 344 088★	—	150	900
DALLAS	K22 466 614A	K26 906 091A	2,807,388	30	100
	K00 241 647★	K00 262 991★	—	150	1,000
SAN FRANCISCO	L08 554 084B	L22 243 980B	5,289,540	30	100
	L01 228 606★	L01 304 745★	—	150	900

Although none are known, it is quite possible mules (back plate below 317) exist in this series.

SERIES 1934C (OLD BACK) GREEN SEAL

The early design has small shrubbery, no balcony, and titled "White House." The later (new) design has a balcony added to the White House with taller shrubbery, and titled "The White House."

SERIAL NUMBERS: All districts continued sequence from previous series.

PLATE NUMBERS: Back numbers up to 587.

SIGNATURES: W.A. Julian, John W. Snyder

Quantities include notes printed with both back varieties.

	Serial Numbers				
	Low	**High**	**Notes Printed**	**VF**	**CH CU**
BOSTON	A42 295 063A	A46 373 548A	7,397,352	$30	$100
	A00 463 255★	A00 470 557★	—	100	750
NEW YORK	B38 676 412B	B50 152 113B	18,668,148	30	70
	B01 531 497★	B01 697 696★	—	100	550
PHILADELPHIA	C50 572 816A	C55 843 968A	11,590,752	30	100
	C00 552 695★	C00 591 991★	—	80	650
CLEVELAND	D71 499 818A	D78 721 934A	17,912,424	30	100
	D00 705 221★	D00 807 221★	—	100	650
RICHMOND	E81 218 620A	—	22,526,568	30	100
	—	E01 832 138B	—	35	125
	E00 784 409★	E00 986 454★	—	100	650
ATLANTA	F54 357 358A	F62 803 437A	18,858,876	30	125
	F00 642 722★	F00 662 748★	—	80	700
CHICAGO	G16 185 385B	G26 057 099B	26,031,660	30	75
	G01 263 515★	G01 455 294★	—	80	500
ST. LOUIS	H35 210 441A	H40 900 929A	13,276,984	30	100
	H00 378 730★	H00 431 121★	—	120	650
MINNEAPOLIS	I19 491 288A	I20 772 004A	3,490,200	35	100
	I-★	—	—	200	1,000
KANSAS CITY	J34 199 254A	J35 607 528A	4,211,904	30	100
	J00 374 799★	J00 380 206★	—	200	750
DALLAS	K25 346 457A	K28 705 809A	3,707,364	$30	100
	K00 301 782★	K00 328 546★	—	200	800
SAN FRANCISCO	L22 220 528B	L29 732 364B	12,015,228	30	100
	L01 312 774★	L01 370 970★	—	200	800

SERIES 1934C (NEW BACK) GREEN SEAL

First note printed with new back - **E**90 480 001**A**. New design has balcony added to the White House, taller shrubbery, and titled "The White House." The first delivery of this redesigned back to the treasurer's vault was on July 27, 1948.

PLATE NUMBERS: Back numbers 588 and higher.

	Serial Numbers				
	Low	**High**	**Notes Printed**	**VF**	**CH CU**
BOSTON	A46 733 962A	A52 528 286A	—	$22.50	$65
	A00 515 662★	—	—	120	800
NEW YORK	B50 380 463B	B55 592 833B	—	22.50	55
	B01 707 021★	B01 744 972★	—	80	600
PHILADELPHIA	C40 943 272A	C66 038 494A	—	22.50	65
	C00 556 864★	C00 670 473★	—	80	600
CLEVELAND	D79 037 088A	—	—	22.50	65
	—	D44 300 344B	—	22.50	65
	D00 805 999★	D00 946 564★	—	100	600
RICHMOND	E90 480 001A	E92 872 408A	—	22.50	65
	official low				
	E06 301 768B	E06 633 116B	—	35	65
	E01 112 542★	E01 205 571★	—	120	600
ATLANTA	F61 618 982A	F73 332 888A	—	22.50	65
	F00 695 886★	F00 800 658★	—	150	800
CHICAGO	G26 178 543B	G40 770 326B	—	22.50	55
	G01 327 744★	G01 559 705★	—	80	400
ST. LOUIS	H41 528 004A	H49 136 987A	—	22.50	65
	H00 453 262★	H00 541 919★	—	120	600
MINNEAPOLIS	I20 837 220A	I22 628 128A	—	30	100
	I00 229 419★	I00 277 546★	—	100	600
KANSAS CITY	J36 196 825A	J41 600 887A	—	22.50	65
	J00 392 834★	J00 461 696★	—	75	600
DALLAS	K31 042 702A	K34 625 505A	—	22.50	65
	K00 332 833★	K00 422 637★	—	150	600
SAN FRANCISCO	L29 876 286B	L43 266 556B	—	22.50	65
	L01 503 904★	L01 589 520★	—	100	600

SERIES 1934D WIDE GREEN SEAL

SERIAL NUMBERS: All districts continued sequence from previous series.

PLATE NUMBERS: The break between wide and narrow backs is found at #669-670.

SIGNATURES: Georgia Neese Clark, John W. Snyder

All collectors are requested to submit High serial number data for 1934D wide, for both regular and star notes.

	Serial Numbers				
	Low	**High**	**Notes Printed**	**VF**	**CH CU**
BOSTON	A41 971 456A	A53 896 892A	4,520,000	—	$95
	A-★	—	—	250	1,350
NEW YORK	B55 961 199B	B63 487 761B	27,894,260	—	75
	B01 750 367★	B01 958 959★	—	—	—
PHILADELPHIA	C62 289 525A	C64 704 659A	6,022,428	—	$95
	C00 660 092★	C00 725 518★	—	—	—
CLEVELAND	D88 751 741A	—	8,981,688	—	95
	D00 984 865★	D01 037 451★	—	$150	1,100
RICHMOND	E04 865 511B	E11 792 135B	14,055,984	—	95
	E00 784 409★	E01 393 165★	—	125	1,000
ATLANTA	F72 717 182A	—	7,495,440	—	95
	F00 820 521★	F00 880 415★	—	—	—
CHICAGO	G41 576 352B	—	15,187,596	—	75
	G01 574 917★	G01 760 204★	—	100	750
ST. LOUIS	H34 055 557A	H51 608 232A	5,923,248	—	95
	H00 614 812★	H00 625 593★	—	—	—
MINNEAPOLIS	22 721 807A	I23 431 437A	2,422,416	25	120
	I-★	—	—	—	—
KANSAS CITY	J42 061 133A	J43 759 966A	4,211,904	—	95
	J00 482 446★	—	—	—	—
DALLAS	K35 095 524A	K38 583 200A	3,707,364	—	95
	K-★	—	—	—	—
SAN FRANCISCO	L42 307 884B	—	12,015,228	—	95
	L01 644 433★	L01 738 012★	—	125	900

WIDE

NARROW

SERIES 1934D NARROW GREEN SEAL

PLATE NUMBERS: Narrow back design starts with #670, and were first printed in July, 1950.

All collectors are requested to submit serial number data to the authors in order to help determine 1934D Narrow back lows and highs for both regular and star notes.

	Serial Numbers Low	High	Notes Printed	VF	CH CU
BOSTON	A53 788 672A	—	—	—	—
	A00 576 815★	—	Incl. in 1934 wide	—	$200
NEW YORK	B63 734 027B	B70 788 131B	—	—	150
PHILADELPHIA	C66 022 173A	C67 697 106A	—	—	200
CLEVELAND	D93 583 819A	D97 055 114A	—	—	200
RICHMOND	E14 882 581A	E18 131 889B	—	—	200
ATLANTA	F76 811 156A	F79 520 333A	—	—	200
CHICAGO	G49 419 303B	G53 814 518B	—	—	150
ST. LOUIS	H53 924 976A	H55 054 801A	—	—	200
MINNEAPOLIS	I23 654 275A	I24 838 904A	—	—	250
KANSAS CITY	J45 709 191A	J45 904 914A	—	—	200
DALLAS	K36 810 156A	K37 549 658A	—	—	200
SAN FRANCISCO	L52 156 687A	L54 955 012B	—	—	200

SERIES 1950 GREEN SEAL

PLATE NUMBERS: Face check numbers begin with #1. Back check numbers continue from series 1934D with #670.

SERIAL NUMBERS: All serial numbers of both regular and star notes begin with 00 000 001.

SIGNATURES: Georgia Neese Clark, John W. Snyder

	Serial Numbers Official				
	Low	**High**	**Notes Printed**	**VF**	**CH CU**
BOSTON	A00 008 518A	A23 184 000A	23,184,000	—	$70
	A00 051 073★	A00 284 214★	—	150	450
NEW YORK	B14 083 033A	B80 064 000A	80,064,000	—	70
	B00 102 147★	B01 134 527★	—	80	400
PHILADELPHIA	C00 719 606A	C29 520 000A	29,520,000	—	70
	C00 006 323★	C00 309 158★	—	100	400
CLEVELAND	D00 183 367A	D51 120 000A	51,120,000	—	60
	D00 043 082★	D00 645 343★	—	80	450
RICHMOND	E03 550 488A	E67 536 000A	67,536,000	—	70
	E00 037 807★	E00 843 597★	—	80	450
ATLANTA	F02 722 006A	F39 312 000A	39,312,000	—	70
	F00 156 842★	—	—	150	700
CHICAGO	G08 969 721A	G70 464 000A	70,464,000	—	50
	G00 000 042★	G00 942 397★	—	80	400
ST. LOUIS	H00 418 292A	H27 352 000A	27,352,000	—	70
	H00 002 807★	H00 319 290★	—	80	550
MINNEAPOLIS	I00 004 730A	I09 216 000A	9,216,000	—	70
	I00 001 796★	I00 109 385★	—	150	700
KANSAS CITY	J00 096 002A	J22 752 000A	22,752,000	—	70
	J00 114 165★	J00 195 219★	—	80	550
DALLAS	K09 339 664A	K22 656 000A	22,656,000	—	90
	K00 124 624★	K00 239 426★	—	100	700
SAN FRANCISCO	L07 823 728A	L70 272 000A	70,272,000	—	65
	L00 007 933★	L00 947 273★	—	100	450

Serial nos. **G**70 464 001**A** thru **G**70 560 000**A**, **H**27 352 001**A** thru **H**27 360 000**A** and **K**22 656 001**A** thru **K**22 752 000**A** were assigned for Chicago, St. Louis and Dallas respectively, but were never used.

SERIES 1950A GREEN SEAL

SIGNATURES: Ivy Baker Priest, G.M. Humphrey

	Serial Numbers Official				
	Low	**High**	**Notes Printed**	**VF**	**CH CU**
BOSTON	A23 184 001A	A42 840 000A	19,656,000	—	$75
	A00 488 034★	A01 771 489★	—	70	250
NEW YORK	B80 064 001A	—	82,568,000	—	50
	—	B62 640 000B	—	—	50
	B01 196 551★	B05 378 648★	—	70	200
PHILADELPHIA	C29 520 001A	C46 080 000A	16,560,000	—	75
	C00 491 484★	C01 435 559★	—	70	250
CLEVELAND	D51 120 001A	—	50,320,000	—	60
	—	D01 440 000B	—	—	85
	D00 741 659★	D03 550 848★	—	70	250
RICHMOND	E67 536 001A	—	69,544,000	—	75
	—	E37 080 000B	—	—	75
	E01 126 803★	E04 928 569★	—	70	250
ATLANTA	F39 312 001A	F66 960 000A	27,648,000	—	75
	F00 846 722★	F02 032 622★	—	70	250
CHICAGO	G70 560 001A	—	—	—	50
	—	G44 280 000B	73,720,000	—	50
	G01 031 678★	G05 023 180★	—	70	200
ST. LOUIS	H27 360 001A	H50 040 000A	22,680,000	—	65
	H00 499 568★	H01 358 531★	—	70	250
MINNEAPOLIS	I09 216 001A	I14 760 000A	5,544,000	—	75
	I00 198 333★	I00 570 430★	—	70	300
KANSAS CITY	J22 752 001A	J45 720 000A	22,968,000	—	65
	J00 337 534★	J02 125 393★	—	70	275
DALLAS	K22 752 001A	K33 480 000A	10,728,000	—	75
	K00 605 026★	K01 094 576★	—	70	275
SAN FRANCISCO	L70 272 001A	—	—	—	65
	—	L55 800 000B	85,528,000	—	65
	L01 165 265★	L07 033 651★	—	70	275

(1) **B**90 236 001**A** to **B**90 240 000**A** and **B**90 252 001**A** to **B**90 256 000**A** were reported missing because of theft. When recovered they were destroyed.

SERIES 1950B GREEN SEAL

SIGNATURES: Ivy Baker Priest, Robert B. Anderson

	Serial Numbers Official				
	Low	**High**	**Notes Printed**	**VF**	**CH CU**
BOSTON	A42 840 001A	A47 880 000A	5,040,000	—	$60
	A-★	—	—	100	500
NEW YORK	B62 640 001B	—	—	—	50
	—	B12 600 000C	49,960,000	—	70
	B05 443 924★	B07 517 857★	—	70	250
PHILADELPHIA	C46 080 001A	C54 000 000A	7,920,000	—	60
	C01 449 489★	C01 633 365★	—	70	350
CLEVELAND	D01 440 001B	D39 600 000B	38,160,000	—	60
	D03 778 734★	D04 522 229★	—	70	300
RICHMOND	E37 080 001B	E79 200 000B	42,120,000	—	60
	E05 817 251★	E06 268 441★	—	70	350
ATLANTA	F66 960 001A	—	40,240,000	—	60
	F00 871 950B	F07 200 000B	—	—	75
	F02 339 040★	F03 624 798★	—	70	350
CHICAGO	G44 280 001B	—	—	—	50
	—	G24 840 000C	80,560,000	—	50
	G05 178 467★	G08 930 902★	—	70	250
ST. LOUIS	H50 040 001A	H69 480 000A	19,440,000	—	60
	H01 655 383★	H02 432 527★	—	70	300
MINNEAPOLIS	I14 760 001A	I27 000 000A	12,240,000	—	60
	I00 578 008★	I01 054 674★	—	70	300
KANSAS CITY	J45 720 001A	J74 160 000A	28,440,000	—	60
	J02 160 802★	J03 910 347★	—	70	350
DALLAS	K33 480 001A	K45 360 000A	11,880,000	—	60
	K01 578 478★	K01 753 037★	—	70	350
SAN FRANCISCO	L55 800 001B	—	—	—	60
	—	L06 840 000C	51,040,000	—	60
	L07 375 803★	L08 946 721★	—	70	350

SERIES 1950C GREEN SEAL

SIGNATURES: Elizabeth Rudel Smith, C. Douglas Dillon

	Serial Numbers				
	Low	**High**	**Notes Printed**	**VF**	**CH CU**
BOSTON	A47 880 001A	A55 080 000A	7,200,000	—	$65
	A01 854 314★	A02 095 356★	—	50	350
NEW YORK	B12 600 001C	B55 800 000C	43,200,000	—	55
	B08 451 632★	B09 629 397★	—	50	350
PHILADELPHIA	C54 000 001A	C61 560 000A	7,560,000	—	65
	C01 944 756★	C02 499 817★	—	50	350
CLEVELAND	D39 600 001B	D68 040 000B	28,440,000	—	55
	D04 720 801★	D05 318 009★	—	50	350
RICHMOND	E79 200 001B	—	—	—	55
	—	E16 200 000C	37,000,000	—	55
	E06 559 116★	E08 000 001★	—	50	350
ATLANTA	F07 200 001B	F26 280 000B	19,080,000	—	55
	F04 176 720★	F04 637 868★	—	50	350
CHICAGO	G24 840 001C	G54 000 000C	29,160,000	—	55
	G09 026 647★	G09 896 513★	—	50	300
ST. LOUIS	H69 480 001A	H82 440 000A	12,960,000	—	55
	H02 551 551★	H02 879 111★	—	50	350
MINNEAPOLIS	I27 000 001A	I33 480 000A	6,480,000	—	55
	I01 120 182★	I01 433 221★	—	50	350
KANSAS CITY	J74 160 001A	J92 520 000A	18,360,000	—	55
	J04 114 718★	J04 599 018★	—	50	350
DALLAS	K45 360 001A	K54 360 000A	9,000,000	—	65
	K01 971 414★	K02 010 051★	—	150	650
SAN FRANCISCO	L06 840 001C	L52 200 000C	45,360,000	—	65
	L09 402 334★	L11 122 650★	—	70	450

SERIES 1950D GREEN SEAL

SIGNATURES: Kathryn O'Hay Granahan, C. Douglas Dillon

	Serial Numbers			
	Low	**High**	**Notes Printed**	**CH CU**
BOSTON	A55 080 001A	A64 440 000A	9,360,000	$75
	A02 283 535★	A02 463 553★	—	225
NEW YORK	B55 800 001C	—	44,200,000	60
	B00 000 001D	B10 080 000D	10,080,000	60
	B08 993 307★	B11 192 003★	—	175
PHILADELPHIA	C61 560 001A	C66 960 000A	5,400,000	75
	C02 572 171★	C02 869 202★	—	200
CLEVELAND	D68 040 001B	D91 800 000B	23,760,000	75
	D05 519 673★	D06 080 612★	—	200
RICHMOND	E16 200 001C	E46 440 000C	30,240,000	75
	E08 350 148★	E09 330 551★	—	225
ATLANTA	F26 280 001B	F48 960 000B	22,680,000	75
	F04 739 303★	F05 029 301★	—	200
CHICAGO	G54 000 001C	G99 999 999C	46,000,000	60
	G00 000 001D	G21 960 000D	21,960,000	65
	G10 110 937★	G12 567 741★	—	150
ST. LOUIS	H82 440 001A	H88 560 000A	6,120,000	75
	H03 003 911★	H03 224 717★	—	250
MINNEAPOLIS	I33 480 001A	I36 720 000A	3,240,000	125
	I-★	—	—	750
KANSAS CITY	J92 520 001A	J96 000 000A	7,480,000	75
	J00 720 000B	J06 400 000B	720,000	125
	J04 865 124★	J05 010 110★	—	250
DALLAS	K54 360 001A	K60 840 000A	6,480,000	75
	K02 250 156★	K02 427 511★	—	200
SAN FRANCISCO	L52 200 001C	L99 999 999C	47,800,000	75
	L00 000 001D	L21 600 000D	21,600,000	75
	L11 251 643★	L13 945 478★	—	200

SERIES 1950E GREEN SEAL

SIGNATURES: Kathryn O'Hay Granahan, Henry H. Fowler

Serial Numbers

	Low	High	Notes Printed	VF	CH CU
NEW YORK	B10 080 001D	B18 720 000D	8,640,000	$50	$100
	B12 389 340★	B13 252 914★	900,000 est.	200	750
CHICAGO	G21 960 001D	G31 320 000D	9,360,000	50	175
	G12 706 343★	G12 919 155★	360,000 est.	200	1,000
SAN FRANCISCO	L21 600 001D	L30 240 000D	8,640,000	$50	175
	L14 196 804★	L14 739 549★	576,000 est.	200	800

SERIES 1963 GREEN SEAL

SERIAL NUMBERS: All serial numbers of both regular and star notes begin with 00 000 001.
PLATE NUMBERS: Face and back begin with 1. Motto "IN GOD WE TRUST" added to back.
SIGNATURES: Kathryn O'Hay Granahan, C. Douglas Dillon

Serial Numbers

	Low	High	Notes Printed	CH CU
BOSTON	A-A	A01 420 510A	2,560,000	$100
	A-★	A00 006 422★	640,000	220
NEW YORK	B-A	B15 461 064A	16,640,000	75
	B00 000 383★	B01 209 593★	1,920,000	125
CLEVELAND	D-A	D03 746 804A	7,680,000	100
	D-★	—	640,000	200
RICHMOND	E-A	—	4,480,000	100
	E-★	E00 407 494★	640,000	200

	Low	High	Notes Printed	CH CU
ATLANTA	F-A	F06 213 222A	12,240,000	$125
	F-★	F00 562 586★	1,280,000	200
CHICAGO	G-A	G00 522 867A	2,560,000	100
	G-★	—	640,000	180
ST. LOUIS	H-A	—	3,200,000	100
	H00 008 918★	H00 639 862★	640,000	200
KANSAS CITY	J00 000 004A	J00 547 957A	3,840,000	125
	J00 000 764★	J00 089 340★	640,000	200
DALLAS	K-A	K02 126 450A	2,560,000	100
	K-★	K00 266 095★	640,000	200
SAN FRANCISCO	L-A	L01 619 168A	7,040,000	100
	L-★	L00 705 956★	1,280,000	150

SERIES 1963A GREEN SEAL

SERIAL NUMBERS: Both regular and star notes continue in sequence from previous series, except Philadelphia and Minneapolis which begin at 00 000 001.

SIGNATURES: Kathryn O'Hay Granahan, Henry H. Fowler

	Serial Numbers			
	Low	High	Notes Printed	CH CU
BOSTON	A02 560 001A	A26 240 000A	23,680,000	$60
	A00 640 001★	A01 920 000★	1,280,000	150
NEW YORK	B16 640 001A	—	93,600,000	60
	—	B10 240 000B	—	60
	B01 920 001★	B05 760 000★	3,840,000	150
PHILADELPHIA	C00 000 001A	C17 920 000A	17,920,000	60
	C00 000 529★	C00 640 000★	640,000	150
CLEVELAND	D07 690 001A	D76 160 000A	68,470,000	60
	D00 640 001★	D03 840 000★	3,200,000	150
RICHMOND	E04 480 001A	—	128,800,000	60
	—	E33 280 000B	—	60
	E00 640 001★	E06 400 000★	5,760,000	150
	E00 123 642★	—	—	—
ATLANTA	F10 240 001A	F53 120 000A	43,880,000	60
	F01 280 001★	F03 200 000★	1,920,000	150
	F02 959 497★	—	—	—
CHICAGO	G02 560 001A	—	156,320,000	60
	—	G58 880 000B	—	60

	Low	High	Notes Printed	CH CU
	G00 640 001★	G07 680 000★	7,040,000	$150
	G03 026 313★	G07 542 909★	—	—
ST. LOUIS	H03 200 001A	H37 760 000A	34,560,000	60
	H00 640 001★	H02 560 000★	1,920,000	150
	H01 961 303★	—	—	—
MINNEAPOLIS	I00 000 001A	I10 240 000A	10,240,000	60
	I00 000 001★	I00 640 000★	640,000	175
	I00 008 091★	I00 414 802★	—	—
KANSAS CITY	J00 000 001A	J40 960 000A	37,120,000	60
	J00 640 001★	J02 560 000★	1,920,000	150
DALLAS	K02 560 001A	K40 960 000A	38,400,000	60
	K00 640 001★	K01 920 000★	1,280,000	150
SAN FRANCISCO	L07 040 001A	—	92,960,000	60
	—	L76 160 000B	76,160,000	60
	L01 280 001★	L09 600 000★	8,320,000	150

SERIES 1969 GREEN SEAL

SERIAL NUMBERS: Both regular and star notes begin with 00 000 001.

SIGNATURES: Dorothy Andrews Elston, David M. Kennedy

	Serial Numbers			
	Low	High	Notes Printed	CH CU
BOSTON	A-A	—	19,200,000	$60
	A00 000 002★	A01 061 777★	1,280,000	140
NEW YORK	B-A	—	99,999,999	60
	B-B	—	6,400,000	60
	B00 280 895★	B01 839 260★	5,108,000	120
PHILADELPHIA	C-A	—	10,880,000	60
	C00 537 783★	C01 039 308★	1,280,000	140
CLEVELAND	D-A	D45 747 313A	60,160,000	60
	D00 000 053★	D02 395 515★	2,560,000	140
RICHMOND	E-A	—	66,560,000	60
	E-★	E02 476 541★	2,560,000	140
ATLANTA	F-A	—	36,480,000	60
	F-★	F00 592 341★	1,280,000	140
CHICAGO	G-A	—	99,999,999	50
	G-B	—	7,680,000	60
	G00 068 237★	G01 447 827★	3,200,000	125

	Low	High	Notes Printed	CH CU
ST. LOUIS	H-A	—	19,200,000	$60
	H-★	H00 014 354★	640,000	150
MINNEAPOLIS	I-A	—	12,160,000	60
	I-★	—	640,000	150
KANSAS CITY	J-A	—	39,040,000	60
	J-★	J01 202 750★	1,280,000	140
DALLAS	K-A	—	25,600,000	60
	K00 000 246★	K00 544 882★	1,280,000	140
SAN FRANCISCO	L-A	—	99,999,999	60
	L-B	—	3,840,000	65
	L-★	L05 079 455★	5,120,000	125

SERIES 1969A GREEN SEAL

SIGNATURES: Dorothy Andrews Kabis, John B. Connally

Serial Numbers

	Low	High	Notes Printed	CH CU
BOSTON	A19 200 001A	A32 640 000A	13,440,000	$80
NEW YORK	B06 400 001B	B76 160 000B	69,760,000	70
	B05 120 001★	B07 680 000★	2,560,000	125
PHILADELPHIA	C10 880 001A	C24 320 000A	13,440,000	80
CLEVELAND	D60 160 001A	D89 600 000A	29,440,000	75
	D02 560 001★	D03 200 000★	640,000	150
RICHMOND	E66 560 001A	—	33,440,000	80
	—	E08 960 000B	8,960,000	90
	E02 560 001★	E04 480 000★	1,920,000	140
ATLANTA	F36 480 001A	F49 920 000A	13,440,000	80
CHICAGO	G07 680 001B	G88 320 000B	80,640,000	70
	G03 200 001★	G05 280 000★	1,920,000	140
ST. LOUIS	H19 200 001A	H33 280 000A	14,080,000	80
	H00 640 001★	H01 280 000★	640,000	160
MINNEAPOLIS	I12 160 001A	I19 200 000A	7,040,000	90
KANSAS CITY	J39 040 001A	J55 680 000A	16,640,000	80
DALLAS	K25 600 001A	K40 320 000A	14,720,000	75
	K00 640 001★	K01 280 000★	640,000	160
SAN FRANCISCO	L03 840 001B	L54 400 000B	50,560,000	70
	L05 120 001★	L06 400 000★	1,280,000	115

SERIES 1969B GREEN SEAL

SIGNATURES: Romana A. Banuelos, John B. Connally

	Serial Numbers			
	Low	**High**	**Notes Printed**	**CH CU**
NEW YORK	B76 160 001B	—	25,040,000	$200
	—	B15 360 000C	15,360,000	200
	B07 200 001★	B07 680 000★	480,000	500
CLEVELAND	D89 600 001A	D96 000 000A	6,400,000	250
RICHMOND	E08 960 001B	E36 480 000B	27,520,000	200
ATLANTA	F49 920 001A	F64 000 000A	14,080,000	200
	F01 280 001★	F01 920 000★	640,000	700
	F01 331 573★	F01 906 648★ (observed)	—	—
CHICAGO	G88 320 001B	—	11,680,000	200
	—	G02 560 000C	2,560,000	250
	G05 280 001★	G07 254 086★ (observed)	1,112,000	600
ST. LOUIS	H33 280 001A	H38 400 000A	5,120,000	250
MINNEAPOLIS	I19 200 001A	I21 760 000A	2,560,000	400
	I19 301 311A	I21 598 131A (observed)		
KANSAS CITY	J55 680 001A	J59 520 000A	3,840,000	300
	J01 280 001★	J01 920 000★	640,000	800
	J01 513 688★	J01 792 223★ (observed)	—	—
DALLAS	K40 320 001A	K52 480 000A	12,160,000	200
	K43 255 555A	K49 61 961A (observed)		
SAN FRANCISCO	L54 400 001B	L80 640 000B	26,240,000	175
	L06 400 001★	L07 040 000★	640,000	800
	L06 681 605★	— (observed)	—	—

SERIES 1969C GREEN SEAL

SIGNATURES: Romana Acosta Banuelos, George P. Shultz
PLATE NUMBERS: All districts continue from previous series.
SERIAL NUMBERS: All districts continue from previous series.

	Serial Numbers			
	Low	**High**	**Notes Printed**	**CH CU**
BOSTON	A32 640 001A	A49 920 000A	17,280,000	$60
	A01 280 001★	A01 920 001★	640,000	135
NEW YORK	B15 360 001C	—	84,640,000	60
	—	B50 560 000D	50,560,000	60
	B07 320 001★	B08 960 000★	1,640,000	120
PHILADELPHIA	C24 320 001A	C65 280 000A	40,960,000	60
	C01 280 001★	C01 920 000★	640,000	135
CLEVELAND	D96 000 001A	—	4,000,000	65
	—	D53 760 000B	53,760,000	60
	D03 200 001★	D03 840 000★	640,000	140
RICHMOND	E36 480 001B	—	80,160,000	60
	—	E16 640 000C	—	60
	E04 480 001★	E06 400 000★	1,920,000	120
ATLANTA	F64 000 001A	F99 840 000A	35,840,000	60
	F01 920 001★	F02 560 000★	640,000	135
CHICAGO	G02 560 001C	G81 280 000C	78,720,000	60
	G06 400 001★	G07 040 000★	640,000	135
ST. LOUIS	H32 320 000A	H69 457 766A	33,920,000	60
	H01 280 001★	H01 920 000★	640,000	170
MINNEAPOLIS	I21 760 001A	I35 840 000A	14,080,000	60
	I00 640 001★	I01 280 000★	640,000	135
KANSAS CITY	J59 520 001A	J91 520 000A	32,000,000	60
	J01 920 001★	J02 560 000★	640,000	170
DALLAS	K52 480 001A	K83 840 000A	32,000,000	60
	K01 280 001★	K03 200 000★	1,920,000	120
SAN FRANCISCO	L80 640 001B	—	19,360,000	60
	—	L62 720 000C	67,720,000	65
	L07 040 001★	L08 320 000★	1,280,000	140

SERIES 1974 GREEN SEAL

SIGNATURES: Frances I. Neff, William E. Simon
SERIAL NUMBERS: Continue from previous series.
PLATE NUMBERS: Continue from previous series.

	Serial Numbers			
	Low	**High**	**Notes Printed**	**CH CU**
BOSTON	A49 920 001A	—	57,120,000	$60
	—	A07 040 000B	—	65
	A01 920 001★	A03 200 000★	768,000	115
NEW YORK	B50 560 001D	—	296,900,000	50
	B-E	—	—	50
	B-F	—	—	50
	—	B47 360 000G	—	50
	B08 960 001★	B17 280 000★	6,976,000	80
PHILADELPHIA	C65 280 001A	—	59,680,000	60
	—	C24 960 000B	—	60
	C01 920 001★	C03 840 000★	1,920,000	125
CLEVELAND	D53 760 001B	—	148,160,000	60
	—	D99 840 000C	—	60
	D03 840 001★	D08 320 000★	4,296,000	125
RICHMOND	E16 640 001C	—	149,920,000	60
	—	E66 560 000D	—	60
	E06 400 001★	E11 520 000★	3,040,000	125
ATLANTA	F99 840 001A	—	53,200,000	125
	—	F53 120 000B	—	60
	F02 560 001★	F03 480 000★	1,120,000	135
CHICAGO	G81 280 001C	—	250,080,000	50
	G-D	—	—	50
	G67 855 304E	—	—	50
	—	G31 360 000F	—	50
	G07 200 001★	G14 080 000★	4,928,000	80
ST. LOUIS	H72 320 001A	—	73,120,000	60
	—	H45 440 000B	—	60
	H01 920 001★	H03 200 000★	1,120,000	110
MINNEAPOLIS	I35 840 001A	I71 680 000A	39,040,000	60
	I01 280 001★	I02 560 000★	1,280,000	110
KANSAS CITY	J91 520 001A	—	74,400,000	60
	—	J65 920 000B	—	60
	J02 720 001★	J04 480 000★	736,000	110

	Low	High	Notes Printed	CH CU
DALLAS	K83 840 001**A**	—	68,640,000	$60
	—	K52 480 000**B**	—	60
	K03 360 001★	K04 480 000★	608,000	110
SAN FRANCISCO	L62 720 001**C**—	—	128,800,000	60
	—	L90 880 000**D**	—	60
	L08 320 001★	L14 080 000★	4,320,000	105

Starting with Series 1963 in the Federal Reserve Notes, star notes are often printed in staggered runs, not consecutive to each other, so that large serial number gaps may exist. This can result in higher star serial numbers found on the notes than may be found in the "Notes Printed" columns.

SERIES 1977 GREEN SEAL

SIGNATURES: Azie Taylor Morton, W.M. Blumenthal

SERIAL NUMBERS: Both regular and star notes begin with 00 000 001.

PLATE NUMBERS: Both face and back continue from previous series.

	Serial Numbers			
	Low	**High**	**Notes Printed**	**CH CU**
BOSTON	A-A	—	94,720,000	$60
	A00 008 001★	A03 840 000★	2,688,000	100
NEW YORK	B-A	B-F	569,600,000	60
	B00 000 001★	B13 440 000★	4,736,000	100
PHILADELPHIA	C-A	C-B	117,320,000	60
	C00 012 001★	C04 480 000★	2,816,000	100
CLEVELAND	D-A	D-B	189,440,000	60
	D00 016 001★	D07 680 000★	5,632,000	100
RICHMOND	E-A	E-C	258,660,000	60
	E00 000 001★	E07 040 000★	6,272,000	100
ATLANTA	F-A	—	70,400,000	60
	F00 000 001★	F03 840 000★	2,688,000	100
CHICAGO	G-A	G-D	358,400,000	60
	G00 012 001★	G10 240 000★	7,552,000	100
ST. LOUIS	H-A	—	98,560,000	60
	H00 012 001★	H03 200 000★	1,792,000	100
MINNEAPOLIS	I-A	—	15,360,000	65
	I00 000 001★	I01 280 000★	512,000	110
KANSAS CITY	J-A	J-B	148,480,000	60
	J00 008 001★	J06 400 000★	4,736,000	100

	Low	High	Notes Printed	CH CU
DALLAS	K-A	K-B	163,840,000	$60
	K00 008 001★	K08 960 000★	3,456,000	100
SAN FRANCISCO	L-A	L-C	263,680,000	60
	L00 012 001★	L09 600,000★	6,528,000	100

SERIES 1981 GREEN SEAL

SIGNATURES: Angela M. Buchanan, Donald T. Regan

PLATE NUMBERS: Back numbers continue from previous series. Face numbers begin at #1.

SERIAL NUMBERS: All regular blocks begin with 00 000 001. Star notes vary, and begin as shown below. Numerous blocks exist with incomplete printings.

Serial Numbers

	Low	High	Notes Printed	CH CU
BOSTON	A-A	—	99,840,000	$75
	A-B	—	17,920,000	80
	A-C	—	73,600,000	75
	A00 008 001★	A01 280 000★	1,024,000	125
NEW YORK	B-A, B-B	B-C	99,840,000 ea.	60
	B-D	—	23,040,000	60
	B-E	—	99,840,000	60
	B-F	—	92,800,000	60
	B00 000 001★	B06 400 000★	2,788,000	125
PHILADELPHIA	C-A	—	72,960,000	75
	C-B	—	28,800,000	75
	C00 008 001★	C00 640 000★	384,000	150
CLEVELAND	D-A	—	98,560,000	75
	D-B	—	48,000,000	75
	D00 000 001★	D01 280 000★	1,280,000	150
RICHMOND	E-A	E-B	99,840,000 ea.	75
	E-C	—	10,240,000	80
	E-D	—	86,400,000	75
	E00 000 001★	E01 280 000★	1,280,000	150
ATLANTA	F-A	—	29,440,000	75
	F-B	—	64,000,000	75
	F00 000 001★	F03 200 000★	3,200,000	140
CHICAGO	G-A	G-B	99,840,000 ea.	75
	G-C	—	23,040,000	80
	G-D	—	99,200,000	75
	G00 000 001★	G03 200 000★	2,688,000	140
ST. LOUIS	H-A	—	47,360,000	75
	H-B	—	28,800,000	75
	H00 012 001★	H01 920 000★	1,536,000	150
MINNEAPOLIS	I-A	—	10,240,000	95
	I-B	—	12,800,000	95
	I00 012 001★	I00 640 000★	256,000	200
KANSAS CITY	J-A	—	99,840,000	75
	J-B	—	19,200,000	80
	J-C	—	28,800,000	75
	J00 000 001★	J01 280 000★	1,280,000	150
DALLAS	K-A	—	60,160,000	75
	K-B	—	35,200,000	75
	K00 000 001★	K01 280 000★	896,000	175

	Low	High	Notes Printed	CH CU
SAN FRANCISCO	L-A	L-B	99,840,000 ea.	$75
	L-C	—	83,200,000	75
	L-D	—	99,840,000	75
	L-E	—	22,400,000	80
	L00 000 001★	L01 560 000★	1,424,000	150

SERIES 1981A GREEN SEAL

SERIAL NUMBERS: Both regular and star notes begin with 00 000 001.

SIGNATURES: Katherine Davalos Ortega, Donald T. Regan

	Serial Numbers			
	Low	High	Notes Printed	CH CU
BOSTON	A-A	A-B	156,800,000	$60
NEW YORK	B-A	B-C	297,600,000	50
	B-D	—	54,400,000	50
PHILADELPHIA	C-A	—	57,600,000	60
CLEVELAND	D-A	—	99,200,000	60
	D-B	—	60,800,000	60
	D-★	D06 400 000★	6,400,000	100
RICHMOND	E-A	E-B	198,400,000	60
	E-C	—	16,000,000	60
ATLANTA	F-A	—	99,200,000	60
	F-B	—	41,600,000	60
	F-★	F03 200 000★	3,200,000	100
CHICAGO	G-A		198,400,000	50
	G-C	—	12,800,000	85
ST. LOUIS	H-A	—	73,600,000	60
MINNEAPOLIS	I-A	—	19,200,000	60
KANSAS CITY	J-A	—	73,600,000	60
DALLAS	K-A	—	99,200,000	60
SAN FRANCISCO	L-A	L-E	457,600,000	60
	L-★	L06 400 000★	6,400,000	100

SERIES 1985 GREEN SEAL

SERIAL NUMBERS: Both regular and star notes begin with 00 000 001, except **C-★**.
SIGNATURES: Katherine Davalos Ortega, James A. Baker III

	Serial Numbers		Notes Printed	CH CU
	Low	**High**	**Notes Printed**	**CH CU**
BOSTON	A-A	A-E	496,000,000	$50
	A00 000 001★	A03 200 000★	2,560,000	75
NEW YORK	B-A	B-S	1,587,200,000	40
	B00 000 001★	B06 400 000★	5,760,000	75
PHILADELPHIA	C-A	C-B	198,400,000	50
	C-C	C25 600 000C	25,600,000	60
	C03 200 001★	C06 400 000★	3,200,000	75
CLEVELAND	D-A	D-F	684, 800,000	50
	D00 000 001★	D06 400 000★	6,400,000	75
RICHMOND	E-A	E-I	864,000,000	50
	E00 000 001★	E06 400 000★	3,456,000	75
ATLANTA	F-A	F-C	278,200,000	50
	F-D	—	16,000,000	70
CHICAGO	G-A	G-H	726,400,000	40
	G00 000 001★	G06 400 000★	2,568,000	75
ST. LOUIS	H-A	H-B	198,400,000	40
	H-C	—	32,000,000	50
MINNEAPOLIS	I-A	—	99,200,000	50
	I-B	I12 800 000B	12,800,000	60
KANSAS CITY	J-A	J-B	204,800,000	50
	J-C	J06 400 000C	6,400,000	70
	J00 000 001★	J03 200 000★	3,200,000	75
DALLAS	K-A	K-B	192,000,000	50
	K00 000 001★	K03 200 000★	1,920,000	75
SAN FRANCISCO	L-A	L-L	1,136,000,000	50
	L00 000 001★	L03 200 000★	3,200,000	75

SERIES 1988A GREEN SEAL

SIGNATURES: Catalina Vasquez Villalpando, Nicholas F. Brady

PLATE NUMBERS: Both face and back numbers begin at #1, with extensive muling from previous series on backs.

SERIAL NUMBERS: Both regular and star notes begin at 00 000 001.

	Serial Numbers			
	Low	**High**	**Notes Printed**	**CH CU**
BOSTON	A-A	A-D	313,600,000	$60
NEW YORK	B-A	B-K	934,400,000	40
	B-★	B12 800 000★	6,560,000	100
PHILADELPHIA	C-A	—	96,000,000	60
	C00 900 266★	C03 200 000★	2,560,000	125
CLEVELAND	D-A	D-D	283,200,000	60
RICHMOND	E45 699 654A	E-C	281,600,000	65
ATLANTA	F-A	F-C	288,000,000	60
	F00 806 276★	F03 200 000★	3,200,000	100
CHICAGO	G-A	G-F	563,200,000	40
	G-★	G03 200 000★	3,200,000	100
ST. LOUIS	H-A	H-B	108,800,000	60
MINNEAPOLIS	I02 857 457A	I11 735 944A	25,600,000	60
KANSAS CITY	J-A	J-B	137,600,000	60
DALLAS	K-A	—	51,200,000	60
	K00 840 794★	K03 200 000★	3,200,000	100
SAN FRANCISCO	L-A	L-H	729,600,000	60

SERIES 1990 GREEN SEAL

SIGNATURES: Catalina Vasquez Villalpando, Nicholas F. Brady

PLATE NUMBERS: Face numbers begin at #1. Back numbers continue sequence from previous series.

SERIAL NUMBERS: Both regular and star notes begin at 00 000 001.

(Series 1990 introduced the anti-counterfeiting security thread and the microsize printing around the portrait.)

	Serial Numbers			
	Low	**High**	**Notes Printed**	**CH CU**
BOSTON	A-A	A-D	345,600,000	$40
	A-★	A03 200 000★	2,560,000	70
NEW YORK	B-A	B-P	1,536,000,000	40
	B-Q	—	6,400,000	45
	B-★	B19 200 000★	16,640,000	70
PHILADELPHIA	C-A	—	96,000,000	45
CLEVELAND	D-A	D-C	279,600,000	45
	D-★	D03 200 000★	3,200,000	70
RICHMOND	E-A	E-D	288,000,000	45
	E-★	E03 200 000★	3,200,000	70
ATLANTA	F-A	F-E	537,600,000	40
	F★ FW	F03 200 000★	1,280,000	125
CHICAGO	G-A	G-G	652,800,000	40
	G-★ FW	G16 000 000★	13,440,000	70
ST. LOUIS	H-A	H-B	172,800,000	45
	H★	H03 200 000★	1,920,000	70
MINNEAPOLIS	I-A	—	70,400,000	45
	I04 113 691★ FW	I06 400 000★	5,120,000	80
KANSAS CITY	J-A	—	83,200,000	45
DALLAS	K-A	—	25,600,000	45
SAN FRANCISCO	L-A	L-E W/FW	416,000,000	40

SERIES 1993 GREEN SEAL

SIGNATURES: Mary Ellen Withrow, Lloyd Bentsen

PLATE NUMBERS: Face numbers begin at #1. Back numbers both continue from previous series, creating mules, and start with #1 simultaneously.

SERIAL NUMBERS: Both regular and star notes begin at 00 000 001.

	Serial Numbers			
	Low	**High**	**Notes Printed**	**CH CU**
BOSTON	A-A - A-C	A96 000 000C	288,000,000	$40
	A-★	A03 840 000★	2,560,000	60
NEW YORK	B-A - B-G	B19 200 000G	595,200,000	40
	B-★	B07 680 000★	5,120,000	50
PHILADELPHIA	C-A	C76 800 000A	76,800,000	45
CLEVELAND	D-A - D-C	D64 000 000C	256,000,000	40
	D-★	D01 920 000★	1,920,000	65
RICHMOND	E-A - E-G	E70 400 000G	646,400,000	40
	E-★	E03 840 000★	3,840,000	60
ATLANTA	F-A	F-D W	352,000,000	40
	F-★ FW	F03 200 000★	3,200,000	70
CHICAGO	G-A - G-D FW	G38 400 000D	326,400,000	40
ST. LOUIS	H-A - H-B W/FW	H89 600 000B	185,600,000	45
KANSAS CITY	J-A FW	J96 000 000A	96,000,000	40
	J-B FW	J06 400 000B	6,400,000	55
DALLAS	K-A - K-B FW	K89 600 000B	185,600,000	45
SAN FRANCISCO	L-A - L-I FW	L38 400 000I	806,400,000	40
	L-★	L09 600 000★	7,680,000	60

SERIES 1995 GREEN SEAL

SIGNATURES: Mary Ellen Withrow, Robert F. Rubin

PLATE NUMBERS: Face numbers begin at #1. Back numbers continue from previous series with the Fort Worth issues.

SERIAL NUMBERS: Both regular and star notes begin at 00 000 001.

	Serial Numbers			
	Low	**High**	**Notes Printed**	**CH CU**
NEW YORK	B-A - B-E W	B19 200 000E	403,200,000	$40
	B-★ W	B08 320 000★	5,760,000	50
PHILADELPHIA	C-A W	C70 400 000A	70,400,000	45
CLEVELAND	D-A - D-B W	D89 600 000B	185,600,000	45
	D-★ W	D05 760 000★	640,000	70
RICHMOND	E-A - E-B W	E25 600 000B	121,600,000	45
ATLANTA	F-A - F-D FW	F19 200 000D	307,200,000	45
	F-★ FW	F03 200 000★	3,200,000	60
CHICAGO	G-A - G-F FW	G12 800 000F	492,800,000	40
ST. LOUIS	H-A - H-B FW	H44 800 000B	140,800,000	45
MINNEAPOLIS	I-A FW	I44 800 000A	44,800,000	45
KANSAS CITY	J-A - J-B FW	J76 800 000B	172,800,000	45
DALLAS	K-A - K-C FW	K57 600 000C	249,600,000	45
SAN FRANCISCO	L-A - L-G FW	L38 400 000G	614,400,000	40

SERIES 1996 GREEN SEAL

SIGNATURES: Mary Ellen Withrow, Robert E. Rubin

PLATE NUMBERS: Both regular and star notes begin at #1.

SERIAL NUMBERS: Both regular and star notes begin at 00 000 001.

	Serial Numbers			
	Low	High	Notes Printed	CH CU
BOSTON	AA-A - AA-I	AA83 200 000I W	883,200,000	$30
	AA-★	AA12 800 000★ W	10,880,000	35
NEW YORK	AB-A - AB-I	AB96 000 000I W	896,000,000	30
	AB-★	AB03 200 000★ W	3,200,000	35
PHILADELPHIA	AC-A - AC-F	AC06 400 000F W	506,400,000	30
	AC-★	AC03 200 000★ W	3,200,000	40
CLEVELAND	AD-A - AD-D	AD64 000 000D W	364,000,000	30
	AD-★	AD06 400 000★ W	6,400,000	40
RICHMOND	AE-A - AE-D	AE83 200 000D W/FW	483,200,000	30
	AE-★	AE03 200 000★ FW	3,200,000	40
ATLANTA	AF-A - AF-J	AF25 600 000J W/FW	925,600,000	30
	AF-★	AF03 200 000★ FW	3,200,000	40
CHICAGO	AG-A - AG-L	AG51 200 000L FW	1,151,200,000	30
	AG-★	AG12 800 000★ FW	12,800,000	35
ST. LOUIS	AH-A - AH-C	AH57 600 000C FW	257,600,000	30
	AH-★	AH00 640 000★ FW	640,000	150
MINNEAPOLIS	AI-A - AI-B	AI12 800 000B FW	112,800,000	30
KANSAS CITY	AJ-A - AJ-C	AJ76 800 000C FW	276,800,000	30
DALLAS	AK-A - AK-C	AK76 800 000C FW	276,800,000	30
SAN FRANCISCO	AL-A - AL-K	AL83 200 000K FW	457,600,000	30
	AL-★	AL07 040 000★	7,040,000	35

SERIES 1999 GREEN SEAL

SIGNATURES: Mary Ellen Withrow, Lawrence H. Summers
PLATE NUMBERS: Both face and back numbers begin at #1.
SERIAL NUMBERS: Both regular and star notes begin at 00 000 001.

	Serial Numbers			
	Low	**High**	**Notes Printed**	**CH CU**
BOSTON	BA-A W	BA51 200 000A	51,200,000	$30
	BA-★ W	BA01 920 000★	1,920,000	60
NEW YORK	BB-A - BB-G W	BB32 000 000G	608,000,000	30
	BB-★ W	BB00 640 000★	640,000	100
	BB03 200 001★ W	BB05 120 000★	1,920,000	45
	BB06 400 001★ FW			
		BB09 600 000★	3,200,000	45
PHILADELPHIA	BC-A - BC-B W	BC96 000 000B	192,000,000	30
CLEVELAND	BD-A - BD-C W/FW	BD32 000 000C	224,000,000	30
	BD-★ W	BD03 840 000★	2,560,000	60
RICHMOND	BE-A - BE-E W	BE32 000 000E	416,000,000	30
ATLANTA	BF-A - BF-F FW	BF12 800 000F	492,800,000	30
CHICAGO	BG-A - BG-H FW	BG32 000 000H	704,000,000	30
	BG-★ FW	BG07 040 000★	7,040,000	40
ST. LOUIS	BH-A FW	BH96 000 000A	96,000,000	30
	BH-B W	BH06 400 000B	6,400,000	35
MINNEAPOLIS	BI-A FW	BI25 600 000A	25,600,000	30
KANSAS CITY	BJ-A FW	BJ70 400 000A	70,400,000	30
SAN FRANCISCO	BL-A FW	BL32 000 000A	32,000,000	30
	BL-★ FW	BL03 200 000★	3,200,000	60

SERIES 2001 GREEN SEAL

SIGNATURES: Rosario Marin, Paul H. O'Neill

PLATE NUMBERS: Both face and back numbers begin at #1.

SERIAL NUMBERS: All districts start both regular and star notes with 00 000 001.

	Serial Numbers			
	Low	**High**	**Notes Printed**	**CH CU**
NEW YORK	CB-A - CB-G W/FW	CB76 800 000G	652,800,000	$30
	CB-★ W	CB00 320 000★	320,000	125
CLEVELAND	CD-A W	CD83 200 000A	83,200,000	30
RICHMOND	CE-A - CE-D W/FW	CE51 200 000D	339,200,000	30
ATLANTA	CF-A - CF-D FW	CF57 600 000D	345,600,000	30
CHICAGO	CG-A - CG-D FW	CG32 000 000D	320,000,000	30
	CG-★ FW	CG03 200 000★	3,020,000	50
ST. LOUIS	CH-A FW	CH89 600 000A	89,600,000	30
MINNEAPOLIS	CI-A FW	CI57 600 000A	57,600,000	30
KANSAS CITY	CJ-A - CJ-B FW	CJ12 800 000B	108,800,000	30
	CJ-★ FW	CJ03 200 000★	3,200,000	50
DALLAS	CK-A - CK-B FW	CK70 400 000B	166,400,000	30
SAN FRANCISCO	CL-A - CL-E FW	CL12 800 000E	396,800,000	30
	CL-★ FW	CL03 200 000★	3,200,000	50

SERIES 2004 GREEN SEAL (COLORIZED)

SIGNATURES: Rosario Marin, John W. Snow
PLATE NUMBERS: Both face and back numbers begin at #1.
SERIAL NUMBERS: All districts start both regular and star notes with 00 000 001.

	Serial Numbers		Notes Printed	CH CU
	Low	**High**	**Notes Printed**	**CH CU**
BOSTON	EA-A - EA-F W	EA96 000 000F	576,000,000	$30
	EA-★ W	EA00 320 000★	320,000	$50
	EA03 200 001★ W	EA03 520 000★	320,000	50
	EA06 400 001★	WEA10 176 000★	576,000	50
NEW YORK	EB-A - EB-L W	EB25 600 000L	1,081,600,000	30
	EB-★ W	EB00 320 000★	320,000	150
PHILADELPHIA	EC-A - EC-G W	EC38 400 000G	614,400,000	30
	EC-★ W	EC03 520 000★	3,520,000	40
	EC06 400 001★	WEC06 720 000★	320,000	80
	EC09 600 001★	WEC12 800 000★	3,200,000	40
CLEVELAND	ED-A - ED-D W/F	WED89 600 000D	377,600,000	30
RICHMOND	EE-A - EE-E W/FW	EE89 600 000E	473,600,000	30
	EE-★ W	EE00 640 000★	640,000	100
	EE03 200 001★ W	EE06 400 000★	3,200,000	50
ATLANTA	EF-A - EF-E W/FW	EF64 000 000E	448,000,000	30
	EF-★ FW	EF06 400 000★	6,400,000	50
CHICAGO	EG-A - EG-F FW	EG96 000 000F	576,000,000	30
	EG-G FW	EG06 400 000G	6,400,000	50
	EG-★ FW	EG03 840 000★	3,840,000	50
	EG06 400 001★ FW	EG07 040 000★	640,000	100
ST. LOUIS	EH-A - EH-B FW	EH32 000 000B	128,000,000	30
MINNEAPOLIS	EI-A FW	EI64 000 000A	64,000,000	30
KANSAS CITY	EJ-A - EJ-B FW	EJ12 800 000B	108,800,000	30
	EJ-★ FW	EJ03 200 000★	3,200,000	50
DALLAS	EK-A - EK-B FW	EK76 800 000B	172,800,000	30
	EK-★ FW	EK03 840 000★ (sheets)	3,840,000	50
SAN FRANCISCO	EL-A - EL-I FW	EL32 000 000I	800,000,000	30
	EL-★ FW	EL06 400 000★	6,400,000	50

SERIES 2004A GREEN SEAL (COLORIZED)

SIGNATURES: Anna Escobedo Cabral, John W. Snow
PLATE NUMBERS: Both face and back numbers begin at #1.
SERIAL NUMBERS: All districts start both regular and star notes with 00 000 001.

	Serial Numbers			
	Low	**High**	**Notes Printed**	**CH CU**
BOSTON	GA-A W	GA38 400 000B	134,400,000	$30
	GA-★ W	GA00 384 000★	384,000	100
NEW YORK	GB-A W	GB96 000 000B	192,000,000	30
	GB-★ W	GB00 320 000★(sheets)	320,000	100
	GB03 2000 001★	WGB05 760 000★	2,560,000	50
PHILADELPHIA	GC-A W	GC96 000 000A	96,000,000	30
CLEVELAND	GD-A W	GD25 600 000B	121,600,000	30
RICHMOND	GE-A W	GE76 800 000D	364,800,000	30
	GE-★ W	GE03 200 000★	3,200,000	50
ATLANTA	GF-A FW	GF96 000 000C	288,000,000	30
	GF00 000 001D	WGF83 200 000D	76,800,000	30
CHICAGO	GG-A W	GG38 400 000A	38,400,000	30
ST. LOUIS	GH-A FW	GH76 800 000A	76,800,000	30
MINNEAPOLIS	GI-A W/FW	GI89 600 000A	89,600,000	30
KANSAS CITY	GJ-A W/FW	GJ96 000 000B	192,000,000	30
DALLAS	GK-AFW	GK83 200 000C	275,200,000	30
	GK-★ FW	GK02 304 000★	2,304,000	60
SAN FRANCISCO	GL-A FW	GL89 600 000B	185,600,000	30

SERIES 2006 GREEN SEAL (COLORIZED)

SIGNATURES: Anna Escobedo Cabral, Henry M. Paulson, Jr.

PLATE NUMBERS: Both face and back numbers begin at #1.

SERIAL NUMBERS: All districts start with 00 000 001.

	Serial Numbers			
	Low	**High**	**Notes Printed**	**CH CU**
BOSTON	IA-A W	IA57 600 000A	57,600,000	$30
NEW YORK	IB-A W	IB06 400 000D	294,400,000	30
PHILADELPHIA	IC-A W	IC44 800 000B	140,800,000	30
CLEVELAND	ID-A W	ID89 600 000A	89,600,000	30
RICHMOND	IE-A W	IE76 800 000B	172,800,000	30
ATLANTA	IF-A W	IF76 800 000A	76,800,000	30
	IF-★ W	IF00 320 000A (Sheets)	320,000	100
KANSAS CITY	IJ-A FW	IJ32 000 000A	32,000,000	30
DALLAS	IK-A FW	IK83 200 000A	83,200,000	30
SAN FRANCISCO	IL-A FW	IL96 000 000C	288,000,000	30

FIFTY DOLLAR NOTES

GOLD CERTIFICATES

SERIES 1928 GOLD SEAL

PLATE NUMBERS: Face range #1 through #41.

SIGNATURES: W.O. Woods, A.W. Mellon

Serial Numbers

Low	High	Notes Printed	VG/F	VF	CH CU	GEM CU
A00 000 001A	A05 520 000A	5,520,000	$350	$750	$3,500	$6,000
★00 000 211A	★00 028 165A	—	1,000	3,000	20,000	—

FEDERAL RESERVE BANK NOTES

SERIES 1929 BROWN SEAL

SERIAL NUMBERS: Both regular and star notes start with 00 000 001.

PLATE NUMBERS: Face numbers begin with #1.

SIGNATURES: Same as $5.00 FRBN

	Serial Numbers					
	Low	**High**	**Notes Printed**	**VF**	**CH CU**	**GEM CU**
NEW YORK	B00 002 557A	B00 594 680A	636,000	$75	$450	$600
	B00 001 201★	B00 015 571★	24,000	625	3,500	—

	Low	High	Notes Printed	VF	CH CU	GEM CU
CLEVELAND	D00 002 867A	D00 679 541A	684,000	$75	$350	$550
	D00 000 182★	D00 006 685★	12,000	750	4,000	—
CHICAGO	G00 000 200A	G00 300 000A	300,000	75	400	550
	G00 002 184★	G00 003 305★	4,000	7,500	—	—
MINNEAPOLIS	I00 000 003A	I00 129 930A	276,000	100	500	800
	I00 001 914★	I00 002 997★	12,000	6,000	—	—
KANSAS CITY	J00 021 424A	J00 273 793A	276,000	$85	350	550

	Low	High	Notes Printed	VF	CH CU	GEM CU
	J00 000 045★	J00 004 854★	12,000	$600	$3,000	—
DALLAS	K00 145 505A	K00 167 221A	168,000	400	4,500	—
	K00 000 578★	not reported	12,000	—	—	—
SAN FRANCISCO	L00 000 420A	L00 570 668A	576,000	100	500	700
	L00 001 953★	L00 002 491★	12,000	5,000	—	—

FEDERAL RESERVE NOTES

SERIES 1928 GREEN SEAL

SERIAL NUMBERS: All serial numbers of both regular and star notes begin with 00 000 001. High official star serial numbers are listed under the High Star serial number column.

PLATE NUMBERS: Both face and back start with #1.

SIGNATURES: W.O. Woods, A.W. Mellon

Serial Numbers

	Low	High	Notes Printed	VF	CH CU	GEM CU
BOSTON	A00 024 935A	A00 345 926A	265,200	$300	$2,000	$2,500
	A00 000 058★	A00 011 959★	—	6,000	—	—
NEW YORK	B00 014 016A	B02 386 257A	1,351,800	$175	600	900
	B00 000 963★	B00 018 980★	76,000	500	2,000	—
PHILADELPHIA	C00 512 342A	C01 472 696A	997,056	200	900	1,200
	C00 004 849★	C00 007 351★	48,000	550	3,000	—
CLEVELAND	D00 000 025A	D01 843 794A	1,161,900	200	700	900
	D00 000 463★	D00 015 894★	48,000	700	3,000	—
RICHMOND	E00 088 672A	E00 779 225A	539,400	200	750	1,100
	E00 001 747★	E00 002 000★	24,000	900	3,500	5,500
ATLANTA	F00 002 865A	F00 412 976A	538,000	200	900	1,250
	F00 001 003★	F00 007 990★	24,000	900	3,000	—
CHICAGO	G00 100 333A	G02 715 649A	1,348,620	175	600	800
	G00 000 129★	G00 042 362★	84,000	500	1,600	2,500
ST. LOUIS	H00 000 346A	H00 316 412A	627,300	175	750	1,000
	H00 000 566★	H00 003 956★	24,000	700	2,000	4,000
MINNEAPOLIS	I00 003 340A	I00 099 867A	106,200	300	2,500	—
	I00 000 069★	I00 002 847★	24,000	5,000	—	—
KANSAS CITY	J00 070 582A	J00 201 963A	252,600	125	900	1,250
	J00 000 254★	J00 006 850★	24,000	2,000	—	—
DALLAS	K00 014 310A	K00 081 870A	109,920	350	2,000	—
	K00 003 342★	—	12,000	3,500	—	—
SAN FRANCISCO	L00 072 461A	L00 471 797A	447,600	175	750	1,000
	L00 000 732★	L00 003 804★	24,000	1,000	—	—

SERIES 1928A DARK GREEN SEAL

Serial Numbers: Continue in sequence from series 1928.

DESIGN CHANGE: District numeral in seal replaced by letter. Face plates begins with #1.

SIGNATURES: W.O. Woods, A.W. Mellon

Serial Numbers

	Low	High	Notes Printed	VF	CH CU	GEM CU
BOSTON	A00 220 836A	A00 719 992A	1,834,989	$80	$300	$500
NEW YORK	B01 392 109A	B02 758 669A	3,392,328	80	300	400
PHILADELPHIA	C00 857 996A	C01 516 053A	3,078,944	80	400	550
CLEVELAND	D01 199 636A	D02 129 955A	2,453,364	80	300	400
RICHMOND	E00 388 711A	E00 904 212A	1,516,500	$80	500	650

	Low	High	Notes Printed	VF	CH CU	GEM CU
ATLANTA	F00 455 771A	F00 543 234A	338,400	100	500	650
CHICAGO	G01 209 277A	G03 172 020A	5,263,956	$80	$300	$400
	G00 040 087★	G00 040 912★	—	4,000	12,500	—
ST. LOUIS	H00 280 205A	H00 653 946A	880,500	90	300	400
MINNEAPOLIS	I00 076 661A	I00 129 520A	780,240	100	650	—
KANSAS CITY	J00 253 917A	J00 287 411A	791,604	125	900	—
DALLAS	K00 104 894A	K00 256 228A	701,496	200	1,300	—
SAN FRANCISCO	L00 442 789A	L00 561 067A	1,522,620	125	1,100	—

SERIES 1928A LIGHT VIVID YELLOW-GREEN SEAL

SERIAL NUMBERS: Continue in sequence from 1928A Dark Green Seal variety.

	Serial Numbers					
	Low	High	Notes Printed	VF	CH CU	GEM CU
NEW YORK	B03 039 046A	B03 634 101A	—	$150	$1,000	—
CHICAGO	G03 523 646A	G03 750 686A	—	150	1,000	—
MINNEAPOLIS	I00 129 518A	I00 163 950A	—	250	1,250	—
KANSAS CITY	J00 492 480A	J00 538 636A	included above	150	1,250	—
SAN FRANCISCO	L01 078 732A	L01 261 965A	included above	150	1,250	—

SERIES 1934 LIGHT VIVID YELLOW-GREEN SEAL

SERIAL NUMBERS: Both regular and stars begin with 00 000 001.

PLATE NUMBERS: Face check numbers start with #1. Back check numbers continue in sequence from Series 1928A

	Serial Numbers				
	Low	High	Notes Printed	VF	CH CU
BOSTON	A00 003 920A	A00 728 854A	2,729,400	$90	$500
	A00 000 043★	A00 009 960★	—	300	1,600
NEW YORK	B00 000 890A	B01 693 309A	17,894,676	85	350
	B00 000 057★	B00 008 680★	—	300	1,600
PHILADELPHIA	C00 189 154A	C00 919 123A	5,833,000	85	350
	C00 004 529★	C00 004 813★	—	300	1,600
CLEVELAND	D00 007 988A	D01 404 274A	8,817,720	85	500
	D00 001 659★	—	—	300	1,600
RICHMOND	E00 000 947A	E00 600 806A	4,826,628	85	500
	E00 005 803★	—	—	300	1,600

	Low	High	Notes Printed	VF	CH CU
ATLANTA	F00 009 969A	F00 247 642A	3,069,348	$85	$500
	F-★	—	—	400	2,000
CHICAGO	G00 001 589A	G00 922 507A	8,675,940	85	300
	G00 002 591★	G00 006 898★	—	400	2,000
ST. LOUIS	H00 038 085A	H00 236 275A	1,497,144	85	350
	H-★	—	—	400	2,000
MINNEAPOLIS	I00 005 105A	I00 092 673A	539,700	100	700
	I-★	—	—	400	2,000
KANSAS CITY	J00 006 550A	J00 043 246A	1,133,520	85	400
	J00 000 921★	—	—	400	2,000
DALLAS	K00 011 067A	K00 160 405A	1,194,876	85	450
	K00 000 438★	K00 000 853★	—	400	2,400
SAN FRANCISCO	L00 008 471A	L00 298 090A	8,101,200	85	450
	L00 001 467★	L00 001 474★	—	400	2,000

SERIES 1934 DARK BLUE-GREEN SEAL

SERIAL NUMBERS: All serial numbers both regular and star continue in sequence from 1934 Light Vivid Yellow Seal variety.

PLATE NUMBERS: Back numbers up to #162.

SIGNATURES: W.A. Julian, Henry Morgenthau, Jr.

Quantities included in Light Vivid Yellow-Green Seal above.

	Serial Numbers				
	Low	High	Notes Printed	VF	CH CU
BOSTON	A00 750 639A	A02 888 879A	—	—	$190
	A00 012 537★	A00 013 474★	—	$105	750
NEW YORK	B02 060 387A	B16 302 878A	—	—	150
	B00 009 593★	B00 132 401★	—	105	525
PHILADELPHIA	C01 026 815A	C05 642 209A	—	—	150
	C00 012 183★	C00 051 088★	—	105	750
CLEVELAND	D01 100 943A	D09 374 113A	—	—	150
	D00 011 932★	D00 078 568★	—	105	750
RICHMOND	E00 853 631A	E06 647 594A	—	—	170
	E00 010 289★	E00 072 987★	—	105	900
ATLANTA	F00 323 667A	F03 528 759A	—	—	170
	F00 005 876★	F00 032 240★	—	105	900
CHICAGO	G01 089 824A	G10 069 519A	—	—	135
	G00 015 086★	G00 080 826★	—	105	600
ST. LOUIS	H00 286 389A	H01 706 620A	—	—	170
	H00 004 089★	H00 023 980★	—	110	900
MINNEAPOLIS	I00 098 398A	I00 673 439A	—	—	210
	I00 004 074★	I00 006 851★	—	110	900
KANSAS CITY	J00 236 102A	J01 182 770A	—	—	150
	J00 004 747★	J00 022 425★	—	110	750
DALLAS	K00 201 846A	K01 419 064A	—	—	190
	K00 004 251★	K00 009 695★	—	110	1,125
SAN FRANCISCO	L00 501 702A	L07 819 924A	—	—	170
	L00 010 964★	L00 090 408★	—	110	750

SERIES 1934A MULE GREEN SEAL

SIGNATURES: W.A. Julian, Henry Morgenthau, Jr.

PLATE NUMBERS: Back numbers 162 and lower (micro size).

SERIAL NUMBERS: All districts continue from previous series.

All observations and reported information indicate that all $50. Federal Reserve notes from 1934A through 1950 are MULES.

	Serial Numbers				
	Low	**High**	**Notes Printed**	**VF**	**CH CU**
BOSTON	A01 441 067A	A02 770 530A	406,200	$75	$340
	A-★	—	—	300	1,125
NEW YORK	B03 737 222A	B17 210 626A	4,710,648	60	225
	B00 021 055★	B00 113 592★	—	110	825
CLEVELAND	D04 859 131A	D07 950 056A	864,168	70	230
	D-★	—	—	300	1,125
RICHMOND	E02 107 772A	E06 327 800A	2,235,372	70	230
	E00 031 768★	E00 040 097★	—	300	975
ATLANTA	F01 975 460A	F03 201 653A	416,100	70	300
	F00 025 815★	—	—	300	1,125
CHICAGO	G02 638 524A	G08 972 632A	1,014,600	65	230
	G00 045 058★	—	—	225	975
ST. LOUIS	H00 759 728A	H01 722 543A	361,944	75	340
	H00 017 769★	H00 021 263★	—	300	1,125
MINNEAPOLIS	I00 266 685A	I00 666 901A	93,300	95	375
	I-★	—	—	300	1,125
KANSAS CITY	J00 595 835A	J01 124 231A	189,300	75	375
	J-★	—	—	300	1,125
DALLAS	K00 394 159A	K01 653 036A	266,700	75	300
	K-★	—	—	300	1,125
SAN FRANCISCO	L00 414 384A	L02 871 431A	—	75	375
	L-★	—	162,000	300	1,125

SERIES 1934B MULE GREEN SEAL

SIGNATURES: W.A. Julian, Fred M. Vinson
PLATE NUMBERS: Back number 162 and lower.
SERIAL NUMBERS: All districts continued from previous series.

	Serial Numbers				
	Low	**High**	**Notes Printed**	**VF**	**CH CU**
PHILADELPHIA	C05 604 319A	C06 450 053A	509,100	$90	$400
	C00 056 617★	C00 064 306★	—	1,000	3,500
CLEVELAND	D09 441 295A	D10 146 571A	359,100	90	400
	D00 108 730★	D00 119 763★	—	1,000	3,500
RICHMOND	E06 906 479A	E07 284 378A	596,700	90	400
	E00 083 474★	E00 090 094★	—	1,000	3,500
ATLANTA	F03 280 429A	F03 763 548A	416,720	90	400
CHICAGO	G09 202 902A	G09 399 017A	306,000	90	400
ST. LOUIS	H01 745 970A	H02 022 571A	306,000	90	400
MINNEAPOLIS	I00 580 912A	I00 695 603A	120,000	200	550
KANSAS CITY	J01 246 543A	J01 495 360A	221,340	90	500
	J00 034 838★	—	—	1,000	3,500
DALLAS	K01 403 267A	K01 460 049A	120,108	150	550
SAN FRANCISCO	L07 831 530A	L08 173 221A	441,000	90	450

SERIES 1934C MULE GREEN SEAL

SIGNATURES: W.A. Julian, John W. Snyder

PLATE NUMBERS: Back number 162 and lower.

SERIAL NUMBERS: All districts continue from previous series.

	Serial Numbers				
	Low	High	Notes Printed	VF	CH CU
BOSTON	A03 019 467A	A03 156 740A	117,600	$100	$300
NEW YORK	B16 487 892A	B19 095 949A	1,556,400	85	220
	B00 144 668★	B00 153 458★	—	500	1,500
PHILADELPHIA	C05 888 759A	C07 789 899A	107,293	100	300
	C00 075 796★	C00 081 801★	—	500	1,500
CLEVELAND	D09 453 708A	D12 183 881A	374,000	90	250
	D00 109 882★	D00 145 476★	—	500	1,500
RICHMOND	E07 527 278A	E08 786 836A	1,821,960	85	220
	E00 097 595★	E00 110 331★	—	500	1,500
ATLANTA	F-A	—	107,640	250	1,000
CHICAGO	G09 166 768A	G09 623 069A	294,432	85	250
	G00 745 810★	—	—	500	1,500
ST. LOUIS	H02 089 607A	H03 577 074A	535,200	85	250
MINNEAPOLIS	I00 721 163A	I00 834 866A	118,800	100	300
	I00 010 437★	I00 011 831★	—	500	1,500
KANSAS CITY	J01 412 982A	J01 806 460A	303,600	85	250
DALLAS	K01 560 306A	K01 941 793A	429,900	85	250
	K00 025 502★	K00 025 507★	—	500	1,500

SERIES 1934D MULE GREEN SEAL

SIGNATURES: Georgia Neese Clark, John W. Snyder
PLATE NUMBERS: Back check number 162 and lower.
SERIAL NUMBERS: All districts continue from previous series. All high numbers are official endings.

	Serial Numbers				
	Low	**High**	**Notes Printed**	**VF**	**CH CU**
BOSTON	A03 129 512A	A03 468 000A	279,600	$125	$300
	A00 030 827★	A00 041 557★	—	1,500	4,000
NEW YORK	B18 147 152A	B19 248 000A	898,776	85	250
	B00 159 698★	B00 171 340★	—	1,200	3,000
PHILADELPHIA	C07 371 807A	C08 004 000A	699,000	85	250
	C00 068 897★	C00 069 641★	—	1,200	3,000
RICHMOND	E09 200 267A	E09 216 000A	156,000	115	400
	E00 109 913★	E00 110 693★	—	1,500	4,000
ATLANTA	F03 835 362A	F04 020 000A	216,000	115	400
	F00 036 681★	F00 043 511★	—	1,500	4,000
CHICAGO	G07 479 216A	G10 188 000A	494,016	85	240
	G00 099 921★	G00 100 066★	—	1,200	3,000
MINNEAPOLIS	I00 750 686A	—	—	$275	600
DALLAS	K01 856 747A	K01 984 000A	103,200	90	400

SERIES 1950 MULE GREEN SEAL

SIGNATURES: Georgia Neese Clark, John W. Snyder

PLATE NUMBERS: Back number 162 and lower (micro size).

SERIAL NUMBERS: All districts begin (both star and regular notes) with 00 000 001.

	Serial Numbers			
	Low	**High**	**Notes Printed**	**CH CU**
BOSTON	A00 277 213A	A01 248 000A	1,248,000	$150
	A00 003 673★	A00 012 550★	—	675
NEW YORK	B00 647 948A	B10 236 000A	10,236,000	135
	B00 041 155★	B00 266 566★	—	450
PHILADELPHIA	C00 002 256A	C02 352 000A	2,352,000	150
	C00 009 124★	C00 031 925★	—	600
CLEVELAND	D00 364 871A	D06 019 325A	6,180,000	170
	D00 014 664★	D00 088 000★	—	490
RICHMOND	E00 287 895A	E05 064 000A	5,064,000	150
	E00 045 108★	E00 048 950★	—	490
ATLANTA	F00 044643A	F01 812 000A	1,812,000	190
	F00 017 620★	—	—	600
CHICAGO	G00 035 208A	G04 212 000A	4,212,000	115
	G00 000 473★	G00 059 216★	—	375
ST. LOUIS	H00 045 774A	H00 892 000A	892,000	135
	H00 002 023★	H00 012 898★	—	675
MINNEAPOLIS	I00 055 202A	I00 379 896A	384,000	320
	I00 008 097★	I00 009 227★	—	1,125
KANSAS CITY	J00 477 370A	J00 696 000A	696,000	150
	J00 002 607★	—	—	675
DALLAS	K00 103 875A	K01 100 000A	1,100,000	150
	K-★	K00 004 300★	—	450
SAN FRANCISCO	L00 048 328A	L03 996 000A	3,996,000	150
	L00 007 897★	L00 049 101★	—	450

Higher serial numbers were assigned to this series, but were not used.

SERIES 1950A GREEN SEAL

SERIAL NUMBERS: Continued sequence from previous series, with small gaps in each district.

SIGNATURES: Ivy Baker Priest, G.M. Humphrey

	Serial Numbers			
	Low	**High**	**Notes Printed**	**CH CU**
BOSTON	A01 296 001A	A02 016 000A	720,000	$190
	A00 155 016★	A00 218 392★	—	450
NEW YORK	B10 368 001A	B16 848 000A	6,480,000	135
	B00 327 121★	B00 861 566★	—	300
PHILADELPHIA	C02 448 001A	C04 176 000A	1,728,000	135
	C00 170 038★	C00 418 696★	—	300
CLEVELAND	D06 192 001A	D08 064 000A	1,872,000	135
	D00 183 149★	D00 415 400★	—	300
RICHMOND	E05 184 001A	E07 200 000A	2,016,000	135
	E00 147 887★	E00 410 849★	—	375
ATLANTA	F01 872 001A	F02 160 000A	288,000	150
	F00 280 895★	—	—	525
CHICAGO	G04 320 001A	G06 336 000A	2,016,000	170
	G00 175 480★	G00 306 562★	—	340
ST. LOUIS	H01 008 001A	H01 584 000A	576,000	150
	H00 240 689★	H00 416 385★	—	300
KANSAS CITY	J00 720 001A	J00 864 000A	144,000	170
	J00 192 270★	J00 272 539★	—	300
DALLAS	K01 152 001A	K02 016 000A	864,000	150
	K00 187 473★	K00 266 449★	—	375
SAN FRANCISCO	L04 032 001A	L04 608 000A	576,000	150
	L00 218 959★	L00 256 794★	—	375

SERIES 1950B GREEN SEAL

SERIAL NUMBERS: Continued sequence from previous series.
SIGNATURES: Ivy Baker Priest, Robert B. Anderson

	Serial Numbers			
	Low	**High**	**Notes Printed**	**CH CU**
BOSTON	A02 016 001A	A02 880 000A	864,000	$115
	A00 339 618★	A00 472 632★	—	265
NEW YORK	B16 848 001A	B25 200 000A	8,352,000	75
	B01 023 417★	B01 800 077★	—	190
PHILADELPHIA	C04 176 001A	C06 768 000A	2,592,000	115
	C00 502 437★	C00 681 219★	—	265
CLEVELAND	D08 064 001A	D09 792 000A	1,728,000	115
	D00 440 077★	D00 617 009★	—	265
RICHMOND	E07 274 001A	E08 784 000A	1,584,000	115
	E00 472 632★	E00 548 566★	—	340
CHICAGO	G06 336 001A	G10 656 000A	4,320,000	75
	G00 432 412★	G00 677 871★	—	240
ST. LOUIS	H01 584 001A	H02 160 000A	576,000	115
	H00 441 493★	H00 560 223★	—	340
KANSAS CITY	J00 864 001A	J01 872 000A	1,008,000	115
	J00 289 624★	J00 427 775★	—	340
DALLAS	K02 016 001A	K03 024 000A	1,008,000	190
	K00 296 427★	K00 560 669★	—	340
SAN FRANCISCO	L04 608 001A	L06 480 000A	1,872,000	115
	L00 294 923★	L00 532 914★	—	340

SERIES 1950C GREEN SEAL

SERIAL NUMBERS: Continued sequence from previous series.

SIGNATURES: Elizabeth Rudel Smith, C. Douglas Dillon

	Serial Numbers Low	High	Notes Printed	CH CU
BOSTON	A02 880 001A	A03 600 000A	720,000	$95
	A00 464 869★	A00 536 983★	—	420
NEW YORK	B25 200 001A	B30 528 000A	5,328,000	75
	B01 945 413★	B02 146 795★	—	375
PHILADELPHIA	C06 768 001A	C08 064 000A	1,296,000	95
	C00 748 575★	C00 848 739★	—	375
CLEVELAND	D09 792 001A	D11 088 000A	1,296,000	95
	D00 734 700★	D00 840 734★	—	375
RICHMOND	E08 784 001A	E10 080 000A	1,296,000	95
	E-★	—	—	525
CHICAGO	G10 656 001A	G12 384 000A	1,728,000	135
	G00 739 171★	G00 985 482★	—	300
ST. LOUIS	H02 160 001A	H02 736 000A	576,000	95
	H00 632 700★	H00 714 238★	—	375
MINNEAPOLIS	I00 432 001A	I00 576 000A	144,000	225
	I00 161 566★	I00 248 473★	—	900
KANSAS CITY	J01 872 001A	J02 304 000A	432,000	210
	J00 488 285★	J00 552 263★	—	450
DALLAS	K03 024 001A	K03 744 000A	720,000	115
	K-★	—	—	525
SAN FRANCISCO	L06 480 001A	L07 632 000A	1,152,000	95
	L00 575 566★	L00 580 030★	—	450

SERIES 1950D GREEN SEAL

SERIAL NUMBERS: Continued sequence from previous series.
SIGNATURES: Kathryn O'Hay Granahan, C. Douglas Dillon

	Serial Numbers			
	Low	**High**	**Notes Printed**	**CH CU**
BOSTON	A03 600 001A	A05 328 000A	1,728,000	$135
	A00 593 199★	A00 692 151★	—	450
NEW YORK	B30 528 001A	B37 728 000A	7,200,000	115
	B02 220 212★	B02 570 310★	—	225
PHILADELPHIA	C08 064 001A	C10 800 000A	2,736,000	95
	C00 881 479★	C01 137 138★	—	300
CLEVELAND	D11 088 001A	D13 968 000A	2,880,000	75
	D00 884 582★	D01 107 811★	—	265
RICHMOND	E10 080 001A	E12 096 000A	2,016,000	95
	E00 600 728★	E00 690 420★	—	300
ATLANTA	F02 160 001A	F02 736 000A	576,000	75
	F00 356 258★	F00 418 019★	—	375
CHICAGO	G12 384 001A	G16 560 000A	4,176,000	75
	G01 009 350★	G01 280 932★	—	225
ST. LOUIS	H02 736 001A	H04 176 000A	1,440,000	115
	H00 757 908★	H00 860 042★	—	300
MINNEAPOLIS	I00 576 001A	I00 864 000A	288,000	135
	I-★	—	—	600
KANSAS CITY	J02 304 001A	J03 024 000A	720,000	135
	J00 600 059★	J00 712 518★	—	300
DALLAS	K03 744 001A	K05 040 000A	1,296,000	190
	K-★	—	—	600
SAN FRANCISCO	L07 632 001A	L09 792 000A	2,160,000	150
	L00 737 388★	L00 936 586★	—	300

SERIES 1950E GREEN SEAL

SERIAL NUMBERS: Districts printed continued sequence from previous series.
SIGNATURES: Kathryn O'Hay Granahan, Henry H. Fowler

	Serial Numbers				
	Low	High	Notes Printed	VF	CH CU
NEW YORK	B37 728 001A	B40 752 000A	3,024,000	$75	$300
	B02 596 329★	B02 860 974★	288,000 est.	300	1,000
CHICAGO	G16 560 001A	G17 568 000A	1,008,000	200	500
	G01 299 826★	G01 430 385★	144,000 est.	800	2,700
SAN FRANCISCO	L09 792 001A	L11 088 000A	1,296,000	175	300
	L01 041 216★	L01 139 838★	144,000 est.	500	1,500

SERIES 1963 GREEN SEAL

None printed

> Starting with Series 1963 in the Federal Reserve Notes, star notes are often printed in staggered runs, not consecutive to each other, so that large serial number gaps may exist. This can result in higher star serial numbers found on the notes than may be found in the "Notes Printed" columns.

SERIES 1963A GREEN SEAL

SERIAL NUMBERS: All serial numbers of both regular and star notes begin with 00 000 001.

PLATE NUMBERS: Face and back both begin with #1. Motto "IN GOD WE TRUST" added on back.

SIGNATURES: Kathryn O'Hay Granahan, Henry H. Fowler

	Serial Numbers			
	Low	**High**	**Notes Printed**	**CH CU**
BOSTON	A-A	—	1,536,000	$80
	A00 000 007★	A00 296 951★	320,000	320
NEW YORK	B-A	—	11,008,000	80
	B00 308 094★	B01 397 635★	1,408,000	200
PHILADELPHIA	C00 992 309A	C-A	3,328,000	180
	C00 112 131★	C00 676 249★	704,000	280
CLEVELAND	D00 988 697A	D-A	3,584,000	80
	D00 000 008★	D00 249 819★	256,000	260
RICHMOND	E-A	—	3,072,000	100
	E00 121 034★	E00 412 061★	704,000	260
ATLANTA	F-A	—	768,000	220
	F00 000 800★	F00 207 449★	384,000	240
CHICAGO	G03 538 396A	—	6,912,000	80
	G00 000 100★	G00 757 624★	768,000	200
ST. LOUIS	H-A	—	512,000	80
	H00 000 007★	H00 114 370★	128,000	320
MINNEAPOLIS	I-A	—	512,000	180
	I00 016 814★	I00 082 882★	128,000	400
KANSAS CITY	J-A	—	512,000	80
	J00 000 003★	J00 028 201★	64,000	340
DALLAS	K-A	—	1,536,000	80
	K00 041 230★	K00 109 683★	128,000	400
SAN FRANCISCO	L01 819 415A	—	4,352,000	80
	L00 120 164★	L00 327 750★	704,000	240

SERIES 1969 GREEN SEAL

SERIAL NUMBERS: All serial numbers of both regular and star notes begin with 00 000 001.

SIGNATURES: Dorothy Andrews Elston, David M. Kennedy

	Serial Numbers			
	Low	**High**	**Notes Printed**	**CH CU**
BOSTON	A-A	—	2,048,000	$150
NEW YORK	B-A	—	12,032,000	115
	B00 236 803★	B00 366 803★	384,000	190
PHILADELPHIA	C-A	C-A	3,584,000	95
	C00 053 603★	C00 057 131★	128,000	225
CLEVELAND	D-A	—	3,584,000	95
	D00 000 990★	D00 137 316★	192,000	225
RICHMOND	E-A	—	2,560,000	150
	E00 016 678★	E00 043 248★	64,000	340
ATLANTA	F-A	—	256,000	75
CHICAGO	G-A	—	9,728,000	150
	G00 061 669★	G00 243 076★	256,000	190
ST. LOUIS	H-A	—	256,000	170
MINNEAPOLIS	I00 082 596A	—	512,000	150
KANSAS CITY	J00 296 378A	—	1,280,000	115
	J-★	—	64,000	375
DALLAS	K01 519 850A	—	1,536,000	170
	K00 061 927★	—	64,000	375
SAN FRANCISCO	L-A	—	6,912,000	115
	L-★	—	256,000	265

SERIES 1969A GREEN SEAL

SERIAL NUMBERS: Continued sequence from previous series.
SIGNATURES: Dorothy Andrews Kabis, John B. Connally

	Serial Numbers			
	Low	**High**	**Notes Printed**	**CH CU**
BOSTON	A02 048 001A	A03 584 000A	1,536,000	$95
	A00 000 001★	A00 128 000★	128,000	190
NEW YORK	B12 032 000A	B21 760 000A	9,728,000	95
	B00 384 001★	B01 088 000★	704,000	190
PHILADELPHIA	C03 584 001A	C06 144 000A	2,560,000	75
CLEVELAND	D03 584 001A	D06 400 000A	2,816,000	75
RICHMOND	E02 560 001A	E04 864 000A	2,304,000	75
	E00 064 001★	E00 128 000★	64,000	340
ATLANTA	F00 256 001A	F00 512 000A	256,000	135
	F00 000 001★	F00 064 000★	64,000	340
	F00 002 330★	—	—	—
CHICAGO	G09 728 001A	G13 312 000A	3,584,000	75
	G00 256 001★	G00 448 000★	192,000	150
ST. LOUIS	H00 256 001A	H00 559 300A	256,000	150
MINNEAPOLIS	I00 512 001A	I01 024 000A	512,000	115
KANSAS CITY	J01 280 001A	J01 536 000A	256,000	150
DALLAS	K01 536 001A	K02 560 000A	1,024,000	75
	K00 064 001★	K00 128 000★	64,000	340
SAN FRANCISCO	L06 912 001A	L12 032 000A	5,120,000	75
	L00 256 001★	L00 512 000★	256,000	225

SERIES 1969B GREEN SEAL

SERIAL NUMBERS: Continued sequence from previous series.
SIGNATURES: Romano Acosta Banuelos, John B. Connally

	Serial Numbers				
	Low	**High**	**Notes Printed**	**VF**	**CH CU**
BOSTON	A03 584 001A	A04 608 000A	1,024,000	$300	$1,250
NEW YORK	B21 760 001A	B24 320 000A	2,560,000	300	1,000
	B21 797 362A	—	—	—	—
PHILADELPHIA	C06 144 001A	C08 192 000A	2,048,000	400	750
RICHMOND	E04 864 001A	E06 400 000A	1,536,000	300	1,000
	E04 917 566A	E05 365 083A	—	—	—
ATLANTA	F00 512 001A	F01 024 000A	512,000	450	1,250
	F00 679 068A	F00 946 207A	—	—	—
CHICAGO	G13 312 001A	G14 336 000A	1,024,000	300	1,000
DALLAS	K02 560 001A	K03 584 000A	1,024,000	325	1,000
	K00 128 001★	K00 256 000★	128,000	1000	2,500
	K00 190 198★	K00 192 260★	—	—	—

SERIES 1969C GREEN SEAL

SERIAL NUMBERS: Continued sequence from previous series, whether if 1969A or 1969B.

SIGNATURES: Romana Acosta Banuelos, George P. Shultz

	Serial Numbers		Notes Printed	CH CU
	Low	**High**		
BOSTON	A04 608 001A	A06 400 000A	1,792,000	$95
	A00 128 001★	A00 192 000★	64,000	340
NEW YORK	B24 320 001A	B31 360 000A	7,040,000	75
	B01 088 001★	B01 280 000★	192,000	265
PHILADELPHIA	C08 192 001A	C09 728 000A	1,536,000	75
	C00 128 001★	C00 384 000★	256,000	225
CLEVELAND	D06 400 001A	D11 520 000A	5,120,000	75
	D00 192 001★	D00 384 000★	192,000	190
RICHMOND	E06 400 001A	E08 704 000A	2,304,000	75
	E00 128 001★	E00 192 000★	64,000	300
ATLANTA	F01 024 001A	F01 280 000A	256,000	135
	F00 064 001★	F00 128 000★	64,000	265
CHICAGO	G14 336 001A	G21 120 000A	6,784,000	55
	G00 448 001★	G01 024 000★	576,000	150
ST. LOUIS	H00 512 001A	H03 200 000A	2,688,000	75
	H00 000 001★	H00 064 000★	64,000	300
MINNEAPOLIS	I01 024 001A	I01 280 000A	256,000	115
	I00 000 001★	I00 064 000★	64,000	300
KANSAS CITY	J01 536 001A	J02 816 000A	1,280,000	95
	J00 064 001★	J00 192 000★	128,000	210
DALLAS	K03 584 001A	K07 040 000A	3,456,000	95
	K00 256 001★	K00 320 000★	64,000	300
SAN FRANCISCO	L12 032 001A	L16 640 000A	4,608,000	75
	L00 512 001★	L00 768 000★	256,000	190

SERIES 1974 GREEN SEAL

SIGNATURES: Francine I. Neff, William E. Simon

PLATE NUMBERS: Face and back check numbers continue from previous series.

SERIAL NUMBERS: All districts continue from previous series.

	Serial Numbers			
	Low	**High**	**Notes Printed**	**CH CU**
BOSTON	A06 400 001A	A10 240 000A	3,840,000	$115
	A00 192 001★	A00 448 000★	768,000	150
NEW YORK	B31 360 001A	B69 760 000A	38,400,000	75
	B01 280 001★	B02 048 000★	768,000	135
PHILADELPHIA	C09 728 001A	C17 280 000A	7,040,000	115
	C00 384 001★	C00 704 000★	320,000	225
CLEVELAND	D11 520 001A	D32 640 000A	21,120,000	75
	D00 384 001★	D01 024 000★	640,000	150
RICHMOND	E08 704 001A	E23 040 000A	14,080,000	75
	E00 192 001★	E00 768 000★	576,000	150
ATLANTA	F01 280 001A	F01 920 000A	1,280,000	75
	F00 128 001★	F00 768 000★	640,000	190
CHICAGO	G21 120 001A	G51 840 000A	30,720,000	55
	G01 024 001★	G02 560 000★	1,536,000	115
ST. LOUIS	H03 200 001A	H05 120 000A	1,920,000	170
	H00 064 001★	H00 192 000★	128,000	265
MINNEAPOLIS	I01 280 001A	I03 840 000A	3,200,000	115
	I00 064 001★	I00 256 000★	192,000	265
KANSAS CITY	J02 816 001A	J07 680 000A	4,480,000	115
	J00 192 001★	J00 384 000★	192,000	265
DALLAS	K07 040 001A	K15 260 000A	8,320,000	115
	K00 320 001★	K00 448 000★	128,000	265
SAN FRANCISCO	L16 640 001A	L24 320 000A	7,680,000	115
	L00 768 001★	L00 832 000★	64,000	300

SERIES 1977 GREEN SEAL

SIGNATURES: Azie Taylor Morton, W.M. Blumenthal

PLATE NUMBERS: Both face and back numbers continue from previous series.

SERIAL NUMBERS: All districts begin with 00 000 001.

	Serial Numbers			
	Low	**High**	**Notes Printed**	**CH CU**
BOSTON	A-A	—	16,640,000	$75
	A00 000 001★	A04 480 000★	1,088,000	135
		A10 257 177★ (observed)		
NEW YORK	B-A	—	49,920,000	55
	B00 000 001★	B12 900 000★	2,112,000	115
PHILADELPHIA	C-A	—	5,120,000	55
	C00 016 001★	C00 064 000★	128,000	225
		C02 056 634★ (observed)		
CLEVELAND	D-A	—	23,040,000	55
	D00 000 001★	D09 600 000★	1,024,000	150
RICHMOND	E-A	E16 579 599A	19,200,000	55
	E00 000 001★	E04 480 000★	640,000	150
ATLANTA	F-A	—	2,560,000	55
	F00 000 001★	F00 640 000★	640,000	150
CHICAGO	G-A	—	47,360,000	55
	G00 000 001★	G14 080 000★	1,152,000	150
		G14 396 599★(observed)	—	—
ST. LOUIS	H-A	—	3,840,000	90
	H00 016 001★	H01 920 000★	512,000	150
MINNEAPOLIS	I00 011 000A	I01 613 900A	3,840,000	75
	I00 016 001★	I00 640 000★	128,000	225
KANSAS CITY	J-A	J08 242 023A (observed)	7,680,000	90
	J00 000 001★	J01 920 000★	256,000	225
		J04 693 384★ (observed)		
DALLAS	K-A	—	14,086,000	90
	K00 000 001★	K03 200 000★	448,000	190
SAN FRANCISCO	L-A	L17 756 210A	19,200,000	55
	L00 000 001★	L04 480 000★	768,000	150

SERIES 1981 GREEN SEAL

SIGNATURES: Angela M. Buchanan, Donald T. Regan

PLATE SERIALS: Both face and back numbers begin with #1.

SERIAL NUMBERS: Regular notes begin with 00 000 001, star notes begin as shown below. All B blocks resumed at 00 000 001 prior to completion of A blocks, making for an unusual two-tiered numbering pattern in each district.

	Serial Numbers			
	Low	**High**	**Notes Printed**	**CH CU**
BOSTON	A-A	—	8,960,000	$115
	A-B	—	9,600,000	115
NEW YORK	B-A	—	46,080,000	95
	B-B	—	32,000,000	95
	B00 004 001★	B01 280 000★	768,000	190
PHILADELPHIA	C-A	—	1,280,000	115
CLEVELAND	D-A	—	15,360,000	115
	D-B	—	12,800,000	115
	D00 012 001★	D00 640 000★	256,000	225
RICHMOND	E-A	—	12,800,000	115
	E-B	—	12,800,000	115
ATLANTA	F-A	—	1,280,000	150
	F-B	—	3,200,000	115
	F00 640 001★	F01 920 000★	768,000	225
CHICAGO	G-A	—	44,800,000	115
	G-B	—	22,400,000	115
	G00 016 001★	G00 640 000★	128,000	190
ST. LOUIS	H-A	—	1,280,000	150
	H-B	—	3,200,000	115
MINNEAPOLIS	I-A	—	2,560,000	115
	I-B	—	3,200,000	115
	I00 016 001★	I00 640 000★	128,000	225
KANSAS CITY	J-A	—	8,960,000	115
	J-B	—	9,600,000	115
	J00 016 001★	J01 280 000★	128,000	225
DALLAS	K-A	—	10,240,000	115
	K-B	—	9,600,000	115
SAN FRANCISCO	L-A	—	25,600,000	115
	L-B	—	9,600,000	115
	L00 012 001★	L00 640 000★	256,000	210

SERIES 1981A GREEN SEAL

SIGNATURES: Katherine Davalos Ortega, Donald T. Regan
SERIAL NUMBERS: Both regular and star notes begin with 00 000 001.

	Serial Numbers			
	Low	**High**	**Notes Printed**	**CH CU**
BOSTON	A-A	—	9,600,000	$100
NEW YORK	B-A	—	28,800,000	100
	B-★	B03 200 000★	3,200,000	275
CLEVELAND	D-A	—	12,800,000	100
RICHMOND	E11 912 216A	—	12,800,000	100
	E00 179 200★	E03 200 000★	704,000	300
ATLANTA	F-A	—	3,200,000	100
CHICAGO	G00 054 404A	G28 174 292A	28,800,000	100
ST. LOUIS	H02 392 052A	—	3,200,000	100
MINNEAPOLIS	I00 000 936A	—	3,200,000	100
KANSAS CITY	J05 987 885A	—	6,400,000	100
DALLAS	K-A	—	6,400,000	100
SAN FRANCISCO	L-A	—	22,400,000	100
	L-★	L00 640 000★	640,000	300

SERIES 1985 GREEN SEAL

SIGNATURES: Katherine Davalos Ortega, James A. Baker III
SERIAL NUMBERS: Both regular and star notes begin with 00 000 001.

	Serial Numbers			
	Low	**High**	**Notes Printed**	**CH CU**
BOSTON	A-A	—	51,200,000	$75
	A00 000 001★	A03 200 000★	64,000	350
NEW YORK	B-A	—	99,200,000	75
	B-B	—	83,200,000	75
	B00 000 001★	B03 200 000★	1,408,000	250
PHILADELPHIA	C-A	—	3,200,000	90
CLEVELAND	D-A	—	57,600,000	75
	D00 000 001★	D03 200 000★	640,000	350
RICHMOND	E-A	—	54,400,000	75
ATLANTA	F-A	—	9,600,000	75
CHICAGO	G-A	—	99,200,000	75
	G-B	—	12,800,000	75
	G00 000 001★	G06 400 000★	1,920,000	250
ST. LOUIS	H-A	—	9,600,000	75
MINNEAPOLIS	I-A	—	12,800,000	75
KANSAS CITY	J-A	—	12,800,000	75
DALLAS	K-A	—	25,600,000	75
SAN FRANCISCO	L-A	—	54,400,000	75

SERIES 1988 GREEN SEAL

SIGNATURES: Katherine Davalos Ortega, Nicholas F. Brady

SERIAL NUMBERS: Both regular and star notes begin with 00 000 001.

	Serial Numbers			
	Low	**High**	**Notes Printed**	**CH CU**
BOSTON	A-A	—	9,600,000	$150
NEW YORK	B-A	B-C	214,400,000	100
	B00 000 001★	B06 400 000★	3,200,000	300
CLEVELAND	D-A	—	32,000,000	150
RICHMOND	E-A	—	12,800,000	150
CHICAGO	G-A	—	80,000,000	100
KANSAS CITY	J-A	—	6,400,000	150
SAN FRANCISCO	L-A	—	12,800,000	150

SERIES 1990 GREEN SEAL

SIGNATURES: Catalina Vasquez Villalpando, Nicholas F. Brady

PLATE NUMBERS: Face numbers begin at #1. Back numbers continue sequence from previous series.

SERIAL NUMBERS: Both regular and star notes begin at 00 000 001.

(Series 1990 introduced the anti-counterfeiting security thread and the micro size printing around the portrait.)

	Serial Numbers			
	Low	**High**	**Notes Printed**	**CH CU**
BOSTON	A-A	—	28,800,000	$75
NEW YORK	B-A	B-C	232,000,000	75
	B00 073 737★	B06 400 000★	3,072,000	100
PHILADELPHIA	C-A	—	41,600,000	75
	C01 872 653★	C03 200 000★	1,280,000	125
CLEVELAND	D-A	—	92,800,000	75
RICHMOND	E-A	—	76,800,000	75
CHICAGO	G-A	G-B	109,600,000	75
	G-★	G03 200 000★	1,032,000	100
ST. LOUIS	H-A	—	16,000,000	75
MINNEAPOLIS	I-A	—	22,400,000	75
KANSAS CITY	J-A	—	35,200,000	75
	J00 596 409★	J03 200 000★	640,000	150
DALLAS	K-A	—	16,000,000	75
SAN FRANCISCO	L-A	L-B	119,200,000	75

SERIES 1993 GREEN SEAL

SIGNATURES: Mary Ellen Withrow, Lloyd Bentsen

PLATE NUMBERS: Face numbers begin at #1. Back numbers continue sequence from previous series. Near end of series, new back numbers starting at #1 appear, and are very scarce.

SERIAL NUMBERS: Both regular and star notes begin at 00 000 001.

	Serial Numbers			
	Low	**High**	**Notes Printed**	**CH CU**
BOSTON	A-A	—	41,600,000	$70
NEW YORK	B-A - B-E	B86 400 000E	483,200,000	70
	B06 861 567★	B07 680 000★	3,200,000	100
CLEVELAND	D-A	—	60,800,000	70
	D-★	D05 120 000★	1,280,000	135
RICHMOND	E-A	—	51,200,000	70
CHICAGO	G-A	—	99,200,000	70
	G-B	—	44,800,000	70
	G-★	G05 120 000★	1,280,000	100
ST. LOUIS	H-A	—	3,200,000	90
KANSAS CITY	J-A	—	12,800,000	70
DALLAS	K-A	—	9,600,000	70

SERIES 1996 GREEN SEAL

SIGNATURES: Mary Ellen Withrow, Robert E. Rubin
SERIAL NUMBERS: Both regular and star notes begin with 00 000 001, except N.Y. stars.
PRINTING FACILITY: All notes printed in Washington, D.C.

	Serial Numbers			
	Low	**High**	**Notes Printed**	**CH CU**
BOSTON	AA-A	AA54 400 000A	54,400,000	$70
NEW YORK	AB-A - AB-F	AB60 800 000F	560,800,000	60
	AB03 200 001★	AB08 320 000★	5,120,000	90
PHILADELPHIA	AC-A	AC76 800 000A	76,800,000	70
CLEVELAND	AD-A - AD-B	AD19 200 000B	119,200,000	70
RICHMOND	AE-A	AE96 000 000A	96,000,000	70
	AE-B	AE06 400 000B	6,400,000	80
ATLANTA	AF-A - AF-B	AF19 200 000B	119,200,000	70
CHICAGO	AG-A - AG-C	AG41 600 000C	241,600,000	60
	AG00 000 001★	AG00 640 000★	640,000	90
	AG00 640 001★	AG05 120 000★(sheets)	640,000	90
ST. LOUIS	AH-A	AH28 800 000A	28,800,000	70
MINNEAPOLIS	AI-A	AI35 200 000A	35,200,000	60
KANSAS CITY	AJ-A	AJ57 600 000A	57,600,000	60
	AJ-★	AJ01 920 000★	1,920,000	95
DALLAS	AK-A	AK92 800 000A	92,800,000	60
SAN FRANCISCO	AL-A - AL-C	AL19 200 000C	219,200,000	60
	AL-★	AL03 200 000★	3,200,000	90

SERIES 2001 GREEN SEAL

SIGNATURES: Rosario Marin, Paul H. O'Neill
PLATE NUMBERS: Both face and back numbers begin at #1.
SERIAL NUMBERS: All districts start both regular and star notes with 00 000 001.
PRINTING FACILITY: All notes were printed in Washington, D.C.

	Serial Numbers			
	Low	**High**	**Notes Printed**	**CH CU**
BOSTON	CA-A	CA06 400 000A	6,400,000	$75
NEW YORK	CB-A	CB54 400 000A	54,400,000	70
	CB-★	CB00 320 000★	320,000	150
PHILADELPHIA	CC-A	CC16 000 000A	16,000,000	70
CLEVELAND	CD-A	CD16 000 000A	16,000,000	70
RICHMOND	CE-A	CE32 000 000A	32,000,000	70
	CE-★	CE00 640 000★	640,000	125
ATLANTA	CF-A	CF28 800 000A	28,800,000	70
CHICAGO	CG-A	CG35 200 000A	35,200,000	70
ST. LOUIS	CH-A	CH03 200 000A	3,200,000	80
MINNEAPOLIS	CI-A	CI03 200 000A	3,200,000	80
KANSAS CITY	CJ-A	CJ03 200 000A	3,200,000	80
DALLAS	CK-A	CK06 400 000A	6,400,000	75
SAN FRANCISCO	CL-A	CL32 000 000A	32,000,000	70

SERIES 2004 GREEN SEAL (COLORIZED)

SIGNATURES: Rosario Marin, John W. Snow
PLATE NUMBERS: Both face and back numbers begin at #1.
SERIAL NUMBERS: All districts start both regular and star notes with 00 000 001.
PRINTING FACILITY: All notes were printed in Fort Worth.

	Serial Numbers			
	Low	**High**	**Notes Printed**	**CH CU**
BOSTON	EA-A	EA09 600 000A	9,600,000	$75
NEW YORK	EB-A	EB41 600 000A	41,600,000	70
PHILADELPHIA	EC-A	EC22 400 000A	22,400,000	70
CLEVELAND	ED-A	ED32 000 000A	32,000,000	70
RICHMOND	EE-A	EE03 200 000A	3,200,000	85
	EE-★	EE00 800 000★	800,000	150
ATLANTA	EF-A	EF44 800 000A	44,800,000	70
CHICAGO	EG-A - EG-B	EG19 200 000B	115,200,000	70
	EG00 000 001★	EG03 840 000★	3,840,000	85
	EG06 400 001★	EG07 040 000★	640,000	100
ST. LOUIS	EH-A	EH09 600 000A	9,600,000	75
MINNEAPOLIS	EI-A	EI12 800 000A	12,800,000	75
KANSAS CITY	EJ-A	EJ22 400 000A	22,400,000	70
DALLAS	EK-A	EK32 000 000A	32,000,000	70
	EK00 000 001★	EK03 200 000★	3,200,000	150
SAN FRANCISCO	EL-A	EL51 200 000A	51,200,000	70

SERIES 2004A GREEN SEAL (COLORIZED)

SIGNATURES: Anna Escobedo Cabral, John W. Snow
PLATE NUMBERS: Both face and back numbers begin at #1.
SERIAL NUMBERS: All districts start with 00 000 001.
PRINTING FACILITY: All notes were printed in Fort Worth.

	Serial Numbers			
	Low	**High**	**Notes Printed**	**CH CU**
BOSTON	GA-A	GA16 000 000A	16,000,000	$75
NEW YORK	GB-A	GB38 400 000A	38,400,000	75
RICHMOND	GE-A	GE60 800 000A	60,800,000	75
	GE-★	GE02 560 000★	2,560,000	100
ATLANTA	GF-A	GF51 200 000A	51,200,000	75
CHICAGO	GG-A	GG54 400 000A	54,400,000	75
KANSAS CITY	GJ-A	GJ19 200 000A	19,200,000	75

SERIES 2006 GREEN SEAL (COLORIZED)

SIGNATURES: Anna Escobedo Cabral, Henry M. Paulson, Jr.
PLATE NUMBERS: Both face and back numbers begin at #1.
SERIAL NUMBERS: All districts start with 00 000 001.
PRINTING FACILITY: All notes were printed in Fort Worth.

	Serial Numbers			
	Low	High	Notes Printed	CH CU
BOSTON	IA-A	IA19 200 000A	19,200,000	$75
NEW YORK	IB-A	IB03 200 000B	99,200,000	75
PHILADELPHIA	IC-A	IC19 200 000A	19,200,000	75
CLEVELAND	ID-A	ID32 000 000A	32,000,000	75
RICHMOND	IE-A	IE09 600 000A	9,600,000	75
ST. LOUIS	IH-A	IH06 400 000A	6,400,000	80
MINNEAPOLIS	II-A	II09 600 000A	9,600,000	75
DALLAS	IK-A	IK22 400 000A	22,400,000	75
SAN FRANCISCO	IL-A	IL48 000 000A	48,000,000	75

ONE HUNDRED DOLLAR NOTES

GOLD CERTIFICATES

SERIES 1928 GOLD SEAL

PLATE NUMBERS: Face range #1 through #24.

SIGNATURES: W.O. Woods, A.W. Mellon

Serial Numbers

Low	High	Notes Printed	VG/F	VF	CH CU	GEM CU
A00 000 001A	A03 240 000A	3,240,000	$450	$1,100	$6,500	$25,000
★00 000 153A	★00 011 566A	12,000	3,000	9,000	30,000	50,000

SERIES 1934 GOLD SEAL

SIGNATURES: W.A. Julian, Henry Morgenthau Jr.

These notes had orange (not green) backs. Their text specified that the $100 was "in gold payable to the bearer on demand as authorized by law." These last four words had been added because the 1934 Gold Notes were for use only among banks and were not to be released into general circulation. The Bureau occasionally exhibits the uncut specimen sheet of these orange-back notes.

FEDERAL RESERVE BANK NOTES

SERIES 1929 BROWN SEAL

SERIAL NUMBERS: Both regular and star notes begin with 00 000 001.

PLATE NUMBERS: Face numbers begin with #1.

SIGNATURES: Same as $5 FRBN

	Serial Numbers					
	Low	**High**	**Notes Printed**	**VF**	**CH CU**	**GEM CU**
NEW YORK	B00 000 260A	B00 477 181A	480,000	$150	$400	$700
	B00 000 581★	B00 003 539★	12,000	2,500	—	—
CLEVELAND	D00 000 002A	D00 258 569A	276,000	160	500	800
	D00 000 016★	D00 006 150★	12,000	3,500	8,000	—
RICHMOND	E00 000 001A	E00 158 862A	192,000	175	800	1,250
	E00 004 488★	E00 006 700★	36,000	4,000	—	—
CHICAGO	G00 001 474A	G00 383 281A	384,000	150	400	700
	G00 000 002★	G00 003 689★	12,000	1,800	4,000	—
MINNEAPOLIS	I00 000 324A	I00 132 337A	144,000	175	650	1,250
	I00 003 001★	I00 003 107★	12,000	9,000	—	—
KANSAS CITY	J00 014 411A	J00 095 909A	96,000	110	500	800
	J00 008 026★	J00 011 953★	12,000	600	1,650	—
DALLAS	K00 001 067A	K00 035 741A	36,000	500	2,500	3,500
	K-★	K00 009 700★	12,000	25,000	—	—

LEGAL TENDER

SERIES 1966 RED SEAL

PLATE NUMBERS: Face numbers begin with #1.

SIGNATURES: Kathryn O'Hay Granahan, Henry H. Fowler

Back design has INDEPENDENCE HALL, Philadelphia, PA, with motto added.

Serial Numbers

Low	High	Notes Printed	VF	CH CU	GEM CU
A00 000 001A	A00 768 000A	768,000	$200	$600	$1,000
★00 000 001A	★00 128 000A	128,000	550	2,000	3,000

SERIES 1966A RED SEAL

SIGNATURES: Dorothy Andrews Elston, David M. Kennedy

Serial Numbers

Low	High	Notes Printed	VF	CH CU	GEM CU
A00 768 001A	A01 280 000A	512,000	$250	$1,400	$2,000
—	A00 870 467A high observed	—	—	—	—

No star notes printed.

FEDERAL RESERVE NOTES

SERIES 1928 GREEN SEAL

SERIAL NUMBERS: Both regular and star notes begin with 00 000 001.
PLATE NUMBERS: Face and back begin with #1.
SIGNATURES: W.O. Woods, A.W. Mellon

	Serial Numbers					
	Low	**High**	**Notes Printed**	**VF**	**CH CU**	**GEM CU**
BOSTON	A00 000 238A	A00 337 097A	376,000	$175	$900	$1,500
	A-★	—	24,000	—	—	—
NEW YORK	B00 038 919A	B00 643 998A	755,400	175	750	1,150
	B00 000 638★	B00 006 749★	48,000	600	2,500	—
PHILADELPHIA	C00 122 452A	C00 418 732A	389,100	175	800	1,200
	C00 000 002★	C00 005 389★	24,000	1,000	2,500	—
CLEVELAND	D00 006 665A	D00 513 817A	542,400	175	900	1,500
	D00 000 005★	D00 003 597★	24,000	600	2,500	—
RICHMOND	E00 041 310A	E00 317 493A	364,416	175	800	1,500
	E00 000 420★	E00 003 933★	24,000	2,000	7,000	—
ATLANTA	F00 042 760A	F00 341 608A	357,000	175	900	1,300
	F00 000 518★	F00 001 658★	24,000	800	4,000	—
CHICAGO	G00 002 494A	G01 331 981A	783,300	175	600	1,000
	G00 000 010★	G00 023 810★	72,000	400	2,500	—
ST. LOUIS	H00 014 740A	H00 187 252A	187,200	185	800	1,200
	H00 000 367★	H00 003 729★	—	900	4,000	—
MINNEAPOLIS	I00 014 321A	I00 083 910A	102,000	500	2,500	3,500
	I00 005 821★	I00 007 606★	24,000	3,500	6,000	—
KANSAS CITY	J00 000 042A	J00 201 963A	234,612	175	750	1,250
	J00 003 341★	—	24,000	3,500	—	—
DALLAS	K00 012 615A	K00 067 002A	80,140	500	2,750	3,500
	K00 001 410★	K00 002 320★	24,000	6,000	—	—
SAN FRANCISCO	L00 200 396A	L00 475 857A	486,000	175	1,000	1,500
	L00 000 073★	L00 008 396★	40,000	2,500	6,000	—

SERIES 1928A DARK GREEN SEAL

SERIAL NUMBERS: All districts continued sequence from previous series.
DESIGN CHANGE: District numeral in seal replaced by letter. Face check begins with #1.
SIGNATURES: W.O. Woods, A.W. Mellon

	Serial Numbers					
	Low	High	Notes Printed	VF	CH CU	GEM CU
BOSTON	A00 399 217A	A00 726 436A	980,400	$150	$350	$450
NEW YORK	B00 704 887A	B01 838 287A	2,938,176	150	250	350
PHILADELPHIA	C00 329 710A	C00 649 889A	1,496,844	150	300	400
CLEVELAND	D00 521 180A	D00 707 570A	992,436	150	375	—
RICHMOND	E00 273 832A	E00 553 895A	621,364	150	325	450
ATLANTA	F00 358 739A	F00 543 232A	371,400	150	500	650
CHICAGO	G00 520 160A	G02 061 704A	4,010,424	150	275	375
ST. LOUIS	H00 153 684A	H00 452 191A	749,544	150	300	425
MINNEAPOLIS	I00 096 312A	I00 145 206A	503,040	150	450	—
KANSAS CITY	J00 210 628A	J00 326 856A	681,804	150	450	600
DALLAS	K00 081 337A	K00 120 472A	594,456	200	450	—
SAN FRANCISCO	L00 498 518A	L00 966 200A	1,228,032	150	400	500

SERIES 1928A LIGHT VIVID YELLOW-GREEN SEAL

SERIAL NUMBERS: Continued in sequence from 1928A Dark Green seal variety.

	Serial Numbers				
	Low	High	Notes Printed	VF	CH CU
NEW YORK	B01 946 633A	B02 342 430A	included above	$200	$750
	B00 038 365★	B00 039 201★	1,200	7,000	15,000
CHICAGO	G02 399 744A	G02 807 844A	included above	—	650
ST. LOUIS	H00 489 113A	H00 598 540A	included above	200	750
	H00 008 083★	H00 010 035★	2,400	7,000	15,000
MINNEAPOLIS	—	I00 191 384A	included above	200	800
KANSAS CITY	J00 399 089A	J00 517 466A	included above	200	800
SAN FRANCISCO	L01 191 078A	L01 339 833A	included above	200	800

SERIES 1934 LIGHT VIVID YELLOW-GREEN SEAL

SERIAL NUMBERS: Both regular and star notes begin with 00 000 001.

PLATE NUMBERS: Face numbers begin with #1. Back numbers continue in sequence from Series 1928A.

SIGNATURES: W.A. Julian, Henry Morgenthau, Jr.

	Serial Numbers				
	Low	**High**	**Notes Printed**	**VF**	**CH CU**
BOSTON	A00 000 564A	A00 895 669A	3,710,000	$120	$500
	A00 001 257★	A00 004 130★	—	400	1,250
NEW YORK	B00 135 280A	B01 642 495A	3,086,000	120	400
	B00 000 557★	B00 013 466★	—	400	1,200
PHILADELPHIA	C00 020 739A	C00 291 703A	2,776,800	120	500
	C00 000 823★	C00 002 010★	—	400	2,000
CLEVELAND	D00 005 436A	D00 323 414A	3,447,108	120	500
	D00 000 001★	D00 003 264★	—	350	1,500
RICHMOND	E00 005 484A	E00 290 248A	4,317,600	120	500
	E-★	—	—	600	2,000
ATLANTA	F00 051 405A	F00 202 766A	3,264,420	120	$500
	F00 001 714★	—	—	600	2,000
CHICAGO	G00 001 081A	G00 490 247A	7,075,000	120	400
	G00 000 716★	G00 002 515★	—	300	1,200
ST. LOUIS	H00 000 418A	H00 236 677A	2,106,192	120	500
	H-★	—	—	600	2,000
MINNEAPOLIS	I00 016 607A	I00 087 524A	852,600	140	600
	I00 003 032★	I00 003 404★	—	400	2,000
KANSAS CITY	J00 006 043A	J00 288 470A	1,932,900	130	500
	J00 001 261★	J00 001 773★	—	600	2,000
DALLAS	K00 001 249A	K00 127 807A	1,506,516	130	600
	K-★	—	—	600	2,000
SAN FRANCISCO	L00 019 304A	L00 448 451A	6,521,940	120	500
	L00 000 001★	—	—	600	2,000

SERIES 1934 DARK BLUE-GREEN SEAL

PLATE NUMBERS: Back number up to 112.

SIGNATURES: W.A. Julian, Henry Morgenthau, Jr.

Serial Numbers

	Low	High	Notes Printed	VF	CH CU	GEM CU
BOSTON	A01 187 136**A**	A03 551 012**A**	see above	$120	$225	$300
	A00 008 478★	A00 038 278★	—	260	1,500	—
NEW YORK	B01 767 403**A**	B03 962 686**A**	see above	120	200	275
	—	B00 111 431★	—	260	1,200	—
PHILADELPHIA	C00 489 332**A**	C03 565 041**A**	see above	120	225	300
	C00 012 798★	C00 031 834★	—	260	1,200	—
CLEVELAND	D00 550 005**A**	D03 390 725**A**	see above	120	225	300
	D00 013 061★	D00 039 854★	—	350	1,800	—
RICHMOND	E00 411 376**A**	E04 230 810**A**	see above	120	250	325
	E00 004 302★	E00 060 459★	—	260	1,600	—
ATLANTA	F00 503 609**A**	F03 216 128**A**	see above	120	250	325
	F00 005 253★	F00 039 929★	—	260	1,500	—
CHICAGO	G00 759 925**A**	G08 177 542**A**	see above	120	200	275
	G00 009 318★	G00 102 951★	—	240	1,200	—
ST. LOUIS	H00 333 913**A**	H02 429 950**A**	see above	120	225	300
	H00 008 658★	H00 069 793★	—	260	1,500	—
MINNEAPOLIS	I00 119 453**A**	I01 006 604**A**	see above	125	250	400
	I00 005 222★	I00 014 620★	—	300	1,500	—
KANSAS CITY	J00 343 302**A**	J01 570 485**A**	see above	120	200	400
	J00 005 681★	J00 036 685★	—	260	1,500	—
DALLAS	K00 130 768**A**	K01 622 956**A**	see above	120	325	500
	K00 005 732★	K00 022 861★	—	260	2,000	—
SAN FRANCISCO	L00 849 165**A**	L07 358 167**A**	see above	120	200	400
	L00 025 535★	L00 081 420★	—	260	1,200	—

SERIES 1934 MULE DARK BLUE-GREEN SEAL

PLATE NUMBERS: Back number 113 and higher.

Quantities included above.

	Serial Numbers				
	Low	**High**	**Notes Printed**	**VF**	**CH CU**
BOSTON	A02 874 576A	A03 282 400A	—	$250	$600
PHILADELPHIA	C02 973 508A	—	—	250	600
CLEVELAND	D03 348 795A	D03 573 728A	—	250	600
RICHMOND	E00 046 483★	E00 051 502★	—	1,000	4,000
ATLANTA	F02 806 595A	F02 874 743A	—	250	600
CHICAGO	G08 548 213A	G10 125 881A	—	200	400
	G00 088 061★	G00 097 205★	—	1,000	4,000
ST. LOUIS	H02 250 525A	H02 292 346A	—	250	600
MINNEAPOLIS	I00 809 498A	I00 825 785A	—	250	600
KANSAS CITY	J01 633 353A	J02 163 457A	—	250	600
	J00 033 296★	—	—	—	Extremely Rare
DALLAS	K01 622 940A	K01 622 959A	—	195	400
SAN FRANCISCO	L05 676 359A	L06 593 880A	—	250	600

SERIES 1934A MULE GREEN SEAL

SERIAL NUMBERS: Continued sequence from previous series.

PLATE NUMBERS: Back number 112 and lower.

SIGNATURES: W.A. Julian, Henry Morgenthau Jr.

Quantities included below under Series 1934A.

	Serial Numbers				
	Low	**High**	**Notes Printed**	**VF**	**CH CU**
BOSTON	A02 334 771A	A02 510 836A	—	$140	$250
	A00 035 608★	—	—	400	1,500
NEW YORK	B03 753 975A	B18 147 245A	—	115	200
	B00 043 123★	B00 149 066★	—	300	700
PHILADELPHIA	C01 647 445A	C02 842 098A	—	115	200
	C00 017 464★	C00 036 124★	—	400	1,500
CLEVELAND	D00 872 940A	D02 783 238A	—	115	200

	Low	High	Notes Printed	VF	CH CU
RICHMOND	E00 899 184**A**	E06 298 291**A**	—	$115	$200
	E00 020 126★	E00 020 985 ★	—	400	1,500
ATLANTA	F00 755 123**A**	F04 009 312**A**	—	115	200
	F00 030 023★	—	—	400	1,500
CHICAGO	G01 729 674**A**	G09 735 335**A**	—	115	200
	G00 036 202★	G00 088 116★	—	225	1,000
ST. LOUIS	H00 931 248**A**	H01 940 941**A**	—	115	200
MINNEAPOLIS	I00 304 577**A**	I00 730 292**A**	—	130	225
KANSAS CITY	J00 914 138**A**	J02 476 621**A**	—	200	1,000
	J00 010 039★	J00 024 584★	—	400	1,500
DALLAS	K00 400 125**A**	K00 510 577**A**	—	125	200
SAN FRANCISCO	L02 525 354**A**	L05 350 891**A**	—	115	225
	L00 033 148★	—	—	400	2,000

SERIES 1934A GREEN SEAL

SERIAL NUMBERS: Continued sequence from previous series.

PLATE NUMBERS: Back number 113 and higher.

SIGNATURES: W.A. Julian, Henry Morgenthau Jr.

	Serial Numbers				
	Low	High	Notes Printed	VF	CH CU
BOSTON	A02 177 526**A**	—	102,000	$200	$475
NEW YORK	B05 525 202**A**	B18 350 345**A**	15,278,892	115	200
	B00 063 693★	B00 155 943★	—	350	1,200
PHILADELPHIA	C01 325 038**A**	C02 586 618**A**	588,000	120	400
CLEVELAND	D03 142 898**A**	—	645,300	125	400
RICHMOND	E-**A**	—	770,100	125	400
ATLANTA	F-**A**	—	589,896	125	400
CHICAGO	G09 657 601**A**	—	3,328,800	125	400
ST. LOUIS	H-**A**	—	434,208	125	400
MINNEAPOLIS	I00 816 356**A**	—	153,000	125	400
KANSAS CITY	J-**A**	—	455,100	125	400
DALLAS	K00 534 394**A**	K00 800 499**A**	226,164	125	400
SAN FRANCISCO	L03 787 578**A**	L04 364 955**A**	1,130,400	125	400

SERIES 1934B MULE GREEN SEAL

SERIAL NUMBERS: Continued sequence from previous series.
PLATE NUMBERS: Back numbers up to 112.
SIGNATURES: W.A. Julian, Fred M. Vinson

	Serial Numbers				
	Low	**High**	**Notes Printed**	**VF**	**CH CU**
BOSTON	A03 628 109A	A03 685 891A	41,400	$150	$425
NEW YORK	B13 971 535A	—	—	—	—
PHILADELPHIA	C03 691 382A	C03 773 271A	39,600	150	450
CLEVELAND	D03 739 079A	D03 909 809A	61,200	150	450
RICHMOND	E04 414 559A	E05 429 922A	977,400	120	450
	E00 062 415★	—	—	1,000	4,500
ATLANTA	F03 529 844A	F04 392 326A	645,000	120	450
CHICAGO	G10 229 062A	G10 720 792A	396,000	120	450
ST. LOUIS	H02 250 860A	H03 287 190A	676,200	120	450
	H00 040 320★	H00 049 907★	—	1,000	4,500
MINNEAPOLIS	I00 900 209A	I01 398 958A	377,000	120	450
	I00 018 986★	I00 020 530★	—	1,000	4,500
KANSAS CITY	J02 298 602A	J02 912 690A	364,500	120	450
DALLAS	K01 618 211A	J02 912 690A	392,700	120	450
	K00 025 669★	K00 029 976★	—	1,000	4,500
SAN FRANCISCO	L07 891 808A	—	—	125	450

SERIES 1934C MULE GREEN SEAL

SERIAL NUMBERS: Continued sequence from previous series.
PLATE NUMBERS: Back number 112 or lower.
SIGNATURES: W.A. Julian, John W. Snyder

	Serial Numbers				
	Low	**High**	**Notes Printed**	**VF**	**CH CU**
BOSTON	A03 632 018A	A03 678 135A	13,800	$150	$500
NEW YORK	None printed.	—	—	—	—
PHILADELPHIA	C03 717 614A	C03 777 657A	13,200	150	500
CLEVELAND	D03 723 564A	D03 944 637A	—	150	500
	D00 052 356★	D00 054 334★	—	1,000	4,500
RICHMOND	E04 574 908A	E06 724 336A	—	150	400
	E00 061 322★	E00 074 977★	—	1,000	4,500
ATLANTA	F03 616 045A	F04 687 110A	493,900	150	400
	F00 054 477★	F00 057 872★	—	1,000	3,750
CHICAGO	G10 209 702A	G11 364 347A	612,000	150	400
	G00 111 525★	G00 119 466★	—	750	3,000
ST. LOUIS	H02 823 377A	H04 196 861A	957,000	150	375
	H00 042 841★	H00 060 718★	—	1,000	3,750
MINNEAPOLIS	I00 967 190A	I01 628 593A	392,904	150	450
	I00 028 121★	I00 030 627★	—	1,000	4,500
KANSAS CITY	J02 282 301A	J03 004 263A	401,100	150	450
DALLAS	K01 896 990A	K02 441 560A	280,700	150	450
SAN FRANCISCO	L07 253 484A	L07 717 988A	432,600	150	400
	L00 089 682★	L00 090 131★	—	1,000	4,500

SERIES 1934D MULE GREEN SEAL

PLATE NUMBERS: Back number 112 or lower.
SERIAL NUMBERS: Continued sequence from previous series.
SIGNATURES: Georgia Neese Clark, John W. Snyder

	Serial Numbers				
	Low	**High**	**Notes Printed**	**VF**	**CH CU**
NEW YORK	B-A	—	156	$2,000	$5,000
PHILADELPHIA	C03 422 462A	C03 686 427A	308,400	300	500
	C00 039 252★	C00 041 919★	—	2,500	6,000
ATLANTA	F04 703 367A	F04 891 533A	260,400	300	750
	F00 061 325★	F00 063 147★	—	2,500	6,000
CHICAGO	G08 504 434A	G11 331 588A	78,000	300	500
	G00 108 325★	G00 112 709★	—	2,000	6,000
ST. LOUIS	H03 852 691A	H04 231 802A	166,800	300	500
DALLAS	K02 334 983A	K02 460 255A	66,000	300	750

SERIES 1950 MULE GREEN SEAL

SERIAL NUMBERS: All serial numbers of both regular and star notes begin with 00 000 001.
PLATE NUMBERS: Back number 112 or lower.
SIGNATURES: Georgia Neese Clark, John W. Snyder

	Serial Numbers				
	Low	**High**	**Notes Printed**	**VF**	**CH CU**
BOSTON	A00 324 811A	—	—	—	$350
NEW YORK	B00 122 127A	B03 835 091A	—	—	250
	B00 036 148★	—	—	200	1,000

	Low	High	Notes Printed	VF	CH CU
PHILADELPHIA	C00 000 001A	C01 084 365A	—	—	$300
	C00 003 529★	C00 004 280★	—	$300	1,200
CLEVELAND	D00 032 581A	D01 589 528A	—	—	300
	D00 003 152★	D00 018 771★	—	—	1,200
RICHMOND	E00 954 669A	E02 641 908A	—	—	300
	E00 020 367★	E00 023 335★	—	200	1,000
ATLANTA	F00 028 319A	F01 781 789A	—	—	300
CHICAGO	G00 000 132A	G04 256 957A	—	—	250
	G00 001 506★	G00 051 993★	—	250	800
ST. LOUIS	H00 008 128A	H01 182 764A	—	—	300
	H00 000 474★	H00 003 088★	—	250	1,200
MINNEAPOLIS	I00 000 097A	I00 505 722A	—	—	500
KANSAS CITY	J00 009 113A	J00 810 832A	—	—	350
	J00 005 039★	J00 008 500★	—	200	800
DALLAS	K00 333 356A	K00 959 412A	—	—	400
SAN FRANCISCO	L00 253 100A	L02 072 699A	—	—	300
	L00 009 491★	L00 017 170★	—	200	800

SERIES 1950 GREEN SEAL

PLATE NUMBERS: Back number 113 and higher.

SIGNATURES: Georgia Neese Clark, John W. Snyder

	Serial Numbers				
	Low	High	Notes Printed	VF	CH CU
BOSTON	A00 000 020A	A00 768 000A	768,000	—	$400
	A00 004 349★	A00 019 600★	—	250	1,300
NEW YORK	B00 072 603A	B03 908 000A	3,908,000	—	300
	B00 002 038★	B00 082 746★	—	200	1,200
PHILADELPHIA	C00 656 433A	C01 332 000A	1,332,000	—	300
	C00 012 034★	—	—	250	1,500
CLEVELAND	D00 414 405A	D01 632 000A	1,632,000	—	350
	D00 024 846★	D00 033 267★	—	250	1,500
RICHMOND	E01 763 376A	E04 076 000A	4,076,000	—	350
	—	E00 051 322★	—	250	1,500
ATLANTA	F00 443 001A	F01 824 000A	1,824,000	—	400
CHICAGO	G00 000 009A	G04 428 000A	4,428,000	—	350

	Low	High	Notes Printed	VF	CH CU
ST. LOUIS	H00 355 263A	H01 284 000A	1,284,000	—	$400
	H00 006 608★	—	—	$250	1,500
MINNEAPOLIS	I00 162 439A	I00 564 000A	564,000	—	550
KANSAS CITY	J00 467 808A	J00 864 000A	864,000	—	450
	J00 001 257★	J00 019 516★	—	250	1,300
DALLAS	K00 918 756A	K01 216 000A	1,216,000	—	450
SAN FRANCISCO	L01 141 614A	L02 524 000A	2,524,000	—	400
	L00 034 860★	—	—	250	1,500

SERIES 1950A GREEN SEAL

SERIAL NUMBERS: Continued sequence from previous series. Numbers between high serial number of Series 1950 and low serial number of this series were not used.

SIGNATURES: Ivy Baker Priest, G.M. Humphrey

	Serial Numbers				
	Low	High	Notes Printed	VF	CH CU
BOSTON	A00 864 001A	A01 872 000A	1,008,000	—	$240
	A00 161 568★	A00 274 778★	—	$200	400
NEW YORK	B04 032 001A	B06 912 000A	2,880,000	—	240
	B00 179 031★	B00 418 672★	—	200	400
PHILADELPHIA	C01 440 001A	C02 016 000A	720,000	—	240
	C00 202 188★	C00 274 827★	—	200	400

	Low	High	Notes Printed	VF	CH CU
CLEVELAND	D01 728 001A	D02 016 000A	288,000	—	$200
	D00 152 431★	D00 232 755★	—	$200	640
RICHMOND	E04 176 001A	E06 336 000A	2,160,000	—	200
	E00 149 662★	E00 337 571★	—	200	400
ATLANTA	F01 872 001A	F02 160 000A	288,000	—	240
	F00 200 421★	F00 280 112★	—	—	—
CHICAGO	G04 464 001A	G05 328 000A	864,000	—	240
	G00 201 943★	G00 257 948★	—	200	400
ST. LOUIS	H01 296 001A	H01 728 000A	432,000	—	240
	H00 169 008★	H00 272 730★	—	200	400
MINNEAPOLIS	I00 576 001A	I00 720 000A	144,000	—	240
	I00 152 712★	I00 256 388★	—	200	520
KANSAS CITY	J00 864 001A	J01 152 000A	288,000	—	240
	J00 184 069★	J00 257 229★	—	200	400
DALLAS	K01 296 001A	K01 728 000A	432,000	—	240
	K00 154 665★	K00 192 541★	—	200	560
	—	K01 791 045A (observed)	—	—	—
SAN FRANCISCO	L02 592 001A	L03 312 000A	720,000	—	240
	L00 200 421★	L00 283 503★	—	200	400
	—	L00 288 000★ (official)	—	—	—

SERIES 1950B GREEN SEAL

SERIAL NUMBERS: Continued sequence from previous series, with exception of Cleveland and Chicago stars, where changeovers exist.

SIGNATURES: Ivy Baker Priest, Robert B. Anderson

	Serial Numbers				
	Low	High	Notes Printed	VF	CH CU
BOSTON	A01 872 001A	A02 592 000A	720,000	—	$200
NEW YORK	B06 912 001A	B13 248 000A	6,336,000	—	160
	B00 434 033★	B00 709 813★	—	$175	280
PHILADELPHIA	C02 016 001A	C02 736 000A	720,000	—	240
	C00 304 528★	C00 336 628★	—	200	320

	Low	High	Notes Printed	VF	CH CU
CLEVELAND	D02 016 001A	D02 448 000A	432,000	—	$200
	D00 177 065★	D00 392 973★	—	$225	400
RICHMOND	E06 336 001A	E07 344 000A	1,008,000	—	180
ATLANTA	F02 160 001A	F02 736 000A	576,000	—	240
	F00 329 298★	F00 395 116★	—	225	400
CHICAGO	G05 328 001A	G07 920 000A	2,592,000	—	160
	G00 218 349★	G00 411 346★	—	200	240
ST. LOUIS	H01 728 001A	H02 880 000A	1,152,000	—	180
	H00 288 537★	H00 417 343★	—	200	320
MINNEAPOLIS	I00 720 001A	I01 008 000A	288,000	—	240
	I00 288 241★	I00 409 637★	—	200	560
KANSAS CITY	J01 152 001A	J01 872 000A	720,000	—	200
	J00 305 847★	J00 416 937★	—	225	400
DALLAS	K01 728 001A	K03 456 000A	1,728,000	—	200
	K00 211 384★	K00 410 156★	—	225	440
SAN FRANCISCO	L03 312 001A	L06 192 000A	2,880,000	—	180
	L00 289 860★	L00 431 628★	—	200	320
	L00 288 001★ (official)		—	—	—

SERIES 1950C GREEN SEAL

SERIAL NUMBERS: Continued sequence from previous series, with exception of Cleveland and Dallas Stars, where changeovers exist.

SIGNATURES: Elizabeth Rudel Smith, C. Douglas Dillon

	Serial Numbers				
	Low	**High**	**Notes Printed**	**VF**	**CH CU**
BOSTON	A02 592 001A	A03 456 000A	864,000	—	$200
	A00 304 758★	A00 417 218★	—	$250	400
NEW YORK	B13 248 001A	B15 696 000A	2,448,000	—	180
	B00 742 926★	B00 952 768★	—	250	440
PHILADELPHIA	C02 736 001A	C03 312 000A	576,000	—	200
	C00 433 365★	C00 536 648★	—	250	440
CLEVELAND	D00 508 001A	D03 024 000A	576,000	—	200
	D00 384 709★	D00 568 222★	—	250	440
RICHMOND	E07 344 001A	E08 784 000A	1,440,000	—	200
	E-★	—	—	250	440
ATLANTA	F02 736 001A	F04 032 000A	1,296,000	—	200
	F00 445 747★	F00 551 864★	—	250	440
CHICAGO	G07 920 001A	G09 504 000A	1,584,000	—	200
	G-★	—	—	250	440
ST. LOUIS	H02 880 001A	H03 600 000A	720,000	—	200
	H00 441 242★	H00 553 500★	—	250	440
MINNEAPOLIS	I01 008 001A	I01 296 000A	288,000	—	220
KANSAS CITY	J01 872 001A	J02 304 000A	432,000	—	200
DALLAS	K03 456 001A	K04 176 000A	720,000	—	200
	K00 266 685★	—	—	250	440
SAN FRANCISCO	L06 192 001A	L08 352 000A	2,160,000	—	180
	L00 441 215★	L00 705 970★	—	250	440

SERIES 1950D GREEN SEAL

SERIAL NUMBERS: Continued sequence from previous series.

SIGNATURES: Kathryn O'Hay Granahan, C. Douglas Dillon

	Serial Numbers				
	Low	**High**	**Notes Printed**	**VF**	**CH CU**
BOSTON	A03 456 001A	A05 328 000A	1,872,000	—	$180
	A00 450 332★	A00 532 049★	—	$175	560
NEW YORK	B15 696 001A	B23 328 000A	7,632,000	—	160
	B01 030 333★	B01 160 446★	—	175	400
PHILADELPHIA	C03 312 001A	C05 184 000A	1,872,000	—	180
	C00 576 331★	C00 688 567★	—	175	560
CLEVELAND	D03 024 001A	D04 608 000A	1,584,000	—	180
	D00 576 408★	D00 699 365★	—	175	480

	Low	High	Notes Printed	VF	CH CU
RICHMOND	E08 784 001A	E11 664 000A	2,880,000	—	$225
	E00 434 032★	E00 558 910★	—	$175	600
ATLANTA	F04 032 001A	F05 904 000A	1,872,000	—	225
	F00 596 822★	F00 692 420★	—	175	600
CHICAGO	G09 504 001A	G14 112 000A	4,608,000	—	200
	G00 433 902★	G00 715 097★	—	175	400
ST. LOUIS	H03 600 001A	H05 040 000A	1,440,000	—	200
	H-★	—	—	175	700
MINNEAPOLIS	I01 296 001A	I01 728 000A	432,000	—	300
	I-★	—	—	250	700
KANSAS CITY	J02 304 001A	J03 168 000A	864,000	—	225
	J00 440 373★	J00 488 321★	—	250	600
DALLAS	K04 176 001A	K05 904 000A	1,728,000	—	250
	K00 512 896★	—	—	175	700
SAN FRANCISCO	L08 352 001A	L11 664 000A	3,312,000	—	225
	L00 783 189★	L00 946 342★	—	175	400

SERIES 1950E GREEN SEAL

SERIAL NUMBERS: Districts printed continued sequence from previous series.

PLATE NUMBERS: Face number range # 24-29. Back range #133-140.

SIGNATURES: Kathryn O'Hay Granahan, Henry H. Fowler

	Serial Numbers					
	Low	High	Notes Printed	VF	CH CU	GEM CU
NEW YORK	B23 328 001A	B26 352 000A	3,024,000	$150	$500	$600
	B01 301 125★	B01 568 256★	288,000 est.	450	2,000	3,000
CHICAGO	G14 112 001A	G14 688 000A	576,000	175	700	1,000
SAN FRANCISCO	L11 664 001A	L14 400 000A	2,736,000	50	600	750
	L01 008 222★	L01 139 505★	144,000 est.	500	3,500	—

SERIES 1963 GREEN SEAL

No $100 notes for Series 1963 were printed.

SERIES 1963A GREEN SEAL

SERIAL NUMBERS: All serial numbers of both regular and star notes begin with 00 000 001.

PLATE NUMBERS: Both face and back numbers begin with #1. Motto "IN GOD WE TRUST" added to back.

SIGNATURES: Kathryn O'Hay Granahan, Henry H. Fowler

	Serial Numbers				
	Low	**High**	**Notes Printed**	**VF**	**CH CU**
BOSTON	A-A	—	1,536,000	$120	$150
	A00 000 639★	A00 014 764★	128,000	200	300
NEW YORK	B-A	—	12,544,000	—	135
	B00 008 646★	B01 472 513★	1,536,000	—	225
PHILADELPHIA	C-A	—	1,792,000	—	150
	C00 024 268★	C00 189 689★	192,000	—	375
CLEVELAND	D-A	—	2,304,000	—	150
	D00 004 880★	D00 172 494★	192,000	—	375
RICHMOND	E-A	—	2,816,000	—	150
	E00 010 671★	E00 164 358★	192,000	—	375
ATLANTA	F-A	—	1,280,000	—	150
	F00 079 074★	—	128,000	—	450
CHICAGO	G-A	—	4,352,000	—	135
	G00 022 647★	G00 339 973★	512,000	—	250
ST. LOUIS	H-A	—	1,536,000	—	150
	H00 050 897★	H00 251 116★	256,000	—	300
MINNEAPOLIS	I-A	—	512,000	—	150
	I00 003 866★	I00 125 448★	128,000	—	450
KANSAS CITY	J-A	—	1,024,000	—	150
	J00 005 078★	J00 123 467★	128,000	—	450
DALLAS	K-A	—	1,536,000	—	150
	K00 003 315★	K00 184 376★	192,000	—	450
SAN FRANCISCO	L-A	—	6,400,000	—	150
	L00 081 197★	L00 641 778★	832,000	—	340

SERIES 1969 GREEN SEAL

SERIAL NUMBERS: All serial numbers of both regular and star notes begin with 00 000 001.

SIGNATURES: Dorothy Andrews Elston, David M. Kennedy

	Serial Numbers			
	Low	**High**	**Notes Printed**	**CH CU**
BOSTON	A-A	—	2,048,000	$140
	A00 000 191★	A00 056 771★	128,000	280
NEW YORK	B-A	—	11,520,000	140
	B00 005 411★	B00 100 414★	128,000	240
PHILADELPHIA	C-A	—	2,560,000	140
	C00 048 141★	C00 127 124★	128,000	280
CLEVELAND	D-A	—	768,000	140
	D00 015 848★	D00 024 301★	64,000	380
RICHMOND	E-A	—	2,560,000	140
	E00 054 950★	E00 141 438★	192,000	280
ATLANTA	F-A	—	2,304,000	140
	F00 076 915★	—	128,000	280
CHICAGO	G-A	—	5,880,000	120
	G00 163 907★	G00 213 637★	256,000	280
ST. LOUIS	H-A	—	1,280,000	140
	H00 000 890★	H00 021 404★	64,000	320
MINNEAPOLIS	I-A	—	512,000	140
	I00 004 043★	I00 100 445★	64,000	360
KANSAS CITY	J-A	—	1,792,000	140
	J00 044 780★	J00 340 637★	384,000	280
DALLAS	K-A	—	2,048,000	140
	K00 000 002★	K00 118 497★	128,000	280
SAN FRANCISCO	L-A	—	7,168,000	140
	L00 132 080★	L00 290 533★	320,000	280

SERIES 1969A GREEN SEAL

SERIAL NUMBERS: Continued sequence from previous series.
SIGNATURES: Dorothy Andrews Kabis, John B. Connally

	Serial Numbers		Notes Printed	CH CU
	Low	**High**	**Notes Printed**	**CH CU**
BOSTON	A02 048 001A	A03 328 000A	1,280,000	$180
	A00 128 001★	A00 448 000★	448,000	260
NEW YORK	B11 520 001A	B22 784 000A	11,264,000	140
	B00 128 001★	B00 768 000★	768,000	220
PHILADELPHIA	C02 560 001A	C04 608 000A	2,048,000	180
	C00 128 001★	C00 576 000★	448,000	260
CLEVELAND	D00 768 001A	D02 048 000A	1,280,000	180
	D00 064 001★	D00 256 000★	192,000	260
RICHMOND	E02 560 001A	E04 864 000A	2,304,600	180
	E00 192 001★	E00 384 000★	192,000	260
ATLANTA	F02 304 001A	F04 608 000A	2,304,000	180
	F00 128 001★	F00 192 000★	64,000	480
CHICAGO	G05 888 001A	G11 264 000A	5,376,000	140
	G00 256 001★	G00 576 000★	320,000	220
ST. LOUIS	H01 280 001A	H02 304 000A	1,024,000	180
	H00 064 001★	H00 128 000★	64,000	320
MINNEAPOLIS	I00 512 001A	I01 536 000A	1,024,000	180
	No Star Notes printed.			
KANSAS CITY	J01 792 001A	J02 304 000A	512,000	180
	No Star Notes printed.			
DALLAS	K02 048 001A	K05 376 000A	3,328,000	180
	K00 128 001★	K00 256 000★	128,000	360
SAN FRANCISCO	L07 168 001A	L11 520 000A	4,352,000	180
	L00 320 001★	L00 896 000★	576,000	260

SERIES 1969C GREEN SEAL

SIGNATURES: Romana Acosta Banuelos, George P. Shultz

	Serial Numbers			
	Low	**High**	**Notes Printed**	**CH CU**
BOSTON	A03 328 001A	A05 376 000A	2,048,000	$150
	A00 448 001★	A00 512 000★	64,000	375
NEW YORK	B22 784 001A	B38 400 000A	15,616,000	135
	B00 768 001★	B01 024 000★	256,000	225
PHILADELPHIA	C04 608 001A	C07 936 000A	3,324,000	150
	C00 576 001★	C00 640 000★	64,000	450
CLEVELAND	D02 048 001A	D07 040 000A	4,992,000	150
	D00 256 001★	D00 320 000★	64,000	450
RICHMOND	E04 864 001A	E12 160 000A	7,296,000	150
	E00 384 001★	E00 512 000★	128,000	300
ATLANTA	F04 608 001A	F07 040 000A	2,432,000	150
	F00 192 001★	F00 256 000★	64,000	450
CHICAGO	G11 264 001A	G17 280 000A	6,016,000	150
	G00 576 001★	G00 896 000★	320,000	265
ST. LOUIS	H02 304 001A	H07 680 000A	5,376,000	150
	H00 128 001★	H00 192 000★	64,000	450
MINNEAPOLIS	I01 536 001A	I02 048 000A	512,000	170
	I00 064 001★	I00 128 000★	64,000	375
KANSAS CITY	J02 304 001A	J07 040 000A	4,736,000	150
	J00 384 001★	J00 576 000★	192,000	375
DALLAS	K05 376 001A	K08 320 000A	2,944,000	150
	K00 256 001★	K00 320 000★	64,000	375
SAN FRANCISCO	L11 520 001A	L21 760 000A	10,240,000	150
	L00 896 001★	L01 408 000★	512,000	300

SERIES 1974 GREEN SEAL

SIGNATURES: Francine I. Neff, William E. Simon

PLATE NUMBERS: Both face and back numbers continued from previous series.

SERIAL NUMBERS: All districts continued from previous series.

	Serial Numbers Low	High	Notes Printed	CH CU
BOSTON	A05 376 001A	A17 280 000A	11,520,000	$135
	A00 512 001★	A00 768 000★	256,000	285
	—	A00 807 574★ (observed)	—	—
NEW YORK	B38 400 001A	—	62,880,000	115
	—	B01 280 000B	1,280,000	150
	B01 024 001★	B02 752 000★	1,728,000	225
PHILADELPHIA	C07 936 001A	C16 000 000A	7,680,000	135
	C00 640 001★	C00 768 000★	128,000	285
CLEVELAND	D07 040 001A	D33 920 000A	26,880,000	135
	D00 320 001★	D00 512 000★	192,000	375
RICHMOND	E12 160 001A	E23 680 000A	11,520,000	135
	E00 512 001★	E00 640 000★	128,000	285
ATLANTA	F07 040 001A	F11 520 000A	4,480,000	135
	F00 256 001★	F00 384 000★	128,000	285
CHICAGO	G17 280 001A	G44 160 000A	26,880,000	115
	G00 896 001★	G02 112 000★	1,216,000	245
ST. LOUIS	H07 680 001A	H13 440 000A	5,760,000	135
	H00 192 001★	H00 384 000★	192,000	285
MINNEAPOLIS	I02 048 001A	I07 040 000A	3,840,000	135
	I00 128 001★	I00 384 000★	256,000	375
KANSAS CITY	J07 040 001A	J12 800 000A	5,760,000	135
	J00 576 001★	J01 024 000★	448,000	285
DALLAS	K08 320 001A	K18 560 000A	10,240,000	135
	K00 320 001★	K00 512 000★	192,000	285
SAN FRANCISCO	L21 760 001A	L51 200 000A	29,440,000	135
	L01 408 001★	L02 304 000★	832,000	265

Starting with Series 1963 in the Federal Reserve Notes, star notes are often printed in staggered runs, not consecutive to each other, so that large serial number gaps may exist. This can result in higher star serial numbers found on the notes than may be found in the "Notes Printed" columns.

SERIES 1977 GREEN SEAL

SIGNATURES: Azie Taylor Morton, W.M. Blumenthal
PLATE NUMBERS: Both face and back numbers continued from previous series.
SERIAL NUMBERS: The regular notes in all districts start at 00 000 001.

	Serial Numbers			
	Low	**High**	**Notes Printed**	**CH CU**
BOSTON	A00 001 237A	—	19,200,000	$115
	A00 014 001★	A01 280 000★	320,000	300
	Low	**High**	**Notes Printed**	**CH CU**
NEW YORK	B-A	—	99,840,000	$115
	B-B	—	66,560,000	115
	B00 000 001★	B08 960 000★	1,664,000	190
PHILADELPHIA	C-A	—	5,120,000	115
	C00 016 001★	C00 640 000★	128,000	225
CLEVELAND	D-A	—	16,640,000	115
	D00 000 001★	D01 280 000★	192,000	225
RICHMOND	E-A	—	24,320,000	115
	E00 000 001★	E01 920 000★	256,000	300
	—	E02 158 077★ (observed)	—	—
ATLANTA	F-A	—	3,840,000	190
	F00 000 001★	F00 064 000★	64,000	450
CHICAGO	G-A	—	33,280,000	115
	G00 000 001★	G05 120 000★	576,000	225
	—	G05 233 997★ (observed)	—	—
ST LOUIS	H-A	—	15,360,000	115
	H00 000 008★	H03 200 000★	448,000	225
MINNEAPOLIS	I-A	—	5,120,000	115
	I00 000 001★	I01 280 000★	192,000	300
KANSAS CITY	J-A	—	20,480,000	115
	J00 000 001★	J03 840 000★	512,000	225
DALLAS	K-A	—	38,400,000	115
	K00 000 001★	K02 560 000★	512,000	300
SAN FRANCISCO	L-A	—	39,680,000	115
	L00 000 001★	L03 200 000★	576,000	225

SERIES 1981 GREEN SEAL

SIGNATURES: Angela M. Buchanan, Donald T. Regan

SERIAL NUMBERS: Both regular and star notes begin with 00 000 001. All B blocks resumed at 00 000 001, prior to completion of A blocks, making for an unusual two-tiered numbering pattern in each district.

	Serial Numbers			
	Low	High	Notes Printed	CH CU
BOSTON	A-A	—	2,560,000	$160
	A-B	—	6,400,000	140
NEW YORK	B-A	—	44,800,000	140
	B-B	—	60,800,000	140
PHILADELPHIA	C-A	—	6,400,000	200
	C-B	—	6,400,000	160
CLEVELAND	D-A	—	2,560,000	160
	D-B	—	3,200,000	160
RICHMOND	E-A	—	7,680,000	220
	E-B	—	16,000,000	140
	E00 005 476★	E00 583 825★	640,000	3,000
ATLANTA	F-A	—	6,400,000	220
CHICAGO	G-A	—	20,480,000	140
	G-B	—	12,800,000	140
ST. LOUIS	H-A	—	2,560,000	140
	H-B	—	3,200,000	140
MINNEAPOLIS	I-A	—	3,200,000	140
KANSAS CITY	J-A	—	7,680,000	140
	J-B	—	16,000,000	140
DALLAS	K-A	—	14,080,000	140
	K-B	—	9,600,000	220
SAN FRANCISCO	L-A	—	15,360,000	140
	L-B	—	9,600,000	180

SERIES 1981A GREEN SEAL

SIGNATURES: Katherine Davalos Ortega, Donald T. Regan

SERIAL NUMBERS: Both regular and star notes begin with 00 000 001.

	Serial Numbers			
	Low	**High**	**Notes Printed**	**CH CU**
BOSTON	A-A	—	16,000,000	$160
NEW YORK	B-A	—	64,000,000	140
PHILADELPHIA	C-A	C10 308 919A	3,200,000	200
CLEVELAND	D-A	—	6,400,000	160
RICHMOND	E-A	—	12,800,000	160
ATLANTA	F-A	—	12,800,000	160
CHICAGO	G-A	—	22,400,000	140
ST. LOUIS	H-A	—	12,800,000	160
MINNEAPOLIS	I-A	—	3,200,000	160
DALLAS	K-A	—	3,200,000	180
SAN FRANCISCO	L-A	—	19,200,000	160
	L00 097 836★	L03 096 188★	3,200,000	1,500

SERIES 1985 GREEN SEAL

SIGNATURES: Katherine Davalos Ortega, James A. Baker III
SERIAL NUMBERS: Both regular and star notes begin with 00 000 001.

	Serial Numbers			
	Low	**High**	**Notes Printed**	**CH CU**
BOSTON	A-A	—	32,000,000	$150
NEW YORK	B-A	—	99,200,000	150
	B-B	—	99,200,000	150
	B-C	—	60,800,000	150
	B00 196 030★	—	—	600
PHILADELPHIA	C-A	—	19,200,000	150
CLEVELAND	D-A	—	28,800,000	150
	D02 563 902★	D03 200 000★	1,280,000	400
RICHMOND	E-A	—	54,400,000	150
ATLANTA	F-A	—	16,000,000	150
CHICAGO	G-A	—	64,000,000	150
ST. LOUIS	H-A	—	12,800,000	150
MINNEAPOLIS	I-A	—	12,800,000	150
KANSAS CITY	J-A	—	12,800,000	150
	J01 274 950★	J03 200 000★	1,280,000	400
DALLAS	K-A	—	48,000,000	200
	K-★	K03 200 000★	640,000	500
SAN FRANCISCO	L-A	—	38,400,000	150

SERIES 1988 GREEN SEAL

PLATE NUMBERS: Face numbers begin with #1. Back numbers continued from previous series.

SERIAL NUMBERS: Both regular and star notes begin with 00 000 001.

SIGNATURES: Katherine Davalos Ortega, Nicholas F. Brady

	Serial Numbers			
	Low	**High**	**Notes Printed**	**CH CU**
BOSTON	A-A	—	9,600,000	$175
NEW YORK	B-A - B-E	B48 000 000E	448,000,000	160
	B00 820 505★	B06 400 000★	4,480,000	450
PHILADELPHIA	C-A	—	9,600,000	175
	Low	**High**	**Notes Printed**	**CH CU**
CLEVELAND	D00 820 000A	—	35,200,000	$175
RICHMOND	E-A	—	19,200,000	175
CHICAGO	G-A	—	51,200,000	175
ST. LOUIS	H-A	—	9,600,000	175
KANSAS CITY	J-A	—	9,600,000	175
SAN FRANCISCO	L-A	—	19,200,000	175

SERIES 1990 GREEN SEAL

SIGNATURES: Catalina Vasquez Villalpando, Nicholas F. Brady

PLATE NUMBERS: Face numbers begin at #1. Back numbers continue sequence from previous series.

SERIAL NUMBERS: Both regular and star notes begin at 00 000 001.

(Series 1990 introduced the anti-counterfeiting security thread and the microsize printing around the portrait.)

	Serial Numbers			
	Low	**High**	**Notes Printed**	**CH CU**
BOSTON	A-A	A76 800 000A	76,800,000	$150
NEW YORK	B-A - B-F	B99 200 000F	595,200,000	140
	B01 116 154★	B09 600 000★	1,880,000	175
PHILADELPHIA	C-A	—	99,200,000	150
	—	C12 800 000B	12,800,000	150
	C02 599 978★	C03 200 000★	2,560,000	225
CLEVELAND	D-A	—	99,200,000	150
	D-B	D16 000 000B	16,000,000	150
RICHMOND	E-A	—	99,200,000	150
	E-B	E09 600 000B	9,600,000	150
ATLANTA	F-A	F64 000 000A	64,000,000	150
CHICAGO	G-A	—	99,200,000	125
	G-B	G35 200 000B	35,200,000	125
	G-★	G03 200 000★	640,000	175
ST. LOUIS	H-A	—	99,200,000	150
	H-B	H22 400 000B	22,400,000	150
MINNEAPOLIS	I-A	I48 000 000A	48,000,000	150
KANSAS CITY	J-A	J76 800 000A	76,800,000	150
	J-★	J03 200 000★	2,560,000	225
	J00 387 597★	J02 566 799★ (observed)	—	—
DALLAS	K-A	—	99,200,000	150
	K-B	K67 200 000B	67,200,000	150
	K-★	K03 200 000★	1,920,000	225
	K00 387 574★	K01 079 730★ (observed)	—	—
SAN FRANCISCO	L-A	—	99,200,000	150
	L-B	L48 000 000B	48,000,000	150
	L-★	L03 200 000★	3,200,000	225

SERIES 1993 GREEN SEAL

SIGNATURES: Mary Ellen Withrow, Lloyd Bentsen

PLATE NUMBERS: Back numbers continued from previous series creating mules with the faces which start over at #1, until very near the end of the run, when new backs starting at #1 appear. These are quite scarce.

SERIAL NUMBERS: Both regular and star notes begin at 00 000 001.

	Serial Numbers			
	Low	**High**	**Notes Printed**	**CH CU**
BOSTON	A-A	—	83,200,000	$160
NEW YORK	B-A - B-C	B25 600 000C	224,000,000	160
	B02 481 699★	B03 200 000★	1,280,000	200
PHILADELPHIA	C-A	(C43 142 207A obsvd.)	41,600,000	160
	C00 830 860★	C01 280 000★	1,280,000	200
CLEVELAND	D-A	—	9,600,000	160
	D-★	D03 200 000★	1,280,000	200
RICHMOND	E-A	—	64,000,000	160
ATLANTA	F-A	—	99,200,000	160
	F-B	—	51,200,000	160
CHICAGO	G-A	—	44,800,000	160
ST. LOUIS	H-A	—	16,000,000	160
	H-★	H03 200 000★	640,000	250
MINNEAPOLIS	I-A	—	9,600,000	200
KANSAS CITY	J-A	—	9,600,000	160
DALLAS	K-A	—	51,200,000	160
SAN FRANCISCO	L-A	—	19,200,000	160

SERIES 1996 GREEN SEAL

SIGNATURES: Mary Ellen Withrow, Robert E. Rubin

PLATE NUMBERS: Both face and back numbers begin at #1.

SERIAL NUMBERS: Both regular and star notes begin at 00 000 001. Prefix letter A is positioned before district letter.

PRINTING FACILITY: All notes printed in Washington, D.C.

See narrative in introduction, describing features of this design.

	Serial Numbers			
	Low	**High**	**Notes Printed**	**CH CU**
BOSTON	AA-A - AA-B	AA25 600 000B	125,600,000	$120
	AA-★	AA03 840 000★	2,560,000	150
NEW YORK	AB-A - AB-Y	AB25 600 000Y	2,325,600,000	120
	AB-★	AB19 200 000★	17,920,000	135
PHILADELPHIA	AC-A	AC86 400 000A	86,400,000	120
CLEVELAND	AD-A - AD-B	AD76 800 000B	176,800,000	120
	AD00 008 700★	AD00 160 000★	160,000	900
RICHMOND	AE-A - AE-C	AE76 800 000C	276,800,000	120
	AE00 885 531★	AE03 200 000★	3,200,000	145
ATLANTA	AF-A - AF-C	AF22 400 000C	222,400,000	120
	AF-★	AF01 920 000★	1,920,000	160
	AF03 200 001★	AF03 840 000★	640,000	200
CHICAGO	AG-A - AG-C	AG44 800 000C	244,800,000	120
	AG-★	AG01 920 000★	1,920,000	160
ST. LOUIS	AH-A - AH-B	AH12 800 000B	112,800,000	120
MINNEAPOLIS	AI-A	AI32 000 000A	32,000,000	125
KANSAS CITY	AJ-A	AJ83 200 000A	83,200,000	120
DALLAS	AK-A - AK-B	AK44 800 000B	144,800,000	120
	AK-★	AK01 920 000★	1,920,000	160
SAN FRANCISCO	AL-A - AL-D	AL96 000 000D	384,000,000	120
	AL-E	AL06 400 000E	6,400,000	160
	AL-★	AL02 560 000★	2,560,000	150

SERIES 1999 GREEN SEAL

SIGNATURES: Mary Ellen Withrow, Lawrence H. Summers
PLATE NUMBERS: Both face and back numbers begin at #1.
SERIAL NUMBERS: Both regular and star notes begin at 00 000 001.
PRINTING FACILITY: All notes printed in Washington, D.C.

	Serial Numbers			
	Low	**High**	**Notes Printed**	**CH CU**
BOSTON	BA-A	BA48 000 000A	48,000,000	$125
	BA-★	BA03 520 000★	3,520,000	150
NEW YORK	BB-B	BB73 600 000B	169,600,000	125
	BB-★	BB01 920 000★	1,920,000	200
	BB03 200 001★	BB05 120 000★	1,920,000	150
PHILADELPHIA	BC-A	BC03 200 000A	3,200,000	150
CLEVELAND	BD-A	BD19 200 000A	19,200,000	135
RICHMOND	BE-A	BE60 800 000A	60,800,000	125
ATLANTA	BF-A	BF16 000 000A	16,000,000	135
CHICAGO	BG-A	BG54 400 000A	54,400,000	130
ST. LOUIS	BH-A	BH22 400 000A	22,400,000	135
MINNEAPOLIS	BI-A	BI70 400 000A	70,400,000	125
KANSAS CITY	BJ-A	BJ25 600 000A	25,600,000	135
DALLAS	BK-A	BK19 200 000A	19,200,000	135

SERIES 2001 GREEN SEAL

SIGNATURES: Rosario Marin, Paul H. O'Neill

PLATE NUMBERS: Both face and back numbers begin at #1.

SERIAL NUMBERS: All districts start both regular and star notes with 00 000 001.

PRINTING FACILITY: All notes were printed in Washington, D.C.

	Serial Numbers			
	Low	**High**	**Notes Printed**	**CH CU**
BOSTON	CA-A	CA32 000 000A	32,000,000	$125
NEW YORK	CB-A - CB-F	CB83 200 000F	563,200,000	125
	CB-★	CB00 320 000★	320,000	300
PHILADELPHIA	CC-A	CC32 000 000A	32,000,000	125
CLEVELAND	CD-A	CD19 200 000A	19,200,000	125
	CD-★	CD01 920 000★	1,920,000	150
RICHMOND	CE-A	CE64 000 000A	64,000,000	125
	CE-★	CE01 920 000★	1,920,000	150
ATLANTA	CF-A	CF96 000 000A	96,000,000	125
	CF-B	CF03 200 000B	3,200,000	250
	CF-★	CF00 320 000★	320,000	400
	CF03 200 001★	CF04 480 000★	1,280,000	175
CHICAGO	CG-A	CG57 600 000A	57,600,000	125
ST. LOUIS	CH-A	CH25 600 000A	25,600,000	125
MINNEAPOLIS	CI-A	CI09 600 000A	9,600,000	140
KANSAS CITY	CJ-A	CJ22 400 000A	22,400,000	130
DALLAS	CK-A	CK60 800 000A	60,800,000	125
SAN FRANCISCO	CL-A - CL-B	CL48 000 000B	144,000,000	125

SERIES 2003 GREEN SEAL

SIGNATURES: Rosario Marin, John W. Snow
PLATE NUMBERS: Both face and back numbers begin at #1.
SERIAL NUMBERS: Districts start both regular and star notes with 00 000 001.
PRINTING FACILITY: All notes were printed in Washington, D.C.

	Serial Numbers			
	Low	**High**	**Notes Printed**	**CH CU**
BOSTON	DA-A	DA35 200 000A	35,200,000	$135
NEW YORK	DB-A - DB-D	DB67 200 000D	355,200,000	125
	DB00 000 001★	DB00 320 000★	320,000	250
	DB03 200 001★	DB05 120 000★	1,920,000	175
PHILADELPHIA	DC-A	DC41 600 000A	41,600,000	135
CLEVELAND	DD-A	DD32 000 000A	32,000,000	135
RICHMOND	DE-A	DE86 400 000A	86,400,000	125
ATLANTA	DF-A - DF-B	DF67 200 000B	163,200,000	125
	DF-★	DF01 280 000★	1,280,000	175
CHICAGO	DG-A	DG80 000 000A	80,000,000	125
ST. LOUIS	DH-A	DH38 400 000A	38,400,000	135
MINNEAPOLIS	DI-A	DI16 000 000A	16,000,000	140
KANSAS CITY	DJ-A	DJ38 400 000A	38,400,000	135
DALLAS	DK-A	DK32 000 000A	32,000,000	135
	DK-★	DK00 128 000★	128,000	300
	DK03 200 001★	DK03 328 000★	128,000	300
	DK06 400 001★	DK07 680 000★	1,280,000	175
SAN FRANCISCO	DL-A	DL89 600 000A	89,600,000	125
	DL-★	DL00 320 000★	320,000	250
	DL03 200 001★	DL03 840 000★	640,000	200

SERIES 2003A GREEN SEAL

SIGNATURES: Anna Escobedo Cabral, John W. Snow
PLATE NUMBERS: Face and back numbers begin at #1.
SERIAL NUMBERS: All districts start both regular and star notes with 00 000 001.
PRINTING FACILITY: All notes were printed in Washington, D.C.

	Serial Numbers			
	Low	**High**	**Notes Printed**	**CH CU**
BOSTON	FA-A	FA12 800 000A	12,800,000	$135
NEW YORK	FB-A	FB28 800 000D	316,800,000	125
	FB-★	FB00 160 000★	160,000 (sheets)	250
	FB03 200 001★	FB04 480 000★	1,280,000	175
	FB06 400 001★	FB06 720 000★	320,000 (sheets)	200
PHILADELPHIA	FC-A	FC28 800 000A	28,800,000	130
CLEVELAND	FD-A	FD16 000 000A	16,000,000	135
RICHMOND	FE-A	FE86 400 000A	86,400,000	125
ATLANTA	FF-A	FF96 000 000C	288,000,000	125
CHICAGO	FG-A	FG35 200 000B	131,200,000	125
	FG-★	FG01 920 000★	1,920,000	175
ST. LOUIS	FH-A	FH64 000 000A	64,000,000	130
	FH-★	FH00 320 000★	320,000 (sheets)	250
	FH03 200 001★	FH04 480 000★	1,280,000	200
MINNEAPOLIS	FI-A	FI19 200 000A	19,200,000	135
KANSAS CITY	FJ-A	FJ64 000 000A	64,000,000	125

	Low	High	Notes Printed	CH CU
DALLAS	FK-A	FK83 200 000B	179,200,000	$125
SAN FRANCISCO	FL-A	FL96 000 000C	288,000,000	125
	FL-D	FL03 200 000D	3,200,000	175
	FL-★	FL01 280 000★	1,280,000	200

SERIES 2006 GREEN SEAL

SIGNATURES: Anna Escobedo Cabral, Henry M. Paulson, Jr.

PLATE NUMBERS: Face and back numbers begin at #1.

SERIAL NUMBERS: All districts start both regular and star notes with 00 000 001, with a print run to 99 200 000.

PRINTING FACILITY: All notes were printed in Washington, D.C.

	Serial Numbers			
	Low	High	Notes Printed	CH CU
NEW YORK	HB-A W/FW	HB80 000 000C	278,400,000	125
PHILADELPHIA	HC-A W	HC32 000 000A	32,000,000	125
CLEVELAND	HD-A W	HD28 800 000A	28,800,000	125
RICHMOND	HE-A W	HE80 000 000A	80,000,000	125
	HE-★W	HE01 920 000★	1,920,000	175
SAN FRANCISCO	HL-A W/FW	HL41 600 000B	140,800,000	125

FIVE HUNDRED DOLLAR NOTES

GOLD CERTIFICATES

SERIES 1928 GOLD SEAL

PLATE NUMBERS: Begin with #1 face and back numbers.
SIGNATURES: W.O. Woods, A.W. Mellon

Serial Numbers

Low	High	Notes Printed	VF	CH CU	GEM CU
A00 000 831A	A00 120 561A	—	$9,500	$45,000	$75,000
A-★	—	4,000	unknown	—	—

FEDERAL RESERVE NOTES

SERIES 1928 DARK GREEN SEAL

SERIAL NUMBERS: All serial numbers both regular and star notes begin with 00 000 001. High official star numbers are listed in the high star serial number column, but the actual notes probably do not exist.

PLATE NUMBERS: Face and back both begin with #1.

SIGNATURES: W.O. Woods, A.W. Mellon

	Serial Numbers					
	Low	**High**	**Notes Printed**	**VF**	**CH CU**	**GEM CU**
BOSTON	A00 003 424A	A00 026 924A	69,120	$10,000	—	—
	A-★	—	360	—	—	—
NEW YORK	B00 000 005A	B00 100 044A	299,400	1,500	$4,000	—
	B-★	—	2,160	—	—	—
PHILADELPHIA	C00 000 001A	C00 019 763A	135,120	1,600	4,000	—
	C00 000 122★	—	1,080	40,000	—	—
CLEVELAND	D00 000 234A	D00 030 771A	166,440	1,600	4,000	$5,500
	D-★	—	1,080	—	—	—

	Low	High	Notes Printed	VF	CH CU	GEM CU
RICHMOND	E00 000 302A	E00 021 387A	84,720	$1,700	$5,750	—
	E-★	—	720	—	—	—
ATLANTA	F00 000 022A	F00 021 935A	69,360	1,600	5,000	—
	F-★	—	360	—	—	—
CHICAGO	G00 000 018A	—	573,600	1,500	4,000	$5,500
	G00 000 064★	—	2,160	40,000	—	—
ST. LOUIS	H00 000 003A	H00 055 477A	66,180	1,400	3,750	5,500
	H-★	—	720	—	—	—
MINNEAPOLIS	I00 000 158A	I00 005 041A	34,680	1,750	7,500	—
	I-★	—	360	—	—	—
KANSAS CITY	J00 002 074A	J00 015 687A	510,720	1,750	5,500	—
	J-★	—	1,080	—	—	—
DALLAS	K00 000 492A	K00 009 443A	70,560	1,750	8,500	—
	K-★	—	360	—	—	—
SAN FRANCISCO	L00 000 363A	L00 036 735A	64,080	1,600	6,500	—
	L-★	—	360	—	—	—

SERIES 1928 LIGHT VIVID YELLOW-GREEN SEAL

SERIAL NUMBERS: Continue in sequence from 1928 Dark Green Seal.

SIGNATURES: Walter O. Woods, A.W. Mellon

	Serial Numbers					
	Low	High	Notes Printed	VF	CH CU	GEM CU
NEW YORK	B00 149 683A	B00 158 748A	included above	$1,900	—	—
CHICAGO	G00 163 228A	G00 209 791A	—	1,900	—	—
KANSAS CITY	J00 040 270A	J00 040 557A	—	1,900	—	—

SERIES 1934 LIGHT VIVID YELLOW-GREEN SEAL

SERIAL NUMBERS: Both regular and star notes begin with 00 000 001.

PLATE NUMBERS: Face and back both begin with #1.

SIGNATURES: W.A. Julian, Henry Morgenthau, Jr.

	Serial Numbers					
	Low	High	Notes Printed	VF	CH CU	GEM CU
BOSTON	A00 000 054A	A00 012 135A	56,628	$1,350	$3,500	—
NEW YORK	B00 000 275A	B00 087 214A	288,000	1,150	2,500	$5,000
PHILADELPHIA	C00 000 197A	C00 017 284A	31,200	1,150	3,500	—
CLEVELAND	D00 000 017A	D00 012 553A	39,000	1,250	2,750	5,000

	Low	High	Notes Printed	VF	CH CU	GEM CU
RICHMOND	E00 000 002A	E00 016 487A	40,800	$1,300	$3,500	—
ATLANTA	F00 001 043A	F00 015 856A	46,200	1,150	2,750	—

	Low	High	Notes Printed	VF	CH CU	GEM CU
CHICAGO	G00 001 424A	—	212,400	1,150	2,500	—
ST. LOUIS	H00 000 060A	H00 017 999A	24,000	1,150	2,750	—
MINNEAPOLIS	I00 000 016A	I00 008 304A	24,000	1,250	3,500	7,500
KANSAS CITY	J00 000 005A	J00 015 772A	40,800	1,150	2,750	—
DALLAS	K00 000 063A	K00 017 926A	31,200	1,700	4,500	—
SAN FRANCISCO	L00 000 018A	L00 022 891A	83,400	1,200	3,000	—

SERIES 1934 DARK BLUE-GREEN SEAL

SERIAL NUMBERS: Continue sequence from 1934 Light Vivid Yellow-Green Seal.

SIGNATURES: W.A. Julian, Henry Morgenthau, Jr.

	Serial Numbers					
	Low	High	Notes Printed	VF	CH CU	GEM CU
BOSTON	A00 020 617A	A00 055 967A	included above	$1,050	$1,750	$2,600
	A-★	—	—	—	—	—
NEW YORK	B00 095 158A	B00 262 007A	included above	1,000	1,750	2,400
	B00 000 100★	B00 004 797★	—	4,000	—	
PHILADELPHIA	C00 021 299A	C00 019 056A	included above	1,150	1,950	2,700
	C00 000 195★	C00 002 892★	—	4,500	—	
CLEVELAND	D00 016 773A	D00 030 418A	included above	1,100	1,950	2,600
	D00 000 059★	D00 001 944★	—	4,000	—	
RICHMOND	E00 021 387A	E00 063 581A	included above	1,250	2,100	4,500
	E00 001 822★	E00 002 209★	—	5,000	—	
ATLANTA	F00 019 087A	F00 063 770A	included above	1,100	1,900	—
	F00 000 104★	F00 003 293★	—	4,000	—	
CHICAGO	G00 042 764A	G00 269 913A	included above	1,050	1,750	2,300
	G00 000 204★	G00 004 122★	—	3,500	15,000	
ST. LOUIS	H00 066 951A	H00 067 368A	included above	1,100	1,900	2,600
	H00 001 971★	H00 002 294★	—	6,000	—	
MINNEAPOLIS	I00 009 705A	I00 012 161A	included above	1,300	3,000	7,500
	I00 000 799★	I00 000 800★	—	6,000	—	
KANSAS CITY	J00 024 132A	J00 078 989A	included above	1,150	1,950	—
	J00 000 001★	—	—	7,000	—	
DALLAS	—	K00 047 749A	included above	1,250	4,000	—
	K00 000 104★	K00 001 443★	—	6,500	—	—
SAN FRANCISCO	L00 029 022A	L00 157 627A	included above	1,150	1,900	—
	L00 000 208★	L00 005 324★	—	4,000	20,000	30,000

SERIES 1934A GREEN SEAL MULE

SERIAL NUMBERS: Continue sequence from previous series.

SIGNATURES: W.A. Julian, Henry Morgenthau, Jr.

	Serial Numbers					
	Low	**High**	**Notes Printed**	**VF**	**CH CU**	**GEM CU**
NEW YORK	B00 247 927A	B00 426 371A	276,000	$1,000	$1,750	$2,500
	B00 003 959★	B00 004 797★	—	6,000	—	—
PHILADELPHIA	C00 025 038A	C00 048 351A	45,300	1,300	2,500	4,000
CLEVELAND	D00 037 408A	D00 057 516A	23,800	1,100	2,000	3,000
RICHMOND	E00 020 037A	E00 064 793A	36,000	1,300	5,500	—
ATLANTA	F00 037 292A	F00 102 801A	—	1,100	1,900	2,750
CHICAGO	G00 131 624A	G00 383 045A	214,800	1,000	1,750	2,250
	G00 002 211★	G00 004373★	—	5,000	—	—
ST. LOUIS	H00 024 593A	H00 070 638A	57,600	1,100	1,900	3,000
	H00 000 602★	—	—	10,000	—	—
MINNEAPOLIS	I00 013 321A	I00 024 957A	14,400	1,500	6,000	9,000
KANSAS CITY	J00 018 095A	J00 078 168A	55,200	1,100	2,000	—
	J00 000 202★	J00 004 905★	—	7,500	—	—
DALLAS	K00 018 984A	K00 048 235A	34,800	1,500	5,500	—
SAN FRANCISCO	L00 063 482A	L00 156 403A	73,000	1,100	2,000	—
	L00 003 621★	L00 004 792★	—	4,500	—	—

SERIES 1934B GREEN SEAL

SERIAL NUMBERS: Continued sequence from previous series.

SIGNATURES: W.A. Julian, Fred M. Vinson

	Serial Numbers				
	Low	**High**	**Notes Printed**	**VF**	**CH CU**
ATLANTA	F-A	—	2,472	—	—

SERIES 1934C GREEN SEAL

SERIAL NUMBERS: Continue sequence from previous series.

SIGNATURES: W.A. Julian, John W. Snyder

	Serial Numbers				
	Low	**High**	**Notes Printed**	**VF**	**CH CU**
BOSTON	A-A	—	1,440	—	—
NEW YORK	B-A	—	204	—	—

ONE THOUSAND DOLLAR NOTES

GOLD CERTIFICATES

SERIES 1928 GOLD SEAL

PLATE NUMBERS: Face and back numbers begin with #1.

SIGNATURES: W.O. Woods, A.W. Mellon

Serial Numbers

Low	High	Notes Printed	VF	CH CU	GEM CU
A00 000 001A	A00 288 000A	288,000	$15,000	$65,000	$90,000
A-★	—	—	unknown	—	—

SERIES 1934 GOLD SEAL

PLATE NUMBERS: Face and back numbers both begin with #1.

SIGNATURES: W.A. Julian, Henry Morgenthau, Jr.

These 1934 notes had orange (not green) backs, and their text specified payment "in gold payable to the bearer on demand as authorized by law." Those last four words have been added because these 1934 gold notes were for use only among banks and were not to be released into public circulation.

The Bureau occasionally exhibits its specimen sheet of these orange-back notes.

Serial Numbers

Low	High	Notes Printed	VF	CH CU	GEM CU
A00 000 001A	A00 084 000A	84,000	—	—	—

FEDERAL RESERVE NOTES

SERIES 1928 DARK GREEN SEAL

SERIAL NUMBERS: All serial numbers of both regular and star notes begin with 00 000 001. High official star serial numbers are listed in the high star serial number column, but the actual notes probably do not exist.

PLATE NUMBERS: Face and back numbers both begin with #1.

SIGNATURES: W.O. Woods, A.W. Mellon

	Serial Numbers					
	Low	**High**	**Notes Printed**	**VF**	**CH CU**	**GEM CU**
BOSTON	A00 000 250A	A00 016 719A	58,320	$30,000	—	—
	A-★	—	360	—	—	—
NEW YORK	B00 000 189A	B00 098 113A	139,200	2,500	$5,300	$7,000
	B00 000 068★	B00 000 111★	160	40,000	—	—
PHILADELPHIA	C00 000 001A	C00 070 731A	96,708	2,500	6,000	8,000
	C00 000 181★	C00 000 301★	720	35,000	—	—
CLEVELAND	D00 000 333A	D00 031 626A	79,680	2,500	6,000	7,500
	D00 000 102★	—	1,080	60,000	—	—
RICHMOND	E00 000 720A	E00 014 715A	66,840	2,500	6,000	8,000
	E00 000 002★	—	360	60,000	—	—
ATLANTA	F00 000 927A	F00 027 630A	47,400	2,350	5,000	6,500
	F-★	—	240	—	—	—
CHICAGO	G00 000 680A	G00 212 733A	355,800	2,400	5,000	6,500
	G00 000 589★	—	1,800	60,000	—	—
ST. LOUIS	H00 000 419A	H00 026 699A	60,000	2,300	5,000	6,500
	H00 000 189★	—	360	60,000	—	—
MINNEAPOLIS	I00 000 056A	I00 004 821A	26,640	3,000	15,000	—
	I00 000 913★	—	360	60,000	—	—
KANSAS CITY	J00 001 729A	J00 012 219A	62,172	3,000	6,000	9,000
	J-★	—	720	—	—	—
DALLAS	K00 000 420A	K00 008 833A	42,960	2,700	15,000	—
	K-★	—	360	—	—	—
SAN FRANCISCO	L00 000 772A	L00 027 466A	67,920	3,000	6,000	—
	L-★	—	360	—	—	—

SERIES 1928 LIGHT VIVID YELLLOW GREEN SEAL

SERIAL NUMBERS: Continue in sequence from 1928 Dark Green Seal.

SIGNATURES: Walter O. Woods, A.W. Mellon

Serial Numbers

	Low	High	Notes Printed	VF	CH CU	GEM CU
RICHMOND	E00 016 637A	E00 032 209A	included above	$3,000	$7,500	$12,000
ST. LOUIS	H00 027 634A	H00 039 815A	included above	2,800	7,000	9,000
KANSAS CITY	J00 030 886A	J00 033 984A	included above	3,000	8,000	—
SAN FRANCISCO	L00 035 180A	L00 035 512A	included above	3,500	8,000	—

SERIES 1934 LIGHT VIVID YELLOW-GREEN SEAL

SERIAL NUMBERS: All serial numbers of both regular and star notes begin with 00 000 001.

PLATE NUMBERS: Face and back numbers both begin with #1.

SIGNATURES: W.A. Julian, Henry Morgenthau, Jr.

Serial Numbers

	Low	High	Notes Printed	VF	CH CU	GEM CU
BOSTON	A00 000 513A	A00 014 598A	46,200	$3,000	$7,500	—
NEW YORK	B00 000 130A	B00 123 094A	332,784	2,700	5,000	—
PHILADELPHIA	C00 001 978A	C00 019 665A	33,000	2,700	7,500	—
CLEVELAND	D00 000 051A	D00 012 531A	35,400	3,000	6,000	—

	Low	High	Notes Printed	VF	CH CU	GEM CU
RICHMOND	E00 000 013A	E00 009 587A	19,560	$3,500	$13,000	—
ATLANTA	F00 000 041A	F00 019 574A	67,800	2,400	5,000	$9,500
CHICAGO	G00 000 135A	G00 028 269A	167,040	2,400	5,000	7,000
ST. LOUIS	H00 000 100A	H00 011 605A	22,440	3,000	6,000	—
MINNEAPOLIS	I00 000 083A	I00 003 903A	12,000	3,400	12,000	—
KANSAS CITY	J00 000 017A	J00 020 557A	51,840	3,000	7,000	—
DALLAS	K00 002 195A	K00 004 584A	46,800	3,400	12,000	—
SAN FRANCISCO	L00 000 040A	L00 016 558A	90,600	3,000	6,000	—

SERIES 1934 DARK BLUE-GREEN SEAL

SERIAL NUMBERS: Continue sequence from 1934 Light Vivid Yellow-Green seal.
SIGNATURES: W.A. Julian, Henry Morgenthau, Jr.

	Serial Numbers					
	Low	**High**	**Notes Printed**	**VF**	**CH CU**	**GEM CU**
BOSTON	A00 020 854A	A00 036 565A	included above	$2,200	$3,900	—
	A00 000 319★	—		— 25,000	—	—
NEW YORK	B00 164 217A	B00 323 288A	included above	2,100	3,700	4,750
	B00 000 181★	B00 001 119★		— 20,000	—	—
PHILADELPHIA	C00 017 296A	C00 020 988A	included above	2,500	4,500	—
	C00 001 986★	C00 002 534★		— 7,500	20,000	27,500
CLEVELAND	D00 021 790A	D00 026 980A	included above	2,200	3,900	5,000
	D00 000 008★	D00 001 390★		— 6,000	—	—
RICHMOND	E00 025 927A	E00 045 009A	included above	2,500	5,000	—
	E00 000 647★	—		— 25,000	—	—
ATLANTA	F00 022 533A	F00 119 866A	included above	2,100	3,900	4,750
	F00 001 150★	F00 004 999★		— 7,500	—	—

	Low	**High**	**Notes Printed**	**VF**	**CH CU**	**GEM CU**
CHICAGO	G00 043 612A	G00 167 426A	included above	$2,100	3,700	4,750
	G00 000 026★	G00 003 519★		— 6,000	15,000	—
ST. LOUIS	H-A	H00 025 972A	included above	2,200	4,000	—
	H00 000 897★	H00 001 586★		— 8,000	—	—
MINNEAPOLIS	I00 006 756A	I00 016 164A	included above	2,700	7,500	—
	I00 000 804★	I00 001 009★		— 12,500	—	—
KANSAS CITY	J00 022 849A	J00 057 596A	included above	2,200	4,500	—
	J00 000 008★	J00 002 300★		— 8,000	—	—
DALLAS	K00 009 755A	K00 050 668A	included above	2,900	12,000	—
	K00 001 011★	—		— 30,000	—	—
SAN FRANCISCO	L00 020 651A	L00 069 325A	included above	2,300	4,500	—
	L00 000 025★	L00 004 176★		— 6,000	—	—

SERIES 1934A GREEN SEAL

SERIAL NUMBERS: Continue sequence from previous series.
SIGNATURES: W.A. Julian, Henry Morgenthau, Jr.

	Serial Numbers					
	Low	**High**	**Notes Printed**	**VF**	**CH CU**	**GEM CU**
BOSTON	A00 023 154A	A00 053 203A	30,000	$2,200	$3,900	$5,000
	A-★	—	—	—	—	—
NEW YORK	B00 312 562A	B00 418 610A	174,348	2,100	3,700	4,750
	B00 002 936★	—	—	25,000	—	—
PHILADELPHIA	C00 024 313A	C00 046 070A	78,000	2,500	4,500	7,500
	C-★	—	—	—	—	—
CLEVELAND	D00 030 853A	D00 046 331A	28,000	2,200	3,900	5,000
	D-★	—	—	—	—	—
RICHMOND	E00 012 200A	E00 028 481A	16,800	2,700	12,000	—
	E-★	—	—	—	—	—
ATLANTA	F00 046 356A	F00 126 363A	80,964	2,100	3,750	4,750
	F-★	—	—	—	—	—
CHICAGO	G00 148 021A	G00 269 046A	134,400	2,100	3,700	4,750
	G00 003 693★	G00 004 094★	—	10,000	25,000	—
ST. LOUIS	H00 022 714A	H00 051 831A	39,600	2,500	3,900	5,000
	H-★	—	—	—	—	—
MINNEAPOLIS	I00 010 950A	I00 012 669A	4,800	3,000	12,000	—
	I-★	—	—	—	—	—
KANSAS CITY	J00 034 236A	J00 056 646A	21,600	2,200	3,900	—
	J-★	—	—	—	—	—
SAN FRANCISCO	L00 071 330A	L00 097 535A	36,600	2,200	3,900	—
	L-★	—	—	—	—	—

SERIES 1934C MULE GREEN SEAL

SERIAL NUMBERS: Continued sequence from previous series.
SIGNATURES: W.A. Julian, John W. Snyder

	Serial Numbers					
	Low	**High**	**Notes Printed**	**VF**	**CH CU**	**GEM CU**
BOSTON	A-A	—	1,200	—	unknown	—
NEW YORK	B-A	—	168	—	unknown	—

FIVE THOUSAND DOLLAR NOTES

GOLD CERTIFICATES

SERIES 1928 GOLD SEAL

PLATE NUMBERS: Face and back numbers both begin with #1.

SIGNATURES: W.O. Woods, A.W. Mellon

Serial Numbers

Low	High	Notes Printed	VF	CH CU
A00 000 001A	A00 024 000A	24,000	—	—

FEDERAL RESERVE NOTES

SERIES 1928 GREEN SEAL

SERIAL NUMBERS: Regular notes begin with 00 000 001. No star notes printed.

PLATE NUMBERS: Face and back numbers both begin with #1.

SIGNATURES: W.O. Woods, A.W. Mellon

	Serial Numbers					
	Low	High	Notes Printed	VF	CH CU	GEM CU
BOSTON	A00 000 107A	A00 000 110A	1,320	$100,000	$125,000	$150,000
NEW YORK	B-A	—	2,640	—	—	—
CLEVELAND	D-A	—	3,000	—	—	—
RICHMOND	E00 000 133A	E00 000 764A	3,984	100,000	150,000	175,000
ATLANTA	F00 000 077A	F00 000 204A	1,440	100,000	—	—
CHICAGO	G00 000 026A	G00 001 179A	3,480	100,000	125,000	150,000
KANSAS CITY	J00 000 117A	—	720	125,000	—	—
DALLAS	K-A	—	360	—	—	—
SAN FRANCISCO	L-A	—	1,300	—	—	—

SERIES 1934 LIGHT VIVID YELLOW-GREEN SEAL

SERIAL NUMBERS: All serial numbers of both regular and star notes begin with 00 000 001.
PLATE NUMBERS: Face and back numbers both begin with #1.
SIGNATURES: W.A. Julian, Henry Morgenthau, Jr.

	Serial Numbers				
	Low	**High**	**Notes Printed**	**VF**	**CH CU**
BOSTON	A00 000 014A	A00 000 176A	9,480	$60,000	—
NEW YORK	B00 000 001A	B00 002 403A	11,520	60,000	$125,000
PHILADELPHIA	C00 000 100A	C00 000 134A	3,000	60,000	—
CLEVELAND	D-A	—	1,680	—	—
RICHMOND	E00 000 114A	E00 000 138A	2,400	60,000	125,000
ATLANTA	F-A	F00 000 167A	3,600	70,000	—
CHICAGO	G00 000 158A	G00 001 272A	6,600	60,000	125,000
ST. LOUIS	H00 000 165A	H00 000 432A	2,400	60,000	125,000
KANSAS CITY	J00 000 012A	J00 000 082A	2,400	60,000	125,000

	Low	**High**	**Notes Printed**	**VF**	**CH CU**
DALLAS	K00 000 032A	K00 000 261A	2,400	$60,000	$125,000
SAN FRANCISCO	L00 000 758A	L00 000 825A	6,000	70,000	—

SERIES 1934A GREEN SEAL

SERIAL NUMBERS: Continued sequence from previous series.
SIGNATURES: W.A. Julian, Henry Morgenthau, Jr.

	Serial Numbers				
	Low	**High**	**Notes Printed**	**VF**	**CH CU**
ST. LOUIS	H-A	—	1,440	—	unknown

SERIES 1934B GREEN SEAL

SERIAL NUMBERS: Continued sequence from previous series.
SIGNATURES: W.A. Julian, Fred M. Vinson

	Serial Numbers				
	Low	**High**	**Notes Printed**	**VF**	**CH CU**
BOSTON	A-A	—	1,200	—	unknown
NEW YORK	B-A	—	12	—	unknown

TEN THOUSAND DOLLAR NOTES

GOLD CERTIFICATES

SERIES 1928 GOLD SEAL

PLATE NUMBERS: Face and back numbers begin with #1.

SIGNATURES: W.O. Woods, A.W. Mellon

Serial Numbers

Low	High	Notes Printed	VF	CH CU
—	—	48,000	—	—

SERIES 1934 GOLD SEAL

PLATE NUMBERS: Begin with #1.

SIGNATURES: W.A. Julian, Henry Morgenthau, Jr.

Serial Numbers

Low	High	Notes Printed
A00 000 001A	A00 036 000A	36,000

These 1934 notes had orange (not green) backs, and their text specified payment "in gold payable to the bearer on demand as authorized by law." The last four words have been added because these 1934 gold notes were for use only among banks and were not to be released into public circulation.

The Bureau occasionally exhibits its specimen sheet of these orange-back notes.

FEDERAL RESERVE NOTES

SERIES 1928 GREEN SEAL

SERIAL NUMBERS: Regular notes begin with 00 000 001.

PLATE SERIALS: Face and back numbers start with #1. No star notes printed.

SIGNATURES: W.O. Woods, A.W. Mellon

	Serial Numbers				
	Low	**High**	**Notes Printed**	**VF**	**CH CU**
BOSTON	A-A	—	1,320	—	—
NEW YORK	B00 000 001A	—	4,680	—	—
CLEVELAND	D00 000 238A	—	960	$150,000	—

	Low	**High**	**Notes Printed**	**VF**	**CH CU**
RICHMOND	E00 000 178A	—	3,024	$150,000	—

	Low	High	Notes Printed	VF	CH CU
ATLANTA	F00 000 016A	F00 000 100A	1,440	$150,000	—
CHICAGO	G-A	—	1,800	—	—
ST. LOUIS	H-A	—	480	—	—
MINNEAPOLIS	I-A	—	480	—	—
KANSAS CITY	J-A	—	480	—	—
DALLAS	K-A	—	360	—	—
SAN FRANCISCO	L00 000 126A	—	360	—	—

SERIES 1934 LIGHT VIVID YELLOW-GREEN SEAL

SERIAL NUMBERS: Both regular and star notes begin with 00 000 001.

PLATE NUMBERS: Face and back check numbers start with #1.

SIGNATURES: W.A. Julian, Henry Morgenthau, Jr.

	Serial Numbers				
	Low	High	Notes Printed	VF	CH CU
BOSTON	A00 000 037A	A00 000 185A	9,720	$70,000	$85,000
NEW YORK	B00 000 097A	B00 004 692A	11,520	60,000	80,000
PHILADELPHIA	C00 000 032A	—	6,000	80,000	—
CLEVELAND	D-A	—	1,480	—	—
RICHMOND	E00 000 082A	—	1,200	80,000	—
ATLANTA	F00 000 017A	F00 000 019A	2,400	75,000	—

	Low	High	Notes Printed	VF	CH CU
CHICAGO	G00 000 112A	G00 001 636A	3,840	$70,000	$85,000
ST. LOUIS	H00 000 112A	H00 000 394A	2,040	75,000	—
KANSAS CITY	J00 000 318A	J00 000 905A	1,200	75,000	—
DALLAS	K00 000 261A	K00 000 271A	1,200	70,000	85,000
SAN FRANCISCO	L00 000 386A	L00 000 448A	3,600	85,000	—

SERIES 1934A GREEN SEAL

SIGNATURES: W.A. Julian, Henry Morgenthau, Jr.

	Serial Numbers				
	Low	High	Notes Printed	VF	CH CU
CHICAGO	G-A	—	1,560	—	unknown

SERIES 1934B GREEN SEAL

SERIAL NUMBERS: Continued sequence from previous series.

SIGNATURES: W.A. Julian, Fred M. Vinson

	Serial Numbers				
	Low	High	Notes Printed	VF	CH CU
NEW YORK	G-A	—	24	—	unknown

ONE HUNDRED THOUSAND DOLLAR NOTES

GOLD CERTIFICATES

SERIES 1934 GOLD SEAL

PLATE NUMBERS: Face and back numbers begin with #1.

SIGNATURES: W.A. Julian, Henry Morgenthau, Jr.

Serial Numbers

Low	High	Notes Printed	VF	CH CU
A00 000 001A	A00 042 000A	42,000	—	—

Like the other 1934 Gold Certificates, this note also has an orange (not green) back and also specifies payment "in gold to the bearer on demand as authorized by law." Also, like the other 1934 Gold Certificates (the $100, $1000, $10,000 notes), these notes were legal for use only among banks, but were not to be released into public circulation.

The Bureau occasionally exhibits its specimen sheet of these high-value orange-back notes.

A00 020 106A Exists

Appendix I

UNCUT SHEETS

Perhaps the most prized and certainly a scarce item in any modern size paper money collection is an uncut sheet printed before 1976. Despite intensive research throughout the Treasury Department, including the records of the Bureau of Engraving and Printing, we find neither validity nor completeness in the records that were examined. Information presented, which is the best available, is contradicted many times by the census of known uncut sheets that follows the list of uncut sheets printed (?) or issued (?). We cannot learn for sure exactly HOW the uncut sheets reached the private collector. We do know that uncut sheets were available to collectors AT FACE VALUE in the Cash Division, Main Treasury Bldg. Washington, D.C. from the start of current size notes, until Secretary Humphrey stopped the sale of uncut sheets during his tenure. Some scant records examined indicate the purchaser signed a "ledger" when making his purchase. Apparently there was no limit, since some signatures appear several times on the same ledger sheet for purchase of separately serial number identified sheets of the same denomination and series. What we have not been able to learn is who requested (or ordered) the uncut sheets from the Bureau and how many were ordered. We have been unable to locate any delivery records of sheets from the Bureau to the Cash Division. We have fairly reliable HEARSAY evidence that IF the sheets remained in the Cash Division unsold, they were eventually cut up and passed over the teller counter as single notes.

Any information relative to either the printing, the issue, or the existence of uncut sheets is welcome.

Listed below is the best information available on the number of uncut sheets printed, followed by a census of uncut sheets known to exist, and their value.

One Dollar

LEGAL TENDER

SERIES 1928 RED SEAL

Signatures	Serial Number Range	# of Sheets
W.O. Woods	A00 000 001A - A00 000 120A	10
W.H. Woodin	A01 872 001A - A01 872 012A	1

SILVER CERTIFICATES

SERIES 1928 BLUE SEAL

Signatures	Serial Number Range	# of Sheets
H.T. Tate	A00 000 001A - A00 004 000A	no record
A.W. Mellon	—	—

SERIES 1928B BLUE SEAL

Signatures	Serial Number Range	# of Sheets
W.O. Woods	V51 000 001A - V51 000 012A	6
Ogden L. Mills	—	—

SERIES 1928C BLUE SEAL

Signatures	Serial Number Range	# of Sheets
W.O. Woods	B29 448 001B - B29 448 120B	10
W.H. Woodin	D23 328 001B - D23 328 012B	1

SERIES 1928D BLUE SEAL

Signatures	Serial Number Range	# of Sheets
W.A. Julian	D82 596 001B - D82 596 720B	60
W.H. Woodin	—	—

SERIES 1928E BLUE SEAL

Signatures	Serial Number Range	# of Sheets
W.A. Julian	F72 000 001B - F72 000 300B	25
Henry Morgenthau, Jr.	—	—

SERIES 1934 BLUE SEAL

Signatures	Serial Number Range	# of Sheets
W.A. Julian	A00 000 001A - A00 000 300A	25
Henry Morgenthau, Jr.	—	—

SERIES 1935 BLUE SEAL

Signatures	Serial Number Range	# of Sheets
W.A. Julian	A00 000 001A - A00 001 200A	100
Henry Morgenthau, Jr.	—	—

SERIES 1935A BLUE SEAL

Signatures	Serial Number Range	# of Sheets
W.A. Julian	V43 128 001A - V43 129 200A	100
Henry Morgenthau, Jr.	F41 952 001C - F41 954 148C N. Africa	25
	F41 964 001C - F41 966 148C Hawaii	25

SERIES 1935B BLUE SEAL

Signatures	Serial Number Range	# of Sheets
W.A. Julian	C93 348 01D - C93 385 200D	100
Fred M. Vinson	—	—

SERIES 1935C BLUE SEAL

Signatures	Serial Number Range	# of Sheets
W.A. Julian	K99 996 001D - K99 997 200D	100
John W. Snyder	—	—

SERIES 1935D BLUE SEAL

12 Subject Sheets

Signatures	Serial Number Range	# of Sheets
Georgia Neese Clark	R88 104 001E - R88 104 200E	100
John W. Snyder	Z33 324 001E - Z33 325 200E	100
	B05 520 001G - B05 521 200G	100

SERIES 1935D BLUE SEAL

18 Subject Sheets

Signatures	Serial Number Range	# of Sheets
Georgia Neese Clark	G00 000 001G - G00 136 100G	100
John W. Snyder	N46 807 999G - N46 944 000G	2

SERIES 1935E BLUE SEAL

Signatures	Serial Number Range	# of Sheets
Ivy Baker Priest	N46 944 001G - N47 080 100G	100
G.M. Humphrey	R95 040 001G - R94 175 100G	100
	U75 168 001G - U75 304 100G	100
	X31 680 001G - X31 816 100G	100

Two Dollars

LEGAL TENDER

SERIES 1928C RED SEAL

12 Subject Sheets

Signatures	Serial Number Range	# of Sheets
W.A. Julian	B09 012 001A - B09 012 300A	25
Henry Morgenthau, Jr.	B83 988 001A - B83 988 500A	50

SERIES 1928D RED SEAL

Signatures	Serial Number Range	# of Sheets
W.A. Julian	—	—
Henry Morgenthau, Jr.	—	

Records indicate 50 sheets Serials B83 988 001A - B83 988 500A were printed for this series, however sheets known with these serials are all Series 1928C. No sheets of this series are known.

SERIES 1928E RED SEAL

Signatures	Serial Number Range	# of Sheets
W.A. Julian	D35 552 001A - D35 532 600A	50
Fred M. Vinson	—	—

SERIES 1928F RED SEAL

Signatures	Serial Number Range	# of Sheets
W.A. Julian	D39 552 001A - D39 553 200A	100
John W. Snyder	—	—

SERIES 1928G RED SEAL

Signatures	Serial Number Range	# of Sheets
Georgia Neese Clark	E07 074 001A - E07 705 200A	100
John W. Snyder	—	—

SERIES 1953 RED SEAL

18 Subject Sheets

Signatures	Serial Number Range	# of Sheets
Ivy Baker Priest	A00 000 001A - A00 136 100A	100
G.M. Humphrey	—	—

Five Dollars

LEGAL TENDER

SERIES 1928E RED SEAL

12 Subject Sheets

Signatures	Serial Number Range	# of Sheets
W.A. Julian	(One sheet offered as item 1111, in A. Kosoff sale of October 26, 1971.)	—
Fred M. Vinson	—	—

SERIES 1928E RED SEAL

Signatures	Serial Number Range	# of Sheets
W.A. Julian	G68 352 001A - G68 353 200A	100
John W. Snyder	—	—

SERIES 1953 RED SEAL

18 Subject Sheets

Signatures	Serial Number Range	# of Sheets
Ivy Baker Priest	A00 000 001A - A00 136 100A	100
G.M. Humphrey	—	—

SILVER CERTIFICATES

SERIES 1934 BLUE SEAL

12 Subject Sheets

Signatures	Serial Number Range	# of Sheets
W.A. Julian	A00 000 001A - A00 000 300A	25
Henry Morgenthau, Jr.	—	—

SERIES 1934A BLUE SEAL

None known.

SERIES 1934B BLUE SEAL

12 Subject Sheets

Signatures	Serial Number Range	# of Sheets
W.A. Julian	—	25*
Fred M. Vinson	—	—

*No record of any issues, however, sheets known to exist indicate an issue of 25 sheets.

SERIES 1934C BLUE SEAL

Signatures	Serial Number Range	# of Sheets
W.A. Julian	L50 808 001A - L50 809 200A	100
John W. Snyder	—	—

SERIES 1934D BLUE SEAL

Signatures	Serial Number Range	# of Sheets
Georgia Neese Clark	Q71 628 001A - Q71 629 200A	100
John W. Snyder	—	—

SERIES 1953 BLUE SEAL

18 Subject Sheets

Signatures	Serial Number Range	# of Sheets
Ivy Baker Priest	A00 000 001A - A00 136 100A	100
G.M. Humphrey	—	—

Ten Dollars

SILVER CERTIFICATES

SERIES 1933 BLUE SEAL

12 Subject Sheets

Signatures	Serial Number Range	# of Sheets
W.A. Julian	A00 372 001A - A00 372 012A	1
W.H. Woodin	—	—

SERIES 1933A BLUE SEAL

Signatures	Serial Number Range	# of Sheets
W.A. Julian	A00 372 013A - A00 372 024A	1
Henry Morgenthau, Jr.	—	—

SERIES 1934 BLUE SEAL

Signatures	Serial Number Range	# of Sheets
W.A. Julian	A00 000 001A - A00 000 120A	10
Henry Morgenthau, Jr.	—	—

SERIES 1953 BLUE SEAL

18 Subject Sheets

Signatures	Serial Number Range	# of Sheets
Ivy Baker Priest	A00 000 001A - A00 136 100A	100
G.M. Humphrey	—	—

CENSUS OF UNCUT SHEETS
RECENTLY KNOWN TO EXIST IN UNCUT CONDITION

We are deeply indebted to Mr. Aubrey E. Bebee for his assistance in supplying much of the sheet information and values. Thanks are also due to Mr. John Morris and Mr. Robert H. Lloyd for their help in this area. Please note that low number sheets will carry much higher values commendurate with their respective low numbers.

One Dollar

LEGAL TENDER

SERIES 1928 RED SEAL

12 Subject Sheets

Value $35,000.

A00 000 025A	-	A00 000 036A
A00 000 037A	-	A00 000 048A
A00 000 049A	-	A00 000 060A
A00 000 061A	-	A00 000 072A
A00 000 073A	-	A00 000 096A
A00 000 097A	-	A00 000 108A
A00 000 109A	-	A00 000 120A

SILVER CERTIFICATES

SERIES 1928 BLUE SEAL

Value $3,000.

A00 000 061A	-	A00 000 072A
A00 000 121A	-	A00 000 132A
A00 000 193A	-	A00 000 204A
A00 000 205A	-	A00 000 216A
A00 000 277A	-	A00 000 288A
A00 000 433A	-	A00 000 444A
A00 000 589A	-	A00 000 600A
A00 000 601A	-	A00 000 612A
A00 000 637A	-	A00 000 648A
A00 000 661A	-	A00 000 672A
A00 000 673A	-	A00 000 684A
A00 000 697A	-	A00 000 708A
A00 000 709A	-	A00 000 720A
A00 000 733A	-	A00 000 744A

SERIES 1928A BLUE SEAL

None known

SERIES 1928B BLUE SEAL

None known

SERIES 1928C BLUE SEAL

Value $10,000.

B29 448 001B	-	B29 448 012B
B29 448 037B	-	B29 448 048B
B29 448 049B	-	B29 448 060B
B29 448 061B	-	B29 448 072B
B29 448 073B	-	B29 448 084B

SERIES 1928D BLUE SEAL

Value $6,000.

D00 000 025B	-	D00 000 036B
D82 596 037B	-	D82 596 048B
D82 596 049B	-	D82 596 060B
D82 596 061B	-	D82 596 072B
D82 596 085B	-	D82 596 096B
D82 596 109B	-	D82 596 120B
D82 596 121B	-	D82 596 132B
D82 596 133B	-	D82 596 144B
D82 596 181B	-	D82 596 192B
D82 596 205B	-	D82 596 216B
D82 596 217B	-	D82 596 228B
D82 596 265B	-	D82 596 276B
D82 596 277B	-	D82 596 288B
D82 596 313B	-	D82 596 324B
D82 596 337B	-	D82 596 348B
D82 596 349B	-	D82 596 360B
D82 596 361B	-	D82 596 372B
D82 596 397B	-	D82 596 408B
D82 596 433B	-	D82 596 444B
D82 596 445B	-	D82 596 456B
D82 596 481B	-	D82 596 492B
D82 596 517B	-	D82 596 528B
D82 596 529B	-	D82 596 540B
D82 596 577B	-	D82 596 588B
D82 596 637B	-	D82 596 648B
D82 596 661B	-	D82 596 672B
D82 596 673B	-	D82 596 684B

SERIES 1928E BLUE SEAL

Value $25,000.

F72 000 049B	-	F72 000 060B
F72 000 097B	-	F72 000 108B
F72 000 133B	-	F72 000 144B
F72 000 145B	-	F72 000 156B
F72 000 217B	-	F72 000 228B
F72 000 241B	-	F72 000 252B
F72 000 277B	-	F72 000 288B
F72 000 289B	-	F72 000 300B

SERIES 1934 BLUE SEAL

Value $3,000.

A00 000 037A	-	A00 000 048A
A00 000 073A	-	A00 000 084A
A00 000 085A	-	A00 000 096A
A00 000 097A	-	A00 000 108A
A00 000 109A	-	A00 000 120A
A00 000 121A	-	A00 000 132A
A00 000 145A	-	A00 000 156A
A00 000 157A	-	A00 000 168A
A00 000 181A	-	A00 000 192A
A00 000 217A	-	A00 000 228A

SERIES 1935 BLUE SEAL

Value $2,000.

A00 000 061A	-	A00 000 072A
A00 000 157A	-	A00 000 168A
A00 000 169A	-	A00 000 180A
A00 000 205A	-	A00 000 216A
A00 000 217A	-	A00 000 228A
A00 000 313A	-	A00 000 324A
A00 000 325A	-	A00 000 336A
A00 000 361A	-	A00 000 372A
A00 000 397A	-	A00 000 408A
A00 000 445A	-	A00 000 456A
A00 000 457A	-	A00 000 468A
A00 000 565A	-	A00 000 576A
A00 000 601A	-	A00 000 612A
A00 000 613A	-	A00 000 624A
A00 000 625A	-	A00 000 636A
A00 000 637A	-	A00 000 648A
A00 000 649A	-	A00 000 660A
A00 000 661A	-	A00 000 672A
A00 000 733A	-	A00 000 744A
A00 000 769A	-	A00 000 780A
A00 000 781A	-	A00 000 792A
A00 000 793A	-	A00 000 804A
A00 000 805A	-	A00 000 816A
A00 000 829A	-	A00 000 840A
A00 000 841A	-	A00 000 852A
A00 000 853A	-	A00 000 864A
A00 000 973A	-	A00 000 984A
A00 001 057A	-	A00 001 068A
A00 001 177A	-	A00 001 188A

SERIES 1935A BLUE SEAL

Value $1,750.

V43 128 025A	-	V43 128 036A
V43 128 469A	-	V43 128 480A
V43 129 045A	-	V43 129 056A
V43 129 069A	-	V43 129 080A
V43 129 081A	-	V43 129 092A
V43 129 093A	-	V43 129 104A
V43 128 205A	-	V43 128 216A
V43 128 109A	-	V43 128 120A
V43 128 313A	-	V43 128 324A
V43 128 325A	-	V43 128 336A
V43 128 373A	-	V43 128 384A
V43 128 505A	-	V43 128 516A
V43 128 529A	-	V43 128 540A
V43 128 656A	-	V43 128 576A
V43 128 589A	-	V43 128 600A
V43 128 601A	-	V43 128 612A
V43 128 613A	-	V43 128 624A
V43 128 661A	-	V43 128 672A
V43 128 817A	-	V43 128 828A
V43 128 901A	-	V43 128 912A
V43 129 153A	-	V43 128 164A

SERIES 1935A MULE BLUE SEAL

Value $2,500.

V43 128 037A	-	V43 128 048A

SERIES 1935A NORTH AFRICA YELLOW SEAL

Value $25,000.

F41 952 007C	-	F41 952 012C left half
F41 954 005C	-	F41 954 010C right half
F41 952 019C	-	F41 952 024C left half
F41 954 017C	-	F41 954 022C right half
F41 952 031C	-	F41 952 036C left half
F41 954 029C	-	F41 954 034C right half
F41 952 049C	-	F41 952 054C left half
F41 954 047C	-	F41 954 052C right half
F41 952 067C	-	F41 952 072C left half
F41 954 065C	-	F41 954 070C right half
F41 952 085C	-	F41 952 090C left half
F41 954 083C	-	F41 954 088C right half
F41 952 091C	-	F41 952 096C left half
F41 954 089C	-	F41 954 094C right half
F41 952 211C	-	F41 952 216C left half
F41 954 209C	-	F41 954 215C right half
F41 952 217C	-	F41 952 222C left half
F41 954 215C	-	F41 954 220C right half
F41 952 223C	-	F41 952 228C left half
F41 954 221C	-	F41 954 226C right half
F41 952 229C	-	F41 952 234C left half
F41 954 227C	-	F41 954 232C right half
F41 952 253C	-	F41 952 258C left half
F41 954 251C	-	F41 954 256C right half
F41 952 265C	-	F41 952 270C left half
F41 954 263C	-	F41 954 268C right half
F41 952 271C	-	F41 952 276C left half
F41 954 269C	-	F41 954 274C right half

SILVER CERTIFICATES

SERIES 1935A HAWAII
BROWN SEAL
Value $10,000.

F41 964 077C	-	F41 964 012C left half
F41 966 005C	-	F41 966 010C right half
F41 964 013C	-	F41 966 018C left half
F41 966 011C	-	F41 966 016C right half
F41 964 019C	-	F41 964 024C left half
F41 966 017C	-	F41 966 022C right half
F41 964 025C	-	F41 964 030C left half
F41 966 023C	-	F41 966 028C right half
F41 966 037C	-	F41 964 042C left half
F41 966 035C	-	F41 966 040C right half
F41 964 043C	-	F41 964 048C left half
F41 966 041C	-	F41 966 046C right half
F41 964 055C	-	F41 964 060C left half
F41 966 053C	-	F41 966 058C right half
F41 964 061C	-	F41 964 066C left half
F41 966 059C	-	F41 966 064C right half
F41 964 067C	-	F41 964 072C left half
F41 966 065C	-	F41 966 070C right half
F41 964 079C	-	F41 964 084C left half
F41 966 077C	-	F41 966 082C right half
F41 964 103C	-	F41 964 108C left half
F41 966 101C	-	F41 966 106C right half
F41 964 127C	-	F41 964 132C left half
F41 966 125C	-	F41 966 130C right half
F41 964 151C	-	F41 964 156C left half
F41 966 149C	-	F41 966 154C right half
F41 964 211C	-	F41 964 216C left half
F41 966 209C	-	F41 966 214C right half
F41 964 229C	-	F41 964 234C left half
F41 966 227C	-	F41 966 232C right half
F41 964 235C	-	F41 964 240C left half
F41 966 233C	-	F41 966 238C right half
F41 964 283C	-	F41 964 288C left half
F41 966 201C	-	F41 966 286C right half
F41 964 301C	-	F41 964 306C left half
F41 966 399C	-	F41 966 304C right half
F41 964 313C	-	F41 964 318C left half
F41 966 311C	-	F41 966 316C right half
F41 964 325C	-	F41 964 330C left half
F41 966 323C	-	F41 966 328C right half

SILVER CERTIFICATES

SERIES 1935B BLUE SEAL
Value $2,000.

C93 384 049D -	C93 384 060D
C93 384 073D -	C93 384 084D
C93 384 097D -	C93 384 008D
C93 384 157D -	C93 384 168D
C93 384 301D -	C93 384 312D
C93 384 313D -	C93 384 324D
C93 384 325D -	C93 384 336D
C93 384 337D -	C93 384 348D
C93 384 349D -	C93 384 360D
C93 384 361D -	C93 384 372D
C93 384 433D -	C93 384 444D
C93 384 493D -	C93 384 504D
C93 384 517D -	C93 384 528D
C93 384 541D -	C93 384 552D
C93 384 553D -	C93 384 564D
C93 384 589D -	C93 384 600D
C93 384 625D -	C93 384 636D
C93 384 637D -	C93 384 648D
C93 384 697D -	C93 384 708D
C93 384 709D -	C93 384 720D
C93 384 841D -	C93 384 852D
C93 384 877D -	C93 384 888D
C93 384 961D -	C93 384 972D
C93 385 009D -	C93 385 020D
C93 385 021D -	C93 385 032D
C93 385 069D -	C93 385 080D
C93 385 141D -	C93 385 152D
C93 385 177D -	C93 385 188D

SERIES 1935C BLUE SEAL
Value $1,750.

K99 996 265D -	K99 996 276D
K99 996 289D -	K99 996 300D
K99 996 313D -	K99 996 324D
K99 996 326D -	K99 996 336D
K99 996 349D -	K99 996 360D
K99 996 361D -	K99 996 372D
K99 996 373D -	K99 996 384D
K99 996 385D -	K99 996 396D
K99 996 409D -	K99 996 420D
K99 996 433D -	K99 996 444D
K99 996 457D -	K99 996 468D
K99 996 529D -	K99 996 540D
K99 996 541D -	K99 996 552D
K99 996 565D -	K99 996 576D
K99 996 577D -	K99 996 588D
K99 996 589D -	K99 996 600D
K99 996 613D -	K99 996 624D
K99 996 637D -	K99 996 648D
K99 996 661D -	K99 996 672D
K99 996 685D -	K99 996 696D
K99 996 709D -	K99 996 720D
K99 996 757D -	K99 996 768D
K99 996 781D -	K99 996 792D
K99 996 817D -	K99 996 828D
K99 996 853D -	K99 996 864D
K99 996 865D -	K99 996 876D
K99 996 889D -	K99 996 900D
K99 996 925D -	K99 996 936D
K99 996 973D -	K99 996 984D

SERIES 1935D BLUE SEAL

12 Subject Sheet

Value $1,500.

R88 104 637E	-	R88 104 648E
R88 104 673E	-	R88 104 684E
R88 104 697E	-	R88 104 708E
R88 104 733E	-	R88 104 744E
R88 104 769E	-	R88 104 780E
R88 104 793E	-	R88 104 804E
R88 104 841E	-	R88 104 852E
R88 104 865E	-	R88 104 876E
R88 104 961E	-	R88 104 972E
R88 104 081E	-	R88 104 092E
R88 104 177E	-	R88 104 188E
R88 104 180E	-	R88 104 200E
R88 105 129E	-	R88 105 140E
Z33 324 073E	-	Z33 324 084E
Z33 324 085E	-	Z33 324 096E
Z33 324 181E	-	Z33 324 192E
Z33 324 325E	-	Z33 324 336E
Z33 324 373E	-	Z33 324 384E
Z33 324 493E	-	Z33 324 504E
Z33 324 505E	-	Z33 324 516E
Z33 324 697E	-	Z33 324 708E
Z33 324 769E	-	Z33 324 780E
Z33 324 781E	-	Z33 324 792E
Z33 324 829E	-	Z33 324 840E

Z33 324 985E	-	Z33 324 996E
Z33 324 853E	-	Z33 324 864E
Z33 324 021E	-	Z33 324 032E
Z33 324 045E	-	Z33 324 056E
Z33 324 153E	-	Z33 324 164E
Z33 324 325E	-	Z33 324 336E
B05 520 049G	-	B05 520 060G
B05 520 337G	-	B05 520 348G
B05 520 361G	-	B05 520 372G
B05 520 505G	-	B05 520 516G
B05 520 601G	-	B05 520 612G
B05 520 709G	-	B05 520 720G
B05 520 733G	-	B05 520 744G
B05 520 745G	-	B05 520 756G
B05 520 757G	-	B05 520 768G
B05 520 769G	-	B05 520 780G
B05 520 793G	-	B05 520 804G
B05 520 817G	-	B05 520 829G
B05 520 889G	-	B05 520 900G
B05 520 997G	-	B05 521 008G
B05 521 033G	-	B05 521 044G
B05 521 105G	-	B05 521 116G
B05 521 117G	-	B05 521 128G
B05 521 129G	-	B05 521 140G
B05 521 141G	-	B05 521 152G
B05 521 153G	-	B05 521 164G
B05 521 165G	-	B05 521 176G

SILVER CERTIFICATES

SERIES 1935D BLUE SEAL

18 Subject Sheets

Value $1,750.

G00 000 011G	-	G00 136 011G
G00 000 012G	-	G00 136 012G
G00 000 013G	-	G00 136 013G
G00 000 014G	-	G00 136 014G
G00 000 015G	-	G00 136 015G
G00 000 016G	-	G00 136 016G
G00 000 017G	-	G00 136 017G
G00 000 018G	-	G00 136 018G
G00 000 019G	-	G00 136 019G
G00 000 020G	-	G00 136 020G
G00 000 021G	-	G00 136 021G
G00 000 025G	-	G00 136 025G
G00 000 053G	-	G00 136 053G
G00 000 055G	-	G00 136 055G
G00 000 056G	-	G00 136 056G
G00 000 057G	-	G00 136 057G
G00 000 058G	-	G00 136 058G

G00 000 059G	-	G00 136 059G
G00 000 060G	-	G00 136 060G
G00 000 070G	-	G00 136 070G
G00 000 071G	-	G00 136 071G
G00 000 072G	-	G00 136 072G
G00 000 073G	-	G00 136 073G
G00 000 078G	-	G00 136 078G
G00 000 080G	-	G00 136 080G
G00 000 085G	-	G00 136 085G
G00 000 086G	-	G00 136 086G
G00 000 087G	-	G00 136 087G
G00 000 088G	-	G00 136 088G
G00 000 089G	-	G00 136 089G
G00 000 090G	-	G00 136 090G
G00 000 091G	-	G00 136 091G
G00 000 092G	-	G00 136 092G
G00 000 097G	-	G00 136 097G
G00 000 099G	-	G00 136 099G
G00 000 100G	-	G00 136 100G

SERIES 1935E BLUE SEAL

18 Subject Sheet

Value $1,300.

N46 944 006G	-	N47 080 006G
N46 944 013G	-	N47 080 013G
N46 944 018G	-	N47 080 018G
N46 944 026G	-	N47 080 026G
N46 944 027G	-	N47 080 027G
N46 944 031G	-	N47 080 031G
N46 944 032G	-	N47 080 032G
N46 944 033G	-	N47 080 033G
N46 944 037G	-	N47 080 037G
N46 944 044G	-	N47 080 044G
N46 944 045G	-	N47 080 045G
N46 944 046G	-	N47 080 046G
N46 944 057G	-	N47 080 057G
N46 944 058G	-	N47 080 058G
N46 944 059G	-	N47 080 059G
N46 944 064G	-	N47 080 064G
N46 944 079G	-	N47 080 079G
R95 040 003G	-	R95 176 003G
R95 040 010G	-	R95 176 010G
R95 040 019G	-	R95 176 019G
R95 040 044G	-	R95 176 044G
R95 040 079G	-	R95 176 079G
N46 944 085G	-	N47 080 085G
N46 944 793G	-	N47 080 793G
R95 040 018G	-	R95 176 018G
R95 040 034G	-	R95 176 034G

R95 040 035G	-	R95 176 035G
R95 040 036G	-	R95 176 036G
R95 040 037G	-	R95 176 037G
R95 040 048G	-	R95 176 048G
R95 040 063G	-	R95 176 063G
R95 040 072G	-	R95 176 072G
R95 040 076G	-	R95 176 076G
R95 040 083G	-	R95 176 093G
R95 040 093G	-	R95 176 093G
R95 040 095G	-	R95 176 095G
R95 040 096G	-	R95 176 096G
R95 040 097G	-	R95 176 097G
U75 168 010G	-	U75 304 010G
U75 168 012G	-	U75 304 012G
U75 168 018G	-	U75 304 018G
U75 168 029G	-	U75 304 029G
U75 168 030G	-	U75 304 030G
U75 168 043G	-	U75 304 043G
U75 168 055G	-	U75 304 055G
U75 168 056G	-	U75 304 056G
U75 168 062G	-	U75 304 062G
U75 168 067G	-	U75 304 067G
U75 168 069G	-	U75 304 069G
U75 168 072G	-	U75 304 072G
U75 168 089G	-	U75 304 089G
U75 168 090G	-	U75 304 090G
X31 680 001G	-	X31 816 001G
X31 680 013G	-	X31 816 013G
X31 680 038G	-	X31 816 038G

FEDERAL RESERVE NOTES

SERIES 1981 GREEN SEAL

32 Subject Sheets

A99 840 001A	-	A99 999 999A
A99 840 001B	-	A99 999 999B
A99 840 001C	-	A99 999 999C
A99 840 001D	-	A99 999 999D
A99 840 001E	-	A99 999 999E
A99 840 001F	-	A99 999 999F
A99 840 001G	-	A99 999 999G
A99 840 001H	-	A99 999 999H
B99 843 875I	-	B99 845 000I
C99 843 875A	-	C99 845 000A
D99 840 001A	-	D99 999 999A
D99 840 001B	-	D99 999 999B
D99 840 001C	-	D99 999 999C
D99 840 001D	-	D99 999 999D
D99 840 001E	-	D99 999 999E
D99 840 001F	-	D99 999 999F
D99 840 001G	-	D99 999 999G
D99 840 001H	-	D99 999 999H
E99 840 001A	-	E99 999 999A
E99 840 001B	-	E99 999 999B
E99 840 001C	-	E99 999 999C
E99 840 001D	-	E99 999 999D
E99 840 001E	-	E99 999 999E
E99 840 001F	-	E99 999 999F

E99 840 001G	-	E99 999 999G
E99 840 001H	-	E99 999 999H
F99 843 875A	-	F99 845 000A
G99 843 875A	-	G99 845 000A
H99 843 875E	-	H99 845 000E
I99 843 875A	-	I99 845 000A
J99 843 875A	-	J99 845 000A
K99 843 875A	-	K99 845 000A
L99 843 875A	-	L99 845 000A

SERIES 1981A GREEN SEAL

B99 840 001B	-	B99 999 999B
C99 840 001B	-	C99 999 999B
F99 840 001B	-	F99 999 999B
G99 840 001B	-	G99 999 999B
H99 840 001B	-	H99 999 999B
I99 840 001B	-	I99 999 999B
J99 840 001B	-	J99 999 999B
K99 840 001B	-	K99 999 999B
L99 840 001B	-	L99 999 999B

SERIES 1985 GREEN SEAL

A99 840 001A	-	A99 999 999A
A99 776 001B	-	A99 999 999B
A99 904 001C	-	A99 999 999C
B99 840 001A	-	B99 999 999A
B99 776 001B	-	B99 999 999B
B99 904 001C	-	B99 999 999C
C99 840 001A	-	C99 999 999A
C99 776 001B	-	C99 999 999B
C99 904 001C	-	C99 999 999C
D99 840 001A	-	D99 999 999A
D99 776 001B	-	D99 999 999B
D99 904 001C	-	D99 999 999C
E99 840 001A	-	E99 999 999A
E99 776 001B	-	E99 999 999B
E99 904 001C	-	E99 999 999C
F99 840 001A	-	F99 999 999A
F99 776 001B	-	F99 999 999B
F99 904 001C	-	F99 999 999C
F99 904 001D	-	F99 999 999D
F99 840 001E	-	F99 999 999E
G99 840 001A	-	G99 999 999A
G99 776 001B	-	G99 999 999B
G99 904 001C	-	G99 999 999C
H99 840 001A	-	H99 999 999A
H99 776 001B	-	H99 999 999B
H99 904 001C	-	H99 999 999C
H99 776 001D	-	H99 999 999D
I99 840 001A	-	I99 999 999A
I99 776 001B	-	I99 999 999B
I99 904 001C	-	I99 999 999C
I99 776 001D	-	I99 999 999D
J99 840 001A	-	J99 999 999A
J99 776 001B	-	J99 999 999B
J99 904 001C	-	J99 999 999C
J99 904 001D	-	J99 999 999D
K99 840 001A	-	K99 999 999A
K99 776 001B	-	K99 999 999B
K99 904 001C	-	K99 999 999C
L99 840 001A	-	L99 999 999A
L99 776 001B	-	L99 999 999B
L99 904 001C	-	L99 999 999C

SERIES 1988 GREEN SEAL

A99 904 001A	-	A99 999 999A
B99 904 001A	-	B99 999 999A
C99 904 001A	-	C99 999 999A
D99 904 001A	-	D99 999 999A
E99 904 001A	-	E99 999 999A
F99 904 001A	-	F99 999 999A
G99 904 001A	-	G99 999 999A
H99 904 001A	-	H99 999 999A
H99 904 001B	-	H99 999 999B
I99 904 001A	-	H99 999 999A
J99 904 001A	-	J99 999 999A
K99 904 001A	-	K99 999 999A

UNCUT HALF SHEETS

SERIES 1981 GREEN SEAL

16 Subject Sheets

B99 840 001A	-	B99 999 999A
B99 840 001B	-	B99 999 999B
B99 840 001C	-	B99 999 999C
B99 840 001D	-	B99 999 999D
B99 840 001E	-	B99 999 999E
B99 840 001F	-	B99 999 999F
B99 840 001G	-	B99 999 999G
B99 840 001H	-	B99 999 999H
B99 842 750I	-	B99 843 875I
C99 842 750A	-	C99 843 875A
F99 842 750A	-	F99 843 875A
G99 842 750A	-	G99 843 875A
H99 840 001A	-	H99 999 999A
H99 840 001B	-	H99 999 999B
H99 840 001C	-	H99 999 999C
H99 840 001D	-	H99 999 999D
H99 842 750E	-	H99 843 875E
I99 842 750A	-	I99 843 875A
J99 842 750A	-	J99 843 875A
K99 842 750A	-	K99 843 875A
L99 842 750A	-	L99 843 875A

Two Dollars

LEGAL TENDER

SERIES 1928 RED SEAL

12 Subject Sheets
Value $8,000.

A00 000 037A - A00 000 048A
A00 000 049A - A00 000 060A

SERIES 1928A RED SEAL

None known

SERIES 1928B RED SEAL

None known

SERIES 1928C RED SEAL

Value $2,000.

B09 012 001A - B09 012 012A
B09 012 013A - B09 012 024A
B09 012 037A - B09 012 048A
B09 012 049A - B09 012 048A
B09 012 073A - B09 012 060A
B09 012 097A - B09 012 084A
B09 012 157A - B09 012 168A
B09 012 181A - B09 012 192A
B09 012 217A - B09 012 228A
B09 012 229A - B09 012 240A
B09 012 253A - B09 012 264A
B09 012 277A - B09 012 288A
B83 988 013A - B83 988 024A
B83 988 085A - B83 988 096A
B83 988 108A - B83 988 120A
B83 988 121A - B83 988 132A
B83 988 145A - B83 988 156A
B83 988 157A - B83 988 168A
B83 988 181A - B83 988 192A
B83 988 253A - B83 988 264A
B83 988 373A - B83 988 384A
B83 988 397A - B83 988 408A
B83 988 409A - B83 988 420A
B83 988 457A - B83 988 468A
B83 988 469A - B83 988 480A
B83 988 481A - B83 988 492A
B83 988 493A - B83 988 504A

SERIES 1928D RED SEAL

None known

SERIES 1928E RED SEAL

Value $3,000.

D35 532 001A - D35 532 012A
D35 532 013A - D35 532 024A
D35 532 037A - D35 532 048A
D35 532 061A - D35 532 072A
D35 532 073A - D35 532 084A
D35 532 085A - D35 532 096A
D35 532 133A - D35 532 144A
D35 532 145A - D35 532 156A
D35 532 157A - D35 532 168A
D35 532 169A - D35 532 180A
D35 532 193A - D35 532 204A
D35 532 205A - D35 532 216A
D35 532 229A - D35 532 240A
D35 532 241A - D35 532 252A
D35 532 289A - D35 532 300A
D35 532 301A - D35 532 312A
D35 532 349A - D35 532 360A
D35 532 361A - D35 532 372A
D35 532 385A - D35 532 396A
D35 532 397A - D35 532 408A
D35 532 409A - D35 532 420A
D35 532 433A - D35 532 444A
D35 532 445A - D35 532 456A
D35 532 469A - D35 532 480A
D35 532 481A - D35 532 492A
D35 532 493A - D35 532 504A
D35 532 541A - D35 532 552A
D35 532 637A - D35 532 648A

SERIES 1928F RED SEAL

Value $2,000.

D39 552 001A - D39 552 012A
D39 552 013A - D39 552 024A
D39 552 025A - D39 552 036A
D39 552 037A - D39 552 048A
D39 552 073A - D39 552 084A
D39 552 061A - D39 552 072A
D39 552 097A - D39 552 108A
D39 552 145A - D39 552 156A
D39 552 169A - D39 552 180A
D39 552 181A - D39 552 192A
D39 552 241A - D39 552 252A
D39 552 265A - D39 552 276A
D39 552 277A - D39 552 288A
D39 552 313A - D39 552 324A
D39 552 337A - D39 552 348A
D39 552 373A - D39 552 384A
D39 552 397A - D39 552 408A
D39 552 541A - D39 552 552A
D39 552 553A - D39 552 564A
D39 552 721A - D39 552 732A
D39 552 937A - D39 552 948A
D39 552 961A - D39 552 972A
D39 553 033A - D39 553 044A
D39 553 069A - D39 553 080A

SERIES 1928G RED SEAL

Value $2,000.

E07 704 037A	-	E07 704 048A
E07 704 073A	-	E07 704 084A
E07 704 097A	-	E07 704 108A
E07 704 121A	-	E07 704 132A
E07 704 145A	-	E07 704 156A
E07 704 169A	-	E07 704 180A
E07 704 181A	-	E07 704 192A
E07 704 193A	-	E07 704 204A
E07 704 229A	-	E07 704 240A
E07 704 325A	-	E07 704 336A
E07 704 397A	-	E07 704 408A
E07 704 481A	-	E07 704 492A
E07 704 493A	-	E07 704 504A
E07 704 541A	-	E07 704 552A
E07 704 649A	-	E07 704 660A
E07 704 661A	-	E07 704 672A
E07 704 709A	-	E07 704 720A
E07 704 781A	-	E07 704 792A
E07 704 829A	-	E07 704 840A
E07 704 841A	-	E07 704 852A
E07 704 853A	-	E07 704 864A
E07 704 877A	-	E07 704 888A
E07 704 961A	-	E07 704 972A
E07 704 973A	-	E07 704 984A
E07 704 985A	-	E07 704 996A
E07 705 021A	-	E07 705 032A
E07 705 057A	-	E07 705 068A
E07 705 081A	-	E07 705 092A
E07 705 117A	-	E07 705 128A
E07 705 177A	-	E07 705 188A
E07 705 189A	-	E07 705 200A

SERIES 1953 RED SEAL

18 Subject Sheets

Value $1,750.

A00 000 028A	-	A00 136 028A
A00 000 032A	-	A00 136 032A
A00 000 034A	-	A00 136 034A
A00 000 039A	-	A00 136 039A
A00 000 040A	-	A00 136 040A
A00 000 041A	-	A00 136 041A
A00 000 043A	-	A00 136 043A
A00 000 045A	-	A00 136 045A
A00 000 048A	-	A00 136 048A
A00 000 051A	-	A00 136 051A
A00 000 052A	-	A00 136 052A
A00 000 053A	-	A00 136 053A
A00 000 055A	-	A00 136 055A
A00 000 058A	-	A00 136 058A
A00 000 062A	-	A00 136 062A
A00 000 063A	-	A00 136 063A
A00 000 067A	-	A00 136 067A
A00 000 071A	-	A00 136 071A
A00 000 073A	-	A00 136 073A
A00 000 074A	-	A00 136 074A
A00 000 078A	-	A00 136 078A
A00 000 079A	-	A00 136 079A
A00 000 080A	-	A00 136 080A
A00 000 084A	-	A00 136 084A
A00 000 087A	-	A00 136 087A

SERIES 1976 GREEN SEAL

32 Subject Sheets

A00 015 001★	-	A00 640 000★
A00 640 001★	-	A00 960 000★
A00 960 001★	-	A01 273 400★
A01 273 401★	-	A01 280 000★
C00 002 001★	-	C01 280 000★
D00 064 001★	-	D00 960 000★
D00 963 001★	-	D01 264 000★
F00 648 001★	-	F01 280 000★
F01 140 001★	-	F02 280 000★
F00 972 897★	-	F01 277 600★
G00 040 046★	-	G00 948 494★
H00 640 001★	-	H01 280 000★
H00 645 001★	-	H00 750 000★
H00 750 001★	-	H01 280 000★
K00 644 001★	-	K01 266 600★
K00 652 001★	-	K01 278 500★
K00 646 601★	-	K01 262 452★
K00 652 001★	-	K01 278 500★
L01 280 001★	-	L01 920 000★

Five Dollars

SILVER CERTIFICATES

SERIES 1934 BLUE SEAL

Value $3,000.

A00 000 013A	-	A00 000 024A
A00 000 025A	-	A00 000 036A
A00 000 049A	-	A00 000 060A
A00 000 061A	-	A00 000 072A
A00 000 073A	-	A00 000 084A
A00 000 084A	-	A00 000 096A
A00 000 097A	-	A00 000 108A
A00 000 157A	-	A00 000 168A
A00 000 169A	-	A00 000 180A
A00 000 217A	-	A00 000 228A
A00 000 229A	-	A00 000 240A
A00 000 265A	-	A00 000 276A
A00 000 289A	-	A00 000 300A

SERIES 1934A BLUE SEAL

None known

SERIES 1934B BLUE SEAL

Value $3,500.

L27 456 001A	-	L27 456 012A
L27 456 013A	-	L27 456 024A
L27 456 049A	-	L27 456 060A
L27 456 085A	-	L27 456 096A
L27 456 097A	-	L27 456 108A
L27 456 121A	-	L27 456 132A
L27 456 157A	-	L27 456 168A
L27 456 169A	-	L27 456 180A
L27 456 193A	-	L27 456 204A
L27 456 217A	-	L27 456 228A
L27 456 229A	-	L27 456 240A

SERIES 1934C BLUE SEAL

Value $2,300.

L50 808 001A	-	L50 808 012A
L50 808 013A	-	L50 808 024A
L50 808 037A	-	L50 808 048A
L50 808 049A	-	L50 808 060A
L50 808 061A	-	L50 808 072A
L50 808 073A	-	L50 808 084A
L50 808 085A	-	L50 808 096A
L50 808 097A	-	L50 808 108A
L50 808 133A	-	L50 808 144A
L50 808 157A	-	L50 808 168A

SERIES 1934D BLUE SEAL

Value $2,000.

Q71 628 001A	-	Q71 628 012A
Q71 628 013A	-	Q71 628 024A
Q71 628 025A	-	Q71 628 036A
Q71 628 037A	-	Q71 628 048A
Q71 628 085A	-	Q71 628 096A
Q71 628 193A	-	Q71 628 204A
Q71 628 205A	-	Q71 628 216A
Q71 628 373A	-	Q71 628 384A
Q71 628 397A	-	Q71 628 408A
Q71 628 409A	-	Q71 628 420A
Q71 628 445A	-	Q71 628 456A
Q71 628 457A	-	Q71 628 468A
Q71 628 469A	-	Q71 628 480A
Q71 628 541A	-	Q71 628 552A
Q71 628 601A	-	Q71 628 612A
Q71 628 649A	-	Q71 628 660A
Q71 628 721A	-	Q71 628 732A
Q71 628 829A	-	Q71 628 840A
Q71 628 961A	-	Q71 628 972A
Q71 628 973A	-	Q71 628 984A
Q71 628 997A	-	Q71 629 008A
Q71 629 021A	-	Q71 629 032A
Q71 629 033A	-	Q71 629 044A
Q71 629 045A	-	Q71 629 056A
Q71 629 057A	-	Q71 629 068A
Q71 629 177A	-	Q71 629 188A

SERIES 1953 BLUE SEAL

18 Subject Sheets

Value $2,500.

A00 000 027A	-	A00 136 027A
A00 000 029A	-	A00 136 029A
A00 000 030A	-	A00 136 030A
A00 000 031A	-	A00 136 031A
A00 000 032A	-	A00 136 032A
A00 000 036A	-	A00 136 036A
A00 000 037A	-	A00 136 037A
A00 000 039A	-	A00 136 039A
A00 000 050A	-	A00 136 050A
A00 000 052A	-	A00 136 052A
A00 000 055A	-	A00 136 055A
A00 000 057A	-	A00 136 057A
A00 000 058A	-	A00 136 058A
A00 000 059A	-	A00 136 059A
A00 000 060A	-	A00 136 060A
A00 000 063A	-	A00 136 063A
A00 000 067A	-	A00 136 067A
A00 000 069A	-	A00 136 069A
A00 000 070A	-	A00 136 070A
A00 000 075A	-	A00 136 075A
A00 000 079A	-	A00 136 079A

LEGAL TENDER

12 Subject Sheets

SERIES 1928 RED SEAL

Value $10,000.

A00 000 049**A**   -   A00 000 060**A**

SERIES 1928A RED SEAL

None known

SERIES 1928B RED SEAL

None known

SERIES 1928C RED SEAL

None known

SERIES 1928D RED SEAL

Value $5,000.

G58 956 001**A**	-	G58 956 012**A**
G58 956 013**A**	-	G58 956 024**A**
G58 956 025**A**	-	G58 956 036**A**
G58 956 037**A**	-	G58 956 048**A**
G58 956 061**A**	-	G58 956 072**A**
G58 956 073**A**	-	G58 956 084**A**
G58 956 109**A**	-	G58 956 120**A**
G58 956 121**A**	-	G58 956 132**A**
G58 956 145**A**	-	G58 956 156**A**
G58 956 169**A**	-	G58 956 180**A**
G58 956 205**A**	-	G58 956 216**A**
G58 956 217**A**	-	G58 956 228**A**
G58 956 241**A**	-	G58 956 252**A**
G58 956 253**A**	-	G58 956 264**A**
G58 956 277**A**	-	G58 956 288**A**

SERIES 1928E RED SEAL

Value $3,500.

G68 352 001**A**	-	G68 352 012**A**
G68 352 013**A**	-	G68 352 024**A**
G68 352 037**A**	-	G68 352 048**A**
G68 352 061**A**	-	G68 352 072**A**
G68 352 073**A**	-	G68 352 084**A**
G68 352 109**A**	-	G68 352 120**A**
G68 352 121**A**	-	G68 352 132**A**
G68 352 145**A**	-	G68 352 156**A**
G68 352 169**A**	-	G68 352 180**A**
G68 352 205**A**	-	G68 352 216**A**
G68 352 217**A**	-	G68 352 228**A**
G68 352 241**A**	-	G68 352 252**A**
G68 352 253**A**	-	G68 352 264**A**
G68 352 277**A**	-	G68 352 288**A**
G68 352 337**A**	-	G68 352 348**A**

SERIES 1953 RED SEAL

18 Subject Sheets

Value $3,500.

A00 000 001**A**	-	A00 136 001**A**
A00 000 031**A**	-	A00 136 031**A**
A00 000 032**A**	-	A00 136 032**A**
A00 000 033**A**	-	A00 136 033**A**
A00 000 035**A**	-	A00 136 035**A**
A00 000 040**A**	-	A00 136 040**A**
A00 000 044**A**	-	A00 136 044**A**
A00 000 046**A**	-	A00 136 046**A**
A00 000 053**A**	-	A00 136 053**A**
A00 000 055**A**	-	A00 136 055**A**

FEDERAL RESERVE NOTES

12 Subject Sheets

SERIES 1928 GREEN SEAL

Value $7,500.

C00 000 025**A**	-	C00 000 036**A**
G00 000 037**A**	-	G00 000 048**A**
K00 000 013**A**	-	K00 000 024**A**
K00 000 025**A**	-	K00 000 036**A**

SERIES 1928B GREEN SEAL

Value $10,000.

I04 692 025**A**	-	I04 692 036**A**
I04 692 049**A**	-	I04 692 060**A**

Ten Dollars

FEDERAL RESERVE BANK NOTES

SERIES 1929 BROWN SEAL

Value $20,000.

B00 000 085A	-	B00 000 096A
B00 000 097A	-	B00 000 108A

FEDERAL RESERVE NOTES

SERIES 1928 GREEN SEAL

Value $12,000.

B00 000 073A	-	B00 000 084A
C00 000 013A	-	C00 000 024A
C00 000 025A	-	C00 000 048A
G00 000 037A	-	G00 000 048A
I02 760 037A	-	I02 760 048A
I02 760 049A	-	I02 760 060A
K00 000 013A	-	K00 000 024A

SILVER CERTIFICATES

SERIES 1934 BLUE SEAL

Value $6,500.

A00 000 013A	-	A00 000 024A
Has been cut		
A00 000 024A	-	A00 000 036A
A00 000 037A	-	A00 000 048A
A00 000 061A	-	A00 000 072A
A00 000 072A	-	A00 000 084A
A00 000 085A	-	A00 000 096A
A00 000 108A	-	A00 000 120A

SERIES 1953 BLUE SEAL

Value $6,500.

A00 000 030A	-	A00 136 030A
A00 000 033A	-	A00 136 033A
A00 000 034A	-	A00 136 034A
A00 000 038A	-	A00 136 038A
A00 000 043A	-	A00 136 043A
A00 000 047A	-	A00 136 047A
A00 000 049A	-	A00 136 049A
A00 000 050A	-	A00 136 050A
A00 000 051A	-	A00 136 051A
A00 000 052A	-	A00 136 052A
A00 000 055A	-	A00 136 055A

Twenty Dollars

FEDERAL RESERVE NOTES

SERIES 1928 GREEN SEAL

12 Subject Sheet

Value $15,000.

B00 000 073A	-	B00 000 084A

C00 000 001A	-	C00 000 012A
C00 000 013A	-	C00 000 024A
C00 000 037A	-	C00 000 048A
G00 000 037A	-	G00 000 048A
I01 800 037A	-	I01 800 048A

One Hundred Dollars

LEGAL TENDER

SERIES 1966 RED SEAL

★00 000 161A   -   ★00 002 161A

This sheet is on permanent loan to the American Numismatic Association and is on display at the Headquarters in Colorado Springs, Colorado.

CHANGEOVER PAIRS

Technically speaking, changeover pairs, sometimes called hold-over or cross-over pairs, should be the highest serial number of one series and the lowest serial number of the following series OF THE SAME DENOMINATION AND CLASS of note. Hence a $1 legal tender note Series 1928 could not be coupled with the next higher serial number of a 1928A $1 silver certificate and qualify as a changeover pair. Also the $5 FRN could not be coupled with the $5 legal tender and fit the criteria of a changeover pair. Pairs of notes where the serial number is higher on the earlier series have been marginally accepted by collectors as so-called changeover pairs, but are referred to as REVERSE CHANGEOVERS.

During the early years (1928-1935) of printing the current size notes, because of the high cost of the engraved plates, and because the signatures were engraved IN the plates, it was customary for the Bureau of Engraving and Printing to use the plates long after the official whose signature appeared in the plate had left office. The result of this practice was that several series were being face printed simultaneously. When a stack of one series was placed on top of another series and sent to the third (serial number) printing, then consecutive numbered notes of different series were produced. An examination of the plate record card usage in BEP indicates quite a number of cases where several series were being printed on the same day. This is substantiated by the existence of known pairs of notes with consecutive serial numbers in various series combinations. For the $1 silver certificate for example, we know that both the 1928 and 1928A series were face printed on the same day. When these stacks were mixed and sent to the third printing, changeover pairs were sometimes in proper sequence, sometimes in reverse sequence. We know also that 28A/28B, 28A/28C, 28A/28D, 28A/28E, 28B/28C, 28B/28D, 28B/28E, 28C/28D, 28C/28E and 28D/28E were run simultaneously, hence we know of or suspect changeover pairs in all of these combinations. For the $2 legal tender we know that Series 1928C/D/E/F were being printed simultaneously and again, we know of or suspect of all of those combinations. The $5 FRN Series 1934-1934D and the $5 silver certificate Series 1934-1934D were printed simultaneously, and finally we know that the $5 legal tender Series 1928D, E and F were face printed simultaneously. Higher denominations too numerous to mention were also printed as is confirmed by the existence of one or more changeover pairs presently known.

The first note will always be an even number, and the second odd. The notes at this time were serial numbered consecutively down the sheet, and there were two columns of six notes. The first note in the first column will be an odd number, and the bottom note will be even. The presses could hold up to four plates, so it is possible to get a changeover pair every six notes.

Because the wide and narrow backs of the $1 silver certificate Series 1935D are found intermingled in packs, changeover pairs of the variety are known in practically all blocks. Because of the relatively high number of changeover pairs in this series, no census is attempted.

And finally, in the current $1 FRN (and higher denominations as well), while NOT being printed concurrently, some of the more astute collectors have managed to get the same serial number packs for consecutive series, and by matching the serial number of the earlier series with the next higher serial number of the later series, have created valid changeover pairs. This of course can be done with any series and any denomination if one worked hard enough at it - or was lucky enough to stumble upon the right combination of packs of notes.

Especially desireable changeover pairs are those that 'skip' series, that is, display consecutive serial numbers on the 28A-28E or 28B-28D despite the fact other series were printed in between. We doubt that collectors would accept a skip in series for current FRN's EXCEPT where NO notes were printed in the intervening series. NO notes were printed for the $1 FRN Boston for Series 1969C, hence consecutive serial numbered notes for Boston Series 1969B/1969D would qualify as so-called changeover pairs.

Census of known changeover pairs follows, the authors earnestly solicit your assistance in reporting any changeover pairs (except the 1935D) not listed.

One Dollar
SILVER CERTIFICATES

CHANGEOVER PAIRS

1928	H15 982 026A	**1928A**	H15 982 027A	$550.00
	H15 982 062A		H15 982 063A	550.00
	H24 067 110A		H24 067 111A	550.00
	H31 865 568A		H31 865 569A	550.00
	H98 174 184A		H98 174 185A	550.00
1928A	F98 281 830A	**1928**	F98 281 831A	550.00
	H15 982 056A		H15 982 057A	550.00
	G87 380 634A		G87 380 635A	550.00
	G99 279 258A		G99 279 259A	550.00
	H98 173 746A		H98 173 747A	550.00
	H98 174 185A		H98 174 184A	550.00
	H98 174 238A		H98 174 239A	550.00
	H99 279 258A		H99 279 259A	550.00
1928A	X62 614 692A	**1928B**	X62 614 693A	550.00
	Y22 437 608A		Y22 437 609A	550.00
	Y22 726 056A		Y22 726 057A	550.00
	Y32 068 044A		Y32 068 045A	550.00
	Y77 437 620A		Y77 437 621A	550.00
	Y77 437 710A		Y77 437 711A	550.00
	Y83 044 722A		Y83 044 723A	550.00
	Y83 044 758A		Y98 044 759A	550.00
	Y91 160 196A		Y91 160 197A	550.00
	Y91 160 436A		Y91 160 437A	550.00
	A11 118 390B		A11 118 391B	550.00
	A20 056 488B		A20 056 489B	550.00
	B40 140 366B		B40 149 367B	550.00
	D33 000 702B		D33 000 703B	550.00
	E14 561 478B		E14 561 479B	550.00
	F17 863 118B		F17 863 119B	550.00
	F17 863 506B		F17 863 507B	550.00
	F17 863 554B		F17 863 555B	550.00
	F18 533 022B		F18 533 023B	550.00
	F22 934 106B		F22 934 107B	550.00
	F22 934 118B		F22 934 119B	550.00
	F22 934 130B		F22 934 131B	550.00
	F22 934 142B		F22 934 143B	550.00
	F22 934 154B		F22 934 155B	550.00
	F86 995 698B		F86 995 699B	550.00
	G03 965 052B		G03 965 053B	550.00
	G08 974 296B		G08 974 297B	550.00
	G09 087 486B		G09 087 487B	550.00
	G10 848 366B		G10 848 367B	550.00
	G29 341 914B		G29 341 915B	550.00
	G30 587 748B		G30 587 749B	550.00
	G52 576 944B		G52 576 945B	550.00
	G65 105 172B		G65 105 173B	550.00
	G72 518 850B		G72 518 851B	550.00
	G84 460 114B		G84 450 115B	550.00
	G90 273 552B		G90 273 553B	550.00
	H02 222 220B		H02 222 221B	550.00
	H14 303 748B		H14 303 749B	550.00
	H23 495 970B		H23 495 971B	550.00
	H27 375 438B		H27 375 439B	550.00
	H38 698 602B		H38 698 603B	550.00
	H38 698 608B		H38 698 609B	550.00
	H55 163 196B		H55 163 197B	550.00
	H59 559 198B		H59 559 199B	550.00

	I04 760 386B		I04 760 387B	450.00
	I20 810 250B		I20 810 250B	550.00
	★34 017 660A		★34 017 661A	3,000.00
	★35 790 882A		★35 790 883A	3,000.00
1928A	★35 168 274A	1928C	★35 168 275A	50,000.00
1928B	Y88 301 814A	1928A	Y88 301 815A	450.00
	A10 358 598A		A10 358 599B	450.00
	A53 342 832B		A53 342 833B	450.00
	B55 757 382B		B55 757 383B	450.00
	C37 209 018B		C37 209 019B	450.00
	C85 181 274B		C85 181 275B	450.00
	F22 934 112B		F22 934 113B	450.00
	F22 934 124B		F22 934 125B	450.00
	F22 934 148B		F22 934 149B	450.00
	F86 995 680B		F86 995 681B	450.00
	F86 995 692B		F86 995 693B	450.00
	F87 881 970B		F87 881 971B	450.00
	G03 152 376B		G03 152 377B	450.00
	G30 587 742B		G30 587 743B	450.00
	G85 881 970B		G85 881 971B	450.00
	H27 375 480B		H27 375 481B	450.00
	H53 342 832B		H53 342 833B	450.00
	H66 205 332B		H66 205 333B	450.00
	H66 205 356B		H66 205 357B	450.00
	H66 205 476B		H66 205 477B	450.00
	I20 810 244B		I20 810 245B	450.00
	I54 899 970B		I54 899 971B	450.00
	★34 169 982A		★34 169 983A	3,000.00
1928B	F03 430 794B	1928C	F03 430 795B	1,400.00
	F41 758 236B		F41 758 237B	1,400.00
	H10 183 452B		H10 183 453B	1,250.00
	H10 183 902B		H10 183 903B	1,250.00
	H45 843 084B		H45 843 085B	1,250.00
	H45 843 270B		H45 843 271B	1,250.00
	H45 843 288B		H45 843 289B	1,250.00
1928B	F48 461 562B	1928D	F48 461 563B	900.00
	H23 667 810B		H23 667 811B	800.00
	H30 383 910B		H30 383 911B	800.00
	H30 383 958B		H30 383 959B	800.00
	H69 719 366B		H69 719 367B	800.00
	H98 188 212B		H98 188 213B	800.00
	I39 766 404B		I39 766 405B	750.00
	I40 504 050B		I40 504 051B	750.00
	I40 504 110B		I40 504 111B	750.00
	I40 504 170B		I40 504 171B	750.00
	I40 504 308B		I40 504 309B	750.00
	I40 504 326B		I40 504 327B	750.00
	I40 504 440B		I40 504 441B	750.00
	I40 504 452B		I40 504 453B	750.00
	I40 504 470B		I40 504 471B	750.00
	I40 504 494B		I40 504 495B	750.00
	I40 504 992B		I40 504 993B	750.00
	I47 647 698B		I47 647 699B	750.00
1928B	I26 386 926B	1928E	I26 386 927B	4,500.00
	I92 908 290B		I92 908 291B	4,500.00
1928C	H99 610 002B	1928B	H99 610 003B	1,300.00
	H99 610 020B		H99 610 021B	1,300.00
	H99 610 068B		H99 610 069B	1,300.00
1928D	H69 717 360B	1928B	H69 717 361B	750.00
	H69 717 372B		H69 717 373B	750.00
	I45 994 416B		I45 994 417B	750.00
	I64 933 206B		I64 933 207B	750.00
	I85 534 092B		I85 534 093B	750.00

1928D	H90 945 102**B**	**1928C**	H90 945 103**B**	2,500.00
1928D	I52 499 060**B**	**1928E**	I52 499 061**B**	5,000.00
1928E	I92 908 296**B**	**1928B**	I92 908 297**B**	4,500.00
1928E	I52 488 054**B**	**1928D**	I52 488 055**B**	5,000.00
1935	(with 1935 back)	**1935**	(with 1935A back) mule	300.00
1935A	(with 1935A back)	**1935A**	(with 1935 back) mule	300.00
			(same as above)	

Pairs of this variety are known in several block combinations. Estimated price would be approximately the sum of the individual blocks doubled.

1935D	wide	**1935D**	narrow
1935D	narrow	**1935D**	wide (same as above)

Pairs are known in all block combinations except U-E, G-G and N-G.

Two Dollars
UNITED STATES NOTES

1928B	B05 689 638**A**	**1928A**	B05 689 639**A**	$6,000.00
1928D	D30 112 452**A**	**1928E**	D30 112 453**A**	400.00
	D30 112 512**A**		D30 112 513**A**	400.00
	D30 112 536**A**		D30 112 537**A**	400.00
	D30 112 896**A**		D30 112 897**A**	400.00
	D31 420 986**A**		D31 420 987**A**	400.00
	D32 341 014**A**		D32 341 015**A**	400.00
	D32 341 062**A**		D32 341 063**A**	400.00
	D32 341 132**A**		D32 341 133**A**	400.00
	D32 341 574**A**		D32 341 575**A**	400.00
	D32 342 340**A**		D32 342 341**A**	400.00
	D32 342 574**A**		D32 342 575**A**	400.00
	D32 342 610**A**		D32 342 611**A**	400.00
	D32 342 730**A**		D32 342 731**A**	400.00
	D32 342 748**A**		D32 342 749**A**	400.00
	D32 343 096**A**		D32 343 097**A**	400.00
	D32 343 132**A**		D32 343 133**A**	400.00
	D32 343 168**A**		D32 343 169**A**	400.00
	D32 343 192**A**		D32 343 193**A**	400.00
	D32 343 354**A**		D32 343 355**A**	400.00
	D32 343 378**A**		D32 343 379**A**	400.00
	D32 343 468**A**		D32 343 469**A**	400.00
	D32 343 480**A**		D32 343 481**A**	400.00
	D32 885 508**A**		D32 885 509**A**	400.00
	D33 598 896**A**		D33 598 897**A**	400.00
1928E	D30 112 260**A**	**1928D**	D30 112 261**A**	400.00
	D30 112 464**A**		D30 112 465**A**	400.00
	D30 112 518**A**		D30 112 519**A**	400.00
	D30 112 548**A**		D30 112 549**A**	400.00
	D31 420 962**A**		D31 420 963**A**	400.00
	D32 341 020**A**		D32 341 021**A**	400.00
	D32 342 778**A**		D32 342 779**A**	400.00
	D32 343 114**A**		D32 343 115**A**	400.00
	D32 343 162**A**		D32 343 163**A**	400.00
	D32 343 198**A**		D32 343 199**A**	400.00
	D32 343 390**A**		D32 343 391**A**	400.00
	D33 599 862**A**		D33 599 863**A**	400.00
1928E	D39 591 132**A**	**1928F**	D39 591 133**A**	600.00
	D39 591 186**A**		D39 591 187**A**	600.00
	D39 591 468**A**		D39 591 469**A**	600.00
1928F	D80 445 094**A**	**1928G**	D80 445 095**A**	700.00

Five Dollars
UNITED STATES NOTES

1928	C91 612 212**A**	**1928A**	C91 612 213**A**	
1928A	C88 431 882**A**	**1928**	C88 431 883**A**	$2,500.00
1928A	D01 359 498**A**	**1928**	D01 359 499**A**	3,500.00
1928B	E54 650 718**A**	**1928B** mule	E54 650 719**A**	800.00
1928B	E55 684 752**A**	**1928C** mule	E55 684 753**A**	800.00
1928B	E56 022 618**A**	**1928C** mule	E56 022 619**A**	750.00
1928B mule	E58 751 094**A**	**1928C**	E58 751 095**A**	750.00
	E65 171 952**A**		E65 171 953**A**	800.00
1928C	E65 171 958**A**	**1928B** mule	E65 171 959**A**	800.00
1928C	E67 242 492**A**	**1928B** mule	E67 242 493**A**	800.00
1928C	E81 416 388**A**	**1928C** mule	E81 416 389**A**	800.00
1928C	F00 703 140**A**	**1928C** mule	F00 703 141**A**	2,500.00
1928C mule	E65 171 946**A**	**1928B** mule	E65 171 947**A**	800.00
1928C mule	E81 416 328**A**	**1928C**	E81 416 329**A**	750.00
	E81 416 358**A**		E81 416 359**A**	750.00
1928C	G54 839 448**A**	**1928D**	G54 839 449**A**	950.00
1928C	G54 848 322**A**	**1928D**	G54 848 323**A**	950.00
1928C	G55 758 066**A**	**1928D**	G55 758 067**A**	950.00
1928C	G56 039 046**A**	**1928D**	G56 039 047**A**	950.00
1928D	G54 848 328**A**	**1928C**	G54 848 329**A**	750.00
1928D	G55 758 072**A**	**1928C**	G55 758 073**A**	750.00
1928D	G55 758 168**A**	**1928C**	G55 758 169**A**	750.00
1928D	G56 058 504**A**	**1928E**	G56 058 505**A**	750.00
1928E	H78 183 018**A**	**1928F**	H78 183 019**A**	750.00

SILVER CERTIFICATES

1934	D72 791 016**A**	**1934A** mule	D72 791 017**A**	$350.00
	D82 075 890**A**		D82 075 891**A**	350.00
	D95 883 624**A**		D95 883 625**A**	350.00
	D95 883 696**A**		D95 883 697**A**	350.00
1934A	G54 669 066**A**	**1934A** mule	G54 669 067**A**	1,000.00
1934 mule	E25 060 764**A**	**1934A**	E25 060 765**A**	400.00
1934A	E25 060 782**A**	**1934A** mule	E25 060 783**A**	4,000.00
1934A	L06 718 356**A**	**1934B**	L06 718 357**A**	400.00
	L06 719 002**A**		L06 719 003**A**	400.00
	L11 507 076**A**		L11 507 077**A**	400.00
	L11 597 976**A**		L11 597 977**A**	400.00
	L12 976 266**A**		L12 976 267**A**	400.00
1934A mule	D75 336 372**A**	**1934**	D75 336 373**A**	400.00
1934A mule	F11 487 672**A**	**1934A**	F11 487 673**A**	300.00
1934A mule	F41 347848**A**	**1934A**	F41 347 849**A**	300.00
1934B	K99 930 672**A**	**1934A**	K99 930 673**A**	2,300.00
1934B	L01 196 490**A**	**1934A**	L01 196 491**A**	400.00
1934B	L26 399 694**A**	**1934A**	L26 399 695**A**	400.00
1934B	L50 330 556**A**	**1934C**	L50 330 557**A**	375.00
	L50 330 568**A**		L50 330 569**A**	375.00
	L51 477 228**A**		L51 477 229**A**	375.00
	L74 667 630**A**		L74 667 631**A**	375.00
	L74 667 702**A**		L74 667 703**A**	375.00
	L80 808 066**A**		L80 808 067**A**	375.00
	L88 153 542**A**		L88 153 543**A**	375.00
	L88 154 544**A**		L88 154 545**A**	375.00
	★12 416 970**A**		★12 416 971**A**	4,500.00
1934C	L80 808 060**A**	**1934B**	L80 808 061**A**	375.00
	L86 524 098**A**		L86 524 099**A**	375.00

	L88 153 446A		L88 153 447A	375.00
	M30 229 668A		M30 229 669A	2,500.00
	★12 416 940A		★12 416 941★	3,000.00
1934C	Q47 622 414A	1934D	Q47 622 415A	275.00
	Q48 088 626A		Q48 088 627A	275.00
	Q48 088 674A		Q48 088 675A	275.00
	Q55 371 070A		Q55 331 071A	275.00
	Q55 331 346A		Q55 331 347A	275.00
	Q55 331 604A		Q55 331 605A	275.00
	Q55 331 910A		Q55 331 911A	275.00
	Q55 331 958A		Q55 331 959A	275.00
	Q56 907 930A		Q56 907 931A	275.00
	Q57 972 972A		Q57 972 973A	275.00
	Q60 674 436A		Q60 674 437A	275.00
	Q60 674 460A		Q60 674 461A	275.00
	★17 397 810A		★17 397 811A	1,000.00
	★17 459 160A		★17 459 161A	1,000.00
	★17 687 718A		★17 687 719A	1,000.00
	★17 700 966A		★17 700 967A	1,000.00
1934D	Q48 175 314A	1934C	Q48 175 315A	300.00
	Q55 331 556A		Q55 331 557A	300.00
	Q55 331 940A		Q55 331 941A	300.00
	Q57 181 422A		Q57 181 423A	300.00
	Q57 972 942A		Q57 972 943A	300.00
	Q57 972 966A		Q57 972 967A	300.00
	★17 448 270A		★17 448 271A	900.00
	★17 448 282A		★17 448 283A	900.00
	★17 459 166A		★17 459 167A	900.00
	★17 459 178A		★17 459 179A	900.00
	★17 459 448A		★17 459 449A	900.00
	★17 459 514A		★17 459 515A	900.00
	★17 687 712A		★17 687 713A	900.00

FEDERAL RESERVE NOTES

1928	G23 163 222A	**1928A**	G23 163 223A	$2,500.00
	G23 163 240A		G23 163 241A	2,500.00
1928	J04 822 494A	**1928A**	J04 822 495A	2,500.00
1928A	G23 163 234A	**1928**	G23 163 235A	2,500.00
1934	B33 072 168A	**1934A**	B33 072 169A	450.00
	G23 511 570A		G23 511 571A	450.00
	G24 527 156A		G24 527 157A	450.00
1934 mule	B01 072 722B	**1934A**	B01 072 723B	450.00
	B29 015 562B		B29 015 563B	450.00
	B83 793 570A		B83 793 571A	450.00
	B96 471 204A		B96 471 205A	450.00
	C52 611 672A		C52 611 673A	450.00
	G24 537 144A		G24 537 145A	450.00
	G39 011 232A		G39 011 233A	450.00
1934A	B83 793 564A	**1934** mule	B83 793 565A	450.00
	C30 365 118A		C30 365 119A	450.00
	G24 437 150A		G24 437 151A	450.00
	L24 794 934A		L24 794 935A	450.00
1934A	B76 314 420B	**1934B**	B76 314 421B	450.00
	B78 089 004B		B78 089 005B	450.00
	B78 604 392B		B78 604 393B	450.00
	B83 602 824B		B83 602 825B	450.00
	B83 602 866B		B83 602 867B	450.00
	C72 036 156A		C72 036 157A	450.00
	C72 036 204A		C72 036 205A	450.00
	C72 036 120A		C72 036 121A	450.00
	C72 036 168A		C72 036 169A	450.00
	C72 036 372A		C72 036 373A	450.00
	C72 036 504A		C72 036 505A	450.00
	C72 036 552A		C72 036 553A	450.00
	D62 128 908A		D62 128 909A	550.00
	D63 026 892A		D63 026 893A	450.00
1934B	B75 425 472B	**1934A**	B75 425 473B	450.00
	B80 562 372B		B80 562 373B	450.00
	B80 562 924B		B80 562 925B	450.00
	B81 038 868B		B81 038 869B	450.00
	B83 602 824B		B83 602 825B	450.00
	B83 602 848B		B83 602 849B	450.00
	C72 036 126A		C72 036 127A	450.00
	C72 036 150A		C72 036 151A	450.00
	C72 036 186A		C72 036 187A	450.00
	C72 036 462A		C72 036 463A	450.00
	D60 932 532A		D60 932 533A	450.00
	D62 128 722A		D62 128 723A	450.00
	G13 872 054B		G13 872 055B	450.00
	G13 872 066B		G13 872 067B	450.00
1934B	L74 667 702A	**1934C**	L74 667 703A	600.00
1934C	D68 122 044A	**1934B**	D68 122 045A	600.00
	D69 301 788A		D69 301 789A	600.00
1934C	B64 863 882C	**1934D**	B64 863 883C	450.00
	B64 863 948C		B64 863 949C	450.00
	B64 863 966C		B64 863 967C	450.00
	B64 863 978C		B64 863 979C	450.00
	B64 863 996C		B64 863 997C	450.00
	C05 063 028B		C05 063 029B	450.00
1950 Wide	H29 999 028A	**1950** Narrow	H29 999 029A	400.00

Ten Dollars

SILVER CERTIFICATES

1934 mule	A77 086 884**A**	**1934A**	A77 086 885**A**	1,250.00
	A87 320 688**A**		A87 320 689**A**	1,250.00
1934A	B18 525 576**A**	**1934B**	B18 525 577**A**	3,000.00
1934B	B18 432 102**A**	**1934A**	B18 432 103**A**	3,000.00

FEDERAL RESERVE NOTES

1928	F06 645 486**A**	**1928A**	F06 645 487**A**	$750.00
	G12 342 348**A**		G12 342 349**A**	1,500.00
1934	J20 907 474**A**	**1934A**	J20 907 475**A**	550.00
1934A	F33 075 792**A**	**1934** mule	F33 075 793**A**	550.00
	G65 813 328**A**		G65 813 329**A**	500.00
	J00 623 940★		J00 623 941★	1,400.00
1934A mule	G66 224 412**A**	**1934**	G66 224 413**A**	400.00
1934A	B79 075 856**D**	**1934B**	B79 076 857**D**	500.00
	B80 851 308**D**		B80 851 309**D**	500.00
	B80 864 112**D**		B80 864 113**D**	500.00
	C23 630 226**B**		C23 630 227**B**	450.00
	C23 630 274**B**		C23 630 275**B**	450.00
	C26 942 310**B**		C26 942 311**B**	450.00
	C26 942 430**B**		C26 942 431**B**	450.00
	C26 942 526**B**		C26 942 527**B**	450.00
	C26 942 580**B**		C26 942 581**B**	450.00
1934B	B77 069 424**D**	**1934A**	B77 069 425**D**	550.00
	C23 630 220**B**		C23 630 221**B**	450.00
	C26 942 304**B**		C26 942 305**B**	450.00
	C26 942 376**B**		C26 942 377**B**	450.00
	C26 942 448**B**		C26 942 449**B**	450.00
	C26 942 520**B**		C26 942 521**B**	450.00
	C26 942 532**B**		C26 942 533**B**	450.00
	C26 942 586**B**		C26 942 587**B**	450.00
	C26 942 928**B**		C26 942 929**B**	450.00
	G37 051 704**B**		G37 051 705**B**	500.00
1934C	C02 424 420★	**1934D**	C02 424 421★	1,250.00
	C02 424 468★		C02 424 469★	1,250.00
	C02 424 492★		C02 424 493★	1,250.00
	C02 424 720★		C02 424 721★	1,250.00
	B27 384 006**F**		B27 384 007**F**	450.00
1934D	C02 424 486★	**1934C**	C02 424 487★	1,100.00
	C02 424 498★		C02 424 499★	1,100.00
	C02 424 648★		C02 424 649★	1,100.00
	C02 425 314★		C02 425 315★	1,100.00
	C02 425 368★		C02 425 369★	1,100.00
	C02 469 096★		C02 469 097★	1,100.00
	C02 469 972★		C02 469 973★	1,100.00
	C02 475 090★		C02 475 091★	1,100.00
	C02 475 102★		C02 475 103★	1,100.00
1950	J19 310 604**A**	**1950**	J19 310 605**A**	250.00

Twenty Dollars
FEDERAL RESERVE NOTES

Series	Serial	Series	Serial	Price
1934	**D**30 843 924**A**	**1934** mule	**D**30 843 925**A**	600.00
1934	**D**53 144 562**A**	**1934A**	**D**53 144 563**A**	500.00
1934	**L**19 857 588**A**	**1934A** mule	**L**19 857 589**A**	600.00
1934 mule	**D**53 144 562**A**	**1934A**	**D**53 144 563**A**	450.00
1934 mule	**D**59 844 186**A**	**1934A**	**D**59 844 187**A**	450.00
1934 mule Hawaii	**L**69 494 322**A**	**1934A** Hawaii	**L**69 494 323**A**	12,500.00
1934A	**D**52 931 742**A**	**1934**	**D**52 931 743**A**	400.00
	E17 813 418**A**		**E**17 813 419**A**	400.00
	E48 966 960**A**		**E**48 966 961**A**	400.00
	H12 146 910**A**		**H**12 146 911**A**	400.00
1934A mule	**B**30 870 654**A**	**1934**	**B**30 870 655**A**	400.00
	D53 171 052**A**		**D**53 171 053**A**	400.00
1934A mule Hawaii	**L**30 855 954**A**	**1934** mule	**L**30 855 955**A**	12,500.00
1934A	**C**34 623 084**A**	**1934** mule	**C**34 623 085**A**	400.00
1934A	**B**18 265 104**B**	**1934B**	**B**18 265 105**B**	350.00
	B18 265 134**B**		**B**18 265 135**B**	350.00
	B18 265 662**B**		**B**18 265 663**B**	350.00
	B18 265 674**B**		**B**18 265 675**B**	350.00
	B18 265 686**B**		**B**18 265 687**B**	350.00
	B18 265 698**B**		**B**18 265 699**B**	350.00
	B18 417 342**B**		**B**18 417 343**B**	350.00
	B34 669 086**B**		**B**34 669 087**B**	350.00
	B34 669 098**B**		**B**34 669 099**B**	350.00
	G06 978 396**B**		**G**06 978 397**B**	350.00
	G07 854 756**B**		**G**07 854 757**B**	350.00
	G07 854 780**B**		**G**07 854 781**B**	350.00
1934B	**B**18 265 128**B**	**1934A**	**B**18 265 129**B**	300.00
	B18 265 140**B**		**B**18 265 141**B**	300.00
	B18 265 656**B**		**B**18 265 657**B**	300.00
	B18 265 668**B**		**B**18 265 669**B**	300.00
	B18 265 680**B**		**B**18 265 681**B**	300.00
	B18 265 692**B**		**B**18 265 693**B**	300.00
	B24 785 304**B**		**B**24 785 305**B**	300.00
	B34 669 956**B**		**B**34 669 957**B**	300.00
	B34 669 080**B**		**B**34 669 081**B**	300.00
	B34 669 092**B**		**B**34 669 093**B**	300.00
	G07 854 744**B**		**G**07 854 745**B**	300.00
	G07 854 762**B**		**G**07 854 763**B**	300.00

Fifty Dollars
FEDERAL RESERVE NOTES

Series	Serial	Series	Serial	Value
1934	B05 072 328A	1934A	B05 072 329A	$1,250.00
	B05 072 364A		B05 072 365A	1,250.00
	B05 072 376A		B05 072 377A	750.00
	B05 072 430A		B05 072 431A	750.00
	D06 698 418A		D06 698 419A	750.00
	G07 928 268A		G07 928 269A	1,500.00
	J00 920 964A		J00 920 965A	750.00
	J00 920 976A		J00 920 977A	750.00
	J00 920 982A		J00 920 983A	750.00
	J00 920 988A		J00 920 989A	750.00
1934A	A01 441 068A	1934	A01 441 069A	900.00
	B05 072 424A		B05 072 425A	750.00
	B05 072 434A		B05 072 435A	750.00
	B10 083 138A		B10 083 139A	750.00
1934A mule	B04 073 802A	1934	B04 073 803A	750.00
	J00 920 970A		J00 920 971A	900.00
1934B	C06 150 792A	1934C	C06 150 793A	1,500.00

One Hundred Dollars
FEDERAL RESERVE NOTES

Series	Serial	Series	Serial	Value
1934	E02 612 556A	1934A mule	E02 312 557A	$1,250.00
	F02 402 610A		F02 402 611A	1,250.00
	H00 993 390A		H00 993 391A	1,250.00
	K00 400 122A		K00 400 123A	1,000.00
	K00 400 128A		K00 400 129A	1,000.00
	K00 400 132A		K00 400 135A	1,000.00
	J01 636 848A		J01 636 849A	1,250.00
1934A mule	D02 453 832A	1934	D02 453 833A	1,250.00
	J01 636 842A		J01 636 843A	1,250.00
	L03 552 924A		L03 552 925A	1,250.00
1934B	H02 938 188A		H02 938 189A	1,250.00
1934B	H03 044 106A	1934C	H03 044 107A	1,250.00
1934C	F03 910 374A	1934B	F03 910 375A	1,250.00
	G10 996 228A		G10 996 229A	1,250.00
	H03 044 124A		H03 044 125A	1,250.00
	J02 520 786A		J02 520 787A	1,250.00
1934C	G11 364 348A	1934D	G11 364 349A	1,750.00
1950 mule	G04 193 802A	1950	G04 193 803A	1,000.00

Five Hundred Dollars
FEDERAL RESERVE NOTES

Series	Serial	Series	Serial	Value
1934	L00 145 416A	1934A	L00 145 417A	$25,000.00
	L00 153 444A		L00 153 445A	25,000.00

One Thousand Dollars
FEDERAL RESERVE NOTES

Series	Serial	Series	Serial	Value
1934A	J00 056 124A	1934	J00 056 125A	$25,000.00

Appendix II

PRESS RELEASES (BY DATE OF ISSUE)

TREASURY DEPARTMENT
BUREAU OF ENGRAVING AND PRINTING
Washington, D.C.
March 14, 1933.

FOR IMMEDIATE RELEASE

The Bureau of Engraving and Printing issued the following statement today:

Late in the day of March 9, 1933, the day that marked the enactment of legislation to provide relief in the banking emergency that had developed, the Bureau of Engraving and Printing was directed to proceed with the physical production of new Federal Reserve Bank Notes. These new bank notes were authorized to meet the need for currency resulting from the panic withdrawals from our banks. They are like our National bank notes in appearance, and they are secured by government bonds or by the obligations of member banks in turn secured by good assets.

The first shipment of the new notes, completed twenty-four hours after the order was received, was delivered in New York at the Federal Reserve Bank on the morning of March 11, 1933. The quick action on the part of the Bureau of Engraving and Printing's getting into production was made possible through the fact that much of the preliminary work was being accomplished at the same time that plans were being considered and the Bill being drafted.

There was not sufficient time to engrave new dies and make new plates for the printing of the Federal Reserve Bank Notes. The standard National bank currency, on which the Bureau of Engraving and Printing was already in production, was therefore pressed into service. First it was necessary to procure facsimile signatures of two officials of each of the twelve Federal Reserve Banks. These were taken from certificates in the files of the Department. Production of special logotype plates, bearing the signature of bank officials, was undertaken at the plant of the American Type Founders Company at Jersey City.

It was necessary to add employees to the staff of the Bureau of Engraving and Printing. On March 13, 1933, 475 persons were recruited in the service. Men whose wives were not employed, women whose husbands were not employed, and veterans were given preference in the large number of former employees who applied for positions.

The initial order for Federal Reserve Bank Notes amounts to 15,524,000 sheets, or 186,288,000 notes, with an approximate face value of $2,000,000,000.

The production at the Bureau of Engraving and Printing will reach its peak within the next week, if demands require it. At peak production over six million notes will leave the bureau every twenty-four hours. These notes will be shipped to the various Federal Reserve Banks throughout the country.

The production program required by the Emergency Bank Act is unprecedented. To meet this program many quick changes had to be made in the methods of handling the currency as it passed from one operation to another. Vaults had to be expanded. The entire staff of the Bureau undertook the task in splendid spirit. Several of the important operations are continuing throughout twenty-four hours of the day.

March 26, 1935

The first sheets of $1 Silver Certificates of the small-size currency were delivered uncut by the Bureau of Engraving and Printing to the Treasury vaults. On July 10, 1929, when the new currency was put into circulation, the first sheet of these uncut sheets of 12 notes each was placed in the archives of the Treasury.

Certain other sheets were distributed to various officials of the Government, the President of the United States, Herbert Hoover, receiving the second sheet; the Secretary of the Treasury, Andrew W. Mellon, receiving the third; the Under-Secretary of the Treasury, Ogden L. Mills, receiving the fourth; the Assistant Secretary of the Treasury, Henry Herrick Bond, receiving the fifth. Other sheets were given to the heads of Treasury bureaus who aided materially in connection with the issue of the small-size currency, and the sheet to which this memorandum is attached is the fifty-first sheet.

A record is kept in the Office of the Treasurer of the United States showing the names of the holders of these sheets. There are only 80 of them in existence.

PLAN OF DISTRIBUTION

Uncut sheets and low-numbered notes of small-size currency series 1928.

$1 SILVER CERTIFICATES

Recipient:	Sheet No.	Note No.
Archives of Office of Treasurer of the United States	1	1-12
Herbert Hoover, President of United States	2	13-24
A.W. Mellon, Secretary of the Treasury	3	25-36
Members of Cabinet (cut)	4	37-48
Ogden L. Mills, Undersecretary of the Treasury	5	49-60
Henry Herrick Bond, Asst. Secretary of Treasury	6	61-72
A.W. Mellon, Secretary of the Treasury	7	73-84
Charles S. Dewey, Former Asst. Secretary of Treasury	8	85-96
Herbert Hoover, President of the United States	9	97-108
A.W. Mellon, Secretary of the Treasury	10	109-120
Henry Herrick Bond, Asst. Secretary of the Treasury	11	121-132
Henry Herrick Bond, Asst. Secretary of the Treasury	12	133-144
Lawrence Richey, Secretary to President Hoover	13	145-156
Ferry K. Heth, Asst. Secretary of the Treasury	14	157-168
A.W. Hall, Director, Bureau of Engraving & Printing	15	169-180
W.S. Broughton, Commissioner of Public Debt	16	181-192
W.O. Woods, Treasurer of the United States	17	193-204
Henry Herrick Bond, Asst. Secretary of the Treasury	18	205-216
Henry Herrick Bond, Asst. Secretary of the Treasury	19	217-228
Henry Herrick Bond, Asst. Secretary of the Treasury	20	229-240

Appendix III

SIGNERS OF U.S. PAPER MONEY

Secretary of the Treasury	Treasurer of the U.S.	Term Start	Term End
Andrew W. Mellon	H. T. Tate	4-30-1928	1-17-1929
Andrew W. Mellon	Walter O. Woods	1-18-1929	2-12-1932
Ogden L. Mills	Walter O. Woods	2-13-1932	3-3-1933
William H. Woodin	Walter O. Woods	3-4-1933	5-31-1933
William H. Woodin	W. A. Julian	6-1-1933	12-31-1933
Henry Morgenthau, Jr.	W. A. Julian	1-1-1934	7-22-1945
Fred M. Vinson	W. A. Julian	7-23-1945	7-23-1946
John W. Snyder	W. A. Julian	7-25-1946	5-29-1949
John W. Snyder	Georgia Neese Clark	6-21-1949	1-20-1953
George M. Humphrey	Ivy Baker Priest	1-28-1953	7-28-1957
Robert B. Anderson	Ivy Baker Priest	7-29-1957	1-20-1961
C. Douglas Dillon	Elizabeth Rudel Smith	1-30-1961	4-13-1962
C. Douglas Dillon	Kathryn O'Hay Granahan	1-3-1963	3-31-1965
Henry H. Fowler	Kathryn O'Hay Granahan	4-1-1965	10-13-1966
Joseph W. Barr	Kathryn O'Hay Granahan	12-21-1968	1-20-1969
David M. Kennedy	Dorothy Andrews Elston*	5-8-1969	9-16-1970
David M. Kennedy	Dorothy Andrews Kabis	9-17-1970	2-1-1971
John B. Connally	Dorothy Andrews Kabis	2-11-1971	7-3-1971
John B. Connally	Romana Banuelos	12-17-1971	5-16-1972
George P. Shultz	Romana Banuelos	6-12-1972	5-8-1974
William E. Simon	Francine I. Neff	6-21-1974	1-19-1977
W. Michael Blumenthal	Azie Taylor Morton	9-12-1977	8-4-1979
G. William Miller	Azie Taylor Morton	8-6-1979	1-4-1981
Donald T. Regan	Angela M. Buchanan	3-7-1981	7-1-1983
Donald T. Regan	Katherine Davalos Ortega	9-23-1983	1-29-1985
James A. Baker III	Katherine Davalos Ortega	1-29-1985	8-17-1988
Nicholas F. Brady	Katherine Davalos Ortega	9-15-1988	6-30-1989
Nicholas F. Brady	Catalina Vasquez Villalpando	12-11-1989	1-20-1993
Lloyd Bentsen	Mary Ellen Withrow	3-1-1994	12-22-1994
Robert E. Rubin	Mary Ellen Withrow	1-10-1995	7-2-1999
Lawrence H. Summers	Mary Ellen Withrow	7-2-1999	1-20-2001
Paul H. O'Neill	Rosario Marin	8-16-2001	12-31-2002
John W. Snow	Rosario Marin	2-3-2003	6-30-2003
John W. Snow	Anna Escobedo Cabral	12-13-2004	6-29-2006
Henry M. Paulson, Jr.	Anna Escobedo Cabral	7-3-2006	—

* During her term of office, Mrs. Elston married Walter L Kabis; the first time the signature of a United States Treasurer had been changed during the term of office.

More Expert Details
More Reliable Pricing

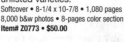

SUBSCRIBE TODAY
AND SAVE 38%! ONE FULL YEAR AT A GREAT LOW RATE

1 YEAR
(12 huge issues)
$37

That's right. Try *Bank Note Reporter* today and discover America's most reliable and authoritative paper money monthly. Each issue is filled to the brim with the valuable information you need to pursue your collecting hobby.

You'll find...

- **The world's largest paper money marketplace to help you find the notes you need, from advertisers you trust**

- **Current market values, featuring *The Paper Money Market*, a U.S. small-size and large-size paper money price guide bound into each issue**

- **Helpful columns, answers to intriguing hobby questions and timely articles to help your paper money knowledge grow**

- **Timely auction reports and a complete list of upcoming shows and auctions**

- **And much, much more!**

DON'T WAIT! Log on to
www.banknotereporter.com and subscribe today.

Or call 866-836-7871. Outside the U.S. and Canada, call 386-246-3416.
You can also write to us at: P.O. Box 420235, Palm Coast, FL 32142-0235. Mention offer code J7AHAD.

In Canada: add $16 (includes GST/HST). Outside the U.S. and Canada: add $26. Outside the U.S., remit payment in U.S. funds with order. Please allow 4-6 weeks for first-issue delivery. Annual newsstand rate $59.88.